Stan Lee PRESENTS

DAREDEVIL

THE MAN WITHOUT FEAR! VOL. 2

ESSENTIAL

DAREDEVIL #26-48 & SPECIAL #1
& FANTASTIC FOUR #73

DAREDEVIL #26
THE MAN WITHOUT FEAR!

WRITER: STAN LEE
ARTIST: GENE COLAN
LETTERER: ARTIE SIMEK

DAREDEVIL #27
THE MAN WITHOUT FEAR!

WRITER: STAN LEE
PENCILER: GENE COLAN
INKER: FRANK GIACOIA
LETTERER: ARTIE SIMEK

DAREDEVIL #28
THE MAN WITHOUT FEAR!

WRITER: STAN LEE
PENCILER: GENE COLAN
INKER: DICK AYERS
LETTERER: SAM ROSEN

DAREDEVIL #29
THE MAN WITHOUT FEAR!

WRITER: STAN LEE
PENCILER: GENE COLAN
INKER: JOHN TARTAGLIONE
LETTERER: SAM ROSEN

DAREDEVIL #30
THE MAN WITHOUT FEAR!

WRITER: STAN LEE
PENCILER: GENE COLAN
INKER: JOHN TARTAGLIONE
LETTERER: ARTIE SIMEK

DAREDEVIL #31
THE MAN WITHOUT FEAR!

WRITER: STAN LEE
PENCILER: GENE COLAN
INKER: JOHN TARTAGLIONE
LETTERER: ARTIE SIMEK

DAREDEVIL #32
THE MAN WITHOUT FEAR!

WRITER: STAN LEE
PENCILER: GENE COLAN
INKER: JOHN TARTAGLIONE
LETTERER: SAM ROSEN

DAREDEVIL #33
THE MAN WITHOUT FEAR!

WRITER: STAN LEE
PENCILER: GENE COLAN
INKER: JOHN TARTAGLIONE
LETTERER: ARTIE SIMEK

DAREDEVIL #34
THE MAN WITHOUT FEAR!

WRITER: STAN LEE
PENCILER: GENE COLAN
INKER: JOHN TARTAGLIONE
LETTERER: ARTIE SIMEK

DAREDEVIL #1
SPECIAL

WRITER: STAN LEE
PENCILER: GENE COLAN
INKER: JOHN TARTAGLIONE
LETTERER: SAM ROSEN

DAREDEVIL #35
THE MAN WITHOUT FEAR!

WRITER: STAN LEE
PENCILER: GENE COLAN
INKER: JOHN TARTAGLIONE
LETTERER: ARTIE SIMEK

DAREDEVIL #36
THE MAN WITHOUT FEAR!

WRITER: STAN LEE
PENCILER: GENE COLAN
INKER: FRANK GIACOIA
LETTERER: ARTIE SIMEK

DAREDEVIL #37
THE MAN WITHOUT FEAR!

WRITER: STAN LEE
PENCILER: GENE COLAN
INKER: JOHN TARTAGLIONE
LETTERER: ARTIE SIMEK

DAREDEVIL #38
THE MAN WITHOUT FEAR!

WRITER: STAN LEE
PENCILER: GENE COLAN
INKER: FRANK GIACOIA
LETTERER: SAM ROSEN

Fantastic Four #73

WRITER: STAN LEE
PENCILER: JACK KIRBY
INKER: JOE SINNOTT
LETTERER: ARTIE SIMEK

DAREDEVIL #39
THE MAN WITHOUT FEAR!

WRITER: STAN LEE
PENCILER: GENE COLAN
INKER: GEORGE TUSKA
LETTERER: ARTIE SIMEK

DAREDEVIL #40
THE MAN WITHOUT FEAR!

WRITER: STAN LEE
PENCILER: GENE COLAN
INKER: JOHN TARTAGLIONE
LETTERER: SAM ROSEN

DAREDEVIL #41
THE MAN WITHOUT FEAR!

WRITER: STAN LEE
PENCILER: GENE COLAN
INKER: JOHN TARTAGLIONE
LETTERER: SAM ROSEN

DAREDEVIL #42
THE MAN WITHOUT FEAR!

WRITER: STAN LEE
PENCILER: GENE COLAN
INKER: DAN ADKINS
LETTERER: SAM ROSEN

DAREDEVIL #43
THE MAN WITHOUT FEAR!

WRITER: STAN LEE
PENCILER: GENE COLAN
INKER: VINCE COLLETTA
LETTERER: ARTIE SIMEK

DAREDEVIL #44
THE MAN WITHOUT FEAR!

WRITER: STAN LEE
PENCILER: GENE COLAN
INKER: VINCE COLLETTA
LETTERER: ARTIE SIMEK

DAREDEVIL #45
THE MAN WITHOUT FEAR!

WRITER: STAN LEE
PENCILER: GENE COLAN
INKER: VINCE COLLETTA
LETTERER: ARTIE SIMEK

DAREDEVIL #46
THE MAN WITHOUT FEAR!

WRITER: STAN LEE
PENCILER: GENE COLAN
INKER: GEORGE KLEIN
LETTERER: ARTIE SIMEK

DAREDEVIL #47
THE MAN WITHOUT FEAR!

WRITER: STAN LEE
PENCILER: GENE COLAN
INKER: GEORGE KLEIN
LETTERER: ARTIE SIMEK

DAREDEVIL #48
THE MAN WITHOUT FEAR!

WRITER: STAN LEE
PENCILER: GENE COLAN
INKER: GEORGE KLEIN
LETTERER: ARTIE SIMEK

REPRINT CREDITS

MARVEL ESSENTIAL DESIGN:
JOHN "JG" ROSHELL OF COMICRAFT
FRONT COVER ART:
GENE COLAN
BACK COVER ART:
JACK KIRBY
COVER COLORS:
AVALON'S ANDY TROY

COLLECTIONS EDITOR:
JEFF YOUNGQUIST
ASSISTANT EDITOR:
JENNIFER GRÜNWALD
BOOK DESIGNER:
JULIO HERRERA
EDITOR IN CHIEF:
JOE QUESADA
PUBLISHER:
DAN BUCKLEY

SPECIAL THANKS TO:
POND SCUM & RALPH MACCHIO

ESSENTIAL

HERE COMES...

DAREDEVIL

MARVEL COMICS GROUP

12¢ IND.

26 MAR

THE MAN WITHOUT FEAR!

IT'S ONE OF OUR LEAST-INSPIRED TITLES... BUT THE STORY'S A BLAST!!

"STILT-MAN STRIKES AGAIN!"

DAREDEVIL, THE MAN WITHOUT FEAR!
STILT-MAN STRIKES AGAIN
HONEST, WE PROMISE YOU, OUR SPELL-BINDING SAGA IS FAR MORE INSPIRING THAN THE SOMEWHAT PEDESTRIAN TITLE WHICH IT BEARS!
WHEN YOU OR I COMMUTE TO WORK, TIGER, WE'RE APT TO TAKE A BUS, A TAXI, OR A TRAIN! IN FACT, WE MIGHT EVEN WALK! BUT, WHEN YOU'RE A SWING-A-DINGIN' SUPER-HERO LIKE OL' DD--WELL, JUST WATCH--
IT WAS GREAT, TAKING THE AFTERNOON OFF SO I COULD SKEEDADDLE AROUND TOWN FOR A WHILE!
BUT, I DIDN'T REALIZE HOW LATE IT WAS GETTING!
I'D BETTER RUSH BACK TO THE OFFICE IN CASE FOGGY OR KAREN NEED MATT MURDOCK FOR ANYTHING!
PULSE-POUNDING PRESENTATION BY: SMILIN' STAN LEE and GENIAL GENE COLAN
LOTS OF LITTLE LETTERING BY: ARTIE SIMEK
1

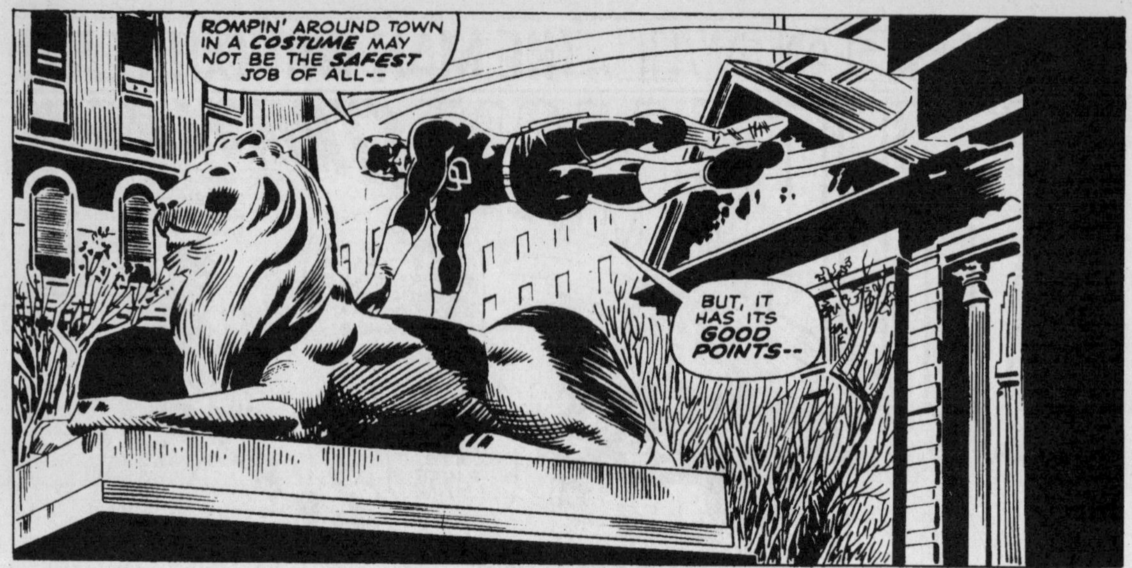
ROMPIN' AROUND TOWN IN A COSTUME MAY NOT BE THE SAFEST JOB OF ALL--
BUT, IT HAS ITS GOOD POINTS--

AT LEAST, I DON'T HAVE TO SQUANDER MY HARD-EARNED SHEKELS ON CAB FARE!
--OR WORRY ABOUT GETTING CAUGHT IN TRAFFIC JAMS!
W 45 ST.
NO PARKING 6AM TO 7PM MON. TO FRI.
WHAT IN THE NAME OF--?!!
OH! ANOTHER SUPER-HERO!
IN THIS TOWN, YOU CAN'T TURN AROUND WITHOUT TRIPPING OVER ONE OF 'EM!

WELL, THIS IS IT!
THONK!
I'LL JUST BOUNCE OFF THE NEAREST TRUCK TOP--ONTO THE BALCONY ABOVE --THEN, A FEW QUICK SOMERSAULTS UPWARD--
--AND IT'S GOT WAITING FOR AN ELEVATOR BEAT A MILE!
ALTHOUGH, IF I EVER FORGET TO LEAVE THIS WINDOW OPEN-- HOOO BOY!

I'D BETTER CHANGE TO MATT MURDOCK FAST, AND THEN-- NO!
JUST FOR KICKS, I'LL BECOME MATTHEW'S FRANTIC, FAST-TALKIN' TWIN BROTHER!
I'M BEGINNING TO ENJOY THE ROLE OF MADCAP MICHAEL MURDOCK!
I GUESS I'M REALLY AS BIG A HAM AS "HE" IS!

ANYWAY, IF ANYONE SAW OL' DD SWINGIN' IN THRU THE WINDOW, THIS'LL HELP TO CONVINCE 'EM THAT THE FEARLESS ONE REALLY IS BROTHER MIKE!
I'M BEGINNING TO FEEL LIKE A ONE-MAN REPERTORY THEATRE!
FIRST, I'M CONSERVATIVE MATT MURDOCK, THE BLIND COURTROOM WHIZ! THEN, I'M ALSO DAZZLIN' DD, THE DARLIN' OF THE SWASHBUCKLIN' SET!
AND FINALLY, TO KEEP ANY-ONE FROM LINKING ME WITH HORNHEAD, I'VE BECOME MIKE MURDOCK, MY OWN MAKE-BELIEVE TWIN BROTHER!
WHEN THEY FINALLY PUT ME OUT TO PASTURE, IN THAT OLD SUPER-HERO HAVEN UP YONDER, THEY'LL PROBABLY GET ALEC GUINESS TO PLAY MY LIFE STORY!

LET'S SEE NOW--I'LL JUST MUSS UP THE MOP, TO GIVE MYSELF THAT CAREFREE TOUSLED LOOK!
A FELLA LIKE MIKE WOULDN'T BE CAUGHT DEAD WITH A SIMPLE IVY-LEAGUE HAIR COMB!

AND, I'LL HAVE TO GIVE MY SPECS A COFFEE BREAK FOR A WHILE, AS I COVER MY SIGHTLESS EYES IN A MORE COLORFUL WAY--
IF THE ATTORNEY-AT-LAW BUSINESS EVER GETS SLOW, I MIGHT JUST DECIDE TO OPEN A SCHOOL OF METHOD ACTING!

YESSIR! STANISLAVSKY HAD NOTHING ON ME!
NOW, ALL I'VE GOTTA DO IS CHANGE MY PERSONALITY!
I FIGURE A CLOWN LIKE MIKE MURDOCK IS SURE TO BE ON ALL THE TIME!

IT'S FUNNY-- I EVEN FEEL LIKE A DIFFERENT GUY WHEN I "BECOME" MIKE MURDOCK!
MAYBE I SHOULD GIVE UP THE COSTUMED CAVORTER JAZZ AND GET INTO SHOW BIZ!
WHO KNOWS? THEY MIGHT BE LOOKING FOR ANOTHER CARY GRANT OUT IN CELLULOID CITY!
I CAN JUST SEE MYSELF NOW--
"DON'T PUT YOUR ARMS AROUND ME, SOPHIA BABY! STOP KISSIN' ME, GINA DOLL--!"
"YOU'RE TICKLIN' THE CLEFT IN MY CHIN!"

UH OH! I HEAR FOGGY AND KAREN PASSING THE DOOR! THEY'RE JUST LEAVING!
WELL, WE'LL SEE IF OL' MIKE CAN DREAM UP SOME WONDROUS WAY TO STOP 'EM!
AFTER ALL-- IF I WENT TO ALL THIS TROUBLE TO BECOME MY OWN TWIN BROTHER, SOME-ONE MIGHT AS WELL CATCH THE ACT!

KAREN! DO YOU HEAR SINGING-- COMING FROM MATT'S OFFICE?
THERE IT IS AGAIN! SOUNDS LIKE THAT IDIOT TWIN BROTHER OF HIS!
FOGGY! HOW CAN YOU CALL THAT FABULOUS DAREDEVIL AN IDIOT?
EASY AS PIE, HONEY!
HE MAY BE A LIVING DOLL TO YOU--
BUT HE'S A LOUD-MOUTHED, SWELL-HEADED SHOWOFF TO ME!

COME IN--COME IN-- WHOOOOOOEVER YOU ARE--!
FOGGY! IT IS MIKE MURDOCK!!
I'M ALL SHOOK-UP ABOUT THE WHOLE THING!
STICKS 'N STONES'LL BREAK MY BONES --BUT WOIIIIIIDS'LL NEVER HOYYYYT ME!

AHH, A MAIDEN FAIR DOTH ENTER THE OFFICE OF BROTHER MATTHEW!
BUT, WHO IS THAT STANDING AT HER SIDE? HE FROWNS --HE SCOWLS--HE MUMBLES UNDER HIS BREATH!!
'TIS CERTAIN HE IS NO MEMBER OF THE MIKE MURDOCK FAN CLUB!
BUT, LET ME WARN YOU, MY CHUBBY FRIEND--

MMMMM-- YOU DIRTY RAT--MIKE MURDOCK IS MY FRIEND-- SO TREAT 'IM NICE--
KAREN--YOU'D BETTER NOTIFY THE FUNNY FARM--HE'S READY FOR A PADDED CELL!
OH, FOGGY! DON'T BE SILLY! CAN'T YOU TELL HE'S IMITATING JAMES CAGNEY?!!

YOU RECOGNIZED IT!! KAREN BABY-- YOU'RE THE GREATEST!
IF YOU COULD ONLY SWING 'ROUND THE ROOFTOPS ON A BILLY-CLUB CABLE, YOU'D BE PERFECT!
NO WONDER MATT NEVER WANTED TO TELL US ABOUT HIM--!
HE'S A FEARLESS, FULL-TIME NUT!
MIKE MURDOCK--TELL ME SOMETHING --AREN'T YOU EVER SERIOUS?

SURE I AM--
C'MON, LET'S GET MARRIED!
SORRY, I CAN'T! I'VE A HAIRDRESSER APPOINTMENT!
SEE? WHEN I'M SERIOUS, NO ONE BELIEVES ME!
KAREN, WE'RE GETTING OUT OF HERE BEFORE YOU GET AS WHACKY AS HE!
WE CAN'T AFFORD TO BE OUT OF OUR TREE BY TOMORROW WHEN COURT CONVENES FOR THE LEAPFROG'S* ARRAIGNMENT!
HOW CAN A MAN LIKE MATT HAVE A TWIN BROTHER WHO'S A REAL MENTAL CASE?!!
*THE LEAPFROG IS THE BADDIE WHOM DD DELIVERED TO THE LAW LAST ISH--AS IF YOU DIDN'T KNOW!--SMILEY!

HEY--HOLD IT, GROUP!
IF YOU'RE GONNA BE IN COURT TOMORROW, SAVE A SEAT FOR ME! I WANNA WATCH YOU LEGAL EAGLES IN ACTION!
AFTER ALL--DON'T FORGET WHO IT WAS WHO OUT-LEAPED THE LEAPFROG!
HE'S RIGHT, FOGGY! HE DESERVES A SEAT AT THE TRIAL!
SURE! SURE! SO DOES PERRY MASON!
LET'S GO!
5

OH! MR. FARNUM --OUR BUILDING MANAGER!
AFRAID WE HAVEN'T MUCH TIME NOW, FARNUM! WE'RE JUST LEAVING FOR THE EVENING!
I WON'T DELAY YOU, NELSON! I WAS JUST LEAVING MYSELF AND NOTICED THAT YOUR LIGHT WAS STILL ON!
WERE YOU-- COMING IN-- TO SEE US!
I READ IN THE PAPER THAT YOU'RE DEFENDING THAT LEAPFROG CHARACTER!
THAT'S RIGHT! THE ARRAIGNMENT IS TOMORROW MORNING!

YOU KNOW, THIS IS A RESPECTABLE OFFICE BUILDING!
I'M NOT VERY HAPPY ABOUT HAVING TENANTS WHO SEEM TO BE INVOLVED WITH SOME OF THE MOST DESPICABLE CRIMINALS OF ALL!
NOW, I'M A BROAD-MINDED MAN, BUT MUST YOU DEFEND SUCH CUT-THROATS AND KNAVES?

WHILE INSIDE, THE CROWDED CORRIDORS ARE RIFE WITH *RUMORS* AND *SPECULATION*--
HOW COME *NELSON* IS DEFENDING THE LEAP-FROG--INSTEAD OF *MATT MURDOCK?*
MISTER, MY JOB IS TO GUARD THIS *DOOR!* ONE LAWYER'S THE SAME AS *ANOTHER* TO ME!
MAYBE *NELSON'S* TIRED OF *MURDOCK* ALWAYS GRABBIN' THE *SPOT-LIGHT?*
I WONDER WHAT'S GOIN' *ON* IN THERE NOW?

AND, ON THE OTHER SIDE OF THE PANELLED OAK DOOR--
THIS IS FOR THE *BIRDS!* A GUY COULD FALL *ASLEEP* IN HERE--
I SUPPOSE THE ROUTINE PROCESS OF COURTROOM PROCEDURE *WOULD* SEEM DULL--TO A MAN LIKE *YOU, MIKE*--!
ALTHOUGH YOUR BROTHER, *MATT,* WOULD BE IN HIS *ELEMENT* HERE!
I STILL DON'T KNOW *WHY* HE ASKED *FOGGY* TO MAKE THE OPENING PRESENTATION?
POOR FOGGY WOULD RATHER SINK HIS TEETH INTO A JUICY CORPORATION *TAX* CASE *ANY* DAY!
MATT COULDN'T BE HERE 'CAUSE I DECIDED TO COME AS *MIKE*--
BUT I CAN'T TELL *YOU* THAT, LITTLE LADY!

AND NOW--IF IT PLEASE THE COURT--I SUBMIT *EXHIBIT "A"*--
--THE ELECTRONICALLY-ACTIVATED *SPRING-SOLED SHOES* WHICH ENABLED THE *LEAP-FROG* TO EXECUTE HIS DAZZLING *HIGH-JUMPS!*
I ASK THE DEFENDANT TO STUDY THIS *SHOE!* IS IT NOT THE SAME ONE YOU WORE WHEN COMMITTING YOUR *CRIMES?*
NAH! I NEVER EVEN *SAW* IT BEFORE!
BUT, IT WAS TAKEN FROM YOUR OWN *FOOT!*
I'M AS *INNOCENT* AS A NEW-BORN BABE! I *COULDN'T* BE THE LEAP-FROG! I'M SCARED OF *HEIGHTS!*
I EVEN GET *AIRSICK* STANDIN' ON A THICK *RUG!*
OBJECTION! COUNCIL IS TRYING TO *BADGER* THE WITNESS!

SAY, DOLL--WHY DOESN'T THE D.A. JUST MEASURE HIS HOOF 'N SEE IF IT'S THE SAME SIZE?--IF IT WAS GOOD ENOUGH FOR CINDERELLA--
WOULD YOU MIND KEEPING YOUR VOICE DOWN, YOUNG MAN? OTHERS WOULD LIKE TO HEAR THE PROCEEDINGS!
COOL IT, POPS! I'LL CLUE YOU IN AS WE GO ALONG!
MIKE! YOU'VE GOT TO BE QUIET --OR THE BAILIFF WILL EVICT YOU! THIS IS A COURTROOM!
NO ONE SHOVES YOURS TRULY AROUND, BABY! THE SUPER-HERO UNION'LL PICKET THE JOINT!

CAN'TCHA SEE THOSE SHOES WOULD NEVER FIT ME? THEY'RE MUCH TOO SMALL!
WITH THE COURT'S PERMISSION, THERE'S ONE WAY TO DISPROVE THAT--!
ALL RIGHT, LEMME HAVE 'EM! I'LL SHOW YOU!

MAN! WHAT A PAIR OF CLOD-HOPPERS THESE ARE--!
HEY! HOLD IT! GRAB THOSE SHOES!! WHAT IF HE--?
MIKE! I WARNED YOU! YOU CAN'T MAKE AN OUTCRY LIKE THAT!

I CAN'T, HUH? SO, I'LL CLAM UP--WHILE THEY HAND THE LEAP-FROG HIS ESCAPE--ON A SILVER PLATTER!
OKAY--YOU WIN YOUR CASE! YOU PROVED I AM THE LEAP-FROG!!
BUT, NOW THAT I'VE GOT MY SPRING-SHOES AGAIN--LET'S SEE WHAT GOOD IT DOES YOU!
STOP, YOU FOOL! YOU'LL NEVER MAKE IT!
BTWANG!

ALAS, EVEN THE CRAFTIEST, MOST CONNIVING OF CRIMINALS CAN MAKE A FATAL MISTAKE--
THEY WERE TOO SMART FOR ME!
MY SPRING-SHOES HAVE TO BE TIGHTLY FASTENED ON MY FEET!
THE D.A. REMOVED THE FASTENERS--!

NOW I'M FALLING-- FROM THREE FLIGHTS UP!!
BUT, EVEN AS ONE MENACE TO SOCIETY IS ABOUT TO BE PUT OUT OF ACTION, ANOTHER SUDDENLY, UNEXPECTEDLY, APPEARS ON THE SCENE-- LIKE SO--
(NEXT PANEL, PLEASE!)

YOU FOOL! WHY DIDN'T YOU WAIT?? I WAS COMING TO GET YOU!!
UHHH--! MY ONE SHOE-- SAVED ME-- BROKE MY FALL--BUT-- CAN'T GET UP-- LEG BROKEN--!
WHO'S THAT-- TOWERING ABOVE ME--?

IT'S THE STILT-MAN!! BUT-- I THOUGHT--YOU WERE DEAD--!
YOU SEEM TO HAVE AN UNCANNY KNACK FOR BEING WRONG!
WHEN I READ OF YOUR CAPTURE, I DECIDED TO HELP YOU ESCAPE-- SO THAT YOU COULD JOIN ME IN A NEW CAREER OF CRIME!
WHAT AN UNBEATABLE TEAM WE'D HAVE MADE-- IF YOU HADN'T BUNGLED EVERYTHING-- LIKE AN AMATEUR!
WHILE BACK IN THE COURTROOM--

HOW ABOUT THAT! THINGS ARE LOOKIN' UP FOR OL' MIKE!
NOW YOU JUST STAY THERE AND CHEER WHILE I START MAKIN' LIKE A HERO!
9

GANGWAY, GUYS! YOU'RE BLOCKIN' TRAFFIC!
HEY! WHERE'S THE FIRE, MAC?
SAY NOW!! THERE'S A GREAT LINE! DIDJA THINK IT UP ALL BY YOURSELF?

SOMEONE OUGHTTA POKE THAT BIG CLOWN!
DON'T TRY IT, SWEETIE --UNLESS YOUR SAW-BONES NEEDS THE BUSINESS!
CAN'T LET THE LEAP-FROG GET AWAY AGAIN--
NOT AFTER ALL THE TROUBLE I WENT THRU TO NAB HIM!

IT LOOKED LIKE I WAS FINALLY GONNA HEAR OL' FOGGY HANDLE A DEFENSE--
I CAN'T LET THAT LEAPIN' LAME-BRAIN SPOIL MY PARTNER'S BIG CHANCE!

SO, I'LL JUST SWING OUT, AND --UH OH!
THERE'S A CROWD DOWN BELOW! I CAN HEAR WHAT THEY'RE SAYING!
HIS SHOE FELL OFF!! HE'S INJURED!
I MIGHT AS WELL SWING RIGHT BACK AND CHANGE TO--
WAIT A MINUTE!!
THERE'S SOMEONE ELSE THERE-- SOMEONE FAR MORE DANGER-OUS!
YOU'LL BE OKAY! I'LL CARRY YOU OUT OF HERE AND GET YOU PATCHED UP! THEN, WE'LL --WAIT!!

YOU!
SORRY, LEAP-FROG! THIS JUST ISN'T YOUR DAY!
I'VE A MORE URGENT MATTER TO ATTEND TO NOW!
HE'S TRYING TO MAKE OFF WITH THE LEAP-FROG! --NO! HE'S DROP-PING 'IM AGAIN!
HE SEES DARE-DEVIL!
SO, YOU'VE RETURNED AT LAST!

HAH! YOU MISSED!!
HAVE YOU FORGOTTEN SO SOON HOW EASILY I CAN CHANGE MY HEIGHT, THANKS TO MY MAGNIFICENT HYDRAULICALLY-OPERATED STILTS?!!
MEBBE SO! BUT I HAVEN'T FORGOTTEN THAT I'M THE GENT WHO WHUMPED YOU GOOD LAST TIME WE FOUGHT!
MAN! IT SURE IS LUCKY I WAS HERE!
IF STILT-MAN EVER MANAGED TO GET THE LEAP-FROG SAFELY AWAY, WHAT A TEAM THOSE TWO WOULD MAKE!

THOP!
AND, IN CASE YOU DON'T BELIEVE ME--!
UNHHH! I BELIEVE YOU! I BELIEVE YOU!

WHEW! WHERE WOULD I BE WITHOUT THESE LOVELY LITTLE LEDGES TO CLING TO?
I'VE GOTTA HANG LOOSE FOR A COUPLE'A SECS UNTIL I GET MY BREATH BACK!
BUT SOMETHING TELLS ME THAT DADDY LONG LEGS OVER THERE ISN'T ABOUT TO WAIT!

AND, IT SEEMS THAT OL' FEARLESS IS A MIGHTY GOOD FORTUNE-TELLER--
COME NOW, MASKED MAN! SURELY YOU DON'T WANT TO DISAPPOINT THE CROWD GATHERED BELOW!
THEY'VE COME TO EXPECT A BETTER PERFORMANCE THAN THAT FROM THE MAN WITHOUT FEAR!
IT DIDN'T FIGURE THAT THE SENSATIONAL STILT-MAN WOULD REAPPEAR WEAPONLESS, DID IT?

ZZAK!
MOVE, YOU CRINGING, COSTUMED CLOWN!! MY NEXT SHOT WON'T MISS!
12

IF THERE'S ONE THING THAT BUGS ME, IT'S A FELLA WHO TALKS NASTY!
SO, IT'S TIME FOR ME TO TEACH YOU WHAT HAPPENS TO BOASTFUL BADDIES WHO ACT IMPOLITE TO US GOOD GUYS--!

IF IT'S ACTION YOU WANT, I'LL TRY TO SEE TO IT THAT YOU'RE NOT DISAPPOINTED!
--SO YOU WON'T GROW UP FRUSTRATED!

AFTER ALL, YOU'VE GOT ENOUGH PROBLEMS GOIN' FOR YOU NOW!
YOK!

YOU CAN'T DEFEAT ME THAT EASILY, DAREDEVIL! MY PROTECTIVE GARB IS MUCH TOO STRONG!

DEFEAT YOU?
HEAVENS TO HARRIET--WHO'D WANNA DO THAT?
--I'LL GIVE YOU THREE GUESSES!
ZOP!

FORGIVE ME FOR ACTING LIKE A ROUGHNECK, OL' BUDDY--
BUT SOMEBODY'S GOTTA SHAKE YOU LOOSE FROM THAT ANTI-SOCIAL BEHAVIOR OF YOURS!
SPOOK
SPECIAL MEDICAL NOTE: ONE OF THE OCCUPATIONAL HAZARDS OF BATTLING A SUPER-HERO IS--EVEN IF YOU SURVIVE THE ENSUING MAYHEM, THERE'S ALWAYS THE CHANCE OF INCURRING A KING-SIZED HEADACHE FROM THE SOUND EFFECTS! --SYMPATHETIC STAN.
AND NOW, BACK TO OUR FANTASY-FRAUGHT FUN-FEST--

WHOOPS! HOLD EVERYTHING! WE JUST THOUGHT OF SOMETHING! IF YOU HAPPEN TO BE ONE OF THOSE FEW UNFORTUNATES WHO NEVER READ DD #8, WE'D BETTER CLUE YOU IN ABOUT THE SENSATIONAL STILT-MAN!

I DIDN'T PLAN IT THIS WAY! IT WAS AN ACCIDENT!

HE WAS ONE OF THE USUAL MAD-SCIENTIST-TYPES WHO USED HIS HYDRAULIC STILTS AS WEAPONS! BUT, HIS MOST DANGEROUS WEAPON WAS A MOLECULAR CONDENSER HE HAD STOLEN--A RAY GUN WHICH COULD SHRINK ANY TARGET INTO ABSOLUTE NOTHINGNESS!!

HOWEVER, IN HIS FINAL BATTLE WITH OUR HAPPY-GO-LUCKY HERO, STILT-MAN HIMSELF WAS HIT WITH THE FATEFUL RAY! SEE--?

I'M GETTING SMALLER!! --STARTING TO FADE AWAY!

THERE'S NO ANTIDOTE-- NOTHING TO STOP ME--!!

HOWEVER, BEFORE RETURNING TO OUR SCENE OF COMBAT, THERE IS STILL ANOTHER DEVELOPMENT WHICH WILL BE OF MORE THAN PASSING INTEREST TO ALL TRUE BELIEVERS--
ONCE I TURN THE CORNER, I'LL BE THERE!
SKREEEEE
AT THIS LATE HOUR, IN THE SHADOWS OF THE DARKENED SIDE-STREET, THERE'LL BE NO ONE TO SEE ME!

SRRRRRRRRRRRRRRRRR
ONLY THE BRILLIANT MASKED MARAUDER COULD HAVE DEVISED THE PERFECT, FOOLPROOF METHOD OF GAINING ACCESS TO ANY WINDOW IN THE CITY!

IT'S ALL SO DEVILISHLY SIMPLE! A HIGH-SPEED HYDRAULIC LIFT, CONCEALED WITHIN MY ARMORED TRUCK--
AND, WITHIN THE LIFT, A SIMPLE VACUUM ELEVATOR OF MY OWN INGENIOUS DESIGN!
AHH! I'VE ALREADY REACHED THE PROPER FLOOR!

AND NOW, THE MASKED MARAUDER CAN SEARCH THE LAW OFFICES OF NELSON AND MURDOCK CALMLY AND SAFELY--
SECURE IN THE KNOW-LEDGE THAT THEY WON'T RETURN UNTIL MORN-ING!

I'VE HAD ENOUGH RUN-INS WITH DAREDEVIL IN THE PAST TO KNOW, BEYOND A SHADOW OF A DOUBT, THAT THERE'S SOME CONNECTION BETWEEN MY COSTUMED ENEMY AND NELSON AND MURDOCK!
NOW, WHEN DAREDEVIL LEAST EXPECTS IT, THE TIME HAS COME TO ATTACK HIM ONCE MORE!
AND, IF I CAN JUST LEARN HIS TRUE IDENTITY, I'LL BE ABLE TO STRIKE WHERE HE'S WEAKEST!!
IF ONLY I COULD FIND SOME CLUE HERE--!

HE CAN'T BE FOGGY NELSON! NELSON'S TOO SOFT, TOO FLABBY!
AND HE COULD NEVER BE A BLIND MAN, LIKE MURDOCK!
BUT, I'M SURE THAT THEY KNOW WHO HE IS--!
PERHAPS THERE'S A NOTE--JUST A CARELESS LINE-- OR A RANDOM PHRASE--!
I'VE GOT TO FIND OUT!!
16

BUT, AFTER MORE THAN AN HOUR OF CAREFUL SEARCHING--
IT'S NO USE! THERE'S NOTHING HERE! I'LL HAVE TO THINK OF ANOTHER WAY!
I'LL CONTACT MY MEN IN THE TRUCK, THRU MY HELMET MIKE--
LOWER THE LIFT! RETURN TO HOME BASE! I'LL REMAIN HERE! THAT IS ALL!

THEN, AS THE MALEVOLENT MASKED MARAUDER CALMLY REMOVES HIS UNIQUE, ELABORATELY-OUTFITTED HELMET, ONLY THE SILENT SHADOWS WITHIN THE DESERTED OFFICE ARE WITNESS TO THE FACT THAT THE FEATURES OF FRANK FARNUM, THE BUILDING'S EVER-PRESENT MANAGER, ARE THUS REVEALED--!*
NO NEED FOR ME TO ACCOMPANY THE TRUCK AGAIN! I'LL MERELY REMOVE MY OUTFIT AND RETURN TO MY NORMAL IDENTITY--REMAINING IN THIS BUILDING, WHERE I BELONG!
AND, I'LL CONTINUE TO OBSERVE NELSON AND MURDOCK--WAITING UNTIL DAREDEVIL CONTACTS THEM AGAIN!
I CAN AFFORD TO BE PATIENT; FOR, NO MATTER HOW LONG IT TAKES, SOONER OR LATER THE MASKED MARAUDER SHALL FIND AND DESTROY THE MAN WITHOUT FEAR!
*WE DON'T REALLY EXPECT YOU TO BE TOO SURPRISED, FAITHFUL ONE, SINCE HE'S ABOUT THE ONLY SUSPECT WE'VE HANDED YOU ALL THESE MONTHS --JUST TO SEE IF YOU WERE PAYING ATTENTION! --SINGLE-MINDED STAN.

BUT, IT SEEMS THAT FARNUM WILL HAVE TO TAKE HIS PLACE IN LINE--
ZAK!
LUCKY FOR ME HE'S NERVOUS--NOT TAKING ENOUGH TIME TO AIM THAT THING!
BLAST IT!! WHAT MUST I DO TO FINISH YOU OFF??!

EVER TRY WISHING ON A STAR?
IT DID WONDERS FOR SNOW WHITE!
AWW! SORRY I MADE YOU DROP YOUR RAY GIZMO! BUT, DON'T DESPAIR--
YOU CAN ALWAYS TRY CALLING ME NASTY NAMES!
17

UH OH! MAYBE THIS'LL TEACH ME NOT TO BE SUCH A BIG MOUTH!
WHILE I'M MAKING WITH THE CORNY CRACKS, STILTY JUST REACHED OUT AND GRABBED THE END OF MY CABLE LINE--!
HE'S UNHOOKING IT!! I CAN FEEL THE TENSION BEING RELEASED!
I'VE ONLY GOT SECONDS TO DO SOMETHING--OR GROW A PAIR OF WINGS!!

EVEN YOU CAN'T STAY ALOFT WITH THE END OF YOUR CABLE UNHOOKED!
I NEEDED YOU TO TELL ME THAT??
GOTTA TWIST MY BODY--BRING MYSELF INTO POSITION FOR ONE LAST THRUST!! NOW--MUST DO IT NOW!!

MADE IT!!

NOW, THE MORE I SWING, THE MORE I TIGHTEN THE CABLE--!!
MY LEGS--BEING PULLED TOGETHER!! --LOSING MY BALANCE--!!

NOW--
ONE FINAL
YANK
OUGHTTA
DO IT!

CAN'T KEEP MY
BALANCE!! I-I'M
FALLING--!!
DON'T
PANIC,
TIN-
TOES!
BY SHIFTING
MY WEIGHT
JUST SO, I
CAN BRING
YOU DOWN
JUST WHERE
I WANT
YOU!
I'VE GOT TO
MAKE HIM
TOPPLE IN THE
ALLEYWAY
BETWEEN THOSE
BUILDINGS--
CAN'T HAVE HIM
LANDING ON ANY OF
THE PROVERBIAL
INNOCENT BYSTANDERS
THAT ALWAYS POP UP
OUT OF THE WOODWORK!
HIS ARMORED OUTFIT
WILL STOP HIM
FROM GETTING
ANYTHING WORSE
THAN A KING-
SIZED NOSE-BLEED!

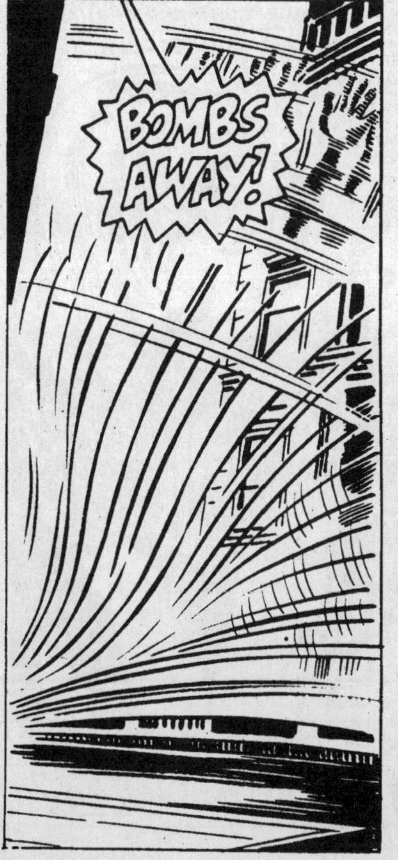
BOMBS
AWAY!

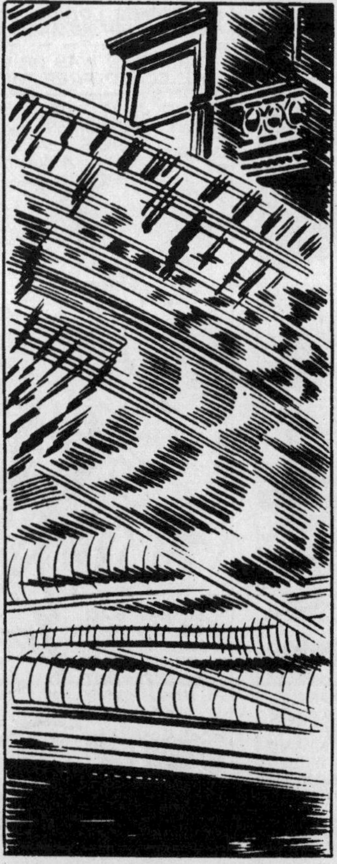

BEEYOONNG!

SECONDS LATER--
STAY BACK, AVERAGE TYPICAL CROWD OF PASSERSBY!
IF STILT-MAN IS STILL CONSCIOUS, HE MIGHT BE MORE DANGEROUS THAN EVER!
SO, LET YOUR EVER-DUTIFUL, DEATH-DEFYING DAREDEVIL BE THE FIRST TO TURN THE CORNER AND CHECK OUT THE ALLEY!

HOWEVER, WHILE DD HOLDS BACK THE WIDE-EYED ONLOOKERS--AND INCIDENTALLY PAUSES TO CATCH HIS OWN BREATH--ANOTHER FIGURE HAS ALREADY REACHED THE FALLEN STILT-MAN--
WHEN I HEARD THE RADIO BULLETIN OF YOUR FIGHT, I REALIZED YOU WERE JUST THE ONE I NEED!
IT'S LUCKY YOUR STILTS AUTO-MATICALLY RETRACTED WHEN YOU FELL--
NOW I'LL BE ABLE TO HIDE YOU IN MY CAR TRUNK BEFORE THAT COSTUMED CLOWN REACHES THE SCENE!

I DID IT! HE'S SAFELY LOCKED INSIDE THE--OH! DAREDEVIL!
STILT-MAN'S GONE! HE MUST HAVE RECOVERED JUST SECONDS AGO!
FARNUM!! GET THAT CAR OUT OF HERE, MAN! THIS AREA IS DANGER-OUS!
STILT-MAN IS ON THE LOOSE! SO TAKE OFF, MISTER!
HE CALLED ME BY NAME! HE KNOWS ME!

HE APPEARED SO SUDDENLY! CAN HE BE--? NO! HIS HEARTBEAT IS DIFFERENT! HE'S NOT LONG-LEGS!
THANKS FOR THE WARNING, DAREDEVIL!
I'M A LOT MORE GRATEFUL THAN YOU SUSPECT, YOU FOOL!
NOW I'M CERTAIN HIS REAL IDENTITY IS THAT OF SOMEONE I KNOW!
ALL I NEED DO IS KEEP THE OFFICE OF NELSON AND MURDOCK UNDER OBSERVATION --AND THEN--
SOONER OR LATER, STILT-MAN AND I WILL HAVE HIM!
20

AND, AT THE COURTHOUSE WINDOW, A PAIR OF SPARKLING BLUE EYES LOOK DOWN WITH ADMIRATION--AND PERHAPS MORE THAN ADMIRATION--
THANKS TO DAREDEVIL, STILT-MAN WAS DRIVEN OFF BEFORE HE COULD FREE THE LEAPFROG!
AND, JUST THINK--WE'RE THE ONLY ONES WHO KNOW HE'S REALLY MIKE MURDOCK!
YEAH! THAT, AND A DIME, WILL GET YOU A CUP OF COFFEE!
IT WAS BAD ENOUGH WHEN SHE HAD A CRUSH ON MATT--BUT NOW--I'VE HAD IT!
NEXT
MIKE MURDOCK MUST DIE!

HERE COMES...
DAREDEVIL
THE MAN WITHOUT FEAR!
APPROVED BY THE COMICS CODE AUTHORITY
MARVEL COMICS GROUP
12¢ IND.
27 APR
GUEST-STARRING: THE ONE, THE ONLY, THE INIMITABLE SPIDER-MAN!
WHO'S AFRAID OF STILT-MAN?
FEATURING THE HONEST-TO-GOSH END OF THE MASKED MARAUDER!
FOGGY! WHAT CAN WE DO?
WELL, WE CAN ALWAYS RESORT TO SHEER PANIC!
AND HOW ABOUT OUR TITANIC TITLE?
"MIKE MURDOCK MUST DIE!"

DAREDEVIL, THE MAN WITHOUT FEAR!
"MIKE MURDOCK MUST DIE!"
NOBODY CAN BE CERTAIN THAT THE SIGHTINGS OF FLYING SAUCERS ARE GENUINE OR NOT! BUT THERE'S ONE THING YOU CAN BET YOUR MMMS BUTTON ON--IF YOU HAPPEN TO SEE A SIGHT LIKE THIS WHEN YOU LEAST EXPECT IT, YOU CAN BET YOUR BOTTOM DOLLAR IT'S OL' DD--AND HE'S FOR REAL--!
STILT-MAN MUST BE SOMEWHERE IN THE CITY --AND SOONER OR LATER I'VE GOT TO FIND HIM!*
ACTUALLY, I'M KIND'A GLAD HE GOT AWAY FROM ME! IT GIVES ME AN EXCUSE TO CATCH UP ON MY EXERCISE WHILE I SEARCH FOR HIM!
GUEST-STARRING: GENIAL GENE'S OWN VARIEGATED VERSION OF: (AWW, WHY BOTHER TELLING YOU? YOU'LL SEE FOR YOURSELF AS SOON AS YOU TURN THE PAGE...!)
*SURELY WE DON'T HAVE TO TELL YOU THAT DD FOUGHT STILT-MAN TO A FARE-THEE-WELL LAST ISH, BUT LOST HIM TO THE SNEAKY MASKED MARAUDER AT THE LAST MINUTE! --SLEEPY STAN.
NOBEL PRIZE COMMITTEE, PLEASE NOTE...
BRAND ECHH WILL LITTLE NOTE NOR LONG REMEMBER WHAT WE SAY HERE... BUT, THE MIGHTY MINIONS OF MARVELDOM SHALL NEVER FORGET THIS BREATH-TAKING BATTLE OF BABBLING BEHEMOTHS, BY--
STAN (THE MAN) LEE and Gentleman GENE COLAN
INDESCRIBABLE INKING BY: FEARLESS FRANKIE GIACOIA
LEVEL-HEADED LETTERING BY: ADORABLE ARTIE SIMEK
1

UH OH! SOUNDS LIKE A FIGHT DOWN THERE BELOW ME!
I HATE TO BE A SPOIL-SPORT, BUT--
I'D BETTER PUT ON THE BRAKES--

AND SEE WHAT'S SHAKIN' DOWN THERE!
IT CAN'T BE STILT-MAN--.
'CAUSE I DON'T HEAR ANYTHING THAT SOUNDS LIKE METAL LEGS!

BUT, THINGS HAVE BEEN SLOW, SO I CAN'T BE TOO PARTICULAR!
IN THIS BUSINESS, YOU JUST TAKE YOUR ACTION AS IT COMES!
SAY! THAT VOICE ON THE STREET BENEATH ME! I'D KNOW IT ANYWHERE!

IT'S SPIDER-MAN!!
THREE TWO-BIT CAR THIEVES ATTACKING YOUR FRIENDLY NEIGHBOR-HOOD WALL-CRAWLER?!!
COME NOW, GENTS--YOU'VE JUST GOTTA BE KIDDING!
KIDDIN' ARE WE? LET'S GO, YOU GUYS--WE CAN TAKE 'IM!
YEAH! HE AINT BUSTIN' UP OUR LITTLE CAPER!

YOU SHOULD BE GRATEFUL THAT IT'S ONLY YOUR CAPER I'M SMASHING!
IF I DIDN'T TAKE THE TROUBLE TO PULL MY PUNCH, YOU'D BE GUMMIN' YOUR FOOD TILL THE COWS COME HOME!
BOK!

HEY, SPIDEY-- IS THIS A PRIVATE FIGHT --OR CAN ANYBODY JOIN THE PARTY?
HORN-HEAD!! WHO INVITED YOU?
WHOOPS! SORRY ABOUT THAT, CHARLIE!
ZAK
WHUMMPHH!

COME TO THINK OF IT, NOBODY INVITED ME!
MAYBE I OUGHTTA TRY A GOOD MOUTH-WASH!
BACK IN LINE, CHUCKLES!
THAT'S A GOOD KID!
THOP!

TELL ME SOME THING, SPIDEY--
SEEN ANYTHING OF A GUY CALLED STILT-MAN?
NO! NOW GET LOST, HUH?
SOMEONE MIGHT THINK IT TOOK TWO OF US TO LICK THREE PENNY-ANTE HOODS!

OKAY, WEB-HEAD-- YOU CAN TAKE THE CREDIT ALL FOR YOURSELF!
BUT, IF YOU HAPPEN TO RUN INTO A SINISTER SCHIZO ON METAL STILTS, SAVE HIM FOR ME, HUH?
WHAT'S WITH YOU, FELLA? DON'T YOU EVER SMILE?
HOW CAN YOU TELL I'M NOT SMILING--UNDER MY MASK?
OH, MATTHEW--YOU LEFT YOURSELF WIDE OPEN FOR THAT ONE!!
HOW DO YOU KNOW I HAVEN'T GOT X-RAY EYES?
IF THAT DOESN'T THROW HIM OFF THE TRAIL, NOTHING WILL!

BUT, SINCE YOU CAN SEE ALL OF SPIDEY YOU WANT TO IN HIS **OWN** MAG, LET'S DO SOME MIGHTY MARVEL **SCENE-SWITCHING** NOW AND JOIN THE MYSTERIOUS **MASKED MARAUDER** AS HE SHOWS HIS SECRET HILLTOP HIDEOUT TO THE MAN HE HAS RESCUED FROM **DAREDEVIL**--

BETWEEN THE **TWO** OF US, IT SHOULD BE **CHILD'S PLAY** TO DEFEAT THE **MAN WITHOUT FEAR!**

AND, AS YOU CAN SEE, I AM NOT WITHOUT THE MOST EFFECTIVE **RESOURCES** TO AID US IN OUR LITTLE ENDEAVOR!

A **HELICOPTER!** BIG DEAL! HOW CAN **THAT** MAKE SOMEONE LIKE **DAREDEVIL** ANY EASIER TO POLISH OFF?

I WAS **HOPING** YOU'D ASK!

DON'T GET CUTE WITH **ME,** MISTER! JUST **ANSWER** THE QUESTION!

SO, YOU THINK THIS IS JUST AN ORDINARY HELICOPTER, EH?
JUST WATCH THE BOX--!

FZZZSSST!
IT--IT DISINTEGRATED!
OH! YOU NOTICED?

STILL THINK WE SHOULDN'T TEAM UP?
OKAY, MASKED MAN--YOU SOLD ME A BILL OF GOODS!
NOW COME WITH ME-- I WANNA SHOW YOU SOMETHING!

JUST SO YOU DON'T THINK THAT FORCE FIELD MAKES YOU TOP DOG, I'LL DEMONSTRATE MY POWER!
I AM FULLY AWARE OF WHAT YOUR STILTS CAN DO!

BUT YOU NEVER SAW THEM IN ACTION!
WAIT'LL I PRESS THIS CONTROL STUD--!
CLICK!

WAS THIS FAST ENOUGH FOR YOU?
IT'S ALMOST UNBELIEVABLE!
YOUR STILTS MOVE FASTER THAN THE EYE CAN FOLLOW!!

NOW DO YOU SEE WHY I'M NOT EXACTLY HELPLESS WITHOUT A PARTNER?!!
HOW DID DAREDEVIL EVER BEAT YOU IN THE FIRST PLACE?
JUST A LUCKY FLUKE! NEXT TIME WE MEET, I'LL WIPE HIM OFF THE FACE OF THE MAP!

NOW THAT'S THE ATTITUDE I LIKE!
WE'LL MAKE A GREAT TEAM, YOU AND I!
NOW, HERE'S MY PLAN--
I KNOW THERE'S SOME CONNECTION BETWEEN THE STAFF OF NELSON AND MURDOCK, ATTORNEYS-AT-LAW-- AND DAREDEVIL HIMSELF!
I'M CONVINCED THAT EITHER MURDOCK, NELSON, OR THE GIRL KNOW THE REAL IDENTITY OF OUR MASKED ENEMY!
THUS, THE WAY FOR US TO LEARN IT IS SIMPLE--WE MERELY CAPTURE THEM ALL!
ONCE WE KNOW WHO THE MAN WITHOUT FEAR REALLY IS, IT SHOULD BE SIMPLE TO ATTACK HIM WHEN HE LEAST SUSPECTS IT!
NOW, THE FIRST THING WE'LL DO IS PAY A VISIT TO THAT OFFICE --TONIGHT--!

AND SO, SHORTLY AFTER SUNSET, ON A SHADOWY SIDE STREET, A STARTLING FIGURE OBSERVES ONE CERTAIN WINDOW--
THEY'RE WORKING OVERTIME TONIGHT! GOOD!

WITH SPLIT-SECOND TIMING, THE WHOLE THING SHOULD BE OVER IN LESS THAN A MINUTE!

WHILE, INSIDE THE OFFICE WHICH IS STILT-MAN'S TARGET--
MATT, I WONDER WHAT HAPPENED TO YOUR BROTHER, MIKE, SINCE STILT-MAN'S ESCAPE?
HE'S PROBABLY OUT SEARCHING FOR HIM-- IN HIS DAREDEVIL GUISE, KAREN!
GOOD OL' "MIKE"! HE SURE GOT THIS REDHEAD OFF THE HOOK!
UH OH WHAT'S THAT?
I HEAR SOME-THING-OUTSIDE THE WINDOW! SOME-THING OMINOUS--!

BUT, BEFORE A WORD CAN BE UTTERED--OR A MOVE MADE--
ALL IT WILL TAKE IS THE ONE LITTLE GAS PELLET WHICH THE MARAUDER GAVE ME!
KAREN! MATT! LOOK OUT! THERE'S SOMEONE AT THE WINDOW!! IT'S STILT-MAN!
HE--THREW SOMETHING--INTO THE OFFICE!!
GAS FUMES! TOO LATE TO DO ANYTHING ABOUT THEM!
IT'S NOT LETHAL! JUST A FORM OF SLEEP GAS!

SINCE MY SENSES--INCLUDING THE SENSE OF SMELL--ARE SO HIGHLY DEVELOPED--I'LL BE FIRST--TO BE OVERCOME--!
HOW IRONIC!--I SEARCHED THE CITY FOR HIM--AND HE'S OUTSIDE--OUR WINDOW--

FIFTEEN SECONDS LATER--
IT'S OVER! WORKED LIKE A CHARM!
I'LL STAY INSIDE THE OFFICE AND WAIT FOR THE HELICOPTER!
MY BREATHING APPARATUS WILL PREVENT THE GAS FROM AFFECTING ME!
I HEAR THE PROPELLER NOW! THE MARAUDER IS AS GOOD AS HIS WORD!

I'VE GOT TO HAND IT TO HIM--HE'S AS BRILLIANT A STRATEGIST AS HE CLAIMED TO BE!
HE'S LOWERING THE INFLATED BALLOON--WITH THE PLATFORM ATTACHED BENEATH IT!
RRRRRRRRRRRR
WE'LL BE SAFELY OUT OF HERE--WITH OUR CAPTIVES--BEFORE ANYONE WHO SAW ME CAN REACH THE OFFICE!
7

AND, WITHIN THE HOVERING SHIP--
SECURE ALL CARGO!
STAND AWAY! I'M HAULING UP PLATFORM--!

IT WENT LIKE CLOCKWORK--!
JUST AS ALL THE PLANS OF THE MASKED MARAUDER DO!
STILT-MAN, PREPARE TO RETRACT!
IT'S TIME TO LEAVE THE AREA!

OKAY! HAUL AWAY! WE GOT WHAT WE CAME FOR!
WHIT!

PERFECT! EVERYONE'S SAFELY ABOARD!
NOW, ALL THAT REMAINS IS TO ACTIVATE THE FORCE FIELD AGAIN!

DID YOU LEAVE THE NOTE FOR DAREDEVIL, AS PLANNED?
YEAH! RIGHT ON THE DESK WHERE HE CAN'T MISS IT!
I'LL JUST TIE OUR PIGEONS UP NOW--
THOUGH WE WON'T HAVETA WORRY ABOUT THE BLIND ONE!

THEN, AS THE CAPTIVES RECOVER CONSCIOUSNESS, AND THE MINUTES TURN TO HOURS--
HEY, THIS IS FOR THE BIRDS!
HOW MUCH LONGER ARE WE GONNA HAVE TO WAIT?
UNTIL DAREDEVIL FINDS THAT NOTE...
OR, UNTIL OUR GUESTS REVEAL HIS IDENTITY TO ME!

IF THAT'S ALL YOU WANT TO KNOW, I'LL TELL YOU!
MATT!! NO! YOU CAN'T!
WHY NOT? ANYTHING TO GET US OUT OF HERE!
DAREDEVIL IS MIKE MURDOCK --MY TWIN BROTHER!
AT LAST! I KNEW WE'D FIND OUT!
THE NOTE IS STILL WHERE YOU LEFT IT-- BUT IT DOESN'T MATTER NOW!
ALL THAT MATTERS IS--
MIKE MURDOCK MUST DIE!

WELL, IN KAREN'S EYES I'VE JUST ELECTED MYSELF HEEL OF THE YEAR-- BUT I HAD TO DO IT!
OUR ONLY CHANCE IS FOR ME TO TURN INTO DAREDEVIL-- BUT I CAN'T DO IT YET!
FIRST, I'VE GOT TO DIVERT THEIR ATTENTION--AND THAT WAS THE ONLY WAY!
DON'T WORRY, KAREN! OL' MIKE WILL BE TOO SMART FOR THEM! THEY WON'T GET HIM!
HE'S BEATEN BETTER MEN THAN THEY BEFORE!
OH, MATT-- MATT! HOW COULD YOU! HOW COULD YOU HAVE BETRAYED YOUR OWN BROTHER?
I NEVER EXPECTED IT OF YOU-- NEVER!
THERE'S AN ESCAPE DOOR AT MY RIGHT! IF I CAN GET THE MARAUDER TO OPEN IT--!
NOW THAT WE KNOW WHO DAREDEVIL IS, WE NEED WAIT NO LONGER!
I'LL BRING THE SHIP LOW ENOUGH FOR YOU TO EXTEND YOUR METAL LEGS AND REACH THE GROUND!
THEN ALL YOU NEED DO IS FIND MIKE MURDOCK!
WELL, MATTHEW BOY--IF YOU EVER HAD A CHANCE WITH KAREN, FORGET IT!
YOU JUST BLEW THE WHOLE BIT!

AND, AS THE WHIRLYBIRD BEGINS ITS SLOW DESCENT--
REMEMBER-- YOUR JOB IS TO FIND MIKE MURDOCK--AND DESTROY HIM!
OKAY! OKAY! I GET THE PITCH! YOU DON'T HAVE TO DRAW ME A PICTURE!

I'VE SHUT OFF THE FORCE FIELD! IT'S SAFE TO LEAVE THE SHIP NOW!
WELL? WHAT ARE YOU WAITING FOR?
ARE YOU KIDDIN'?
BRING 'ER DOWN LOWER, MISTER! THESE STILTS OF MINE DON'T EXTEND FOREVER!
ALL RIGHT! THAT'S LOW ENOUGH! NOW HOLD HER STEADY--!

IF I DO THIS FAST ENOUGH--
I'LL BE ON THE GROUND--
AND SAFELY OUT OF SIGHT--
BEFORE ANYONE KNOWS WHAT HAPPENED!

SAY, BILL--DID YOU JUST SEE SOMETHING FLASH OUT OF THE SKY?
AWW, COME ON, CHUCK! NOT ANOTHER FLYING SAUCER?
OR, WAS IT SANTA'S SLEIGH?
NO--I COULD'A SWORN I SAW SOME-THING METAL--!
NO STAN
MUSTA BEEN A REFLECTION, I GUESS!

I MADE IT!
LUCKY IT'S LATE--AND THE STREETS ARE DESERTED!
I'LL JUST FIND MYSELF A LONELY PHONE BOOTH AND LOOK UP THE HOME ADDRESS OF MIKE MURDOCK!
THE REST WILL BE A BREEZE!
HIS BROTHER, MATT, MUST BE A REAL YELLA-BELLY TO PULL THE RUG OUT FROM UNDER DAREDEVIL LIKE THAT!
SOME GUYS'LL DO ANYTHING TO SAVE THEIR OWN SKIN!

BUT, A SHORT TIME LATER, STILT-MAN FINDS HIS TASK A BIT MORE DIFFICULT THAN HE HAD EXPECTED--
NUTS! WHAT AM I GONNA DO NOW?
I'M NO BLASTED BLOOD-HOUND--
HOW DO YOU FIND ONE GUY IN A CITY OF MILLIONS??
THERE'S NO MIKE MURDOCK LISTED IN THE PHONE BOOK!
THE MARAUDER WOULD SAY-- "MAKE HIM COME TO YOU!"

WELL, WELL! THAT LOOKS LIKE THE GENT DAREDEVIL WAS AFTER!
LUCKY I HAPPENED TO BE CRAWLIN' BY!
THIS JEWELRY STORE MAY DO THE TRICK!
IF I BREAK IN--AND MY PIGEON'S IN THE NEIGHBOR-HOOD--
--IT MIGHT BRING HIM ON THE RUN!
BUT, NO SOONER DOES OUR STILT-WEARING SCOUNDREL TAKE PRECIPITOUS ACTION, WHEN--

WHAT ARE YOU TRYING TO DO, CHUM--WAKE UP THE NEIGHBORHOOD?
WE'VE GOT ANTI-NOISE LAWS AROUND HERE!
HOW ABOUT GIVING UP NOW, AND SAVING US THE USUAL SORDID FIGHT ROUTINE?
SPIDER-MAN!
AWW, SOMEONE MUSTA TOLD YOU!

YOU FAST-TALKING FOOL! DID YOU THINK STILT-MAN WOULD BE SO EASY TO CAPTURE?
ALL I NEED DO IS ATTAIN MY FULL HEIGHT TO GET SAFELY AWAY FROM YOU!
OH, A REAL TRICKY LITTLE RASCAL, AREN'T YOU?
WELL, YOUR FRIENDLY NEIGHBORHOOD SPIDER-MAN CAN GO ALONG WITH A GAG--!

AND, WHEREVER YOU CAN STRETCH TO, OL' SPIDEY CAN SWING TO!
THAT'S IT!! JUST HOLD THAT POSE --!

THANKS AWFULLY!
I TRUST YOU'VE NOTICED THAT AT NO TIME DO THE FINGERS LEAVE THE HAND!
SPOOOINNK!

FORGIVE ME IF I TRY TO MAKE THIS QUICK!
I'M GETTING KINDA AIRSICK UP HERE!
FPAK!
YOU WEBBED WEASEL! I DIDN'T WANT TO FIGHT YOU-- BUT NOW--!

YOU'RE GOING FOR A BREATH OF AIR--
RIGHT THRU THE EXIT DOOR!
NO! YOU CAN'T!
IT'S WHAT I WAS HOPING FOR! NOW--IF ONLY NOTHING HAPPENS TO PREVENT IT!
IT'S COLD-BLOODED MURDER! YOU'LL NEVER GET AWAY WITH IT! YOU'RE MAD! MAD!
WHEN DAREDEVIL LEARNS OF THIS--YOU'LL NEVER ESCAPE! HE'LL FIND YOU--HE'LL MAKE YOU PAY--!
I CAN'T BELIEVE IT! IT'S LIKE A NIGHTMARE! IT CAN'T REALLY BE HAPPENING!
IT'S HAPPENING, ALL RIGHT! THE MASKED MARAUDER NEVER GOES BACK ON HIS WORD!

ALL RIGHT, MURDOCK! JUST LEAN YOURSELF FORWARD! THE DOOR IS RIGHT IN FRONT OF YOU!
I'VE UNLATCHED IT, SO ONE LITTLE PUSH IS ALL IT WILL TAKE!
CAN'T ACT TOO EAGER! I'VE GOT TO MAKE THIS LOOK GOOD!
LOOK-- I HAVE MONEY!! I CAN PAY YOU--!
I SAID LEAN FORWARD-- OR I'LL SHOOT!

THEN I'VE NOTHING MORE TO LOSE!
HE DIDN'T EXPECT ME TO BUTT HIM WITH MY HEAD!
NOW, IF HE'LL JUST FALL BACK AT THE RIGHT ANGLE--!
THUD
NEXT, I'VE GOT TO MAKE HIM FIRE HIS GUN--JUST ONCE!
YOU FOOL! YOU'RE ONLY PROLONGING YOUR FINAL FATE!

IT WORKED!
HE STUMBLED BACK AGAINST THE FORCE FIELD BUTTON--HE DE-ACTIVATED IT!
HIS FINGER IS TIGHTENING! HE'S ABOUT TO FIRE! IT'S NOW--OR NEVER!
BLAM!

MOVING WITH A SKILL AND PRECISION WHICH NO SIGHTED MAN COULD MATCH, MATT MURDOCK--AFTER PREDICTING THE TRAJECTORY OF THE MARAUDER'S BULLET --SPINS HIMSELF AROUND SO THAT THE ROPES WHICH BIND HIM ARE DIRECTLY IN THE PATH OF THE FATEFUL SHELL, AND THEN...
FTHWK
I DID IT!! MY HANDS ARE FREE!

NOW TO HURL MYSELF BACK-- AGAINST THE DOOR!
IT'LL SEEM AS THOUGH THE SHOT SENT ME REELING --!
MATT!

YOU MURDERER!! YOU KILLED HIM!!
SO FAR, EVERYTHING'S GONE WITHOUT A HITCH!!
THOUGH I HATE TO THINK HOW TOUGH THIS MUST BE FOR KAREN!

YOU FIEND!! YOU HEARTLESS, MERCILESS BEAST!!
I'M GLAD YOU'RE SHOWING SOME FIGHT, YOUNG LADY--!
IT WILL MAKE IT EASIER FOR ME TO DO WHAT I MUST!

KAREN!! HOLD ON! STAND AWAY FROM THAT DOOR!! KAREN--!!
IT'S NO USE! SHE CAN'T HEAR ME OVER THE ROAR OF THE SPINNING BLADES!
I CAN ONLY PRAY THAT I WON'T BE-- TOO LATE!

DAREDEVIL!! BUT--HOW--??
SIMPLE, PRETTY GIRL! I WAS HITCH-HIKIN' OUTSIDE ALL THE TIME!
AND YOU NEEDN'T WORRY ABOUT MATTY BOY! I CAUGHT HIM AND LOWERED 'IM TO A ROOFTOP WITH MY CABLE!

KPAK
AS FOR YOU, YOU CLOAKED CORNBALL, I HEAR YOU WANTED TO FIND ME!
WELL, YOU GOT YOUR WISH, CREEP!

AND PUT THAT POPGUN AWAY WHEN I'M TALKING TO YOU!
WHOOM!
PAY ATTENTION --THERE'LL BE A TEST LATER!

I--NEVER NOTICED BEFORE! HIS HEARTBEAT--HIS PULSE RATE--I RECOGNIZE THEM!
AT LAST--I KNOW WHO HE IS!
UH OH!! HE FELL BACK AGAINST A CONTROL SWITCH!
CLAKK!

IT WAS THE AUTOMATIC PILOT--HE RELEASED IT!
THE SHIP'S OUT OF CONTROL!
WHIRR

KAREN!! FOGGY!! HANG ON--!
I'LL GET 'ER RIGHTED--SOME-HOW!

THE CONTROLS!! GRAB THE CONTROLS--BEFORE WE CRASH!
FOGGY! HE CAN'T! THE MARAUDER'S ATTACKING HIM AGAIN!

YOU WON'T ESCAPE ME NOW--!
YOU FOOL! DROP THAT--BEFORE WE'RE ALL KILLED!

NO!! I'VE PLANNED--I'VE WAITED--I'VE SCHEMED TOO LONG TO ACCEPT ANOTHER FAILURE!!
NO MATTER WHAT HAPPENS--NO MATTER HOW MANY OTHERS DIE WITH YOU--YOU MUST BE DESTROYED!

THE SHIP'S STEADY NOW!! FOGGY RIGHTED IT!
SO, I'VE ONLY THE MARAUDER TO WORRY ABOUT!
I KNOW WHO YOU ARE, DAREDEVIL!
AND THE SAME GOES FOR ME-- FARNUM!!
WHAT?!! HOW-HOW DID YOU FIND OUT??
I THOUGHT THAT WOULD GRAB YOU!

THEN, THERE'S NO LONGER ANY NEED FOR CONCEALMENT!
REMOVE MY HELMET, GIRL!! REMOVE IT, I SAID!
IT-IT IS-- MR. FARNUM!
THANK YOU FOR MAKING MY TASK EASIER!
NOW, I CAN'T POSSIBLY LET ANY OF YOU LIVE--!

WHA-WHAT ARE YOU DOING?
DISINTEG
CLICK!
MERELY REACTIVATING THE SHIP'S DEADLY FORCE FIELD ONCE MORE!

WANNA LEAVE NO EVIDENCE AFTER YOU TOSS US OUT, EH?
WELL, I'VE GOT NEWS FOR YOU--!

I'M BETTING MY LIFE THAT YOU CAN'T SQUEEZE THAT TRIGGER BEFORE I CLIP YA--!
AHHH!-- TOO BAD WE WEREN'T BETTING FOR DOUGH!

FARNUM!! WATCH IT!! THAT OPEN DOOR --BEHIND YOU-- FARNUM!!
YOU STILL LOSE! I'VE ANOTHER GUN IN MY-- MY--A A
AARGHHHHHH

QUICK! THE FORCE FIELD LEVER--THERE MAY STILL BE TIME--
NO--!

IT'S TOO LATE!
NOTHING CAN SAVE HIM-- NOW!
FOGGY SMASHED THE WHOLE MECHANISM! IT CAN'T HARM ANYONE ELSE!
BUT-- WHAT ABOUT-- FARNUM?
HE'LL NEVER MENACE US AGAIN!

HOWEVER, HUNDREDS OF FEET BELOW, STILT-MAN IS STILL VERY MUCH A DANGER--
EVEN YOUR SPIDER STRENGTH CAN'T PROTECT YOU FROM A STUN GAS PELLET!
NO ONE WILL EVER RECAPTURE ME NOW!

IT'S NOT SAFE HERE! IF NOT FOR THE GAS, HE'D HAVE WON!
I'VE GOT TO GET BACK TO THE 'COPTER!

AND, AS STILT-MAN HEADS FOR THE WATERFRONT WITH GIANT-SIZED STRIDES--
SPIDER-MAN! LOOK, I'M A REPORTER! WAIT-- HOLD IT!
SORRY, MISTER! I NEED PUBLICITY LIKE ROCKEFELLER NEEDS A LOAN!
STILT-MAN TOOK OFF-- AND THAT'S JUST WHAT SPIDEY'S GONNA DO!
IF YOU RUN INTO HORNHEAD, BE SURE TO GIVE 'IM MY WORST!

NEXT: AN ALIEN ON EARTH!

MARVEL COMICS GROUP

12¢ IND.

28 MAY

HERE COMES...

DAREDEVIL™

THE MAN WITHOUT FEAR!

APPROVED BY THE COMICS CODE CA AUTHORITY

"THOU SHALT NOT COVET THY NEIGHBOR'S PLANET!"

DAREDEVIL, THE MAN WITHOUT FEAR!
"THOU SHALT NOT COVET THY NEIGHBOR'S PLANET!"
OH, MATT... MATT! HOW COULD YOU REVEAL THAT YOUR OWN BROTHER, MIKE, IS REALLY DARE-DEVIL?*
LUCKILY, THE MARAUDER DIED BEFORE HE COULD USE THAT SECRET--- BUT HOW... HOW COULD YOU HAVE BEEN SO... WEAK?
KAREN, BABY! YOU'RE JUST TOO MUCH..!
HOW CAN ANY CHICK SOUND SO BLECCH WITH A LOVER-BOY LIKE OL' MIKE AROUND?
*IT HAPPENED LAST ISH, REMEMBER? BUT, CUDDLY KAREN DOESN'T KNOW THAT MATT, MIKE, AND DD ARE ALL THE SAME SWINGER! ...STARRY-EYED STAN.
NOW LOOK, DAD... WE WENT TO A LOT OF TROUBLE TO HIRE THESE GUYS... SO BE SURE THAT YOU MEMORIZE THEIR NAMES, HEAR?
PHILOSOPHICALLY PRODUCED BY:
SMILIN' STAN LEE and GENIAL GENE COLAN
INKED BY: DICK AYERS
LETTERED BY: SAM ROSEN
OKAY! NOW THAT THAT'S OVER, LET'S SEE WHAT'S SHAKIN' UP AHEAD...

AND, IF YOU'RE WASTIN' TIME MOONIN' OVER MATT, FORGET IT!
MATTY BOY'S GONNA BE OUT OF TOWN FOR A WHILE, LECTURIN' AT CARTER COLLEGE!
HONESTLY, MIKE... AREN'T YOU EVER SERIOUS?
AT LEAST STOP JUGGLING THAT SILLY BALL LONG ENOUGH TO TELL ME WHAT MATT'S LECTURING ABOUT!
I'M SURE GLAD THAT TWINNY GOT ALL THE BRAINS IN THE FAMILY...'N YOURS TRULY GOT STUCK WITH THE GOOD LOOKS!
HE DIDN'T SAY A WORD ABOUT IT TO ME!

I HATE GIVING MY BEST FRIEND SUCH A HARD TIME, BUT I HAVE TO!

I CAN'T LET HIM GET FRIENDLY ENOUGH WITH MIKE TO EVER REALIZE THAT MATT'S "BROTHER" IS ALSO BLIND!

NUTS! THE CITY'S TOO QUIET FOR ME TONIGHT!

NO POLICE SIRENS! NO CRIES FOR HELP!.. NOTHING!

NOT EVEN SOME LITTLE KID BLOWING HIS DICK TRACY WHISTLE!

IF THIS KEEPS UP, I MAY END UP CHASING A LITTERBUG... IF I'M LUCKY!

FACE IT, DD! THIS JUST ISN'T YOUR DAY!
THE UNMISTAKABLE SOUND OF A HANSOM CAB!

MIGHT AS WELL GO HOME AND START PACKING, AND--- UH OH!
I'D KNOW THOSE VOICES ANYWHERE!

THEY'RE TALKING ABOUT MY FAVORITE SWASHBUCKLER..!
I'D BETTER GET OUT OF SIGHT AND GIVE A LISTEN!

NEVER KNEW FOGGY WAS SUCH A ROMANTIC DEVIL!
I WONDER WHAT MATT WILL SAY DURING HIS LECTURE, FOGGY?
DO YOU HAVE ANY IDEAS?
CLOPPITTY CLOP!

YOU BET I HAVE, KAREN..!
BUT, THEY'VE NOTHING TO DO WITH MATT, OR MIKE, OR DARE-DEVIL!
I THOUGHT, IF WE TOOK THIS RIDE IN THE MOONLIGHT, YOU MIGHT-- KAREN! YOU'RE NOT EVEN LISTENING!
HOW CAN MIKE BE SO UNCONCERNED ABOUT MATT ALMOST GIVING AWAY HIS SECRET?
IF HIS HIDDEN IDENTITY IS SO IMPORTANT TO HIM, DAREDEVIL SHOULD HAVE BEEN MORE UPSET!
UNLESS--- THERE'S ANOTHER--- A MORE IMPORTANT REASON..! SOMETHING WE HAVEN'T GUESSED!
WHAT IF IT'S MATT, NOT MIKE, WHO'S REALLY..! OH, NO! IT'S TOO MAD!
IT COULDN'T BE WHAT I'M THINKING--- FOR WE KNOW THAT MATT IS BLIND!
BUT, THERE'S SOMETHING ABOUT ALL THIS THAT JUST DOESN'T ADD UP!
4.

KAREN IS GETTING TOO DANGEROUSLY CLOSE TO THE TRUTH!
I'D BETTER JUST INTERRUPT THEM--!
HI, GROUP! IT'S LIKE OLD HOME WEEK HERE, ISN'T IT?
DAREDEVIL!! STAY AWAY FROM HERE!! GO CHASE CROOKS, WILLYA?
LOOK OUT, MISTER! DON'T SCARE MY HORSE!
HOW'S ABOUT GIVING YOUR FEAR-LESS FRIEND A LIFT?

THAT'S GREAT! SHE'S STILL INTERESTED IN ME AS MATT!
IT'S SIMPLE, PRETTY GIRL! I'LL SPELL IT OUT FOR YOU..!
MATT'S A LAWYER, RIGHT?
OF COURSE HE IS!

WELL, IF ANY ALIENS LAND ON EARTH, THERE'LL BE A LOT OF LEGAL PROBLEMS!
DO THEY PAY TAXES? CAN THEY BE DRAFTED? SHOULD THEY RECEIVE DIPLOMATIC IMMUNITY?
YOU SOUND LIKE A LAWYER YOURSELF, MIKE!

WHOOPS! CAREFUL, DD! ONE SLIP AND SHE'LL HAVE YOU!
I SHOULD SOUND LIKE A LEGAL EAGLE! TWINNY TOLD ME ALL ABOUT THAT JAZZ LAST TIME I SAW 'IM!
WELL, FAR BE IT FROM ME TO HORN IN ON ANOTHER CAT'S DATE... SO I'LL BE HITTIN' THE THE ROAD NOW!
MEBBE I'LL SCOOT UP TO CARTER AND KEEP MATTY BOY COMPANY WHILE HE PUTS THOSE POOR KIDS TO SLEEP!

BUT, IF YOU WANNA KNOW THE REAL REASON I'M CUTTIN' OUT NOW...
THESE THREADS OF MINE WERE NEVER MEANT TO DOUBLE FOR A SNOW SUIT!
JUST BETWEEN US, KIDDIES.. IT'S COLD OUT HERE!

WAIT! WHAT ABOUT MY FARE?
FOGGY'LL PAY YOU! HE'S LOADED!
DON'T WORRY, DAREDEVIL! WE'LL MAKE SURE HE GETS PAID!
IF YOU SEE MATT, TELL HIM---EH--
NEVER MIND! PERHAPS IT'S BEST NOT TO MENTION ME TO HIM!
6

OKAY, FRANTIC ONE... NOW THAT ONE OF THE LONGEST PROLOGUES ON RECORD IS FINALLY OVER, LET'S HEAD FOR CARTER COLLEGE WITH OUR SIGHTLESS STALWART...
ALTHOUGH SHE HATES HERSELF FOR IT, KAREN IS HURT... AND DISAPPOINTED IN ME FOR THE WEAKNESS I SHOWED BY SEEMING TO BETRAY "MIKE" TO THE MASKED MARAUDER!
AND I CAN'T REVEAL THE TRUE STORY WITHOUT GIVING MY SECRET AWAY!
MATT, OL' BUDDY... HOW'D YOU EVER GET YOURSELF IN THIS THREE-IDENTITIES-TANGLE?
OH, WELL, I'LL WORRY ABOUT IT SOME OTHER TIME!

BUT, AS MATT REACHES THE CAMPUS, HE IS SOON TO FIND A NEW, MORE INCREDIBLE PROBLEM TO CONCERN HIM...
THAT MUST BE THE GUEST LECTURER FROM NEW YORK! I DIDN'T THINK HE'D BE SO YOUNG-- OR HANDSOME!
YOU'VE SURE GOTTA HAND IT TO HIM!
IMAGINE A BLIND MAN BECOMING ONE OF THE GREATEST TRIAL LAWYERS OF HIS TIME!
I'VE SPENT HARDLY ANY TIME WORKING ON MY SPEECH--!
BUT I'M SURE I'LL THINK OF SOMETHING!
TAXI
I HOPE HE'S NOT AS FANATICAL ABOUT FLYING SAUCERS AS PROFESSOR BREWSTER IS!
I HEAR THE PROF HAS STARTED CARRYING A REVOLVER IN CASE HE MEETS ANY LITTLE GREEN MEN FROM MARS!
BREWSTER'S BEEN WORKING TOO HARD! HE SWEARS HE'S SEEN SAUCERS FLYING AROUND HERE!

GOOD OF YOU TO COME, MR. MURDOCK! I'M DEAN SMITH! LET ME TAKE YOUR BAG!
YOU'LL HAVE A CAPACITY CROWD FOR YOUR TALK!
I HOPE I'LL SAY SOMETHING TO DESERVE IT!
I UNDERSTAND YOU HAVE A PROFESSOR HERE WHO CLAIMS TO HAVE SEEN SOME SAUCERS LATELY?
YES.. THAT'S TOM BREWSTER! I'M AFRAID HE'S GETTING TOO WRAPPED-UP IN THE SUBJECT!
HE'S OUT SEARCHING RIGHT NOW!

I'LL TALK TO HIM ANOTHER TIME THEN!
YOU GONNA TAKE IN THE LECTURE, SAL?
WASN'T GOING TO...
BUT I'VE SUDDENLY CHANGED MY MIND!
--JUST LIKE ALL THE OTHER GALS!
ACTUALLY, I SPECIALIZE IN CRIMINAL LAW MORE THAN MATTERS LIKE THIS...
BUT, I MUST ADMIT THAT THE LEGAL RAMIFICATIONS OF ALIENS LANDING ON EARTH COULD BE VERY, EH, UNUSUAL!
WELL, THEN, LET'S GET ON WITH IT, SHALL WE?
7.

A FEW MINUTES LATER, A TALL, COMMANDING FIGURE MOUNTS THE PODIUM..AS THE VOICE WHICH HAS SWAYED JUDGE AND JURORS ALIKE IN COURTROOMS THROUGHOUT THE NATION BEGINS TO SPEAK...
ONLY THE LAW STANDS BETWEEN JUSTICE AND TOTAL ANARCHY..!
AND THAT LAW MUST OFFER EQUITABLE PROTECTION TO ALL.. REGARDLESS OF RACE, CREED, OR COLOR...

NOW, IN THIS AGE OF SPACE EXPLORATION, WE MAY NEED A FOURTH QUALIFICATION...
WITHOUT REGARD TO PLANET OF ORIGIN, AS WELL!
BUT, THERE IS ALWAYS THE POSSIBILITY THAT VISITORS FROM SPACE MAY HAVE DIFFERENT STANDARDS OF VALUES ...A DIFFERENT MORAL CODE! OUR PRESENT LAWS MAY NOT ALWAYS APPLY..!
GOSH! TO HEAR HIM TALK, MAYBE PROFESSOR BREWSTER ISN'T A MENTAL CASE!
HE MAKES IT SOUND LIKE HE REALLY EXPECTS SOME BEMS* TO DROP IN FOR TEA!
*BUG-EYED-MONSTERS...WHAT ELSE?... SOLICITOR STAN.

AND, EVEN AS OUR ROGUISH, RED-HEADED HERO HOLDS HIS AUDIENCE SPELLBOUND...
I KNOW THEY'RE UP THERE.. WATCHING!
I'VE GOT TO FIND PROOF! I'VE GOT TO MAKE THE OTHERS REALIZE I'M NOT MAD!
I EVEN BROUGHT A PISTOL.. JUST IN CASE!
STRANGE... I'VE NEVER HEARD THE WOODS SO QUIET BEFORE!
THEN, ENTERING A CLEARING, TOM BREWSTER GAZES DOWN... AND SUDDENLY SEES...

TRACKS!
BUT..OF WHAT??!
LOOK BEHIND YOU...AND.. YOU..WILL.. SEE!

N-NO!
WHY..SO.. SHOCKED? IS.. THIS..NOT..WHAT.. YOU..WERE.. SEEKING?

YOUR..WORTHLESS.. WEAPON... CANNOT... AFFECT..ME!
TRY..IT..AND.. YOU..SHALL.. SEE..!
I..COMMAND.. YOU..TO.. FIRE!

KRAK!
BTAM!
GUNFIRE!! FROM THE WOODS, BEYOND THE CAMPUS!!
WHERE PROFESSOR BREWSTER WAS SUPPOSED TO BE SEARCHING!

SECONDS LATER...
I SAW HIM! I SAW HIM..!
TOM! IN HEAVEN'S NAME..WHAT HAPPENED?
THAT GUN! WAS IT YOU WHO FIRED IT? WHY..WHY?

I HAD TO! IT COMMANDED ME TO SHOOT!
IT? IT WHO? WHAT ARE YOU TALKING ABOUT, MAN?
THE ALIEN! IT WASN'T HUMAN! IT HAD AN AURA..OF SHEER, DEADLY EVIL!
IT STOOD AND LAUGHED.. AS I FIRED..!
THEN IT WALKED AWAY...INTO THE WOODS..!
ITS LAST WORDS WERE..WE'RE DOOMED! THE WHOLE HUMAN RACE IS..DOOMED!

WITHIN MINUTES, A HASTILY-SUMMONED SQUAD CAR REACHES THE SCENE...
LOOK, MISTER...YOU CAN SPOT ALL THE FLYING SAUCERS YOU WANT TO...IT'S A FREE COUNTRY!
BUT THERE'S A LAW AGAINST SHOOTIN' UP THE LANDSCAPE! THIS IS A CAMPUS, NOT A TARGET RANGE!
I'VE GOTTA TAKE YOU IN, FOR A HEARING!
BUT WE'RE WASTING TIME! THERE'S SOME-ONE OUT THERE, I TELL YOU! SOMEONE DANGEROUS!
PD
SURE, SURE, I KNOW ALL ABOUT IT!
SOON AS WE GET YOU NICE 'N COZY, I'LL GRAB MY RAY GUN AND SHOO 'IM AWAY!
MY NAME IS MURDOCK, PROFESSOR! I'LL BE GLAD TO REPRESENT YOU IN COURT, IF YOU SHOULD NEED ME!
9.

LATER...
THE POLICE SEARCHED THE WOODS AND FOUND NO TRACKS, NO ALIEN NOTHING!
AND YET, I COULD SENSE THAT BREWSTER WAS TELLING THE TRUTH... AT LEAST, THE TRUTH AS HE BELIEVED IT!
MY INSTINCTS HAVE NEVER FAILED ME YET!
AND, MY INSTINCT TELLS ME... WITH-OUT ANY DOUBT... THAT TOM BREWSTER IS NOT MAD!

ALL OF WHICH MAKES ME REAL GLAD THAT I BROUGHT MY LITTLE FUN COSTUME WITH ME!
I'VE JUST GOTTA HOPE THAT NO ONE GETS TOO SUSPICIOUS ABOUT DD POPPING UP OUT OF TOWN AT THE SAME PLACE AS MATT MURDOCK!

BUT, I DID TELL KAREN AND FOGGY THAT MIKE MURDOCK MIGHT SCOOT UP TO CARTER U., ALSO!
THAT OUGHT TO ALLAY ANY OF THEIR SUSPICIONS, ANYWAY!
AS FOR ANYONE ELSE CATCHING WISE, I'LL JUST HAVETA TAKE MY CHANCES!

THIS IS THE PATH THAT BREWSTER SAID HE TOOK... BUT THE POLICE WERE RIGHT..
ACCORDING TO MY RADAR SENSE, THERE'S NO TRACE OF ANY...
WAIT A MINUTE!
THERE'S SOMETHING UP AHEAD! SOMETHING BIG... AND UNMOVING!
IT'S NOT NATIVE TO THIS AREA! I CAN TELL BY THE DIS-RUPTION OF THE AIR MOLECULES AROUND ME!

IT'S MADE OF SOME FANTASTICALLY STRONG METAL... LIKE NOTHING I'VE EVER ENCOUNTERED BEFORE!
AND I HEAR THE MUFFLED HUM OF GENERATORS... CAPABLE OF DEVELOPING ENOUGH POWER TO LIFT A THOUSAND TONS TO THE STARS!
PROFESSOR BREWSTER WAS RIGHT! WHATEVER IT IS THAT'S WAITING THERE-- IT WAS NEVER SPAWNED ON THE PLANET EARTH!
10

AND THEN, IT ARRIVES!! ...THE GLORIOUS MOMENT THAT EVERY TRUE SCIENCE-FICTION AFICIONADO SO DESPERATELY LONGS FOR.. THE INEXPRESSIBLY INCREDULOUS INSTANT WHEN EARTHLING AND ALIEN DRAMATICALLY CONFRONT EACH OTHER...
A HATCH OPENING UP..! A FIGURE SLOWLY..CONFIDENTLY.. EMERGING!
SO! ANOTHER HUMAN HAS DISCOVERED OUR PRESENCE ON THIS PRIMITIVE PLANET!
BUT, IT MATTERS NOT! ..THIS TIME WE SHALL TAKE STRONGER PREVENTIVE MEASURES.. FAR FAR STRONGER THAN WE HAVE TAKEN BEFORE!
ADDITIONAL SOUNDS.. BEHIND HIM! HE ISN'T ALONE!
THE OTHERS ARE PREPARING TO ATTACK ME, ALSO!
FACE IT, FEARLESS ONE... YOU'RE IN FOR IT NOW!
11.

HE'S SHINING SOME STRANGE BEAMS AT ME--!
TRYING TO BLIND ME!--- I'LL PLAY ALONG--- PRETEND TO BE AFFECTED!
ZZZZZZZZZZ
WITHIN A MERE FOUR NOMAMETERS HE WILL BE TOTALLY SIGHTLESS, AND THEN ---
NO! WAIT! SOMETHING IS AMISS!
MY VISIONATORY SENSORS TELL ME THAT OUR RAY IS INEFFECTUAL! HE IS ONLY PRETENDING TO BE STRICKEN!
THAT CAN MEAN BUT ONE THING--- HE IS ALREADY BLIND!
THERE IS NO NEED FOR FURTHER DELAY! LET US PUT AN END TO THE HUMAN'S LIFE CYCLE AT ONCE!

THOK!
STAY BACK, GENTS! WE CAN FIGHT EACH OTHER ANY TIME!
WHY DON'T WE TALK THINGS OVER FIRST?

TALKING IS USELESS!
WE MUST CARRY OUT THE PLAN--- AND NO HUMAN MAY STOP US!
THEREFORE, OUR FIRST TASK IS TO RENDER YOU TOTALLY HELPLESS!
ZAK!
A SUDDEN ICY BLAST.. CHILLING ME TO THE MARROW!!
BUT, THE EFFECT ONLY LASTED FOR A SECOND!
WHAT CAN IT MEAN?
12

OH WELL... I'LL FIND OUT SOONER OR LATER...
RIGHT NOW, IT'S TIME TO MAKE LIKE A HERO...
BAM!!
--WHILE I STILL CAN!
ONE THING IS CERTAIN--THESE CATS DIDN'T DROP IN JUST TO BE SOCIABLE!
I'VE GOT TO LEARN WHAT THEY'RE AFTER.. IF I CAN HOLD THEM OFF LONG ENOUGH!

PTOWW!
SPECIAL NOTE: PLEASE BE ADVISED, IN READING THIS STORY ALOUD, THAT THE FIRST LETTER IN THE ABOVE SOUND EFFECT IS PRESUMED TO BE SILENT!
--STICKLER STAN.

IT'S NO GOOD! THERE ARE TOO MANY OF THEM!
JUST A MATTER OF TIME BEFORE ONE OF 'EM MAKES ME BITE THE DUST!
BUT, WHAT DO YOU DO WITH A BATCH OF WEIRDIES WHO WON'T LISTEN TO REASON?!!
UH OH! THEY'RE STARTING TO EASE UP!.. BUT WHY?
THE TIME IS COME!

YOU BATTLED BRAVELY, EARTHLING.. BUT, ALAS, IN VAIN!
THE WEAPON WE FIRED AT YOU... HAD A DELAYED-ACTION EFFECT! WITHIN SECONDS YOU WILL BE UNABLE TO MOVE!
A CASING OF ICE... FORMING ALL OVER ME..!

THEY'RE RIGHT!
IT'S LIKE BEING ENCLOSED IN CEMENT! I..I'M A LIVING STATUE!
QUICKLY TO THE SHIP WITH HIM!

WE MUST NOT LEAVE HIM HERE, WHERE HE MAY BE FOUND!
TRUE! THE TIME IS NOT YET COME FOR OUR PLAN TO BE MADE KNOWN!
I CAN'T LET IT END THIS WAY! IT'S NOT JUST MY LIFE NOW--- ALL OF EARTH IS IN DANGER!
AND YET--- WHAT CAN I DO? I CAN'T EVEN MOVE!

FASTER! OUR INSTRUMENTS TELL OF OTHER HUMANS APPROACHING!
THEY MUST NOT FIND US!

TO THE MAIN CONQUEST SITE--- IMMEDIATELY!
WE CAN DELAY THE PLAN NO LONGER
SHOOSH!

BEFORE ANOTHER NOMAMETER HAS PASSED, EARTH SHALL BE OURS!!

THEN, SECONDS AFTER THE SOARING SHIP HAS FADED FROM SIGHT...
THAT SUDDEN FLASH!! I SAW IT SHOOT INTO THE SKY! I SAW IT!
IT CAME FROM THE TOP OF THAT RIDGE... JUST AHEAD!
THIS MEANS... PROFESSOR BREWSTER WAS RIGHT! THERE WAS SOMETHING HERE!
THAT'S WHERE IT WAS! YOU CAN STILL SMELL THE FUMES!
HOLY COW! LOOK AT THE GROUND JUST AHEAD-- LOOK AT IT--!!
THOSE TRACKS!! NOTHING FROM EARTH EVER MADE ANY MARKS LIKE THAT!

BUT-- WHO WERE THEY-- AND WHERE DID THEY GO?
THERE ARE HUMAN PRINTS HERE, TOO! I WONDER-- WHAT REALLY HAPPENED?
IF VINCENT PRICE SHOWS UP... I'LL SCREAM!

WHILE, TRAVELLING AT SONIC SPEED IN THE IONOSPHERE ABOVE...
THE ICE HAS MELTED! YOU CAN MOVE ONCE MORE!
BUT I'M STILL YOUR PRISONER ABOARD THIS TUB, EH?
NATURALLY! WE COULD NOT AFFORD TO LEAVE YOU BEHIND!
HOWEVER, WE ARE MOST IMPRESSED WITH YOUR COURAGE... AND WISH TO MAKE YOU AN OFFER---!
I MIGHT AS WELL HEAR THEM OUT! I DON'T SEEM TO HAVE MUCH CHOICE!
BEFORE WE DO ANY BARGAINING, TELL ME SOMETHING... HOW DO YOU HAPPEN TO SPEAK OUR LINGO?

A SIMPLE MATTER! WE HAVE HOVERED ABOVE THIS PLANET FOR MONTHS, MONITORING YOUR VARIOUS TONGUES AND DIALECTS!
THEN, WITH THE AID OF OUR ADVANCED MEMORY FIXATION RECORDERS, WE MASTERED ALL WE HAD TO KNOW!
BUT NOW, WE HAVE REACHED OUR CONQUEST SITE... AND THERE IS A FAR MORE FATEFUL TASK TO BE PERFORMED... WHILE YOU SHALL MAKE THE GRAVEST DECISION OF YOUR LIFE!

THEN, SOON AFTER LANDING...
ACTIVATE THE SIGHT-STEALING RAY!
SET IT FOR CONTINUAL INCREASE.. TILL MAXIMUM INTENSITY IS ACHIEVED!
THIS IS WHY WE NEED NO LARGE, INVADING ARMY!
WE MERELY MAKE A PLANET'S POPULATION UNABLE TO SEE...AS WE GO ABOUT OUR NECESSARY TASK!

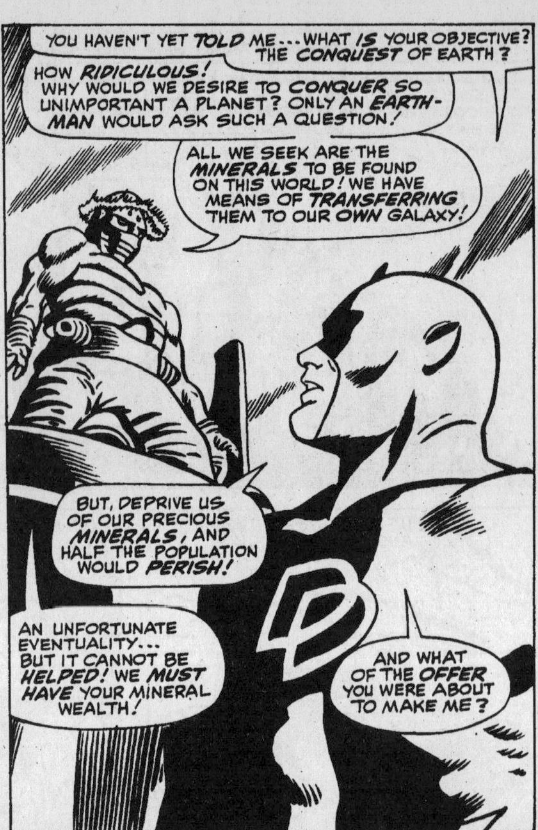
YOU HAVEN'T YET TOLD ME...WHAT IS YOUR OBJECTIVE? THE CONQUEST OF EARTH?
HOW RIDICULOUS! WHY WOULD WE DESIRE TO CONQUER SO UNIMPORTANT A PLANET? ONLY AN EARTH-MAN WOULD ASK SUCH A QUESTION!
ALL WE SEEK ARE THE MINERALS TO BE FOUND ON THIS WORLD! WE HAVE MEANS OF TRANSFERRING THEM TO OUR OWN GALAXY!
BUT, DEPRIVE US OF OUR PRECIOUS MINERALS, AND HALF THE POPULATION WOULD PERISH!
AN UNFORTUNATE EVENTUALITY... BUT IT CANNOT BE HELPED! WE MUST HAVE YOUR MINERAL WEALTH!
AND WHAT OF THE OFFER YOU WERE ABOUT TO MAKE ME?

WE HAVE GREAT RESPECT FOR COURAGE! IF YOU JOIN US, WE WILL SPARE YOUR LIFE!
AND, WE CAN OFFER YOU THE GREATEST GIFT...
WE POSSESS THE MEANS TO RESTORE YOUR SIGHT TO YOU! SAY THE WORD, AND YOU WILL SEE ONCE MORE!
THINK OF THE MATCH-LESS WONDERS YOU MIGHT BEHOLD... TRAVELLING WITH US THROUGH THE ENDLESS GALAXIES.. RAVAGING ENTIRE PLANETS AT WILL!

STRIPPING OTHER WORLDS OF THEIR MINERALS... NOT CARING HOW MUCH DAMAGE YOU DO.. HOW MUCH DISASTER YOU CAUSE?
HAVE A CARE! THE WRONG ANSWER MEANS YOU DIE!
MAYBE SO... BUT I'LL DIE LIKE A MAN...NOT A MURDEROUS SCAVENGER!

BOK!
AND, IN CASE YOU DIDN'T GET THE MESSAGE!..
THIS'LL SPELL IT OUT FOR YOU!
16

BAM!
GOTTA KEEP MOVING... FAST!
IF ANOTHER ICY BLAST HITS ME, THAT'LL BE THE BALL GAME!

THERE'S ONE LUCKY THING, ANYWAY--- THEY'RE NO STRONGER THAN ORDINARY HUMANS, REGARDLESS HOW ADVANCED THEIR SCIENCE MAY BE!
YOK!

ANOTHER ONE... ALL SET TO MAKE A HUMAN ICE CUBE OUT OF ME AGAIN!
ZAK!

SORRY, CHARLIE! I'VE GOT OTHER PLANS THIS TIME!
WUP!
I CAN'T HOLD OUT HERE FOREVER!! I'VE GOT TO REACH THEIR SHIP ITSELF..!
THEY'VE ALREADY STARTED THEIR SIGHT-STEALING RAY!
NO TELLING HOW MUCH DAMAGE IT'S DOING.. RIGHT NOW..!

AND, AS THOUGH TO LEND EMPHASIS TO DD'S RANDOM THOUGHT...
I STILL THINK IT'S RIDICULOUS FOR US TO CHASE UP HERE AFTER MATT JUST BECAUSE OF THAT RADIO REPORT, KAREN!
EVEN IF A FLYING SAUCER WAS SIGHTED.. WHAT CAN THAT HAVE TO DO WITH HIM?
BUT, FOGGY... MATT'S BLIND! DON'T YOU UNDERSTAND? IF THERE'S ANY DANGER... HE'LL NEED SOMEONE --- TO LOOK AFTER HIM..!
OH! WHAT'S THAT!!!
LOOK OUT!!
SOMETHIN' HAPPENED! ALL OF A SUDDEN... I CAN'T SEE!! GOTTA SLAM ON THE BRAKES.. FAST..!!
SKREEEE!
TAXI

AND, THROUGHOUT THE GLOBE, THE EFFECT IS THE SAME! NOT A SINGLE INHABITED AREA ESCAPES THE ALIENS' UNCANNY RAY...!

I'm Blind!

I CAN'T SEE! I CAN'T SEE!

THE LIGHT IS GONE! I AM SIGHTLESS!

MUHAMMUD HAS TURNED HIS FACE AWAY!

What have The Kapitalists Done To Us??

WHILE, BACK AT THE ALIENS' SO-CALLED CONQUEST SITE, THE GRIM BATTLE ENTERS ITS FINAL DESPERATE STAGE...
HUMAN... YOU ARE A FOOL!
WE OFFERED YOU THE GIFT OF SIGHT... BUT YOU CHOSE TO DEFY US INSTEAD OF BETRAYING YOUR OWN, DOOMED RACE!
IT'S NO GOOD! NO MATTER HOW MANY I OVERCOME, THERE'S ALWAYS ANOTHER TO TAKE HIS PLACE!

OUR PATIENCE HAS FINALLY REACHED ITS LIMIT..!
THEREFORE, YOU MUST NOW PREPARE TO DIE!
SKLAKK

NOT WHILE I CAN STILL SLING A MEAN OL' SNOWBALL, I WON'T!
WHOP!

ANOTHER ONE... SNEAKING UP BEHIND... READY TO HURL A KING-SIZE ICE BLAST!!

NO TIME TO TACKLE 'IM!!
ALL I CAN DO.. IS... DUCK!!
ZAK!
...AND HOPE THAT I WAS IN EXACTLY THE POSITION I WANTED TO BE!!

IT WORKED!
BY FAST, SPLIT-SECOND REFLEX CALCULATING, I ARRANGED FOR THE BLAST TO GO OVER MY HEAD...
...AND TO STRIKE THEIR OWN SIGHT-STEALING RAY!
SPLANNGG!

OUR WEAPON SUPREME IS COMPLETELY FROZEN... BY OUR MOST POWERFUL ICE BLAST!
SO SENSITIVE IS THE MACHINE, THAT.. ONCE FROZEN--IT WILL TAKE A THOUSAND THOUSAND NOMAMETERS TO DEFROST IT!
AND WE CANNOT SPARE THE TIME!
THUS, WE MUST FLEE.. FROM THE SCENE OF OUR FIRST, OUR ONLY... DEFEAT!

THEY'RE LEAVING! IT'S OVER... AT LAST!
AND, WITH THE FATEFUL FROZEN MACHINE ONCE MORE ON BOARD, HURTLING FROM OUR GALAXY FOREVER, THE PRICELESS GIFT OF SIGHT RETURNS TO MANKIND'S STARTLED MILLIONS...

KAREN! I..I CAN SEE AGAIN!
SO CAN I! WHATEVER AFFLICTED US.. IS GONE!
LOOK AT THE CROWDS! EVERYONE'S OKAY AGAIN!
LET'S FIND MATT! I FEEL LIKE CELEBRATING!

C'MON, ADMIT IT NOW-- DON'T YOU FLIP FOR A HAPPY ENDING THE SAME WAY WE DO?
PROFESSOR BREWSTER'S BEEN VINDICATED! HE WON'T NEED US TO DEFEND HIM! HE--UH!?---
HMMM... MIGHT AS WELL BE TALKING TO THE WALL!
NEXT
"CAPTURED BY... THE BOSS!"

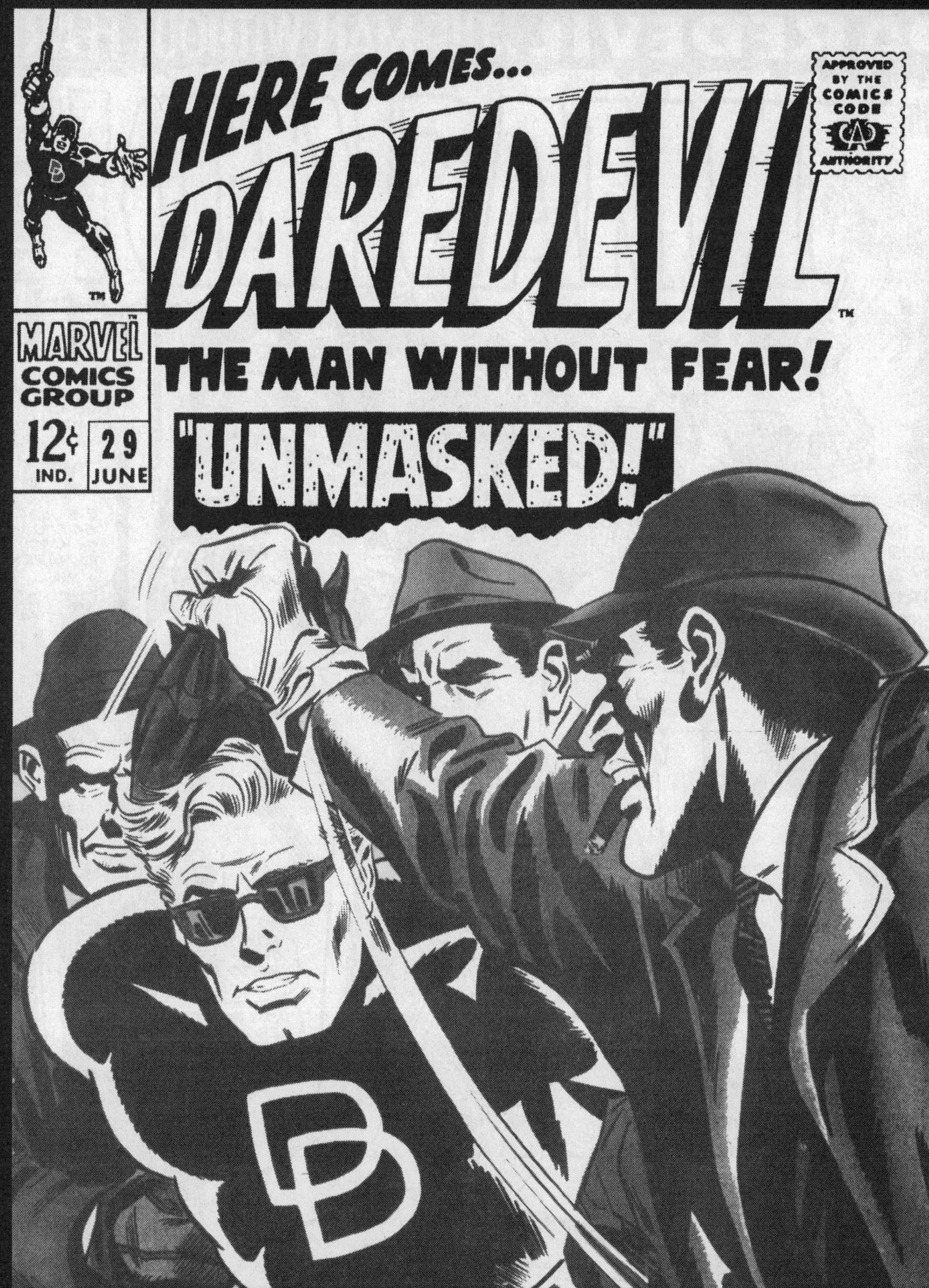
HERE COMES...
DAREDEVIL
THE MAN WITHOUT FEAR!
MARVEL COMICS GROUP
12¢ IND.
29 JUNE
APPROVED BY THE COMICS CODE AUTHORITY
"UNMASKED!"

DAREDEVIL, THE MAN WITHOUT FEAR!
"UNMASKED!"
IN WHICH D.D. IS CAPTURED BY THE HEINOUS HIRELINGS OF THE HEARTLESS HOOD THEY CALL... THE BOSS!
MY MIND'S MADE UP!! I WON'T--- I CAN'T WAIT ANY LONGER!
I'VE JUST GOT TO ASK KAREN TO MARRY ME!
NOW, THE ONLY THING LEFT FOR ME TO DECIDE IS---
DO I PROPOSE TO HER AS MATT MURDOCK ---OR AS MY OWN "TWIN BROTHER", MIKE?
GARNISHED WITH GREATNESS and GLAZED WITH GLORY by: SMILIN' STAN LEE and GENIAL GENE COLAN
INKED BY: J. TARTAGLIONE LETTERED BY: SAM ROSEN

I CAN'T LET MY BLINDNESS COME BETWEEN US ANY LONGER!
I'VE LOVED HER SINCE THE TIME I FIRST HEARD HER VOICE... SINCE SHE FIRST WALKED INTO THE OFFICE, TO TAKE THE JOB OF SECRETARY TO FOGGY AND ME!
AND, UNLESS I CAN'T BELIEVE THE EVIDENCE OF MY OWN SUPER-KEEN SENSES... UNLESS I'M TOTALLY, HOPELESSLY MISTAKEN... I KNOW SHE FEELS THE SAME WAY ABOUT ME!
A MAN JUST CAN'T KEEP DENYING THE LONGING IN HIS HEART!
...NOT EVEN THE MAN CALLED... DAREDEVIL!

KAREN, MY DARLING.. EVEN THOUGH I CANNOT SEE YOU.. YOUR BEAUTY IS LIKE A LIVING THING TO ME!
IN MY MIND'S EYE I'VE DEVOURED YOUR FEATURES HUNGRILY... GREEDILY... LIKE A STARVING MAN!
AND NOW, THE SO-CALLED MAN WITHOUT FEAR IS SUDDENLY NERVOUS!

I FEEL AS JITTERY AS A SCHOOL-BOY, HEADING FOR HIS FIRST DATE!
I'VE GOT TO CALM DOWN... RELAX A BIT... BEFORE I PROPOSE!
I'D BETTER HEAD FOR MY PRIVATE GYM... FOR A LAST-MINUTE WORKOUT!

SECONDS LATER, IN THE SOUND-PROOFED APARTMENT WHICH MATT SECRETLY RENTS, DIRECTLY BELOW HIS OWN LIVING QUARTERS, WE FIND...
IF THIS DOESN'T CLEAR OUT THE OL' COBWEBS, NOTHING WILL!
NOTHING LIKE A LITTLE HIGH-BAR HIJINKS TO MAKE A FELLA FEEL AS GOOD AS NEW AGAIN!
2.

IT'S JUST BARELY POSSIBLE THAT DD IS SHOWING OFF A BIT, BECAUSE A QUIET DEEP-BREATHING EXERCISE MIGHT CALM HIM DOWN JUST AS EFFECTIVELY! BUT, THAT'S THE WAY IT IS WITH SOME SWINGIN' SUPER-HEROES...!
SMILEY WANTED TO PUT A ZILLION NUTTY SOUND EFFECTS AND THOUGHT BALLOONS ON THIS PAGE, BUT GENTLEMAN GENE THREATENED TO KILL HIM IF HE DID! SO, YOU'LL HAVE TO STUDY IT IN SILENCE, TIGER, AS WE GIRD OURSELVES FOR THE THRILLS TO COME!

OKAY NOW, FACE FRONT! WHILE MERRY MATTHEW KNOCKS HIMSELF OUT, LET'S SEE WHAT'S SHAKIN' WITH THE MASKED MARAUDER'S NOW-LEADERLESS GANG OF GUNMEN..
WE AIN'T HEARD FROM THE MARAUDER FOR OVER A MONTH... EVER SINCE HE WENT AFTER THAT CREEP, DAREDEVIL!
WE MIGHT AS WELL FACE IT! HORN-HEAD MUSTA POLISHED OFF THE BOSS... WHICH LEAVES US HERE, HIGH 'N' DRY!
BUT WHAT ABOUT THAT NOTE THE MARAUDER LEFT--?
YEAH! I WAS JUST THINKIN' ABOUT IT MYSELF!

CLICK!
IN CASE ANY-THING HAPPENED TO 'IM, WE WERE SUPPOSED TO OPEN HIS VAULT AND FOLLOW THE INSTRUCTIONS WAITIN' INSIDE!
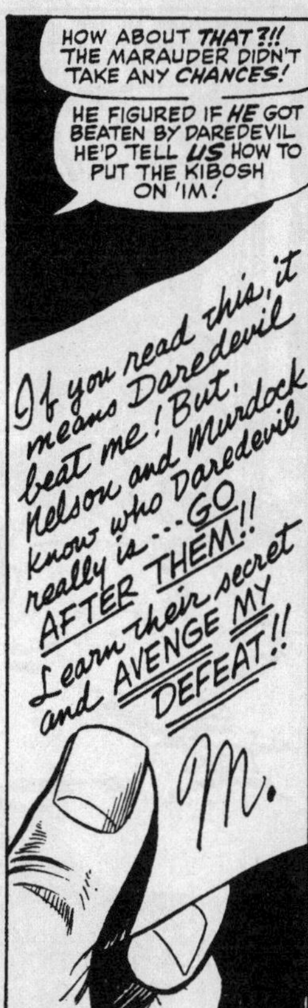
HOW ABOUT THAT?!! THE MARAUDER DIDN'T TAKE ANY CHANCES!
HE FIGURED IF HE GOT BEATEN BY DAREDEVIL HE'D TELL US HOW TO PUT THE KIBOSH ON 'IM!
If you read this, it means Daredevil beat me! But, Nelson and Murdock know who Daredevil really is...GO AFTER THEM!! Learn their secret and AVENGE MY DEFEAT!!
M.

EXACTLY ONE HOUR LATER, DIRECTLY ACROSS TOWN ---
SO YOU'RE GONNA TELL ME HOW I CAN TAKE OVER THE MARAUDER'S MOB, EH?
OKAY, START TALKIN'!
I JUST CAME FROM A MEETING OF HIS BOYS!
MY LIFE WOULDN'T BE WORTH A PLUGGED NICKEL IF THEY KNEW I WAS SPILLIN' THE BEANS TO--THE BOSS!
BUT I FIGGER... WITH THE MARAUDER GONE--THAT YOU'RE THE ONLY ONE BIG ENOUGH TO FILL HIS SHOES!

ALL YOU GOTTA DO IS HIJACK HIS SPECIAL TRUCK TONIGHT! IT'LL BE HEADIN' FOR THE OFFICE OF NELSON AND MURDOCK!
IT SOUNDS INTERESTIN', PAL! YEAH... REAL INTERESTIN'!
GRAB YER HATS, YOU GUYS!
BEFORE THIS EVENING'S OVER, THE MARAUDER'S MEN'LL BE WORKIN' FER ME... THE BOSS!
AND IF THIS STOOLIE IS LEVELLIN' WITH US, WE'LL BE ABLE TO DUST OFF DAREDEVIL, ALSO!
4.

LATER THAT NIGHT, IN THE BEST GANGLAND TRADITION, A HIGH-POWERED SEDAN SILENTLY WAITS IN THE SHADOWS AS A MYSTERIOUS TRUCK LUMBERS THROUGH THE DESERTED STREETS...
HERE THEY COME!
YOU GUYS ALL KNOW WHAT TO DO!
AND REMEMBER, DON'T MUSS 'EM UP TOO MUCH UNLESS YA HAVE TO! I DON'T WANT NO WRECKS WORKIN' FOR ME!
OKAY, LOUIE... GIT YER POP-GUN 'N' SLOW 'EM DOWN!

KRAK!
ONE SHOT IS ALL IT'LL TAKE!

PWEEEOWWW

SKREEEEEE
GOOD SHOOTIN', LOUIE!
OKAY... LET'S GIT IT OVER WITH!
TAKE 'EM!

END O' THE LINE, PAL.. COMPLIMENTS OF.. THE BOSS!
BOK
HEADS UP! HERE COME THE REST OF 'EM!

ZUK!
HEY! IT'S THE BOSS!
WE AIN'T GOT A CHANCE AGAINST HIS MOB!
YOU CAN SAY THAT AGAIN!
OKAY, YOU GUYS-- COOL IT! IT'S OUR BALL GAME!
YOU HEARD THE BOSS, DIDN'T YA?
C'MON...ON YER FEET! THE PARTY'S OVER!
IT WAS A REAL BREEZE! THEY NEVER EVEN KNEW WHAT HIT 'EM!

FROM NOW ON, YOU CREEPS ARE WORKIN' FOR ME!
NOW GIT BACK IN THAT TRUCK! YOU'RE STILL GOIN' AFTER DAREDEVIL---
BUT IT'S GONNA BE THE BOSS WHO WHISTLES THE TUNE FOR YA!
AND, AS CONTROL OF THE MARAUDER'S MOB THUS CHANGES HANDS---

CAN'T WAIT ANY LONGER! I'VE JUST GOT TO SEE HER NOW!

KAREN AND FOGGY WERE GONNA WORK LATE TONIGHT, SO I KNOW SHE'LL BE THERE!
IF ONLY I COULD REACH HER FASTER!! THE SUSPENSE IS KILLING ME!
BUT, SHE JUST HAS TO SAY "YES"!
I COULDN'T FEEL THE WAY I DO ABOUT HER IF SHE DIDN'T FEEL THE SAME ABOUT ME!
AT LEAST...THAT'S WHAT I KEEP TELLING MYSELF!

BUT, I STILL HAVEN'T FIGURED OUT... DO I PROPOSE TO HER AS MATT MURDOCK...OR SHOULD I POP THE QUESTION AS MIKE?
IF ONLY I MYSELF KNEW WHICH ONE OF US IS THE REAL ME!!
BUT, WHAT'S THE DIFFERENCE... AS LONG AS SHE SAYS YES!!

I'LL TAKE A SHORT-CUT OVER THIS BUILDING ON MADISON AVENUE AND--UH OH!
DAREDEVIL! MAN, WHAT A SURPRISE THIS IS! YOU'RE THE LAST FELLA I EXPECTED TO SEE!
CAN'T STOP NOW, STAN... I'M IN A HURRY!
BUT, WAIT! IF OL' GENE FINDS OUT HE MISSED YOU..!
HE'LL GET OVER IT! SEE YOU AROUND, TIGER!
OKAY! HANG LOOSE, HERO!

FINALLY...
SNAP
SNAP!
I'M HERE!! THIS IS IT! IT'S DD'S BIG MOMENT!
VA-VOOM!
I FEEL AS GIDDY AS A GUPPY IN A GOBLET!

OKAY, MASKED MAN...CALM DOWN!
JUST MAINTAIN YOUR COOL LONG ENOUGH TO REACH INTO YOUR OFFICE WINDOW AND HOOK YOUR WORKING DUDS!
AHHH... GOT 'EM!

A WINDOW LEDGE, HIGH OVER THE HEART OF TOWN, MAY NOT BE THE BEST DRESSING ROOM IN THE WORLD...
BUT AT LEAST A FELLA ISN'T LIKELY TO GET CLAUSTROPHOBIA OUT HERE!
LOOKS LIKE I'LL HAVE TO PROPOSE IN THE IDENTITY OF MATT MURDOCK...SINCE I JUST REMEMBER THAT I LEFT MY LOUD MIKE MURDOCK THREADS BACK AT THE APARTMENT!
WELL, KAREN HONEY.. READY OR NOT--HERE I COME!
7.

CAN'T RUSH IN.. FOGGY'S CONSCIOUS ... WATCHING ME...!
HAVE TO PLAY THE ROLE OF A BLIND MAN ... NO MATTER HOW MUCH I WANT TO GO INTO ACTION!
FOGGY! WHY DON'T YOU ANSWER ME? ARE YOU THERE? WHERE'S KAREN? WHY DOESN'T SOMEONE SPEAK?
I HEAR SOMEONE MOANING... AS IF THE SOUND IS COMING FROM THE FLOOR!
HE'S BOUND AND GAGGED! I'VE GOT TO UNTIE HIM... QUICKLY!
MMMMM! MMMPPFFF!
MMMMFFFTFF!

8.

I'VE GOT TO CONTINUE MOVING SLOWLY... GROPING ABOUT, THE WAY AN UNSEEING MAN WOULD! CAN'T HAVE FOGGY SUSPECT-ING THE TRUTH..!
WHAT'S THIS? SOMETHING ON THE FLOOR! IT FEELS LIKE--A BODY!
FOGGY! YOU MUST HAVE TRIPPED... AND FALLEN! I'LL BEND DOWN--TRY TO HELP YOU UP--!
MMMM! MMMFF! MMMPPPFFF!

IT FEELS AS THOUGH THERE'S SOMETHING OVER YOUR MOUTH! HERE...I'LL REMOVE IT..!
FTAHH! SAY, IT'S A GOOD THING YOU ARRIVED WHEN YOU DID, MATT!
A WHOLE BUNCH OF HOODS BROKE IN HERE...THEY LOOKED LIKE THE MARAUDER'S MOB---
THEY TIED ME UP.. AND RAN OFF WITH KAREN!
WHY? WHY WOULD THEY DO THAT?
BEATS ME! THEY MUMBLED SOMETHING ABOUT USING HER TO TRAP DARE-DEVIL!

THEY LEFT A NOTE.. FOR ME TO GIVE TO DAREDEVIL--- TELLING HIM WHERE HE COULD FIND KAREN!
THEY WERE CONVINCED THAT WE KNOW THAT COSTUMED CLOWN'S REAL IDENTITY!
I CAN "READ" THESE DIRECTIONS BY MERELY RUNNING MY FINGERS OVER THE DRIED INK!
YOUR GIRL
THEN..THAT MEANS THEY'RE AFTER..MY BROTHER MIKE!

HERE...YOU'D BETTER MAKE SURE MIKE GETS THAT NOTE!
HOLD IT, MATT! WHAT ABOUT YOU? WHERE ARE YOU GOING?
BACK TO MY APARTMENT! YOU NEVER CAN TELL..MIKE MAY STOP IN THERE, FIRST!
OKAY, PARTNER.. BUT BE SURE TO LOCK YOURSELF IN..JUST IN CASE!
THOSE GUN-HAPPY GOONS WILL STOP AT NOTHING TO GET HOLD OF YOUR BRO-THER..SO BE CAREFUL!
KAREN..IN DANGER AGAIN!.. BECAUSE OF ME! IT'S THE ONE THING.. THE ONLY THING I'VE EVER FEARED!

A SHORT TIME LATER... ON THE OUTSKIRTS OF TOWN...
THEY SOMEHOW LEARNED HOW DAREDEVIL FEELS ABOUT KAREN... THEY KNOW I'LL RISK ANYTHING TO SAVE HER!
BUT, EVEN THOUGH I'M HEADING STRAIGHT FOR A DEADLY TRAP.. I'VE GOT TO PLAY IT THEIR WAY!
I CAN'T RISK THE SAFETY OF THE GIRL I LOVE!
TAXI
WE'RE GETTIN' CLOSE TO THE ADDRESS YOU GAVE ME, MAC! BUT, IT'S LIKE THE MIDDLE OF NOWHERE!
I SURE WOULDN'T WANNA BE HERE ALONE AT NIGHT... OR ANY TIME!

MIDNIGHT RD.
SAY, DON'TCHA WANT I SHOULD WALK YOU TO THE DOOR?
NO THANKS! I'LL BE ALL RIGHT!
I, EH, I KNOW THE WAY! YOU'D BETTER LEAVE, NOW!
TAXI
OKAY, PAL... YOU DON'T HAVETA TELL ME TWICE!

THERE MUST BE A DOZEN ARMED HOODS WAITING TO DROP ME AS SOON AS I ENTER THAT HOUSE!
BUT, I'VE GOT ONE SLIM CHANCE... IF I PLAY MY CARDS RIGHT!

THEY DON'T KNOW WHO I REALLY AM... BUT THERE'S ONE THING THEY'D NEVER BELIEVE...
THEY'D NEVER BELIEVE THAT THE OL' DARING DAZZLER COULD BE A BLIND MAN!
SO, IT'S TIME FOR ME TO GIVE THE GREATEST PERFORMANCE OF MY LIFE...!

WHILE, WITHIN THE GLOOMY, DESOLATE HOUSE...
LOOK ALIVE, YOU GUYS! HE'S RIGHT OUTSIDE... HEADIN' THIS WAY!
I DON'T GET IT! HE MUST KNOW IT'S A TRAP...
SO WHY'S HE WALKIN' RIGHT INTO IT?
HAH! HE'S LIKE A CLAY PIGEON!
WHAT'S THE DIFFERENCE? MEBBE HE'S JUST TIRED OF LIVIN'!
SOMETHIN'S WRONG! HE'S WALKIN' KINDA FUNNY... ALMOST LIKE HE CAN'T SEE!
PROBABLY 'CAUSE HIS KNEES ARE SHAKIN'... WITH FRIGHT!

I--I'M INSIDE!!
KAREN! THIS IS DAREDEVIL! WHERE ARE YOU?? SAY SOMETHING--!!
HE MUST BE NUTS, BOSS!
SHUDDUP! LET'S SEE WHAT HE DOES...!
I DON'T HEAR ANYONE! THE HOUSE MUST BE---EMPTY!! BUT...WHERE IS KAREN?

WAIT! I HEARD SOMEONE GROAN!! --THE SOUND OF A STRUGGLE!
THERE IS SOMEONE HERE!! I KNOW IT!
DON'T ANYONE TRY ANYTHING!! I'VE GOT A GUN!

A FAT LOTTA GOOD THAT'LL DO YA!
YOU BEEN WAVIN' IT IN THE WRONG DIRECTION!
HEY, BOSS.. WHAT GIVES HERE?
THIS HORN-HEADED HEEL ACTS LIKE HE'S BLIND!
HOLD 'IM THERE!! WE'LL GET THAT MASK OFF, AND SEE..!

HEY!! WHAT IS THIS? I'D KNOW THIS GUY ANY-WHERE..!
IT'S MATT MURDOCK ...THE BLIND LAWYER!! IF HE'S DAREDEVIL, I'M PETER PAN!
START TALKIN', MURDOCK.. AND MAKE IT GOOD!!
I SHOULD HAVE KNOWN IT WOULDN'T WORK! BUT... I HAD TO TRY..!

I KNEW THE REAL DAREDEVIL WAS ON HIS WAY HERE! I KNEW YOU'D BE WAITING!
I THOUGHT---IF I COULD IMPERSONATE HIM... GET YOU TO SHOOT ME FIRST..THEN, YOU'D THINK HE WAS FINISHED...AND YOU WOULDN'T BE EXPECTING HIM!
IT WAS THE ONLY THING I COULD THINK OF THE ONLY WAY..TO REPAY HIM...! BUT.. I'VE FAILED!
MATT! YOU WERE WILLING TO GIVE YOUR LIFE...TO SAVE DAREDEVIL!
STOW IT, LADY! I'M GITTIN' ALL CHOKED UP!
OKAY, BOYS... NO HARM DONE!
TAKE YER PLACES AGAIN! WE'LL JUST WAIT TILL THE REAL DAREDEVIL COMES CALLIN'!

LEAVE MURDOCK WHERE HE IS! AIN'T NOTHIN' A BLIND MAN CAN DO TO STOP US!

MATT.. MATT!! YOU POOR, BRAVE, WONDERFUL FOOL!
TO THINK...YOU WERE WILLING TO SACRIFICE YOURSELF...IN ORDER TO SAVE ANOTHER!
BUT NOW.. WE'RE BOTH PRISONERS ..UNABLE TO WARN DAREDEVIL!

KAREN...DO WHATEVER THE BOSS TELLS YOU...AND TRY NOT TO WORRY!
DAREDEVIL'S BEEN COUNTED OUT BEFORE...BUT SOMEHOW HE USUALLY MANAGES TO END UP ON TOP!

NOW AIN'T THAT TOUCHIN'?!!
WE BETTER SEPARATE THESE TWO ...JUST IN CASE!
OKAY, BOSS!

I'LL PUT THE DAME IN THE OTHER ROOM ...SO SHE CAN'T SHOUT A WARNIN' WHEN OUR PIGEON SHOWS UP!
AND I'LL TIE THE MOUTHPIECE'S HANDS ... TO MAKE SURE HE STAYS OUTTA TROUBLE!

JUST SIT TIGHT THERE, LAWYER MAN! WE'LL BE BACK FOR YA LATER... AFTER WE POLISH OFF THE REAL DAREDEVIL WHEN HE COMES WALTZIN' IN!
DON'T COUNT ON IT, BUDDY BOY!
THEY'VE GONE! NOW, ALL I HAVE TO DO IS WIGGLE OUT OF THESE ROPES!

POSSESSING AN INDESCRIBABLY ACUTE SENSE OF TOUCH, IT'S A MATTER OF MERE SECONDS FOR THE MAN WITHOUT FEAR TO APPLY MUSCULAR PRESSURE IN SUCH A WAY THAT...
I DID IT! I'M FREE!

AND NOW, I'LL SEE TO IT THAT THOSE TRIGGER-HAPPY HOODS GET JUST WHAT THEY'RE WAITING FOR...
BUT, THEY'LL GET IT DAREDEVIL STYLE...!

HEY, CREEPS... I'VE GOT NEWS FOR YOU--!!
YOU'VE BEEN FACING THE WRONG DIRECTION!
I DECIDED TO SWING IN THROUGH THE BACK ENTRANCE...
OR MAYBE YOU'VE ALREADY NOTICED!
FTOOK!
KP
HKK!
HEADS UP, BLAST IT!! IT'S HIM!
THUMP!
14.

BTOP!
SORRY I'M LATE, GUYS!
IF I'D KNOWN THERE WAS A PARTY GOING ON, I'D HAVE GOTTEN HERE SOONER!
AS FAR AS YOU'RE CONCERNED, WISE GUY--- THE PARTY'S OVER!

KRAK!
HEY...YOU FELLAS SURE PLAY ROUGH!! NO WONDER YOU HAVE A TOUGH TIME MAKING UP A GUEST LIST!

MISTER, WHEN YOU TRY TO SNEAK UP ON A GENT FROM BEHIND...
DON'T DO IT WHILE YOU'RE WEARING SIZE 12 CLOD-HOPPERS!

AND, AS FOR YOU, CHUCKLES...
ZAK!
FWOOP!

I'M DRUMMING YOU OUT OF THE DAREDEVIL DEVOTEES FAN CLUB HERE AND NOW!!

...BECAUSE I'M BEGINNING TO SUSPECT THAT YOU DON'T LIKE ME!

AND IF THERE'S ONE THING I CAN'T STAND...
..IT'S A HOSTILE HOOD!

IT'S TIME YOU REALIZED HOW UNHEALTHY PENT-UP AGGRESSIONS CAN BE!

BOK!
I WISH YOU KIDS WOULD STOP LONG ENOUGH TO TAKE SOME NOTES WHILE I'M TALKING!

SO YOU'RE THE GUYS WHO WANTED TO TAKE OVER THE MARAUDER'S MOB, HUH?
HE'D NEVER LET DAREDEVIL WALK ALL OVER 'IM... LIKE HE'S DOIN' TO THE WHOLE BUNCH OF YA!
YER ALL JUST A BUNCHA PUNKS!

WHO DO YA THINK YOU'RE CALLIN' PUNKS?!!
IF YOU GUYS WERE SO GREAT, MEBBE THE MARAUDER WOULDN'TA BIT THE DUST AWREADY!
WRASSK

HEY! WHA--?? NOOO! DON'T!! ...LEGGO!! LOOK OUT!! YEEEEOW!
CAN'T AFFORD TO WASTE MUCH MORE TIME! I'VE GOT TO END THIS QUICKLY!
CAN'T CHANCE THE BOSS REALIZING HE'S FAILED, AND RUNNING OFF WITH KAREN!
STOP!
OKAY, ALL OF YOU!! YOU WANTED ME.. NOW COME AND GET ME!!
THIS IS PAY DIRT, YOU PACK-RATS!

AWRIGHT, MASKED MAN... NOW THE GLOVES ARE OFF!
EVEN IF WE CAN'T USE OUR BLASTERS BECAUSE WE'RE FIGHTIN' TOO CLOSE, THAT DON'T MEAN WE'RE HELPLESS!
I GOT 'IM!! I GOT 'IM!!
THAT'S IT!! DON'T LET 'IM GET AWAY..!!
THANKS A HEAP, GUYS!
IT'S NICE OF YOU TO COME TO ME... SO I DON'T HAVE TO CHASE AROUND AFTER YOU!
ROOM
CAN'T KEEP GOING AT THIS PACE MUCH LONGER!
I'M GETTING EXHAUSTED.. MY ARMS... BEGINNING TO FEEL HEAVY AS LEAD..!
BUT I HOPE MY LITTLE PLAYMATES DON'T SUSPECT IT!
BEHIND ME.. SOME-ONE ABOUT TO STRIKE! I CAN HEAR HIM..!
NOW I'VE GOT YOU, YOU RED-GARBED GOON! YOU WON'T BE ABLE TO.. TO..!!
NICE TRY, SWEETIE... BUT YOU'RE STILL ONLY SECOND BEST!
ZTAK!

HE'S SURROUNDED! HE AIN'T GOT A CHANCE NOW!
YOU GOT 'IM NOW! IN ANOTHER COUPLE'A MINUTES THE WHOLE WORLD'LL KNOW IT WAS THE BOSS'S MOB THAT MADE MINCEMEAT OUTTA DAREDEVIL!
C'MON!! LET'S ALL RUSH 'IM AT ONCE!
COMING AT ME.. FROM ALL SIDES! AND THEY'RE NOT JUST OUT FOR AUTOGRAPHS!
MAN! IF EVER THERE WAS A TIME WHEN I FELT LIKE TRADING MY LITTLE HEAD-HORNS FOR A TICKET TO ANYWHERE..!
CAREFUL, YOU GUYS! HE'S STILL TRICKY!
OUR TIMING'S PERFECT!!
THERE'S NOTHIN' THAT SMIRKIN' SLOB CAN DO NOW!
BIG DEAL! A LOT OF GOOD BEIN' TRICKY IS GONNA DO HIM IN A SPOT LIKE THIS!
19.

CORRECTION, PLEASE! THERE'S ONE THING I CAN DO..!
BY SPLIT-SECOND TIMING, I CAN LEAP OVER YOUR HEADS JUST BEFORE IMPACT... LETTING THE FORCE OF YOUR CHARGE FINISH THIS LITTLE PICNIC FOR ME!
AWW, SHUCKS! I DON'T THINK YOU HEARD A WORD I SAID!
THONK!

AND NOW, BIG MOUTH..!
SAVE IT, MASKED MAN! I AIN'T TANGLIN' WITH YOU!
ANY GUY WHO CAN LICK TWO GANGS AT ONCE... SINGLE-HANDED... AIN'T EVEN HUMAN!
I'M KINDA SORRY YOU CHICKENED OUT! I WANTED TO SHOW YOU HOW I HANDLE A BIG, TOUGH BAD-MAN WHO THREATENS A FEMALE..!
BUT, THE POLICE WILL FINISH YOUR EDUCATION! GET MOVING, PUNK!

A SHORT TIME LATER...
MATT, YOU HAD CALLED ME EARLIER.. SAYING THERE WAS SOMETHING YOU WANTED TO TELL ME..!
YES! I.. REMEMBER!
HER VERY LIFE WAS THREATENED... BECAUSE SOME-ONE MERELY SUSPECTED SHE KNEW ME!
IF SHE BECAME MY WIFE... SHE'D NEVER BE SAFE FOR A MINUTE!

I LOVE HER.. TOO MUCH.. TO TAKE SUCH A RISK!
...EVEN IF IT MEANS... MY OWN LIFE WILL BE... ETERNALLY EMPTY!
IT WAS NOTHING, KAREN! JUST SOME BUSINESS TO DISCUSS.. BUT... IT CAN WAIT..!
SURE.. IT CAN WAIT, ALL RIGHT..
LIKE.. FOREVER!
NEXT: "The COBRA and MR. HYDE!"
20

HERE COMES...
DAREDEVIL
MARVEL COMICS GROUP
12¢ IND.
30 JULY
APPROVED BY THE COMICS CODE AUTHORITY
THE MAN WITHOUT
GUEST-STARRING
THE MIGHTY THOR!

DAREDEVIL, THE MAN WITHOUT FEAR!
"IF THERE SHOULD BE A THUNDER GOD!"
SAY, MATT! DID YOU HEAR ABOUT THE ROBBERY THIS MORNING? IT SEEMS UNBELIEVABLE!
THE DOOR OF A TWO-TON SAFE WAS TORN FROM ITS HINGES LIKE A TOY!
TWO SETS OF FOOTPRINTS WERE FOUND OUTSIDE THE BUILDING...ONE SET WAS NORMAL-SIZED, BUT THE OTHER--ENORMOUS!!
SOUNDS LIKE A NEW TEAM OF SUPER-POWERED MENACES AT LARGE IN THE CITY!
DAILY BUGLE
FANTASTIC ROBBERY!
SAFE DOOR RIPPED FROM HINGES
I'M SURE GLAD IT'S GOT NOTHING TO DO WITH US!
I WOULDN'T LAY ODDS ON THAT, MR. NELSON!
HANG LOOSE, HALLOWED ONE!
SMILIN' STAN LEE and GENIAL GENE COLAN
HAVE COME UP WITH ANOTHER BLOCK-BUSTER, AIDED AND ABETTED BY:
J. TARTAGLIONE, INKER & ARTIE SIMEK, LETTERER
1

A FUNNY THING ABOUT THE CASE-- THE OUTSIDE BANK DOOR WASN'T DAMAGED AT ALL!
THAT MEANS THEY MANAGED TO GET IN SOME OTHER WAY, AND THEN OPENED IT EASILY FROM THE INSIDE!
BUT, THE ONLY OTHER OPENING IS A WINDING AIR VENT-- WHICH NO NORMAL HUMAN COULD POSSIBLY SLITHER THRU!
SLITHER!! THAT'S THE KEY WORD, OLD BUDDY!
ONE OF THE MYSTERY MEN HAS THE ABILITY TO SLITHER INTO A PLACE...
WHILE THE OTHER POSSESSES THE POWER TO DO THE JOB ONCE HE'S INSIDE!

SUPER-HUMAN SKILL--AND SUPER-POWERED STRENGTH! QUITE A COMBO, EH, FOGGY?
I DON'T LIKE YOUR TONE OF VOICE, MATTHEW!
YOU'RE BEGINNING TO SOUND TOO INTERESTED!
WE'VE ENOUGH CASES NOW-- WITHOUT HAVING TO DEFEND THEM ONCE THEY'RE CAUGHT!
DON'T WORRY, PARTNER-- I'M NOT INTERESTED IN DEFENDING THEM!
WELL, THAT'S A RELIEF!
I JUST WANNA TAKE OFF AND FIGHT 'EM!

HOWEVER, I DO HAVE A HUNCH ABOUT OUR UNKNOWN FRIENDS!
WHAT SAY YOU JUST LEND A HAND WITH A LITTLE RESEARCH DURING LUNCH HOUR?
I KNEW IT! I KNEW IT!
A GUY WHO CAN COAX, AND CAJOLE LIKE YOU-- OUGHTTA BE-A-A-LAWYER!
OKAY, COUNSELOR --LET'S GO!

MINUTES LATER--
THIS IS WHAT YOU WANT, MATT!
IT TOOK PLACE MONTHS AGO--!
IT'S ALL HERE--THE COMPLETE ACCOUNT OF THOR'S BATTLE WITH THE COBRA-- AND MR. HYDE! WANT ME TO READ IT TO YOU?
EVERY LAST, LITTLE SYLLABLE, PAL!
I COULD READ IT TWICE AS FAST BY MERELY RUNNING MY FINGERS OVER THE PAGE--BUT WHY SPOIL FOGGY'S BIG MOMENT?

FINALLY, AS MATT'S EXHAUSTED PARTNER RETRIEVES THEIR COATS--
NOW CAN I GET BACK TO MY OWN CASE?
I'M RIGHT IN THE MIDDLE OF A ROUSING CORPORATE PROXY BATTLE TAX LITIGATION!
BE MY GUEST, LAD! I'VE GOT THE INFO I CAME FOR!
NOW, I'LL JUST TURN IT OVER TO MY BROTHER-- MIKE!
IT'S MADE TO ORDER FOR A FULL-TIME NUT LIKE DARE-DEVIL!
YOU CAN SAY THAT AGAIN, MR. NELSON!

AND, EVEN AS THE LESS-THAN-ADVENTUROUS **FOGGY NELSON** LEADS HIS SIGHTLESS LAW PARTNER BACK TO THEIR EAST SIDE OFFICE, **ANOTHER** EVENT OF SOMEWHAT MORE THAN CASUAL INTEREST IS TAKING PLACE JUST A FEW MERRY MILES AWAY--

NO SAFE CAN PROTECT ITS CONTENTS FROM THE POWER OF-- **MR. HYDE!**

NEVER MIND THE **SPEECHES,** STRONG MAN--JUST GET THE **LOOT!**

JUPITER FINANCE CO.

POWER ISN'T **EVERYTHING!**

WITHOUT THE **COBRA'S** SUPERIOR **STEALTH** YOU'D STILL BE LANGUISHING IN **JAIL!**

BUT, DESPITE THE COBRA'S SOMEWHAT IMMODEST PRONOUNCEMENT, THERE IS ONE SIGHTLESS STALWART WHO'S ITCHING FOR A CHANCE TO TANGLE WITH THE DEADLY DUO--!
IT MIGHT TAKE DAYS FOR DAREDEVIL TO TRACK THEM DOWN--
AND THERE'S NO TELLING HOW MUCH DAMAGE THEY'D DO IN THAT TIME!
I'VE GOT TO MAKE THEM COME TO ME!
AND METHINKS OL' MATTHEW KNOWS JUST HOW TO DO IT!
HYDE STRIKES AGAIN

THUS, A BRIEF, UNEVENTFUL TAXI RIDE LATER--
WANT I SHOULD HELP YA GET ACROSS THE STREET, MISTER?
COSTUM
TAXI
TAXI
THAT'S VERY KIND OF YOU-- BUT I THINK I CAN MAKE IT!
IF THEY HAVE WHAT I'M AFTER IN THAT COSTUME SHOP, I'LL BE HALF-WAY HOME!

IT'S FOR A LITTLE PARTY I'VE BEEN INVITED TO!
SURE, BUDDY-- I CAN HELP YOU OUT!.
I'VE GOT A BRAND-NEW THOR COSTUME --COMPLETE WITH A FULL-SIZE HAMMER!

BY NOW, MATTHEW'S LITTLE PLAN SHOULD BE CRYSTAL CLEAR TO ALL TRUE BELIEVERS--BUT, LET'S STAY WITH IT AND SEE WHAT DEVELOPS ANYWAY--
NOW ALL I'VE GOTTA DO IS SWING AROUND TOWN LIKE A DYED-IN-THE WOOL THUNDER GOD, HOPING HYDE AND THE COBRA WILL SPOT ME!
SINCE THOR IS THE ONE WHO ORIGINALLY DEFEATED EACH OF THEM, THEY'LL BE SURE TO ZERO IN ON HIM AS SOON AS HE'S SIGHTED!
MY ONLY PROBLEM IS TO FIGURE OUT A WAY TO GET THE COSTUME OVER MY OWN DD DUDS--WITH NO ONE BEING THE WISER!
I CAN EASILY COVER THE RED PORTIONS OF MY EXPOSED ARMS AND LEGS WITH SKIN-COLORED PLASTIC--
AND EVERYTHING ELSE OUGHTTA WORK OUT JUST FINE!
I MAY NOT BE AS MUSCULAR AS A THUNDER GOD--BUT I'M NOT EXACTLY A 99-POUND WEAKLING MYSELF!
AND I'LL BE MOVING TOO FAST FOR ANYONE TO NOTICE THE DIFFERENCE!

AND THEN--
VIOLA!!
MAN! IF IT LOOKS AS GOOD AS IT FEELS-- I'M IN BUSINESS!
THE FLESH-COLORED PLASTIC SHOULD ADD JUST ENOUGH TO MY BULK TO MAKE ME SEEM ALMOST AS MUSCULAR AS GOLDILOCKS HIMSELF!
AND THIS HAMMER'S THE CRAZIEST! I CAN'T WAIT TO GET GOING!
THE ONLY THING I DON'T DIG IS HOW THOR MANAGES TO FLY!
BUT, I GUESS A RAZZLE-DAZZLER LIKE HIM IS ENTITLED TO SOME SECRETS!
HOLD IT, HEROIC ONE! BEFORE YOU TURN THE PAGE, WE'VE GOT A LITTLE GUESSING GAME FOR ALL OF THOR'S THUNDEROUS FANS-- (LIKE EVERYBODY)
CAN YOU SPOT THE ONE LITTLE DETAIL IN MATT'S DISGUISE WHICH IS INCORRECT ??
IF NOT, DON'T PANIC! YOU'LL LEARN WHAT IT IS ON THE VERY NEXT PEERLESS, PRICELESS, PULSATIN' PAGE--
5

UH OH! I JUST THOUGHT OF SOMETHING!
THE HAMMER!
UNLESS THOR HAPPENS TO BE A LEFTY--

CHANCES ARE HE'D HOLD IT IN HIS RIGHT HAND!

NOW I'VE GOTTA MAKE SURE I CAN MANEUVER IN THIS GETUP!
I FEEL LIKE A FELLA WEARING TWO SUITS OF CLOTHES--
IT BETTER NOT CUT DOWN MY SPEED!
WELL, THERE'S JUST ONE WAY TO FIND OUT--

ONE FAST BACK-FLIP OUGHTTA TELL THE STORY!
IT MAY NOT BE DIGNIFIED ENOUGH FOR A LONG-HAIRED AVENGER--
BUT I WON'T COMPLAIN IF HE DOESN'T!

ALLEZ OOOOP! A PERFECT LANDING!
MAYBE I'M IN THE WRONG BUSINESS! MAYBE THUNDER GODDING IS MORE IN MY LINE!
THUP!

MY NEXT PROBLEM IS TO FIGURE OUT HOW TO FLY!
SAY! I'LL BET IF I PRESS MY BILLY CLUB AGAINST THE HAMMER HANDLE--AND THEN CLICK THE CABLE RELEASE--!
WHEN I SWING FROM THE ROOFTOPS, IT'LL LOOK AS THOUGH THE HAMMER IS PULLING ME THRU THE AIR!
KLAK
I LIKE IT! THE WHOLE THING'S JUST NUTTY ENOUGH TO WORK!

FIRST THING TO DO IS TEST IT OUT ON KAREN AND FOGGY!
SO, I'LL JUST BECOME MIKE MURDOCK UNDER THE MASK!
BOY! MY BIGGEST PROBLEM'LL BE KEEPING ALL THESE IDENTITIES STRAIGHT!

IF I CAN MOVE FAST ENOUGH, I MAY JUST GET AWAY WITH IT!
LUCKY IT'S GETTING DARK NOW--
CHANCES ARE NO ONE WILL EVEN NOTICE THE CABLE I'M HOLDING ONTO!

LOOK! UP THERE--IT'S THOR!
HE MUST'A LOST HIS BUS FARE!
I'LL BET HE'S AFTER THE COBRA --AND HYDE!
TOO BAD I HAVE TO WEAR THIS NUTTY CAPE!
BY FLUTTERING THIS WAY, IT MUFFLES SOME OF THE SOUND VIBRATIONS THAT GUIDE ME!

BUT, IT DIDN'T MUFFLE THEM ENOUGH! I'M LANDING RIGHT ON TARGET!
OH!
FOGGY-- LOOK! IT-IT'S THOR!
LOOK OUT, DARN IT!
WHAT'S GOING ON? THIS IS AN OFFICE--NOT A SILLY SUPER-HERO HAVEN!

FORSOOTH! HAVE YE NO WORD OF GREETING FOR THE MIGHTY THOR?
WHAT-- SHOULD WE-- SAY??
SAY IT ISN'T SO, PUSSYCAT!
WAIT A MINUTE! HE ISN'T THOR!
7

NO, BUT I MIGHT BE THOR--IF I WENT NORTHBACK RIDING!
OR, WOULD'JA BELIEVE-- MIKE MURDOCK?
MIKE! I DON'T UNDERSTAND!! WHY THAT RIDICULOUS DISGUISE?
IN THE WORDS OF A FAMOUS PHILOSO-PHER--
--WHOSE NAME ESCAPES ME--
WHY NOT?

ACTUALLY, KIDDIES --I'M MERELY A STALE PIECE OF CHEESE IN THE OL' MOUSE-TRAP OF LIFE!
I'M SETTIN' MYSELF UP AS BAIT-- TO CATCH ME A COUPLE OF RATS!
YOU MEAN-- YOU'RE DISGUISED AS THOR--SO THAT THE COBRA--AND HYDE--WILL ATTACK YOU?
THE LITTLE LADY WINS A BIIIIIIIG CIGAR!

MIKE MURDOCK--IN THE IDENTITY OF DAREDEVIL--DISGUISED AS THOR --IN ORDER TO TRAP TWO OTHER LOONS!
HOW CAN ANYONE TELL WHO'S WHO AROUND HERE ANY MORE??!
SIMPLE! JUST BUY ONE OF MY LITTLE ALL-PURPOSE MIKE MURDOCK SCORE CARDS!

HOW DID A NUT LIKE YOU EVER HAVE A BROTHER LIKE MATT?
IT WASN'T EASY, TUBBY!
AND NOW, AS YOU GAPE IN WIDE-EYED WONDER-- HERE'S WHERE I GO INTO MY ACT--!
DON'T BE BASHFUL! YOU CAN APPLAUD, IF YOU WANNA!
8

BUT, EVEN DAREDEVIL'S PLANS CAN HIT A SNAG WHEN A FRIVOLOUS FATE STEPS IN--FATE, IN THE PERSON OF--DR. DON BLAKE--!
I HAD INTENDED TO REMAIN IN MY OFFICE TONIGHT, TO CONDUCT SOME PATHOLOGICAL LAB TESTS--
BUT, THAT LITTLE NEWS ITEM ON THE RADIO MEANS A CHANGE OF PLAN!
BULLETIN! THE MIGHTY THOR HAS BEEN SEEN HURTLING ABOVE THE CITY'S ROOF-TOPS! PEOPLE EVERYWHERE ARE WONDERING--

IF ANYONE IS IMPERSONATING THE GOD OF THUNDER--THERE MUST BE SOME SINISTER MOTIVE BEHIND IT.!
AND I'VE GOT TO LEARN WHAT IT IS!!

IN ALL THE UNIVERSE, THERE'S ONLY ONE TRUE THUNDER GOD--!
BAM

AND, BY THE GOLDEN GATES OF ASGARD, NONE OTHER SHALL USURP MY PLACE!

SOON, YON BASE IMPOSTER SHALL ANSWER TO MIGHTY THOR, HIM-SELF!

SO BE IT!

FLY, MIGHTY MJOLNAR!! FLY, THOU ENCHANTED HAMMER! LEAD THY MASTER TO HIS PREY!
BY THE BRISTLING BEARD OF ODIN, HOW MY LIMBS DO LONG FOR BATTLE!

WHILE, DIRECTLY AROUND THE CORNER--
THIS HAMMER BIT IS THE GREATEST!
I WONDER IF THOR WAS EVER A CARPENTER--!
UH OH! MY RADAR SENSE IS RECEIVING SOME-THING--!

IT'S COMING TOWARD ME--AT GREAT SPEED--FASTER THAN THE COBRA--OR HYDE COULD EVER MOVE!
10

THE IMPOSTER! I HAVE FOUND THEE!
IT'S THE REAL THOR!!
MOVING TOO FAST-- LIKE A HUMAN COMET!
IF I CAN'T DODGE HIM SOMEHOW --I'LL BE STEAM-ROLLERED!
WHEW! JUST MADE IT-- BY CONTORTING MY ENTIRE BODY!
WHAT WITCHERY IS HERE AFOOT?
VERILY, THOU COULDST BE MY MIRROR IMAGE!
BUT, SINCE I AM I--AND THOU A KNAVE--
THEN, LET THERE BE A RECKONING!
BUT, EVEN AS THE THUNDER GOD SPEAKS, OUR FEARLESS FRIEND, HAVING LOST HIS MOMENTUM, DUE TO THE NEAR COLLISION, HURTLES THRU THE WINDOW OF A NEARBY BUILDING--
CRASH
CAN'T CHANGE DIRECTION!! TOO LATE TO USE CABLE AGAIN
UNNHHH--!
11

JUST MY LUCK! OF ALL THE GENTS TO RUN INTO, I HADDA PICK THE REAL THOR!
GOOD THING NO ONE'S HOME! EVEN I'D HAVE A TOUGH TIME EXPLAINING THIS!
MY DISGUISE SEEMED LIKE A STROKE OF GENIUS WHEN I THOUGHT OF IT--
NOW, ALL OF A SUDDEN, I FIGURE I SHOULD'A HAD MY HEAD EXAMINED!

OH WELL-- IT'S TOO LATE TO TURN BACK NOW!
I'VE GOT TO PLAY OUT THE HAND!
BUT, I SURE HOPE THE COBRA AND HYDE DIDN'T SEE WHAT HAPPENED!
EVEN THEY MIGHT NOT WANNA TACKLE A SET OF TWO MATCHED THUNDER GODS!
ANYWAY, I'D BETTER LOSE MYSELF IN THE PARK, OUTSIDE--!

HOLD, IMPOSTER! DIDST THOU THINK TO ESCAPE MIGHTY THOR THUS EASILY?
NOW THAT YOU MENTION IT, FELLA-- NO!
LOOK-- I HAVE A JOB TO DO--
WHY DON'T YOU GO AND LIFT SOME WEIGHTS FOR A WHILE, OR SOME-THING?

HAVING BEEN CAUGHT IN THY DECEPTION, THOU STILL DAREST MAKE LIGHT OF THE MATTER?
WHAT MANNER OF MORTAL ART THOU?
WELL, MY FRIENDS CALL ME A REAL PUSSYCAT-- BUT THEY MAY BE PREJUDICED!

ENOUGH! EVEN THE PATIENCE OF THOR DOTH HAVE ITS LIMITS!
'TIS TIME TO DIVEST THEE OF THY COSTUME AND LEARN THY TRUE IDENTITY!
STAND THEE BACK, BASE DECEIVER! THE MALLET OF THOR NOW SPEAKS IN SILENT THUNDER!

HE'S CREATING AN ACTUAL TORNADO-- BY MERELY SWINGING HIS HAMMER!
I'VE NEVER FACED SUCH FORCE--SUCH SHEER, UNCONTROLL-ABLE POWER!

THE FURY OF HIS STORM IS LIKE A LIVING THING --SAVAGE-- UNCONTROLL-ABLE--!
IT'S STRIPPING OFF MY OUTER COSTUME-- PEELING THE FABRIC FROM ME LIKE A BANANA SKIN!

I'LL SAY ONE THING FOR YOU, CURLY--
WHEN YOU MAKE UP YOUR MIND TO DO SOMETHING--
--YOU SURE DON'T KID AROUND!

DAREDEVIL! 'TIS THOU WHO HAST PRESUMED TO STEAL MY ROLE!
BUT WHY? SPEAK, MORTAL! I DESIRE TO KNOW THY MOTIVE!
THEN WHY DIDN'T YOU JUST COME OUT AND ASK ME?
I SAID SPEAK, MASKED ONE!
AND, HAVE A CARE, LEST I FIND THY NARRATIVE NOT TO MY LIKING!
US MEN WITHOUT FEAR DON'T BELIEVE IN KEEPING SECRETS FROM THUNDER GODS!

NO NEED TO MAKE A BIG THING ABOUT IT! I'M ON THE TRAIL OF MR. HYDE AND THE COBRA--AND I THOUGHT I'D SMOKE THEM OUT EASIER IF THEY THOUGHT I WAS YOU!
THY WORDS HAVE THE TINGE OF MADNESS!
HOW COULDST THOU HOPE TO MATCH THE POWER OF TWO SUCH AS THEY?
I'M NOT EXACTLY A PUSHOVER, PAL!
BUT, DON'T TAKE MY WORD FOR IT--TRY ME, AND SEE!

SO BE IT!
I SHALL PROVE THE FOLLY OF THY WAYS!
ZOK!
BUT, SINCE THOU ART MERELY MORTAL, I SHALL APPLY BUT A FRACTION OF MY ASGARDIAN STRENGTH!
BY RAGNAROK! THY REFLEXES DEFY UNDER-STANDING!

DO NOT COMPEL ME TO CAUSE THEE INJURY! I HAVE NO DESIRE TO INFLICT BODILY HARM!
THUD!
DON'T WORRY ABOUT IT, FELLA! I'VE NO DESIRE TO BE HARMED!
I JUST WANNA SHOW YOU WHAT I CAN DO AGAINST THOSE TWO EX-PLAYMATES OF YOURS!
THY PERFORMANCE IS OF GREAT CREDIT TO THY SKILL AND DARING! AND YET--
IT SHALL AVAIL THEE NAUGHT!
SEE WHAT DOTH OCCUR WHEN ONE, POSSESSED OF SUPER-HUMAN STRENGTH, CAN SEIZE THY CABLE!
THOU MUST HELPLESSLY HURTLE TO THE GROUND BELOW!
OOOF! YOU'VE GOT A POINT THERE--PAL!
THUMP!
YET, THOUGH I HAVE BESTED THEE, I AM SINGULARLY IMPRESSED!
THY SKILL IS GREATER BY FAR THAN I SUPPOSED!
THEREFORE, I SAY THEE-- YEA!
YEA??

SINCE I HAVE MATTERS OF STILL GREATER URGENCY--I GRANT THEE LEAVE TO BATTLE IN MY STEAD--
PROVIDED THOU DOST NOT WEAR AGAIN THE IMMORTAL RAIMENT OF THOR!
THUPP!
IF YOU MEAN HANDS OFF YOUR THREADS--THE ANSWER IS--OKAY!
--THOUGH IT'LL BE A WHALE OF A JOB TRACKING THOSE TWO DOWN AS PLAIN OL' DAREDEVIL!

HOWEVER, WE HAVE JUST WITNESSED ONE OF THE FEW SHINING MOMENTS WHEN OUR HORN-HEADED HERO IS DEAD WRONG--!
WHAT RARE GOOD LUCK FOR US TO SPY OUR IMMORTAL ARCH-ENEMY BATTLING THE MAN WITHOUT FEAR!
IT WOULD HAVE BEEN BETTER LUCK IF THOR HAD REMAINED--SO I COULD CRUSH HIM WITH MY NEW, GREATLY-ENLARGED STRENGTH!
BUT, SINCE HE IS NOW OUT OF REACH, LET US DO THE NEXT BEST THING AND DESTROY DAREDEVIL!
OTHERWISE, HE MAY PROVE TO BE A SOURCE OF GREAT ANNOYANCE TO US IN THE FUTURE!

AND SO...
SOMEONE RUSHING ME--FROM BEHIND!
I'LL PRETEND TO BE UNAWARE--AND SEE WHAT HAPPENS!

HAH! IT WAS EASIER THAN I THOUGHT!
NONE CAN BREAK THE IRON GRIP OF MR. HYDE!
HYDE! STRENGTH!
IT'S TOO GOOD TO BE TRUE!
IF ONLY THE COBRA'S WITH HIM, TOO--!

NO NEED TO BREAK YOUR GRIP, STRONG MAN--
NOT WHEN I CAN SLIP OUT OF IT BY SOME SIMPLE MUSCLE CONTRACTION!

HE'S GONE! WHERE DID HE GO? WHERE DID HE GO??
CALM DOWN! HE'S BOUND TO BE NEAR HERE!
I'VE TOLD YOU NOT TO RELY ON YOUR BESTIAL STRENGTH ALONE!
NEXT TIME, LET THE COBRA HANDLE THE STRATEGY!

OR, BETTER STILL-- WHY NOT LET OL' DD HANDLE IT?
THERE HE IS-- RIGHT ABOVE US!
AWW, SOMEONE MUSTA TOLD YOU!
DON'T JUST STAND THERE! RUSH HIM!
RUSH HIM-- BEFORE HE CAN GET AWAY!

BTOK!
HOW MANY TIMES DO I HAVETA TELL YOU--??
I'M NOT LEAVING! I LIKE IT HERE!

UH OH! HYDE SEVERED MY BRANCH IN TWO--WITH JUST ONE SWEEP OF HIS APE-LIKE HAND!
ZLOP!
YOUR SPEED --YOUR ACROBATIC SKILL--ARE MEANINGLESS AGAINST THE POWER OF MR. HYDE!
TOO BAD YOU HAVEN'T A PARTNER NAMED SEEK! THAT'D REALLY BE A SWINGIN' COMBO!
THAT'LL BRING YOU DOWN TO EARTH! NEVER AGAIN WILL YOU TAUNT US!

HYDE-- WAIT! HE'S TRYING TO GET YOU MAD! DON'T FALL FOR IT!
SILENCE, COBRA! NOBODY CAN SPEAK TO ME THE WAY HE DID--AND LIVE TO BRAG OF IT!
SO FAR, SO GOOD! NOW, IT'S ALL UP TO MY SPLIT-SECOND TIMING--!

MAN! THAT WAS A CLOSE ONE!
HAPPY LANDINGS, HYDIE!
THE NAKED FORCE OF HIS LEAP CLEAN SHATTERED THAT OAK LIKE A MATCHSTICK!
KRAKK
IF THAT HAD BEEN ME HE HIT--!
SHEEESH! CAN'T EVEN LET MYSELF THINK ABOUT SUCH THINGS!

THERE THEY GO--INTO A GETAWAY CAR!
I HEAR THE DOORS OPENING! THEY HAVEN'T EVEN STARTED THE MOTOR YET!
I'LL REACH THEM EASY!

THERE'S JUST ONE THING THAT DOESN'T ADD UP!
THE COBRA DOWNED ME WITH ONE PUNCH FROM BEHIND!
BUT, THEY RAN OFF! WHY? WHY DIDN'T THEY TRY TO FINISH ME?
BUT, CAN'T AFFORD TO LET 'EM GET AWAY NOW!
MAYBE I'LL FIND THE ANSWERS I WANT LATER ON!
THEY'RE HEADING FOR HAUNTED HILL -- WHERE THERE'S AN OLD DESERTED BARN!

SECONDS LATER, WITHIN THAT "DESERTED-LOOKING" STRUCTURE...
WHY DOESN'T HE TRY TO BREAK IN? WHERE IS HE?
I DON'T LIKE THIS PLAN, HYDE! I DON'T LIKE IT AT ALL!
PATIENCE, COBRA! HE'LL BE HERE! HE'S GOT TO BE HERE!
AND, WHEN HE ARRIVES, MY FORMULA WILL BE READY!

HEADS UP, GROUP!
CRASH!
YOU!
YOU CRASHED IN THRU THE SKYLIGHT!

I KNOW! I DIDN'T WANNA DISTURB YOU BY RINGING THE BELL!
HEY! - WHAT IN THE--??!
YOU DIDN'T REALIZE HOW FAST THE COBRA CAN ATTACK!
GOTTA GET HIM OFF!
HE CAN WRAP HIMSELF AROUND A VICTIM JUST LIKE HIS NAMESAKE!

HOLD HIM! HOLD HIM! THAT'S IT-- GOOD!
JUST FOR ANOTHER SECOND--
AND THEN, AFTER THAT, IT WILL NO LONGER MATTER!

WHILE, OUTSIDE THE DESOLATE STRUCTURE--
COBRA! HYDE! THIS IS THE POLICE! WE KNOW YOU'RE IN THERE!
WE SAW YOU FIGHTING DAREDEVIL-- AND THEN WE FOLLOWED YOU!
WE'VE GOT YOU SURROUNDED! COME OUT WITH YOUR HANDS UP!
SURRENDER--NOW! YOU HAVEN'T A CHANCE!
WE'RE READY TO CLOSE IN AT A MINUTE'S NOTICE, CHIEF!
THEY'LL NEVER SURRENDER! BUT I'VE GOT TO GIVE 'EM THE CHANCE!

BUT, WITHIN THE COLD, DANK WALLS--
WE DID IT!
IT'S TOO LATE FOR HIM TO SAVE HIMSELF NOW!
SPLOOSH!
NOW-- RELEASE HIM, COBRA!

NOTICE ANYTHING DIFFERENT ABOUT YOURSELF, MASKED MAN?
WHAT-- DID THEY DO-- TO ME??

NO MATTER HOW GREAT A CRIME-FIGHTER IS--
IF HE CANNOT SEE-- HE'S HELP-LESS!
WHAT-- IS HE-- TALKING ABOUT?

THE CHEMICAL I POURED OVER YOU WAS SPECIALLY DESIGNED --FOR ONLY ONE PURPOSE--
TO TAKE AWAY ANY MAN'S EYESIGHT!
NO! NO!
HE'S RIGHT-- I--I CAN'T SEE!

BUT, I WAS BLIND ALL THE TIME! SO, HOW COULD THE CHEMICAL--? WAIT! I KNOW!
I'M AS SIGHTLESS AS I EVER WAS-- BUT THERE'S A DIFFERENCE--!
THE CHEMICAL WAS SUPPOSED TO AFFECT MY OPTIC NERVE, BUT SINCE I'M ALREADY SIGHTLESS...
...IN SOME STRANGE WAY, IT AFFECTED MY SENSES INSTEAD-- DEADENING THEM ALL!

SO NOW--TO ALL INTENTS AND PURPOSES--
DAREDEVIL-- IS--REALLY-- AND--TRULY-- BLIND!
MORE NEXT ISSUE!

HERE COMES...

DAREDEVIL

THE MAN WITHOUT FEAR!

APPROVED BY THE COMICS CODE AUTHORITY

MARVEL COMICS GROUP

12¢ IND.

31 AUG

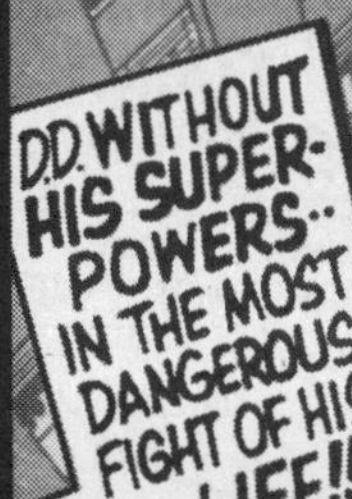

"BLIND MAN'S BLUFF!"

DAREDEVIL, THE MAN WITHOUT FEAR!
"BLIND MAN'S BLUFF!"
I'VE ALWAYS BEEN BLIND... BUT I HAD MY SUPER SENSES TO MAKE UP FOR IT! YET, NOW--
THE POWER WHICH MADE ME DAREDEVIL--IS GONE! I'M AS HELPLESS AS ANY BLIND MAN!
A STAN (THE MAN) LEE and GENE (THE DEAN) COLAN THRILL-A-MINUTE TRIUMPH!
EMBELLISHED BY: JOHN TARTAGLIONE
LETTERED BY: ARTIE SIMEK
LAST ISH, WE SAW THE FIENDISH MR. HYDE HURL A POTENT CHEMICAL AT DAREDEVIL, HOPING TO DESTROY HIS EYESIGHT! BUT, SINCE THE MAN WITHOUT FEAR IS ALREADY BLIND, HYDE'S FORMULA AFFECTED HIS SUPER SENSES INSTEAD--MAKING THEM TOTALLY USELESS! BUT THAT'S NOTHING! THINGS REALLY GET RUGGED FOR OUR HERO IN THIS INCREDIBLE ISH--!!
HANG LOOSE, HALLOWED ONE! YOU'RE ABOUT TO READ THE MOST UNUSUAL SAGA OF ALL--!
1.

I'VE GOT TO GET AWAY!
GOT TO RUN-- SOMEWHERE-- ANYWHERE--!
THE WORLD MUST NEVER SUSPECT THAT DAREDEVIL IS REALLY A BLIND MAN!

WE'VE WAITED LONG ENOUGH! LET'S RUSH 'EM!
DON'T TAKE ANY CHANCES!
IF HYDE-- OR THE COBRA ARE STILL IN THERE-- ANYTHING CAN HAPPEN!
I HEAR THE POLICE-- THEY'RE HEADING THIS WAY!
THERE MUST BE A WAY OUT FOR ME-- BEFORE THEY GET HERE!

I KNOW THERE'S A DOOR BACK HERE SOMEWHERE-- A HIDDEN ESCAPE ROUTE!
I HEARD THEM RUNNING OUT-- JUST SECONDS AGO!
BUT-- HOW DO I FIND IT??

I'VE GOT TO DO WHAT ANY BLIND MAN DOES--
FEEL MY WAY AS I GO!!
IT HAS TO BE HERE-- IT HAS TO!!

WHAT'S THIS? A DOOR-KNOB!! IT MUST BE IT!
AND--ONE WAY OR ANOTHER-- I'VE GOT TO CHANCE IT!
CLICK!

WHILE, SECONDS LATER--
ARE THEY *IN* THERE, LEW?
NOT A *SIGN* OF 'EM!
LOOKS LIKE WE'RE *TOO LATE!*
SLAM!
SPRAK!
FAN OUT, MEN! GO OVER THIS PLACE WITH A *FINE-TOOTH COMB!*
I WANNA KNOW WHO WAS *IN* HERE-- AND *WHY!*
THEY *COULD* HAVE GOTTEN OUT *THIS* WAY!
OR THRU THIS HIDDEN *TRAP DOOR!*
I GET THE FEELING SOMEONE *ELSE* WAS WITH THE COBRA AND HYDE!
BUT-- *WHO??*
FOR THE ANSWER TO *THAT* QUESTION, LET'S VISIT A DARKENED SIDE-STREET IN THE EARLY, SILENT HOURS BEFORE DAWN--
MY *LUCK* IS STILL HOLDING OUT!
I'VE HEARD ALMOST NO TRAFFIC--NO SOUNDS OF PEDESTRIANS!
THAT MEANS IT'S *STILL* EARLY IN THE MORNING-- BEFORE THE SUNRISE!
I *STILL* HAVE A CHANCE OF REACHING HOME --WITHOUT BEING SEEN!
BUT--*WHA-?!!* I'M *FALLING!* I WAS TOO *CARELESS*-- MOVED TOO *FAST!*

UHHH-- CAUGHT MYSELF JUST IN TIME!
I'VE GOT TO BE MORE CAREFUL NOW--FEEL MY WAY ALONG THE BUILDING WALLS--
IF ONLY--I COULD BE SURE I'M GOING IN THE RIGHT DIRECTION--!
I THINK--I'VE FINALLY BITTEN OFF--MORE THAN I CAN CHEW!
I'VE-- GOT TO-- GET HELP!

AND, AS THE LONELY MINUTES DRAG ON--STRETCHING INTO HOURS--THE GALLANT COSTUMED FIGURE STUMBLES THRU THE CITY STREETS--TOTALLY TRAPPED IN A WORLD OF UTTER AND COMPLETE DARKNESS--UNTIL, AT LAST--
IT'S DAREDEVIL!
BUT--SOME-THING'S HAPPENED TO HIM!!
I KNEW IT WAS HOPELESS!--BEEN WALKING FOR HOURS--DON'T KNOW WHERE I AM--
AND NOW--THERE ARE PEOPLE ON THE STREETS--THEY MUST SEE ME--!

HE LOOKS LIKE HE'S BEEN HURT!
THAT'S MY ANSWER--WHAT THAT MAN SAID! I'LL CLAIM I WAS INJURED IN A FIGHT!
HE MUSTA JUST FINISHED ROUNDIN' UP SOME HOODS!
ARE YOU OKAY, FELLA? ANYTHING WE CAN DO? SHOULD WE CALL THE COPS?
NO--EVERY-THING'S FINE NOW! I JUST TOOK A LITTLE SHELLACKIN'!
I'LL BE GOOD AS NEW AGAIN--WHEN MY HEAD CLEARS!

AND NOW--IF SOMEONE WILL BE GOOD ENOUGH TO TELL ME --WHERE I AM--!
AWW--DON'T PUT US ON, DAREDEVIL!
YOU KNOW THIS NEIGHBOR-HOOD BETTER'N WE DO!
WELL, SO MUCH FOR THAT GAMBIT!

IF ONLY I COULD ADMIT THAT I CAN'T SEE! BUT IT WOULD MEAN MY LIFE!
IT WOULD BE OPEN SEASON ON DARE-DEVIL THRUOUT THE ENTIRE UNDERWORLD!
LET ME THRU!! I'VE GOT TO GET NEAR HIM--I'VE GOT TO--!
A GIRL'S VOICE-- COMING CLOSER--!

NO ONE WILL BELIEVE I WAS THIS CLOSE TO DARE-DEVIL!!
BUT--IF I CAN GET A PIECE OF HIS MASK--FOR PROOF--!
SO THAT'S WHAT-- WAIT! NO! --DON'T!!

I GOT IT! I GOT IT!!
DON'T--TRY-- THAT-- AGAIN-- LADY!
I CAN'T EVEN TELL-- HOW BIG A PIECE SHE TORE OFF--!

HEY! NO NEED TO GET SO ROUGH, BIG MAN!
MAYBE NOT--BUT I DON'T WEAR THIS MASK FOR FUN!
SHE DIDN'T MEAN ANY HARM!
NEXT TIME YOU WANNA RIP SOME APPAREL, GO FIND A SCREEN STAR!
BUT NONE ARE AS GLAMOROUS AS YOU!
MAN! I WOULDN'T WANNA FACE THAT JOKER IF HE WAS EVER REALLY MAD!

NOW THAT YOU GOT IT, WHAT'LL YOU DO WITH IT?
PUT IT IN MY HOPE CHEST, OF COURSE!
CAREFUL! DON'T GET TOO CLOSE TO IT! DON'T EVEN BREATHE ON IT!
IF MY SENSES HAD BEEN OPERATING NORMALLY, I'D HAVE KNOWN THAT GIRL WAS REACHING FOR MY MASK ALMOST BEFORE SHE KNEW IT!
WELL, I'D BETTER GET GOING-- ANYWHERE--
IF I KEEP WALKING-- KEEP MOVING-- THERE'S LESS CHANCE OF ANYONE ELSE GRABBING FOR MY MASK!

UNHHH!
ALTHOUGH THERE'S **MORE** CHANCE OF ME BREAKING MY FOOL **NECK** BY BUMPING **INTO** SOMETHING!
IT--FEELS LIKE--A **PARKING METER!**
THAK!

THAT MEANS I'M NEAR THE **CURB!**
SAY! WAIT! A MINUTE!
WHY DIDN'T I THINK OF THIS **BEFORE**--??!
IT'S THE EASIEST WAY IN THE **WORLD** TO REACH MY PAD--

ALL I HAVE TO **DO** IS--
CALL A--
TAXI!

HEY, WADDAYA **KNOW!**
I NEVER PICKED UP A **SUPER-HERO** BEFORE!
HOW COME YA AINT JUST **SWINGIN'** THRU THE STREET?
I JOINED A **UNION!** THIS IS MY **COFFEE BREAK** TIME!
TAXI
UH OH! I WONDER HOW MY **CREDIT** IS?
I DON'T HAVE A **RED CENT** WITH ME!

APPARENTLY, **DD's** CREDIT IS OKAY--BECAUSE, A FEW MINUTES LATER--
I TOLD HIM I WANTED TO VISIT **MATT MURDOCK**, BECAUSE I NEEDED A **LAWYER!**
I EVEN HAD **HIM** LOOK UP THE ADDRESS--AS THOUGH I DIDN'T **KNOW** IT!
NOW--IF I **REMEMBER** RIGHTLY--MY **STAIRWAY** SHOULD BE JUST AHEAD--!
MAN! WHAT A **RELIEF!** FOR A WHILE THERE, I NEVER THOUGHT I'D **MAKE** IT THIS FAR!
THE ONLY PROBLEM **IS**--WHAT DO I DO **NEXT??**

WELL, ONE THING I MUSTN'T DO IS SIT AROUND FEELING SORRY FOR MYSELF!
I'VE ALREADY CONVINCED FOGGY AND KAREN THAT DAREDEVIL IS REALLY MY "TWIN BROTHER", MIKE MURDOCK!
I CAN'T GO IT ALONE ANY MORE--I'VE GOT TO DEPEND ON THEM NOW--
BUT PERHAPS I CAN STILL MAINTAIN THE FICTION THAT DD AND MIKE ARE ONE AND THE SAME!

THE IMPORTANT THING IS--NO ONE MUST EVER KNOW THAT DAREDEVIL IS REALLY MATT MURDOCK!
THEREFORE, IF I ADMIT TO KAREN AND FOGGY DD IS NOW BLIND, THEY MUST BELIEVE THAT MIKE HAS GONE BLIND, ALSO!
IF I CARRY THIS OFF, IT'LL BE A MIRACLE!
BUT THE WHOLE THING IS JUST NUTTY ENOUGH THAT THEY'LL HAVE TO BELIEVE IT!
NO ONE COULD DREAM UP A FANTASY LIKE THIS!

AND SO--
HERE'S A TAXI FOR YOU, MISTER!
I'M GLAD I WAS ABLE TO HELP!
MUCH OBLIGED, FRIEND!

MINUTES LATER--
YOU SURE FIND OUT HOW MANY DECENT PEOPLE THERE ARE IN THE WORLD WHEN YOU REALLY NEED HELP!
IN MY LINE OF WORK, A FELLA TENDS TO FORGET ABOUT THINGS LIKE THAT!
MURDOCK AND NELSON ATTY.
THAT'S THE OFFICE YOU ASKED FOR--RIGHT IN FRONT OF YOU--!

ANYTHING ELSE I CAN DO FOR YOU?
NOT A THING, THANKS!
I'LL BE OKAY NOW!
ELEV
JUST CALL ME IF YOU NEED ANYTHING, MR. MURDOCK!

OKAY, GROUP-- LET'S HEAR IT FOR OL' MIKE!
WHAT HAPPENED TO THE BRASS BAND? ARE THEY OUT TO LUNCH?
WOULDN'T YOU KNOW IT? I'VE A MILLION CASES WAITING TO BE DISCUSSED WITH MATT-- AND HIS IDIOT BROTHER MIKE DROPS BY INSTEAD!
SAY! WHAT'S WITH THE CANE--AND THE UNSTEADY WALK BIT??
IF THAT'S YOUR IDEA OF A GAG, YOU CAN GO PEDDLE IT ELSEWHERE!
LOOK OUT--!
WHAT'S A DESK DOING HERE?
IT--USED TO BE-- ON THE OTHER SIDE-- OF THE ROOM!
KLOP!
LEVEL WITH ME, MIKE-- WHAT'S GOING ON?
WHAT'S HAPPENED TO YOU, FELLA?
EVER HEAR OF A BLIND SUPER-HERO?
WELL, I'M INTRODUCING YOU TO ONE RIGHT NOW!
IN A NUTSHELL, LAWYER MAN-- I CAN'T SEE!!
BUT--MATT'S THE BLIND ONE! I--I DON'T GET IT--!
FIGURE IT OUT, SON--I'M MATT'S BROTHER, RIGHT?
MAYBE WE BOTH WERE BORN WITH A WEAKNESS IN OUR EYES-- ONLY MINE DIDN'T HIT ME TILL YEARS AFTER MATT'S!
TROUBLE WITH YOUR EYES! THEN --THAT'S WHY YOU ALWAYS WORE THOSE SUNGLASSES! IT WAS MORE THAN JUST AN ACT!
IT'S WORKING! HE'S SWALLOWING IT! HE STILL DOESN'T SUSPECT THAT I'M REALLY MATT!!
8

ALAS, IT'S TIME TO TEAR OURSELVES *AWAY* FROM MATT AND FOGGY FOR A WHILE--AS THE *COBRA* AND *MR. HYDE* ENGAGE IN SOME UNUSUAL ACTIVITIES WHICH MAY SOON BE OF SOME INTEREST TO *DAREDEVIL*--AND TO *YOU*--

DOWN, HYDE.!! GET *DOWN*, I SAY!!

IF THERE'S A *GUARD* IN THE AREA, HE'S LIABLE TO *SEE* YOU RUNNING ACROSS THE ALLEY THAT WAY!!

SHUDDUP, YOU SPINELESS, CRINGING *COWARD*!!

WITH MY MATCHLESS *STRENGTH*, DO YOU THINK *I* FEAR ANY PUNY *GUARD*?!!

SPLUSHH!

WAIT! YOU CAN'T MAKE IT THRU THAT PIPE!!
IT BENDS TOO SHARPLY-- AT A 90° ANGLE!!
THE COBRA CAN SLITHER THRU ANYTHING --WATCH!
HE'S CRAWLING INTO THE PIPE WITHOUT ANY EFFORT--
LIKE HE HASN'T A BONE IN HIS BODY!

HOW SIMPLE THIS SORT OF THING CAN BE--FOR THE COBRA!
EVEN HYDE, WITH ALL HIS STRENGTH, CAN'T MATCH MY OWN SERPENTINE STEALTH!

EXACTLY SEVEN SECONDS LATER--
ARE YOU THERE, HYDE?
NOW, WITHOUT ANY STRAIN-- WITHOUT ANY TROUBLE--YOU MAY ENTER IF YOU WISH!
--WITH THE COMPLIMENTS OF--THE UNBEATABLE COBRA!

BAH! YOU AND YOUR STUPID SPEECHES!!
HAVE YOU FORGOTTEN WHICH OF US IT WAS THAT DEFEATED DAREDEVIL??
YOU BRAINLESS BRAGGART!!
YOU COULD NEVER HAVE DONE IT WITHOUT MY HELP!

AND I STILL SAY YOU SHOULD HAVE FINISHED HIM OFF--INSTEAD OF LEAVING HIM THE WAY YOU DID!
WE LEFT HIM BLINDED, DIDN'T WE?
WHAT CAN WE EVER HAVE TO FEAR FROM A BLIND MAN?!!
NOW--FOLLOW ME!! THE SAFE IS JUST AHEAD!
FRAGI

HMMM-- ANOTHER QUARTER HOUR AND IT'LL BE TIME TO CHECK IN AGAIN!

THIS SURE IS AN EASY JOB!
--IF ONLY IT WASN'T SO DULL!

PERHAPS THIS WILL LIVEN UP YOUR EVENING FOR YOU!
HURRY! SHUT 'IM UP FAST SO WE CAN MAKE A CLEAN HAUL!
HEY!! WHAT'S GOIN' ON--??!

DON'T WORRY, HYDE--!
THE COBRA MAKES NO SLIP-UPS!
FTOK

HE'S OUT LIKE A LIGHT!
NOW, LET'S GO! THIS PLACE WILL BE SWARMING WITH COPS WHEN IT GETS PAST HIS CHECK-IN TIME!
WE'VE GOT TO GET WHAT WE CAME FOR, AND BE GONE BY THEN!!
EVERYTHING DEPENDS UPON HOW FAST YOU CAN GET THE SAFE OPEN! --SO MOVE!

IT'S A *NEW* TYPE!! I CAN'T FEEL THE *TUMBLERS* CLICK!

SO! AFTER ALL YOUR BIG TALK, YOU *FAIL* US WHEN THE CHIPS ARE DOWN!

SAY THAT *AGAIN*, AND I'LL SHUT YOU UP FOR *GOOD!* HYDE *NEVER* FAILS!!

YOU SAW WHAT I DID TO THAT STEEL DOOR--!
JUST THINK WHAT I COULD DO TO YOU--IF YOU EVER CROSS ME!
I WOULDN'T JUST STAND THERE--AS HELPLESS AS A DOOR, HYDE!
BUT NEVER MIND THE USELESS THREATS! LET'S DIVVY UP THE LOOT!
WE'LL DO OUR DIVVYING LATER! THE NIGHT'S STILL YOUNG!
THERE'S TIME TO PULL A COUPLE MORE JOBS!

AND SO--
WHAT DRIVES YOU, HYDE? DON'T YOU EVER REST--?
--EVER TAKE THE TIME TO SPEND ANY OF YOUR HAUL?
THE MONEY MEANS NOTHING TO ME! I CRAVE EXCITEMENT!
IT'S MY STRENGTH AGAINST THE WHOLE WORLD!!
MANKIND MUST PAY FOR WHAT THEY'VE DONE TO MR. HYDE!!

OH NO!! IT--IT'S MR. HYDE!!
HE'S HOLDING A HUGE CORNICE AT THE EDGE OF THE ROOF--
THREATENING TO HURL IT AT THE PEOPLE BELOW!

DROP YOUR GUNS AND GET OUT OF HERE,--OR THIS STONE GOES FLYING!
IT'S UP TO YOU!!
DON'T DO IT, HYDE!!
HAH!! JUST TRY AND STOP ME!!

WE'VE GOTTA DO SOMETHING--FAST!
EITHER THOSE COPS WILL BE INJURED--OR SOME INNOCENT BYSTANDERS WILL GET IT!
BUT, WHAT CAN WE DO??
REMEMBER--YOU CAN'T SEE NOW!
LISTEN! I'LL TELL YOU--!

LUCKILY, I KEPT MY EXTRA SET OF RED ROMPERS UNDER MY SUIT!
MIKE! ARE YOU MAD?
YOU CAN'T GO OUT THERE!
ONLY A MADMAN WOULD BE A COSTUMED CLOWN IN THE FIRST PLACE!
WISH ME LUCK, PRETTY GIRL! UNCLE MIKE IS SURE GONNA NEED IT!
ONLY A DIVERSION WILL PREVENT A TRAGEDY OUT THERE!
BUT--HOW--???
AND MERRY MICHAEL IS GONNA PROVIDE THAT DIVERSION!
THAT'S WHERE YOU COME IN, FOGGY!
THE COBRA AND HYDE HAVE TO SEE ME--HAVE TO BELIEVE I'M NOT BLIND ANY MORE!
I'LL TRY TO BLUFF IT THRU--IF YOU GUIDE ME!
GRAB MY ARM--JUST GET ME TO THE ROOF, AND I'LL TAKE IT FROM THERE!
I ALWAYS THOUGHT YOU WERE OUT OF YOUR TREE!
NOW I'M SURE OF IT!
BUT, IF SOMEONE HAS TO LEND YOU A HAND--IT MIGHT AS WELL BE ME!

CROUCH DOWN--BEHIND THE LEDGE, FOGGY! NO ONE MUST SEE YOU!
HYDE!! LOOK--UP THERE! IT'S DAREDEVIL!
HE'S REGAINED HIS SIGHT AGAIN! HE'S COMING AFTER US!

LOOK! THERE ON THE ROOF! ISN'T THAT--DAREDEVIL??

WHAT CHANCE WILL HE HAVE--AGAINST BOTH HYDE--AND THE COBRA??

BUT, IF OUR EMOTIONAL FEMALE SPECTATOR IS WORRIED ABOUT DD NOW, HOW WOULD SHE FEEL IF SHE KNEW HE WAS ALSO TOTALLY BLIND--??

IN FACT, HOW DOES HE FEEL--AT A TIME LIKE THIS--?

I--I MISJUDGED THE WIDTH OF THE LEDGE!

I'M SLIPPING--!

MY ANKLE!! GRAB IT, FOGGY--HOLD ON!! HOLD ON!!

I KNEW THIS WAS INSANE! YOU HAVEN'T A CHANCE, MIKE!! I CAN'T KEEP HOLDING YOU!

SOONER OR LATER YOU'LL TAKE ONE WRONG STEP--!

YOU'VE GOT TO QUIT!! YOU'VE GOT TO COME BACK!!

THKK!
I DID IT!
IT ISN'T POSSIBLE!! MY FORMULA WAS FOOLPROOF!
IT DID MAKE HIM BLIND!! I SAW IT-- I KNOW IT!!
YOU'RE AN IDIOT, HYDE! THERE HE IS! DO YOU DOUBT YOUR EYES??
THEN WHAT-- DO WE DO-- NOW?
I DON'T KNOW! WE'VE GOT TO WAIT! LET HIM MAKE THE NEXT MOVE!
EVEN WITHOUT MY SUPER SENSES, I'VE TRAINED MYSELF IN ACROBATICS FOR YEARS!
IF I WAS ABLE TO DO THIS BEFORE-- WHY SHOULDN'T I BE ABLE TO DO IT NOW?!!
I'VE GOT TO MAKE THE COBRA AND HYDE ABSOLUTELY CONVINCED THAT I'M THE SAME OLD DAREDEVIL!
16

I NEVER APPRECIATED MY HYPER-KEEN SENSES ENOUGH BEFORE!
I USED TO BE ABLE TO DO THIS WITHOUT GIVING IT A SECOND THOUGHT!!
BUT NOW-- IT'S PROBABLY A LUCKY THING THAT I CAN'T SEE OR I WOULDN'T HAVE THE NERVE TO GO ON!

CAN'T HOLD ON--! I'M FALLING!!
BUT, IF I CAN REACH OUT--FAR ENOUGH--!
HOOO BOY!!
HYDE--AND THE COBRA MUST HAVE BEEN WATCHING--!
THIS IS ONE PERFORMANCE I WOULDN'T WANNA REPEAT!
I'VE GOT TO ACT NONCHALANT--AS THOUGH I DID IT FOR KICKS!
YOU WERE RIGHT, COBRA!! HE CAN SEE!
NO ONE BUT DAREDEVIL WOULD HAVE THE NERVE TO CLOWN AROUND THAT WAY TWENTY STORIES ABOVE THE GROUND!!
WE CAN'T FIGHT HIM AND THE POLICE--!
SO LET'S TAKE OFF--WHILE THEY'RE ALL WATCHING HIS ACT!!
SAY, LEN--DO YOU THINK DAREDEVIL IS--HEY!!
WHAT'S WITH HYDE--AND THE COBRA?
THEY'RE TRYIN' TO GET AWAY!
NOW! LET'S MOVE--!
DON'T WORRY ABOUT ME!
MY SPEED IS TWICE AS FAST AS YOURS!
HOLD IT, YOU TWO!
STOP--OR I'LL SHOOT!
KRAK!
I SAID STOP!!
ZISK!
MADE IT!
WE'LL FIND TIME FOR DAREDEVIL--LATER!
ZAK!
ZAK!

DAREDEVIL--THEY'VE GONE! YOU CAN COME BACK NOW!
GOOD DEAL, FOGGY!

IF ONLY IT WAS AS EASY...
--AS YOU MAKE IT SOUND!

GLAD YOU'RE BACK! MY FINGERS ARE HURTING!
I KNOW! YOU'LL GET YOUR MEDAL IN THE MORNING!

IT'S STILL HARD FOR ME TO BELIEVE THAT YOU CAN'T SEE!
THAT SO? I CAN BELIEVE IT EASY AS PIE!
LEND ME YOUR HAND, COUNSELOR!
I'D HATE TO BREAK MY NECK ON THE STAIRS--AFTER ALL I'VE JUST BEEN THRU!

A FEW SECONDS LATER--
OH, MIKE--YOU WERE SIMPLY SENSATIONAL!
THERE'S NO WAY OF KNOWING HOW MANY PEOPLE OWE THEIR VERY LIVES TO YOU!
TO HEAR HIM TELL IT, THAT INCLUDES ABOUT HALF THE POPULATION!
BUT, WHAT HAPPENS NOW? YOU CAN'T CONTINUE TO FACE DANGER WITHOUT BEING ABLE TO SEE!
I DON'T INTEND TO KAREN!
I HAVE A NEW PLAN--WHICH'LL REQUIRE FOGGY'S HELP AGAIN!

THUS, WHEN DARKNESS HAS FALLEN--AND THE CROWDS HAVE ALL DISPERSED--
JUST LEAD ME TO MATT'S HOUSE WHILE I TELL YOU WHAT I'VE THOUGHT OF--!
YEAH--SURE!
I'M NOT EXACTLY ONE OF YOUR FAVORITE PEOPLE, AM I FOGGY?
AND I THINK I KNOW WHY!

IT'S BECAUSE OF KAREN! YOU THINK SHE'S SWEET ON ME, DON'T YOU?
IT USED TO BE YOUR BROTHER MATT-- BUT NOW, YOU'VE EVEN PUSHED HIM OUT OF THE RUNNING!
ANYWAY, WHO CAN COMPETE WITH A SWASH-BUCKLING COSTUMED DO-GOODER?
YOU MADE YOUR POINT, MAN!

BUT THINGS MAY NOT BE AS BAD AS YOU THINK--!
MAYBE KAREN HAS A SISTER!
-MPFFF!-
DON'T MUMBLE, SON!
IF YOU'VE SOMETHING TO SAY, JUST SPEAK RIGHT UP!

FOGGY??!
WHY DON'T YOU ANSWER ME?
FOGGY! WHERE ARE YOU? DO YOU HEAR ME? WHAT HAPPENED??
20

NOTHING TO WORRY ABOUT... I'M OKAY!
I JUST FORGOT FOR A SECOND--THAT YOU STILL ARE REALLY BLIND!
NEXT
THE REAL DAREDEVIL!

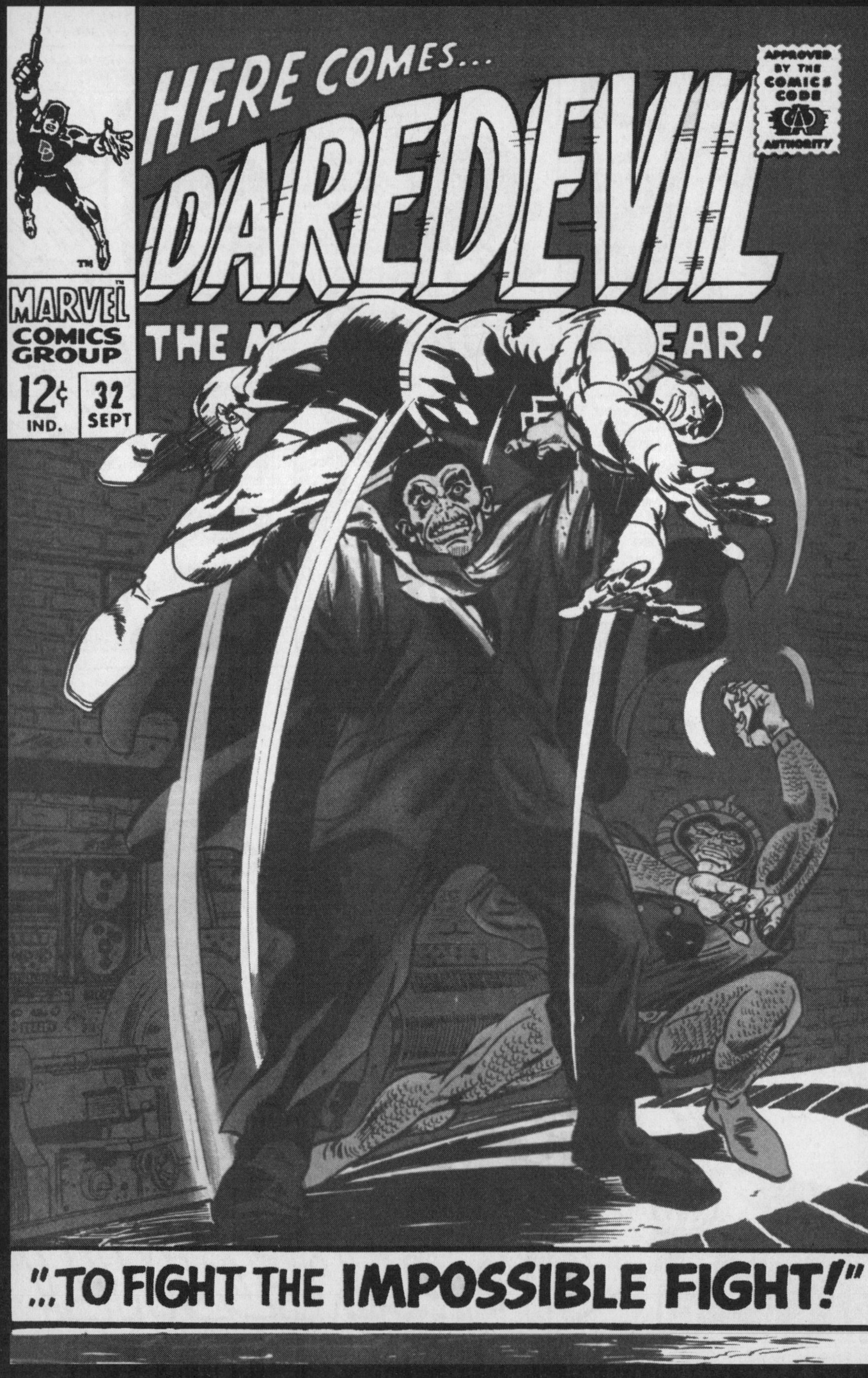

HERE COMES...

DAREDEVIL

THE M... EAR!

MARVEL COMICS GROUP

12¢ IND. 32 SEPT

"...TO FIGHT THE **IMPOSSIBLE FIGHT!**"

DAREDEVIL, THE MAN WITHOUT FEAR!
"...TO FIGHT THE IMPOSSIBLE FIGHT!"
CAN ANY MAN--- EVEN DAREDEVIL--- SUCCESSFULLY BATTLE TWO DEADLY, SUPER-POWERED FOES WHEN HE HIMSELF IS TOTALLY BLIND... AND HIS OWN SUPER SENSES ARE LOST TO HIM?
THE ANSWER TO THAT QUESTION BETTER BE "YES"... OR THIS MAY BE THE LAST WE'LL SEE OF OUR FEARLESS FRIEND... LIKE FOREVER!
DD
HOW FORTUNATE THAT I WAS PASSING BY... IN TIME TO SEE YOU BEING LED THROUGH THE STREET-- LIKE THE SIGHTLESS FRAUD THAT YOU ARE!
THE VOICE OF-- THE COBRA!
I THOUGHT I HEARD SOMEONE ATTACK POOR FOGGY!
OKAY, BRIGHT BOY-- NOW YOU KNOW I'M REALLY BLIND! SO WHERE DO WE GO FROM HERE?
HOW DO THEY DO IT, MONTH AFTER MONTH? SMILIN' STAN LEE and GENIAL GENE COLAN HAVE ANOTHER WINNER ON THEIR HANDS!!
INKED BY: JOHN TARTAGLIONE
LETTERED BY: SAM ROSEN
INSTANT UPDATE DEPARTMENT!
• THE EVIL MR. HYDE TOSSED A POTENT CHEMICAL AT DD, IN ORDER TO BLIND HIM!
• BUT, SINCE OUR HERO IS ALREADY BLIND, THE CHEMICAL DEADENED HIS SUPER SENSES INSTEAD!
• NOW, MORE HELPLESS THAN EVER BEFORE, DD IS CAPTURED BY HYDE'S POWER-MAD PARTNER, THE COBRA!
AND THIS IS ONLY THE BEGINNING..!!

I MUST ADMIT YOU HAD US FOOLED FOR A WHILE, DAREDEVIL!
IT WAS CLEVER OF YOU TO DO THOSE STUNTS IN PUBLIC... SO WE'D THINK YOU COULD SEE!
OF COURSE, I WAS MORE SUSPICIOUS OF YOU THAN THE BESTIAL HYDE!
HOWEVER, JUST IN CASE THIS IS ANOTHER OF YOUR LITTLE TRICKS...

...MAKE ONE SUDDEN MOVE, AND I'LL PRESS THIS NERVE ON YOUR NECK IN SUCH A WAY THAT YOU'LL NEVER MOVE AGAIN!
THANKS FOR THE WARNING, SLIMY!
BY THE WAY, WHAT HAPPENED TO YOUR MUSCLE-BOUND PLAYMATE?
I'M BRINGING YOU TO HIM RIGHT NOW!
HE'S WAITING FOR US... IN HIS CAR!
NO

SECONDS LATER...
WHY BOTHER DRIVING HIM ANYWHERE?
WHY NOT FINISH HIM OFF RIGHT NOW?
DAREDEVIL FOOLED US!! HYDE DOES NOT LIKE THAT!
THEREFORE, I MUST PLAN A FITTING REVENGE!! WE'LL TAKE HIM TO OUR NEWEST LABORATORY..
THERE WE'LL DEVISE A FITTING FATE FOR THE HELPLESS FOOL!
NO NEED TO RUSH ON MY ACCOUNT! ...I'VE GOT TIME!

THIS IS WHAT I'VE BEEN HOPING FOR!
I WANT TO BE TAKEN TO THEIR LAB!
MY ONLY CHANCE FOR SURVIVAL IS TO REGAIN MY SUPER SENSES...
IF HYDE CREATED THE POTION WHICH CAUSED ME TO LOSE THEM, HE MUST HAVE ALSO CREATED AN ANTIDOTE!
AND, IF THE ANTIDOTE EXISTS, IT'S BOUND TO BE HIDDEN SOMEWHERE IN HIS LAB...
...WHERE MY VERY LIFE DEPENDS UPON ME FINDING IT... IN TIME!

MEANWHILE, A DAZED FOGGY NELSON SLOWLY COMES TO HIS SENSES AFTER HAVING BEEN ATTACKED BY THE SLITHERING COBRA...
IT WAS HYDE'S SNAKE-LIKE PARTNER... I'D RECOGNIZE HIM ANYWHERE!
THE LAST I REMEMBER.. HE GRABBED DAREDEVIL AND HEADED DOWN THE STREET WITH HIM!
BUT, DD IS BLIND NOW.. UNABLE TO DEFEND HIMSELF..!

HIS LIFE WON'T BE WORTH A PLUGGED NICKEL...
UNLESS SOMEONE CAN FIND THEM!!
I CAN'T STAND AROUND... DOING NOTHING..!

I'LL ALERT THE POLICE!
AN ALL-POINTS ALARM MAY DO THE TRICK!
IF ONLY I'M NOT.. TOO LATE!

SERGEANT... YOU'VE GOT TO DO SOMETHING!
THE COBRA'S CAPTURED DAREDEVIL! I SAW HIM..!
GIVE ME THE DETAILS! WE'LL SLAP A CORDON OVER THE WHOLE CITY!
EVERY SECOND COUNTS! DAREDEVIL IS HELPLESS! HE'S BEEN BLIND.. FOR DAYS..!
DAREDEVIL.. BLIND?
WHAT ARE YOU TRYIN' TO PULL, MISTER?

YOU LOOK LIKE YOU'VE HAD A LITTLE TOO MUCH PARTYING, PAL!
BETTER GO HOME AND SLEEP IT OFF!
YOU'LL FEEL BETTER IN THE MORNING!
DAREDEVIL... BLIND!! THAT'S LIKE SAYIN' THE HULK IS ANEMIC!
OR HOW ABOUT SPIDER-MAN! IS IT TRUE THAT HE'S AFRAID OF HEIGHTS?
BOY! I SURE MEET ALL KINDS ON THIS JOB!
3.

I SAW HIM ON THAT TIGHT-ROPE A FEW HOURS AGO... HAMMIN' IT UP FOR THE CROWD LIKE A BORN ACROBAT!
I EVEN SAW THE ACT HE PUT ON WHEN HE PRETENDED TO LOSE HIS BALANCE A COUPLE OF TIMES!
I'D SURE LIKE TO SEE A BLIND MAN HANDLE HIMSELF LIKE THAT!
MAN! IF WE HAD A FEW LIKE HIM ON THE FORCE!

ARE YOU STILL HERE?
TAKE OFF, MISTER... AND DON'T TRY TO PULL ANY FAST ONES AGAIN WITH ANY NUTTY STORIES ABOUT BLIND SUPERHEROES!
WHEN WE WANNA HEAR A FAIRY TALE, WE'LL LETCHA KNOW!
IT'S NO USE! I'M JUST WASTING MY TIME!

HOW CAN I EXPECT THEM TO BELIEVE THAT DAREDEVIL IS BLIND?
WOULD I BELIEVE A YARN LIKE THAT IF SOMEONE ELSE TOLD IT TO ME?
NOT IN A MILLION YEARS!
AT LEAST HE WAS ORIGINAL!
YEAH! MOST OF 'EM COME IN CLAIMIN' THEY'RE NAPOLEON!

WHAT DO I DO NOW?
MAYBE I SHOULD TRY TO FIND MATT... AND LET HIM KNOW..!
BUT, WHAT'S THE POINT? WHAT COULD HE DO ABOUT IT?
12
UH-OH! IT'S STARTING TO RAIN!
AND FROM THE LOOKS OF THAT SKY, IT'S GONNA BE A BEAUT!
WELL, THIS IS A PERFECT DAY FOR IT!

AT THAT MOMENT SOMEWHERE IN NEW ENGLAND -- AFTER A NON-STOP DRIVE AT TURNPIKE SPEED -- WE FIND---
I NEVER REALIZED BEFORE HOW MUCH I TOOK MY SUPER-SENSES FOR GRANTED!
A FEW DAYS AGO, I'D HAVE BEEN ABLE TO TELL EXACTLY WHERE WE ARE... MERELY BY USING MY RADAR SENSE, COUPLED WITH MY SUPER-KEEN HEARING!
BUT NOW... I ONLY KNOW IT'S SOMEWHERE NEAR THE SHORE... BECAUSE I CAN HEAR THE ROLLING SEA AT MY RIGHT!
DON'T GET TOO COMFORT-ABLE, DAREDEVIL! WE'VE ALMOST REACHED THE END OF THE LINE!
AND, FROM HIS TONE OF VOICE, I CAN TELL IT'LL REALLY BE THE END OF THE LINE FOR ME..
..UNLESS I CAN MANAGE TO FIND THAT ANTIDOTE WHEN WE REACH HIS LAB!
...IF HE LETS ME LIVE LONG ENOUGH!
OUT, MASKED MAN! AND WATCH YOUR STEP!
WE WOULDN'T WANT YOU TO TRIP AND FALL ...YOU MIGHT HURT YOURSELF!
THE SURF SOUNDS LOUDER THAN EVER!
ARE THEY PLANNING TO DROWN ME..?
THAT'S IT, COBRA! TAKE REAL GOOD CARE OF HIM!
AFTER ALL, WE INVITED HIM HERE! HE'S OUR GUEST!
FASTER, HYDE! THERE'S A STORM COMING UP... AND I DON'T LIKE RAIN!
I'VE GOT 'ER AT FULL THROTTLE NOW!
NO STORM IS GONNA CHANGE OUR PLANS!
I'M IN A SPEEDBOAT OF SOME SORT! THEY MUST BE TAKING ME TO A LARGER SHIP! OR ELSE..TO WHAT..?
RRRRRR
I STILL THINK THIS IS A WASTE OF TIME!
WHY DON'T WE JUST DUMP HIM OVERBOARD NOW--- AND FORGET ABOUT IT?!!

NOW, IT'S REALLY UP TO ME... ALONE!
THERE'S NO CHANCE OF ANYONE FINDING US... IN TIME TO SAVE ME!
SO, IF I DON'T WANNA LEAVE THE WORLD DAREDEVIL-LESS, I'VE GOT TO GET THAT ANTIDOTE... IF THERE IS ONE!
CAREFUL, HYDE!! WATCH OUT FOR THOSE ROCKS AHEAD!
SHUT UP, COBRA! I CAN DO THIS WITH ONE HAND BEHIND ME!
IT'S DAREDEVIL WHO SHOULD BE WORRY-ING.. NOT US!

SECONDS LATER...
COME ON! COME ON! WHAT'S TAKING YOU SO LONG?
LOOK WHO'S TALKING!! REMEMBER... EVERYONE HASN'T GOT THE SAME SUPER-HUMAN STRENGTH AS YOU DO!
JUST KEEP THAT GRIP OF YOURS--- AND DON'T LET GO TILL WE'RE SAFELY INSIDE, YOU UGLY APE!
IF YOU TWO ARE SUPPOSED TO BE CHUCKLIN' CHUMS.. I'D HATE TO HEAR THE WAY YOU'D ACT AS ENEMIES!
DON'T WORRY, DAREDEVIL---YOU'LL FIND OUT HOW WE TREAT OUR ENEMIES-- AS SOON AS WE REACH HYDE'S LAB!
7.

FELLAS, IF I DIDN'T KNOW BETTER, I'D THINK YOU DIDN'T LIKE ME!
STILL A WISE-GUY, HUH?
OKAY, HAVE YOUR FUN NOW.. YOU'LL SING A DIFFERENT TUNE IN A FEW MINUTES!

I'M NOT MUCH OF A SINGER.. BUT PERHAPS I COULD HUM A FEW BARS FOR YOU!
DON'T TRY MATCHING WITS WITH HIM, COBRA!
YOU'RE ONLY HALF-EQUIPPED FOR THAT!
THEY'RE FORCING ME UP STEEP, WINDING STAIRS..!
HYDE'S LAB MUST BE AT THE VERY TOP OF THE LIGHTHOUSE!
AN INTERESTING BIT OF INFORMATION WHICH DOES ME ABSOLUTELY NO GOOD!

GETTING NERVOUS, DAREDEVIL? BEGINNING TO FEEL FRIGHTENED??
YOU SHOULD BE.. BECAUSE YOU CAN COUNT THE REMAINING MINUTES OF YOUR LIFE ON THE FINGERS OF ONE HAND!

MOVE, COBRA! I'M BEGINNING TO GET IMPATIENT NOW! INTO THE LAB WITH HIM!
WHATEVER I ATTEMPT IN THERE.. I'VE GOT TO DO IT FAST!
YOU MUST BE REAL PROUD OF YOURSELVES, GENTS...
WITH A LITTLE LUCK, YOU MAY ACTUALLY DEFEAT A BLIND MAN... IF YOU WORK TOGETHER!

TALKING CAN'T HELP YOU NOW, SMART GUY! IT'S TOO LATE FOR THAT!
NOTHING THAT LIVES CAN ESCAPE FROM HYDE AND ME ONCE WE ENTER THIS ROOM..!

NOW, DAREDEVIL.. WE ARE YOUR JUDGE..AND YOUR JURY!
AND WE SENTENCE YOU..TO DEATH!
GO GET THE CABLES AND WRAP THEM AROUND HIM, COBRA!
DON'T TALK TO ME IN THAT TONE, YOU GARGOYLE!
NOBODY ORDERS THE COBRA AROUND.. NOT EVEN MR. HYDE!

WHATEVER THEY'RE PLANNING TO DO, IT PROBABLY INVOLVES ELECTRICITY!
AND WHERE THERE'S ELECTRICITY IN A PLACE LIKE THIS... THERE MUST BE A GENERATOR!
IF I CAN JUST REACH IT--WHILE THEY'RE ARGUING..!

CALL ME A GARGOYLE, WILL YOU?? WHY, YOU SERPENTINE FOOL...
NOW'S MY CHANCE! I HEAR A STEADY HUM BEHIND ME! IF I CAN SILENTLY MOVE BACKWARDS..!
TAKE YOUR HAND OFF ME, HYDE... OR ELSE..!!

IF THEY'LL JUST KEEP ARGUING.. FOR A FEW MINUTES MORE..!
WHAT'S THIS? IT FEELS LIKE... A DOOR! AND THE HUM IS COMING FROM THE OTHER SIDE!
IT MUST BE THE GENERATOR! IF I CAN JUST REACH IT...!
YOU MAY BE STRONGER THAN ME, HYDE... BUT..!
STRONGER THAN YOU?!!
I'M STRONGER THAN ANYBODY, YOU SLITHERING, SPINELESS WEAKLING!!
NOW GET THAT CABLE.. WHILE YOU STILL CAN!

I'M IN LUCK! THE DOOR WAS UNLOCKED!
AND THEY'RE SHOUTING TOO LOUD TO HEAR ME PUSH IT OPEN--!
NOW--THERE'S GOT TO BE A CONTROL BOX NEARBY--WITH A SHUT-OFF SWITCH--!

IF I CAN MANAGE TO STOP THE GENERATOR...

IT'LL KILL ALL THE ELECTRICAL POWER THROUGHOUT THE LIGHTHOUSE--!

I FOUND IT!

HYDE!! WAIT!! STOP!! LOOK WHAT HAPPENED...!!
DAREDEVIL.. HE'S GONE!
WHAT?!

SPLASK!
THE LIGHTS.. THEY'RE OUT!!

DAREDEVIL DID IT!
COBRA.. QUICK.. GO AFTER HIM! THERE'S NO PLACE HE CAN RUN TO HERE!
I'VE GOT TO GET THE ANTIDOTE, AND PUT IT OUT OF HIS REACH!
CAN'T TAKE A CHANCE OF HIM STUMBLING ONTO IT AND GETTING HIS SIGHT BACK!!

THAT'S WHAT I WANTED TO HEAR!
THERE IS AN ANTIDOTE --- AND HYDE'S GONNA GET IT!
BUT, IF I PLAY MY CARDS RIGHT... HE'LL BE GETTING IT FOR ME!
EVEN THOUGH I'VE LOST MY SUPER POWERS, SO LONG AS THE LIGHTS STAY OUT, THE ODDS ARE IN MY FAVOR...
I'VE HAD A LIFETIME OF LEARNING TO MANEUVER IN THE DARK!

...CAN'T SEE... BUT, I KNOW THE ANTIDOTE IS HERE SOMEWHERE ...
AHH! I GOT IT!
NOW WITH MY MATCHLESS STRENGTH... SO LONG AS I HOLD IT.. DAREDEVIL CAN NEVER GET IT FOR HIMSELF!

THUMP!
UNHHH! MY SHOULDER..!
THAT SOUND!! IT MUST BE HIM!! HE'S TRYING TO ATTACK US!

IT WAS A NICE TRY, MASKED MAN... BUT NOBODY CAN FREE HIMSELF FROM THE COBRA'S GRIP!
I'VE GOT TO GET FREE! GOT TO REACH HYDE.. AND THE ANTIDOTE!!

SO NOBODY CAN FREE HIMSELF FROM THE COBRA'S GRIP, EH--??

WELL, I'VE GOT NEWS FOR YOU, SNAKE MAN! FROM NOW ON---

...JUST CALL ME NOBODY!!

I KNOW YOU'RE THERE, DAREDEVIL!
EVEN THOUGH THE LIGHTS ARE OUT, I CAN HEAR YOU STUMBLING AROUND!
IT'S HYDE!
DOES HE HAVE..THE ANTIDOTE?!!

ALL I NEED DO IS KEEP SWINGING!! SOONER OR LATER I'LL FIND MY TARGET!
THE DARKNESS CAN'T HELP YOU NOW!

THE ONLY THING THAT COUNTS IS STRENGTH...
AND NONE CAN MATCH THE POWER OF HYDE!!
12.

BUT THEN, SUDDENLY...
I HAVE HIM, HYDE!
YOUR WAY IS TOO CRUDE, TOO FUMBLING! THIS CALLS FOR STEALTH.. AND SKILL!
EVEN IN THE DARK, ALL I NEED DO IS KEEP HIM FROM ESCAPING WHILE I STRIKE AT HIS HELPLESS FORM---AS ONLY THE COBRA CAN!
HELPLESS FORM? MISTER, YOU MUST BE TALKIN' ABOUT A COUPLE OF OTHER DAREDEVILS!
NOW--WITH HIS ARM UPRAISED--IF I CAN SHIFT MY WEIGHT SUDDENLY---WHILE HE'S OFF-BALANCE--!

HE'S AT MY RIGHT.. BUT I CAN'T JUDGE HOW FAR!
I'VE GOT TO STALL FOR TIME!..I'LL PRETEND TO BE PANICKY... TRY TO MAKE HIM OVERCONFIDENT!
THE ANTIDOTE!! I MUST HAVE IT! I CAN'T FIGHT IN THE DARK.. I'M HELPLESS WITHOUT MY EYES..HELPLESS!
I CAN HEAR YOU SWINGING! YOU'RE GIVING YOURSELF AWAY WITH THAT COWARDLY WHINING!

DON'T YOU REALIZE IT WOULDN'T HELP YOU EVEN IF YOU DID LAND A LUCKY PUNCH?
THAT'S IT, HYDE! KEEP TALKING! I'VE A GOOD IDEA WHERE YOU ARE NOW!
THE STRENGTH OF MR. HYDE IS FAR TOO GREAT!
HE MUST BE HOLDING THE ANTIDOTE---IN HIS HAND!--- BUT, IF I MAKE HIM LASH OUT.. IF HE SHOULD SWING AT ME..!
I'LL START EDGING CLOSER.. SO THAT HE CAN'T RESIST..!
I WARNED YOU TO STOP THAT SENSELESS THRASHING..!

NOW THIS WILL SHOW YOU THE FOLLY OF ANY FURTHER RESISTANCE!
WHA..? YOU WERE EXPECTING THAT BLOW!!
YOU DREW YOUR ARM BACK..JABBING MY FIST WITH YOUR ELBOW..
..MAKING ME DROP THE ANTIDOTE!!
BUT IT'LL DO YOU NO GOOD!!

I'LL CRUSH YOU LIKE A WORM BEFORE YOU CAN EVEN HOPE TO FIND THAT VIAL!!
NOW I'VE GOT TO CHANGE MY TACTICS..!!
ONLY ABSOLUTE SILENCE CAN HELP ME!
HE MUSTN'T SUSPECT I'VE FLATTENED MYSELF HERE ON THE FLOOR!!
14.

THERE! EVEN IF I CAN'T SEE YOU IN THE DARK--- I CAN'T MISS YOU--- WITH THIS!!
SURE YOU CAN'T!
I'LL TEAR THIS WHOLE LIGHTHOUSE APART.. WITH MY BARE HANDS.. TILL I'VE DESTROYED YOU!!
SKRAK
HE'S COMING TOO CLOSE FOR COMFORT!
I'VE GOT TO STOP HIM BEFORE HE DROPS A SLAB ON ME BY SHEER DUMB LUCK!
HAH! SO THERE YOU ARE!!
AND YOU DARE PIT YOUR PUNY SINEWS AGAINST MINE!!?!
THUS, YOU HAVE JUST SEALED YOUR DOOM!!
UNHH!!..HE WASN'T KIDDING ABOUT HIS STRENGTH!
HERE'S WHERE I CAN USE SOME HELP---IF I CAN JUST TRICK THE COBRA INTO BOTCHING THINGS UP!!
HAH! I TOLD YOU I'D GET FREE! AND NOW, IT'S MY TURN, HYDE! YOU AND THE COBRA HAVEN'T A CHANCE!
FREE? BUT-- YOU'RE NOT--!
OH NO, DAREDEVIL! WE'RE NOT BEATEN YET.. NOT WHILE I CAN STILL FOLLOW THE SOUND OF YOUR VOICE!
COBRA! STAY BACK! I'LL HANDLE HIM!
DO YOUR WORST, COBRA! YOU CAN'T HURT ME!
I CAN'T TAKE ANY CHANCES! GOT TO STRIKE...IN THE DIRECTION OF HIS VOICE!
15.

SPEEYOK!
IT WORKED! I FIGURED HE'D STRIKE WHERE HE EXPECTED ME TO BE---NOT REALIZING HYDE WAS HOLDING ME ABOVE HIS HEAD!!
COBRA!! YOU BLASTED, BRAINLESS IDIOT!! I'LL RIP YOU APART FOR THAT!!
AND THE SUDDEN FORCE OF IMPACT MADE HIM LOOSEN HIS GRIP--- RELEASING ME!!

WHAT?!! YOU DARE SPEAK THAT WAY TO YOUR OWN SUPER-POWERED PARTNER!??
NOW--IF ONLY HE DROPPED THE ANTIDOTE NEAR HERE!!

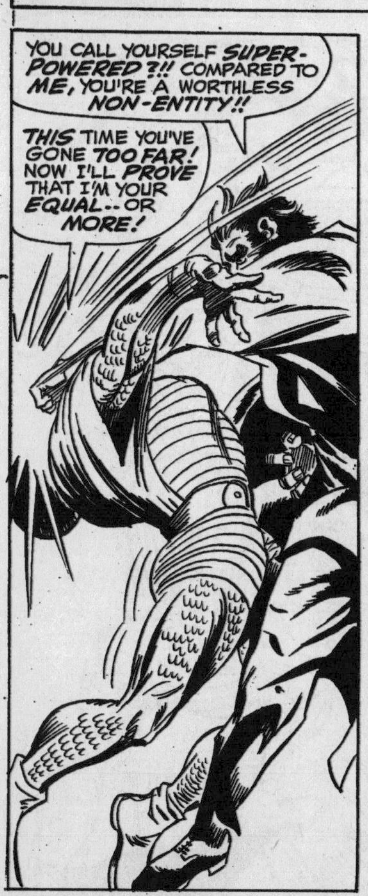
YOU CALL YOURSELF SUPER-POWERED?!! COMPARED TO ME, YOU'RE A WORTHLESS NON-ENTITY!!
THIS TIME YOU'VE GONE TOO FAR! NOW I'LL PROVE THAT I'M YOUR EQUAL--OR MORE!

IT'S NO USE!! I DON'T FEEL IT HERE!!
EVEN IF IT WERE INCHES AWAY--HOW WOULD I KNOW?? HOW COULD I TELL?

IT MIGHT BE ANYWHERE!!
...MIGHT BE RIGHT AT MY FINGERTIPS!!
BUT--WITH MY POWERS GONE... I'M HELPLESS... UNABLE TO SENSE IT!!
THE NOISE STOPPED!! COBRA AND HYDE--- NO LONGER FIGHTING..!

WE'LL SETTLE ACCOUNTS LATER!
OUR FIRST JOB IS TO FIND THAT ANTIDOTE... BEFORE DAREDEVIL DOES!
YES! BUT, AS SOON WE DO--WE'LL FINISH WHERE WE LEFT OFF!

IS LIFE SO VALUELESS TO YOU THAT YOU DON'T MIND LOSING IT AT THE HANDS OF HYDE??!
BAH!! YOUR MINDLESS STRENGTH CAN'T SAVE YOU FROM...
THE VIAL!! I'VE GOT IT!!

GOOD! THEN I'VE NO FURTHER USE FOR YOU!!
LOOK OUT, YOU FOOL! THE BOTTLE..!
I DROPPED IT!! YOU MADE ME DROP IT!

AND, WHILE THE TWO ARCH-VILLAINS AWKWARDLY STRIVE TO UNTANGLE THEMSELVES... A DESPERATE FIGURE POUNCES LIKE A RED-GARBED STREAK IN THE DIRECTION OF THE FALLING BOTTLE..!
IT'S MINE..AT LAST!!

THEN, BEFORE HE CAN POSSIBLY BE STOPPED...
IT HAS TO WORK! IT HAS TO!
IT IS! I CAN ALREADY HEAR THE HEARTBEAT OF A FIGURE SNEAKING UP BEHIND ME!

OH, MAN! IT'S LIKE SOMEONE JUST TURNED THE LIGHTS BACK ON.
HYDE!! HE.. CAN SEE AGAIN!! UNGHHHH!
SO WHAT?!! HE'S STILL NO BETTER OFF THAN WE ARE...
NOT AS LONG AS IT STAYS DARK IN HERE!

IT'S STILL NOT AS DARK AS IT'S GONNA BE..!
FOR YOU, THAT IS, STRONG MAN!
I'VE WAITED TOO LONG FOR THIS TO LET ANYTHING BOTCH IT UP NOW!

YOU MAY BE ABLE TO FIGHT RINGS AROUND THE SLOW-WITTED HYDE... BUT NOT THE COBRA!
OH NO! NOT YOU AGAIN!
YOU MUST ENJOY BEING A PERMANENT LOSER!

AND, AS FOR YOU, MY MUSCLE-BOUND FRIEND...

I WOULDN'T LET YOU FEEL NEGLECTED AROUND HERE FOR ANYTHING!

NOW BE SURE TO CLOSE YOUR PINK LITTLE EYES..

..'CAUSE WE WOULDN'T WANT YOU TO GET DIZZY..WOULD WE??

OHH! CLUMSY ME! I MUST HAVE LOST MY GRIP!

BUT DON'T WORRY.. WE CAN ALWAYS TRY AGAIN!
HOW?? HOW CAN YOU SEE WHAT YOU'RE DOING.. HERE IN THE DARK??!
OH, IS IT DARK?
SHUCKS! YOU SHOULDN'T HAVE TOLD ME...
NOT WHEN I WAS GETTING ALONG SO WELL

NOW YOU'VE GOT ME ALL CONFUSED!!
SEE? I CAN'T EVEN HOLD ON TO YOU?!!
19

NEXT: "BEATEN BY... The BEETLE!"

HERE COMES...
DAREDEVIL
THE MAN WITHOUT FEAR!
APPROVED BY THE COMICS CODE AUTHORITY
MARVEL COMICS GROUP
12¢ IND.
33 OCT
FEATURING: THE GREATEST CHASE OF ALL TIME!
"BEHOLD THE BEETLE!"

DAREDEVIL, THE MAN WITHOUT FEAR!
BEHOLD... THE BEETLE!
DAREDEVIL!!
HOW DID HE KNOW I WAS ATTACKING AN ARMORED TRUCK??
ACTUALLY, OL' HORN-HEAD DIDN'T KNOW! HE WAS JUST SWINGING BY AND HEARD THE SOUND OF SCREETCHING TIRES AS HIS SUPER-SENSITIVE NOSTRILS SMELLED THE ODOR OF THE BEETLE'S NERVE GAS!--BUT, WHY DWELL ON THAT WHEN IT'S ACTION TIME AHEAD--
WHY DO WE BOTHER TELLING YOU? WHO ELSE BUT STAN (THE MAN) LEE and GENE (THE DEAN) COLAN COULD HAVE PRODUCED THIS ACTION-PACKED SPECTACULAR?
AND WHO, BUT IRVING FORBUSH COULD HOPE TO EQUAL JOHN TARTAGLIONE'S INKING, OR ARTIE SIMEK'S LETTERING?
1

YOU CAN'T BOWL THE BEETLE OVER LIKE SOME ORDINARY CRIMINAL, YOU FREE-SWINGING FOOL!
THWAM!
NOT WHEN I CAN USE MY HEAVY METAL WING AS A PROTECTIVE SHIELD!
UNHHH! HE'S NOT KIDDIN'!
IT'S LIKE SLAMMING INTO A SHERMAN TANK!
IT'S HIGH TIME THAT YOU MASKED DO-GOODERS REALIZED THERE ARE SOME FOES FAR MORE POWERFUL THAN YOU!
AND, IN YOUR CASE, THE BOMBASTIC BEETLE IS OBVIOUSLY SUCH A FOE!
LOOK, MISTER-- IT'S BAD ENOUGH HAVING TO FIGHT A NUT LIKE YOU--
AM I GONNA HAVE TO LISTEN TO SPEECHES, TOO?
SO! YOU THINK I'M SOMEONE TO BE BRUSHED ASIDE WITH A FEW SNEERING REMARKS, EH?
WELL, PERHAPS THIS WILL CHANGE YOUR MIND--!
HIS FINGERS!! HE CAN EXTEND THEM-- HYDRAULICALLY!!
I'M STUCK TO THE SUCTION CUPS WHICH HE PRESSED AGAINST ME!
BTAM!
THE FAMOUS DAREDEVIL-- HAH!!
YOU DON'T EVEN POSSESS THE SUPER-STRENGTH OF OTHERS I'VE FOUGHT IN THE PAST!

HE'S UNCONSCIOUS! AND ONE BLOW WAS ALL IT TOOK!
EITHER MY LONG, ENFORCED LAY-OFF HAS IMPROVED MY PROWESS--
OR, HE'S BY FAR THE WEAKEST ONE I'VE EVER BATTLED!
I'LL TAKE MY LOOT AND BE OFF NOW, FOR ONE THING IS CERTAIN--
HE WILL NEVER DARE TO TACKLE THE BEETLE AGAIN!

THEN, MOMENTS AFTER THE WINGED WRONGDOER HAS MADE GOOD HIS ESCAPE--
I MUST HAVE BEEN--OUT OF MY MIND--TO TACKLE HIM THAT WAY--!
I'VE GONE WITHOUT SLEEP FOR TWO DAYS--FIGHTING HYDE AND THE COBRA--*
I WAS TOO TIRED--TOO WEAK...
*JUST LAST ISH--A FEW HOURS AGO TO DD! --SCOREKEEPER STAN.

HOWEVER, ONE CHANGE OF CLOTHES LATER--
MIKE, I THINK IT'S SIMPLY WONDERFUL THAT YOUR EYESIGHT RETURNED TO YOU IN TIME TO DEFEAT THAT HORRIBLE HYDE AND HIS SNAKE-LIKE PARTNER!
IT MUST HAVE BEEN JUST A TEMPORARY AFFLICTION!
IF ONLY YOUR BROTHER MATT COULD BE SO LUCKY!
MATHEW'S HAD IT, HONEY! HIS EYE-SIGHT'S GONE --FOREVER!
BUT AT LEAST OL' TWINNY'S LEARNED TO LIVE WITH IT!
Y'KNOW SOMETHIN'? I'M BUSHED!
HOW'S ABOUT THE THREE OF US TAKIN' AN OVERNIGHTER TO MONTREAL AND DIGGIN' EXPO '67?
YOU THINK WE CAN LEAVE THE OFFICE AS EASY AS THAT?

SURE YOU CAN! MERRY MATTHEW CAN HANG AROUND TO LOOK AFTER THINGS!
NO, MIKE! WE CAN'T LEAVE HIM BEHIND!
AND HE SURE CAN'T TAG ALONG IF I'M GOING TOO!
HE WON'T MIND, BABY! I'LL PROVE IT! I'LL PHONE HIM AND ASK HIM!
I'LL ADMIT WE HAVEN'T HAD A VACATION IN MONTHS!
AND, THE WAY I LET THE BEETLE SLIP THRU MY FINGERS, I NEED ONE FAST!

TELL YA WHAT--YOU CALL HIM SO YOU WON'T THINK HE'S LETTING HIS BROTHER TALK HIM INTO IT!
AN UNEXPECTED VACATION--AND IN CANADA!
I CAN HARDLY BELIEVE IT!
I DIALED HIS NUMBER, KAREN--YOU ASK HIM!
IF NOTHING ELSE, THIS WILL DELAY THEM FROM EVER GUESSING THAT MATT AND MIKE ARE THE SELF-SAME MAN!
I'M ALWAYS AFRAID THEY'LL SUSPECT SOMETHING BECAUSE THEY NEVER SEE US TOGETHER!

MATT? THIS IS KAREN!
MIKE HAS SUGGESTED US VISITING EXPO '67--AND HE SAID YOU'D BE HAPPY TO MIND THE STORE! I WANTED TO MAKE SURE--WHAT'S THAT?
IT WAS YOUR IDEA? YOU SUGGESTED IT TO MIKE?!!
YOU THOUGHT THE THREE OF US SHOULD GO?
BOSS MAN--YOU'RE A DOLL!

FORTUNATELY, WE HAVEN'T ANY PENDING CASES NOW, AND--OH!
HE MUST HAVE THOUGHT I WAS FINISHED TALKING! I THINK HE HUNG UP!
AND DON'T FEEL YOU HAVETA WORRY ABOUT MATTHEW, KIDS--
YOU KNOW HIM--HE'S ALWAYS HAPPIEST WHEN HE CAN REVUE HIS BRAILLE LAW BOOKS WITH NO ONE ON HIS BACK!
WELL, WHAT ARE WE WAITING FOR? LET'S START PACKING, LADY!

IT WORKED LIKE A CHARM! NOTHING LIKE A TAPE RECORDER FOR A FELLA TRYING TO BE IN TWO PLACES AT ONCE!
WILL YOU TAKE YOUR DAREDEVIL COSTUME, MIKE?
WOULD A TIGER BRING HIS STRIPES, BABY?

THUS, ALMOST BEFORE YOU CAN SAY "THE MAN WITHOUT FEAR"--
BUT WHY DO YOU INSIST ON TAKING A TRAIN-- INSTEAD OF FLYING, MIKE?
WITH YOU ALONG... WHO'S IN A HURRY, HONEY!
ALSO, I HEARD OVER THE RADIO THAT THE WORLD'S MOST PRECIOUS NECKLACE IS BEING BROUGHT TO THE EXPOSITION--ON THIS TRAIN!
AND IF THAT'S NO ENOUGH TO TEMPT THE BEETLE--THEN I DON'T KNOW MY INSECTS!
HEY, HERO MAN! WHY AM I CARRYING THE EXTRA BAGS?
WHY NOT, TUBBY?
--PROBABLY THE SAME REASON YOU'RE CARRYIN' THE EXTRA WEIGHT!

I--NEVER HEARD YOU TALK THAT WAY BEFORE--MIKE--!
SOMETIMES EVEN US DARING, DASHING, DO-GOODERS HAVE OUR MOMENT OF TRUTH!
SERVICE
ANYWAY, THAT'S ENOUGH OF THAT!
WHO BROUGHT THE CARDS? I FEEL LIKE SOME POKER!

SPEAKING OF CARDS, IN ANOTHER COMPARTMENT ON THE SAME, SPEEDING TRAIN, TWO PLAINCLOTHES GUARDS WHILE AWAY THE TIME AS A LOCKED METAL BOX LIES SILENTLY BETWEEN THEM--NEVER OUT OF THEIR SIGHT--!
EASIEST ASSIGNMENT WE EVER HAD, EH, TOM?
YOU SAID IT! IT WOULD TAKE AN ARMY TO GET THAT NECKLACE AWAY FROM US--
CONSIDERING THE SECURITY MEASURES THAT HAVE BEEN TAKEN ALL OVER THE TRAIN!
IT'S LIKE GETTING PAID TO PLAY CARDS!
AND I'M NOT COMPLAINING!
YOU ALREADY OWE ME A BUCK SEVENTY-FIVE!

WHILE, IN A FORWARD SECTION OF THE SLEEK STREAMLINER, A TEAM OF TECHNICIANS CHECKS THE TRACKS AHEAD WITH SPECIAL RADAR DEVICES--
ALL CLEAR SO FAR, CHRIS!
GOOD! WITH THE CARGO WE'RE CARRYING, WE CAN'T AFFORD TO TAKE ANY CHANCES!

AND, IN THE CORRIDOR ITSELF, SHARP EYES WATCH THE DOINGS OF EVERY PASSERBY--
ANY CROOK--OR TEAM OF CROOKS--WOULD HAVE TO BE CRAZY TO MAKE A TRY FOR THE REGINA NECKLACE!
NOT EVEN A BUG COULD GET ABOARD WITHOUT ONE OF US SPOTTING HIM!

BUT, THERE IS ONE BUG THAT THINKS DIFFERENTLY! FOR, AS THE THUNDERING EXPRESS ROARS INTO A STYGIAN TUNNEL--THE BEETLE IS ABOUT TO STRIKE--!!
WHERE? WHEN? HOW? OKAY, FRANTIC ONE--LET'S TURN THE PAGE AND SEE--

--AND EFFORTLESSLY HAULING IT THRU THE NOW-OPEN AIR VENT!

SOUNDS LIKE THEY'RE PLAYIN' MY SONG, KIDDIES!
MIKE-- WAIT! YOU CAN'T--!
WANNA BET?
YOU ACT-- AS THOUGH YOU WERE EXPECTING THIS TO HAPPEN-- ALL ALONG--!

NOT JUST EXPECTING, LOVELY LADY-- HOPING!
I HOPED I'D BE AROUND IF THE NECKLACE WAS SNATCHED--
AND I'M HOPING THE BEETLE'S THE ONE WHO TOOK IT!
YOU TWO STAY WHERE YOU ARE--BUT YOU CAN CHEER IF YOU WANNA!

WELL, WELL! IT IS YOU!
HOW LUCKY CAN A FEARLESS FELLA BE?!!
DAREDEVIL! AGAIN YOU CHOOSE TO DEFY YOUR BETTERS!
--AND AGAIN YOU SHALL LIVE TO REGRET IT!

I NEED MERELY EXTEND MY WHIP-LIKE FINGERS, AND--
UH UH! NOT THIS TIME, YOU OVER-GROWN BEDBUG!
THOK

I WOULD LIKE TO STAY LONG ENOUGH TO FINISH YOU FOR-EVER, BUT ALAS--I CANNOT!
I MUST BE ON MY WAY BEFORE THE POLICE CAN CONVERGE UPON THIS SPOT!
SO, FAREWELL, MASKED MAN!
IT'S A PITY YOU ARE EARTHBOUND --UNLIKE THE BEETLE!

I MAY BE WINGLESS --BUT HE'S NOT GETTING AWAY AGAIN!
THAT IS-- IF I CAN MANAGE TO SURVIVE A LEAP LIKE THIS--!

I'VE GOTTA LAND JUST RIGHT--
AND ROLL WITH THE IMPACT, LIKE A HUMAN BOUNCING BALL--
--STAYING LOOSE AND LIMBER--TO KEEP THE BONES FROM SNAPPING!

JUST AS I THOUGHT!
THOSE HEAVY METAL WINGS CAN LIFT HIM INTO THE AIR OKAY--
BUT HIS SPEED IS NOTHING TO BRAG ABOUT!
WITH LUCK, I SHOULD BE ABLE TO FOLLOW HIM EASILY-- FROM THE GROUND!
MY RADAR SENSE WILL BE FAR MORE USEFUL THAN A SIGHTED MAN'S EYES--
FOR IT CAN'T BE FOOLED BY DISTANCE-- THE GLARE OF THE SUN--OR CLOUD COVER!
AND, SO LONG AS I HAVE MY BILLY CLUB CABLE--!

--EVEN THE MOUNTAINOUS TERRAIN SHOULDN'T SLOW ME DOWN TOO MUCH!
THE ONLY THING NUTTY ABOUT THIS WHOLE BUSINESS, IS--

HE TROUNCED ME THE FIRST TIME WE MET--BECAUSE I WAS JUST PLAIN TIRED!
AND NOW-- I'M TACKLING HIM AGAIN, WITHOUT HAVING HAD ANY REST YET--
SO I'M EVEN MORE TIRED THAN EVER!

BUT, I CAN'T LET THAT STOP ME!
I'LL JUST HAVE TO BE ON MY GUARD --TAKE NO FOOLISH CHANCES--!
--WHICH IS A HECKUVA POLICY FOR DAREDEVIL!

UH OH! I CAN HEAR SOMEONE BREATHING HARD--ABOVE ME! MY RADAR SENSE READS HIM, TOO!
IT'S HIM!! --ABOUT TO THROW SOMETHING DOWN ON ME!!
YOU OUT-SMARTED YOURSELF THIS TIME, YOU FOOL!
NOW YOU HAVE NO PLACE TO RUN!

A MOST ADMIRABLE EFFORT, DAREDEVIL!

AS A REWARD, I'LL TOY WITH YOU A WHILE LONGER!

BUT, REMEMBER-- --THE FURTHER YOU FOLLOW ME, INTO THE WILDS--THE LESS CHANCE YOU HAVE OF EVER RETURNING --ALIVE!

IF THAT LITTLE THREAT WAS INTENDED TO SCARE ME--IT SUCCEEDED!

I'M SCARED, ALL RIGHT!

SCARED HE'LL TALK HIMSELF TO DEATH BEFORE I CAN REACH HIM!

UH OH! MY EVERY SENSE DETECTS A WATERFALL UP AHEAD!
AND, FROM THE SOUND OF IT-- IT'S A LULU!
BUT, IF THE BEETLE CAN REACH THE OTHER SIDE--
THEN I'VE GOT TO FIND A WAY TO DO IT TOO!

SOMETHING WRONG, DAREDEVIL?
YOU'RE NOT AFRAID OF A LITTLE WATER, ARE YOU?
12

NOT AFRAID, EXACTLY!
I JUST HATE TO WASTE IT--
WHEN IT'S NOT EVEN SATURDAY NIGHT!

BUT, KNOWING HOW LONELY YOU MUST BE--

IN YOUR CASE--
I'LL MAKE AN EXCEPTION!

HAH! I WAS WAITING FOR YOU TO DO THAT!
THIK!
SNAP!
HE CUT THE CABLE!!

AND, IF ANYONE CAN WRITE A CAPTION--OR DIALOGUE--WHICH WILL DO JUSTICE TO THIS GREAT ILLUSTRATION OF GENE'S, THEN GO AHEAD--BE STAN'S GUEST!
14

MY CABLE STILL MAY SAVE ME--
IF I CAN LOOP THE REMAINING LENGTH AROUND A JUTTING PIECE OF SHALE!
GOT IT!

UNHHHH! IT'S NO GOOD!
MY WEIGHT IS TOO MUCH-- THE LEDGE SNAPPED OFF!
BUT, IT STILL SLOWED ME DOWN--WHICH WAS ALL I NEEDED--!

NOW IT'S UP TO ME--
--TO DO--
--THE REST!

I--MANAGED TO--SURVIVE THE PLUNGE--
--BUT--I DOVE-- TOO DEEP!--LOST-- TOO MUCH--BREATH--!
CAN I MAKE IT--BACK TO-- THE SURFACE-- IN TIME??

AND, YOU KNOW HOW IT IS WITH CARD-CARRYING SUPER HEROES--
AIR!
JUST IN TIME!
COULDN'T HAVE HELD --MY BREATH --A SECOND LONGER!

THE BEETLE IS PROBABLY HALF-WAY TO THE NEXT COUNTY BY NOW!
BUT I'M STILL GOING AFTER HIM --'CAUSE THERE'S ONE THING IN MY FAVOR--
HE PROBABLY THINKS I'M A GONER--AND WON'T BE BOTHERING TO HIDE HIS TRAIL!

MEANWHILE, AS DD GETS FURTHER AND FURTHER FROM THE NOW-STATIONARY TRAIN--
THIS TRAIN'S NOT MOVING TILL WE GET SOME MORE CLBES TO THAT ROBBERY!
A GREAT VACATION THIS IS--STRANDED IN THE MIDDLE OF NOWHERE--
WHILE THAT MASKED MISFIT IS OFF HAVING HIMSELF A BALL!
BUT WHAT ABOUT THE DANGER DAREDEVIL MAY BE FACING?
WHAT DANGER? HE ONLY TACKLES GUYS HE KNOWS HE CAN BEAT!

FOGGY NELSON! THAT'S NOT TRUE--IT'S NOT FAIR--AND YOU KNOW IT!
OKAY, LADY--I ADMIT I WAS OFF-BASE! LET THE JURY DISREGARD THAT REMARK!
I MIGHT AS WELL LEVEL WITH YOU AND ADMIT I'M JEALOUS OF HIM--JEALOUS AS ALL GET-OUT!
BUT--YOU'RE A SUCCESSFUL LAWYER, AND--
LET'S DROP IT! WHY I'M JEALOUS HAS NOTHING TO DO--WITH OUR PROFESSIONS!
16

BUT NOW--LET'S TODDLE BACK TO THE MAN OF THE HOUR--
LUCKY THERE'S HARDLY ANY WILDLIFE AROUND HERE!
SO ANY MOVING OBJECT MY RADAR SENSE DETECTS IS APT TO BE THE BEETLE!

AND, SINCE IT'S SO QUIET--AND OPEN HERE--MY SENSES CAN OPERATE AT THEIR MAXIMUM RANGE!
WHOOP! HOLD IT, DD--!
THERE'S SOMETHING DOWN BELOW!
I GET THE IMAGE OF --A CLUSTER OF BUILDINGS!
MUST HAVE REACHED A SMALL VILLAGE!
IT CAN BE A BREAK!
PERHAPS SOMEONE THERE HAS SEEN HIM GO BY!

THERE'S NO ONE ON THE STREET!
AND YET--I CAN HEAR HEARBEATS ALL AROUND ME!
SO THEY MUST ALL BE INDOORS!
GROCERY
WELL, HERE'S ONE WAY TO GET A LITTLE ATTENTION AROUND HERE!
SUMPTER'S CHEWING TOBACCO

IT WORKED! I HEAR THEM COMING NOW!
BUT WAIT A MINUTE--!
I SENSE ENOUGH HOSTILITY TO START A WAR!
HE MUST BE CRAZY--COMIN' HERE ALONE LIKE THIS!

FACE IT, HORNHEAD! WHOEVER THESE CHARACTERS ARE, YOU'LL NEVER GET 'EM IN YOUR FAN CLUB!
UH OH! THEY'RE STARTING TO RUSH ME!

THEY'RE CARRYING GUNS--LIKE THEY MEAN TO USE 'EM! THESE JOKERS JUST AREN'T KIDDIN' AROUND!
BUT, I STILL DON'T GET IT!
THERE'S NO FAMILIAR HEARTBEAT OR VOICE IN THE BUNCH!
WHO ARE THEY?? AND WHAT'S THE DEAL??
UHH!!
LOOK OUT! HE'S GONNA-- OOFFF!
GRAB 'IM!!

I DUNNO WHO YOU CUTIES ARE--
BUT ONE THING'S FOR SURE--
YOU'RE NOT WORKING FOR THE WELCOME WAGON!
THONK!

NOW LOOK--SUPPOSE WE TALK THIS OVER FOR A WHILE--?
KLIK!
SURE! TALK ALL YOU WANT TO--!

ARGHHH!
NOT WITH THAT BLASTER IN YOUR HAND, WISE GUY!

WHAT'S WITH YOU GUYS?? HE'S ALL ALONE--AND UNARMED!
SO LET'S FINISH 'IM OFF!
LOOK! I DUNNO WHO YOU THINK I AM--
BUT YOU'RE BARKING UP THE WRONG TREE!
I DON'T EVEN KNOW YOU!

I'M JUST HERE LOOKING FOR SOMEONE!
IF YOU'LL-- UMMFFFF!
MISTER, YOU TALK TOO MUCH!
OKAY, WHITEY--GET A BEAD ON 'IM! HURRY --HE'S A LOT STRONGER'N HE LOOKS!

DON'T FRET ABOUT IT NONE!
'LESS'N YA THINK HE'S STRONG ENUFF TO STOP A .30 CALIBER SHELL!
YA CAN LET UP ON 'IM NOW! HE AINT LIKELY TO TRY ANYTHING WHEN I GOT 'IM DEAD IN MY SIGHTS!

ONE FAST BACK-FLIP, KICKING UP WITH MY HEELS, COULD PROBABLY--BUT WHY BOTHER?
I MIGHT AS WELL PLAY IT COOL --TILL I GET THE LAY OF THE LAND!
LOOK--MAYBE YOU HEARD THERE'S A FUGITIVE IN THESE PARTS--A KILLER IN A CONCEALING COSTUME!
BUT WHAT-EVER YOU THINK--I'M NOT HIM!

WELL, WELL! MY ONE-TIME PURSUER STILL LIVES, DOES HE?
BUT, NEVER FEAR--WE WILL VERY QUICKLY ATTEND TO THAT LITTLE MATTER!
UNLIKE THE OTHER FOES WHOM YOU'VE DEFEATED IN THE PAST --THE BEETLE IS FAR MORE CAUTIOUS!
YOU WILL BE GUARDED EVERY MINUTE--UNTIL I SELECT THE MOST FITTING FATE--FOR A DOOMED DAREDEVIL!

NEXT: AMONG ONE OR TWO OTHER THINGS--
The ORIGIN of the BEETLE!

HERE COMES...
DAREDEVIL
THE MAN WITHOUT FEAR!
APPROVED BY THE COMICS CODE AUTHORITY
MARVEL COMICS GROUP
12¢ IND.
34 NOV
MCG
LOOK! DAREDEVIL'S HELPLESS!
THE BEETLE IS ABOUT TO UNMASK HIM!
"TO SQUASH A BEETLE!"

DAREDEVIL, THE MAN WITHOUT FEAR!
"TO SQUASH A BEETLE!"
BONE WEARY...ON THE VERGE OF COMPLETE EXHAUSTION... DAREDEVIL HAS FOLLOWED THE METAL-WINGED BEETLE ON FOOT, WHILE THE HIGH-FLYING ARCH-VILLAIN HAS REACHED HIS FAR NORTH HIDEOUT WITH THE STOLEN, PRICELESS REGINA NECKLACE, WHICH HAD BEEN EN ROUTE TO EXPO '67 FOR DISPLAY! AND NOW, AS THE BEETLE'S MEN CLOSE IN, DD DESPERATELY STRIKES BACK--
LET'S HEAR IT FOR: STAN (THE MAN) LEE and GENE (THE DEAN) COLAN WHO BRING YOU THIS ACTION-PACKED THRILLER-CHILLER!
ABLY ASSISTED BY:
JOHN TARTAGLIONE, INKER
ARTIE SIMEK, LETTERER
THE BEST TIME TO ACT IS WHEN THEY LEAST EXPECT IT--LIKE NOW!
SOK!
WHOP!
HOLD ONTO YOUR HATS, HEROES! WE'RE GONNA MOVE...
1

OKAY, MASKED MAN--YOU *ASKED* FOR IT!
NO MATTER *HOW* MUCH OF A HOT SHOT YOU ARE, YOU HAVEN'T A *CHANCE* AGAINST--
UNNNHH!!
QUIET, LOUDMOUTH! DON'T SAY A *WORD!*
JUST DRINK IN THE SHEER *POETRY* OF THIS LITTLE MANEUVER!
BTAM!

DON'T BE *IMPATIENT,* BEETIE!
I HAVEN'T FORGOTTEN ABOUT *YOU!*
I WAS JUST SAVING THE *BEST* FOR THE *LAST!*
THOSE HYDRAULICALLY-POWERED TIN *MITTENS* OF YOURS ARE *FAST,* SONNY--
BUT NOT FAST *ENOUGH!*
THAT REMAINS TO BE *SEEN,* YOU SWAGGERING *SIMPLETON!*

DID ANYONE EVER TELL YOU THAT YOU HAVE A HOSTILITY SYNDROME??
I'D BETTER SHOW YOU WHAT HAPPENS TO PEOPLE WHO TALK 'SO NASTY!
FOR YOUR OWN GOOD, OF COURSE!
THAP!

NOW PAY ATTENTION! --THERE MAY BE A TEST LATER!

THIS'LL TEACH YOU NOT TO GO POKING AROUND AT PEACE-LOVING DAREDEVILS--!
UH OH! FOOTSTEPS RACING UP BEHIND ME!
THIS WON'T BE AS EASY AS I'M TRYING TO MAKE IT SOUND!
HOTEL
KRASH!

WE'LL SHUT YOUR MOUTH NOW--FOR GOOD!
NOT IF I CAN HELP IT, SWEETIE!

AND HELP IT I CAN!
UNGGHHTT!

I'M GETTING TIRED--TOO DANGEROUSLY TIRED!
CAN'T KEEP UP THE PACE MUCH LONGER!
DON'T YOU FELLAS EVER STOP FOR A COFFEE BREAK?

THE ONLY THING THAT'LL BREAK AROUND HERE IS--HEY!!
HOW'D YOU MOVE SO FAST??
I HAD TO!! YOU'VE GOT BAD BREATH!
4

YOU DON'T REALLY EXPECT TO SWAT A SWINGIN' SUPER-HERO THAT EASY, DO YOU?
MY ARMS AND LEGS-- FEEL LIKE THEY'RE MADE OF LEAD--!
IF I COULD JUST SLOW DOWN-- EVEN FOR A MINUTE--!
KEEP YAPPIN', PAL! YOU GOTTA SLIP UP SOONER OR LATER!
WHHHHT

I GOT HIM!
BUT, WHAT GOOD WILL IT DO?
THE OTHERS ARE REGROUPING AGAIN!

A SOUND--SOMETHING FLUTTERING ABOVE ME!
THE BEETLE!! HE'S RECOVERED-- ATTACKING AGAIN!
BUT--CAN'T FOCUS MY SENSES--TOO TIRED--CAN'T PINPOINT HIS LOCATION!!
EVERYTHING'S GETTING LIKE A HAZY BLUR TO ME--!

THEN, AS THE GALLANT GLADIATOR VAINLY TRIES TO CLEAR AWAY THE COBWEBS--
THONK

STAY BACK!
I DON'T WANT HIM HARMED!
WADDAYA MEAN, BOSS?
YOU GOTTA BE KIDDIN'!
HE ALMOST FLATTENED US ALL! WE CAN'T GIVE 'IM ANOTHER CHANCE!
5

QUIET, YOU FEEBLE-WITTED FOOLS!
I SAID NOTHING ABOUT GIVING HIM ANOTHER CHANCE!
INSTEAD, I SHALL MAKE HIM PAY FOR DARING TO ATTACK US-- AS HE HAS NEVER PAID BEFORE!
WE WILL DISGRACE HIM--BEFORE THE EYES OF THE ENTIRE WORLD!
SOUNDS REAL JAZZY, BOSS!
BUT I STILL THINK WE OUGHTTA JUST VENTILATE 'IM--LIKE NOW!
I DO THE THINKING HERE! OR, DO YOU DISPUTE THAT??
WHO, ME? NO SIR, BEETLE! WHAT-EVER YOU SAY GOES! YOU'RE TOP MAN HERE!
AND DON'T EVER FORGET IT!
TIE HIM UP! PUT HIM IN THE VAN!
THE VAN? WHERE ARE THEY TAKING ME?
THAT'S IT!
PUT HIM ON THE FLOOR-- AND GET IN AFTER HIM!
THERE'LL BE A GUN POINTING AT HIM EVERY MILE OF THE WAY!
THAT'S OKAY WITH ME! THE LONGER THE TRIP, THE MORE TIME I'LL HAVE TO REST UP! I CAN AFFORD TO BE PATIENT!
I HOPE HE TRIES TO MAKE A BREAK!
IT'LL GIVE US AN EXCUSE TO LET 'IM HAVE IT!
THE PUNK'S HOLDIN' HIMSELF RIGID--TO MAKE IT TOUGH TO CARRY 'IM!
A FAT LOTTA GOOD IT'LL DO HIM!
GOOD! THEY DON'T SUSPECT I'M MERELY FLEXING MY MUSCLES--
SO THAT THERE'LL BE ENOUGH SLACK TO LOOSEN MY BONDS WHEN THE TIME COMES!
I STILL THINK WE SHOULD'A POLISHED HIM OFF!
JUST DRIVE, MAC! THE BEETLE KNOWS WHAT HE'S DOING!

IN CASE YOU'VE BEEN WONDERING, DAREDEVIL-- WE'RE HEADED FOR EXPO '67!
I PLAN TO PUBLICLY UNMASK YOU THERE--IN A TELEVISED CEREMONY WHICH WILL BE MY GREATEST TRIUMPH!
THAT SOUNDS GREAT, BOSS! I ALWAYS WANTED TO BE ON TELEVISION!
ALL OF A SUDDEN, BIG MOUTH AINT GOT ANYTHING TO SAY!
YEAH! HE AINT LAUGHIN' ANY MORE NOW THAT HE KNOWS WHAT'S WAITIN' FOR HIM!

WHILE DAREDEVIL IS BLINDFOLDED, I'LL STORE THE STOLEN NECKLACE IN THE SECRET COMPARTMENT HERE IN THE VAN!
EVEN IF HE SHOULD TEMPORARILY GET FREE, HE WON'T KNOW WHERE TO LOOK FOR IT!

BUT, LITTLE DOES THE BEETLE SUSPECT--
I HEARD HIM OPEN A PANEL ABOVE US!
HE MUST HAVE STASHED THE NECKLACE THERE!
BOSS, YOU'RE THE EVER-LOVIN' GREATEST!
HOW DO YA EVER DREAM UP ALL THEM SCHEMES OF YOURS, ANYWAY?

I'VE ALWAYS BEEN A THINKER-- A SCHEMER-- A SUPREME STRATEGIST!
THAT'S HOW I BECAME THE SUPER-POWERFUL BEETLE IN THE FIRST PLACE--
I WASN'T SATISFIED WITH MERELY BEING A MASTER MECHANIC IN THE FACTORY I ONCE WORKED FOR--!
AND NOW, AS ALL MARVEL MADMEN KNOW, FLASHBACK TIME IS FAST APPROACHING--SO READY YOURSELF, FRANTIC ONE, FOR A SWINGIN' SINGLE-PAGE SUMMARY OF BEETIE'S ORIGIN--

"SLYLY, SECRETLY, I WORKED ON A NEW TYPE OF TESTING DEVICE THAT EVALUATED THE TENSILE STRENGTH OF METALS AND CERAMICS--!"
I'VE DONE IT! THIS NEW METAL ALLOY WILL BE PERFECT FOR THE TYPE OF WINGS I'M AFTER!
HAH! ALL THESE MONTHS, AND NOBODY'S SUSPECTED WHAT I'VE BEEN UP TO!
AND NOW-- IT'S TOO LATE TO STOP ME!
"I CONDUCTED THE MOST EXHAUSTIVE TESTS POSSIBLE, TILL I WAS SATISFIED THAT--"
NEITHER COLD, NOR HEAT, NOR ANYTHING CAN DAMAGE THESE WINGS!!
WITH THEM ON MY SHOULDERS, I'LL BE UNBEATABLE!
"THEN, TO COMPLEMENT MY BEETLE WINGS, I DEVISED A FORM OF METAL, HYDRAULIC-POWERED FINGERS--TIPPED WITH HEAVY-DUTY SUCTION-FEELERS!
THAT DOES IT! NOW I'M READY FOR ANYTHING!!
"THUS, I BURST FORTH UPON THE WORLD--NO LONGER A DRAB, COLORLESS FIGURE, BUT--GARBED IN MY HIGHLY-SOPHISTICATED METAL HELMET, WITH ITS BUILT-IN CONTROL DEVICES--I WAS THE BRIGHT-COLORED, FLYING BEETLE--MASTER OF CRIME!"
"TRUE, I LOST A BATTLE OR TWO IN THE BEGINNING--BUT I WAS YOUNGER, LESS EXPERIENCED! NOW, AT THE HEIGHT OF MY POWER--NO ONE CAN DEFY ME! THE BEETLE IS SUPREME!"

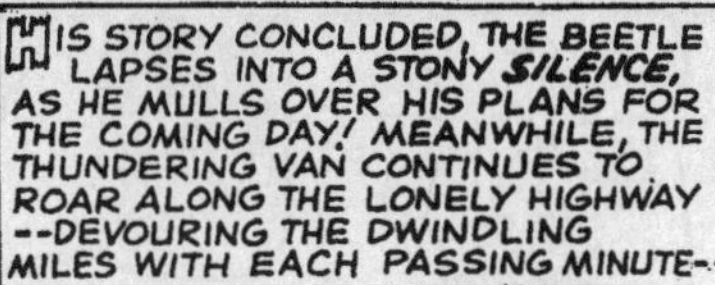
His story concluded, the Beetle lapses into a stony *silence*, as he mulls over his plans for the coming day! Meanwhile, the thundering van continues to roar along the lonely highway --devouring the dwindling miles with each passing minute--

And, all the while, Daredevil *sleeps*-- as the strength and stamina flow back into his lithe-muscled frame--
Until, at last--

Everybody *up!* We're nearly *there!*
Slip into the identity-concealing *masks* which I've provided for each of you!
Man! This is *one* caper I'm looking *forward* to!
The whole blamed *underworld* will applaud us when we rip that red *hood* off Daredevil's head!
They'll probably even make a *movie* about this some day!

That *rest* was just what I *needed!* I feel like the ol' *Daredevil* again!
But there's no need to let my prancin' *playmates* know about it yet!

It's lucky I *tensed* my muscles before!
Now, when I *relax* them, there's enough *slack* to make it easy for me to work the ropes *loose!*

But I won't wriggle *out* of them yet! Not till the right *time* arrives!
Look sharp back there, boss!
We're comin' to the *main gate!*

IT'S LUCKY IT'S SO LATE! THE WHOLE PLACE IS EMPTY!
THE CROWDS WON'T BE SHOWIN' UP TILL MORNING!
ONCE WE GET INSIDE, PICK ANY BUILDING THAT WILL SUIT OUR PURPOSES!

HOLD IT RIGHT THERE!
NO DELIVERIES ARE MADE AT THIS HOUR WITHOUT A SPECIAL PERMIT!
THAT'S OKAY! WE'VE GOT A PERMIT!
THEN LET ME SEE IT!

SURE! TAKE A GOOD LOOK--!
YOU DON'T SEE SLEEPING GAS LIKE THIS EVERY DAY!
SHOOOSH

OKAY, THAT DOES IT!
NOW MOVE-- THIS JOINT'S GONNA BE CRAWLIN' WITH MOUNTIES BEFORE YA KNOW IT!
AND WE GOTTA BE OUT OF SIGHT BEFORE THEY GET HERE!
CLANG!

THERE'S A PERFECT BUILDING FOR US! IT WON'T BE OPEN TO THE PUBLIC FOR A FEW MORE DAYS--
OR SO THEY THINK!
NOW QUICKLY-- FOLLOW ME!
SLOW IT DOWN, WILLYA, BOSS? THIS GUY'S NO FEATHER!
AND WE AINT ALL GOT WINGS LIKE YOU!
IF YA ASK ME, HE'S ONLY FAKIN' IT! I'M BETTIN' HE AIN'T ASLEEP NO MORE!

WHAT DIFFERENCE DOES IT MAKE?
WITHIN A FEW HOURS HE'LL BE THE MOST THOROUGHLY BEATEN SUPERHERO WHO EVER LIVED!
OR--WHO WAS EVER FATED TO DIE!

NOW, PUT HIM DOWN! FOR DAREDEVIL, THIS WILL BE THE LAST STOP!
AND HE SOUNDS AS THOUGH HE MEANS IT!
THUD!

MINUTES LATER--
DON'T WORRY, BOSS! WE'LL HAVE IT FINISHED 'WAY BEFORE THE GATES OPEN TOMORROW MORNING!
THE GREATEST EXHIBIT OF ALL— SEE DAREDEVIL UNMASKED BY THE BEE
MY BONDS ARE JUST THE WAY I WANT THEM NOW!

IT WAS REAL NICE OF THEM TO CARRY ME AROUND THAT WAY! THE REST WAS JUST WHAT I NEEDED!
THE ONLY PROBLEM LEFT IS PICKING JUST THE RIGHT INSTANT TO GO INTO ACTION!

BUT WHAT OF KAREN AND FOGGY, WHOM WE HAD LAST SEEN ON THE TRAIN, EN ROUTE TO MONTREAL--?
I HOPE THAT CLOWN BROTHER OF MATT'S STAYS AWAY TILL WE'RE READY TO RETURN HOME!
BUT AREN'T YOU EVEN WORRIED ABOUT--FOGGY!! LOOK!!

CAN'T WE EVER GET AWAY FROM THAT CONCEITED CORNBALL??!
HEY--WAIT! THAT SIGN READS AS THOUGH THE BEETLE'S CAPTURED HIM!
OH NO! IT CAN'T BE! IT JUST CAN'T!
SEE THE GREATES EXHIBIT OF ALL— SEE DAREDEVI UNMASKED BY
EXPO 67
WE'D BETTER GET OVER THERE, LITTLE LADY-- BUT FAST!

AND, ONCE INSIDE, THE STARTLED COUPLE SEE--

IT'S *HIM*--WITH THE *BEETLE!* HE LOOKS LIKE--A *PRISONER!*

BUT, THE *CROWDS*--THE *CAMERAMEN*--HOW DOES THE BEETLE EXPECT TO GET *AWAY* WITH IT??

LADIES AND GENTLEMEN--GIVE ME YOUR *ATTENTION*--

YOU ARE ABOUT TO WITNESS A SIGHT YOU'LL NEVER *FORGET!*

THE BEETLE'S *COSTUME*--AND *DAREDEVIL'S*--

AND THOSE MEN--WITH *GUNS*--!

IT ALMOST LOOKS *REAL!*

FOGGY! NOBODY'S *DOING* ANYTHING BECAUSE THEY THINK IT'S JUST A *SHOW*--SOME SORT OF *PAGEANT!*

WHAT CAN ANYONE DO *ANYWAY*--AGAINST ALL THE *GUNS* THEY'RE CARRYING?!!

BEFORE YOUR VERY EYES--I, THE *BEETLE*, SHALL *UNMASK* MY HELPLESS VICTIM--THE TOTALLY-DEFEATED *DAREDEVIL!!*

THOUGH MANY HAVE *ATTEMPTED* THIS FEAT--NONE BUT THE *BEETLE* HAS EVER *SUCCEEDED!*

HIS HYDRAULIC *FEELERS* ARE REACHING TOWARDS MY FACE! LOOKS LIKE THIS IS *IT!*

WOK!
I'M SURPRISED AT YOU, BEETIE!! YOU FORGOT THE MOST IMPORTANT THING--!
A GOOD SHOWMAN NEVER STARTS OFF WITH HIS MAIN ATTRACTION! LET'S GIVE THE FOLKS A LITTLE WARM-UP FIRST!
AFTER ALL, IF YOU'VE DECIDED TO TRY YOUR HAND AT SHOW BIZ, I WOULDN'T WANT YOU TO BE AS BIG A FLOP AS YOU ARE AT CRIME!
HE GOT HIS HANDS FREE!! DON'T LET HIM-- UNNHHH!!
DON'T WORRY, BOSS! HE AINT GOT A CHANCE!
14

MAN! THEY LOOK AS IF THEY REALLY MEAN IT!
AND IF YOU'D LIKE TO SEE HOW DD'S LITTLE DONNEYBROOK LOOKS THRU THE CAMERAMAN'S LENS, BE OUR GUEST--

HOW'D THEY EVER FIND AN ACTOR AS ATHLETIC AS THE REAL DAREDEVIL??
THOSE OTHER ONES ARE NO SLOUCHES, EITHER!!
THEY LOOK AS IF THEY'RE PLAYING FOR KEEPS!!

PHTOP!

C'MON, FELLAS-- LET'S PUT SOME OF THE OL' MOXIE IN IT, HUH?

AFTER ALL, WE DON'T WANNA DISAPPOINT THE CASH CUSTOMERS, DO WE?
ZAK!
15

QUICK! WE CAN GRAB 'IM NOW--BEFORE HE GETS AWAY!
NOW I REALIZE I COULD NEVER GIVE UP BEING DD!
I FEEL ALIVE AGAIN--FOR THE FIRST TIME SINCE I WAS CAPTURED!

GUESS AGAIN, LITTLE FRIENDS!
I'VE NO INTENTION OF GETTING AWAY!
WHERE ELSE CAN A FELLA GET SUCH ENERGETIC SPARRING PARTNERS--ALL FOR FREE?
SPTONK!

UH OH! THE BEETLE'S ATTACKING AGAIN!
YOU'RE ONLY PROLONGING YOUR ULTIMATE FATE, DAREDEVIL!
THERE'S NO WAY TO OUT-FIGHT, OR OUT-RUN THE POWER OF THE BEETLE!

SEE HOW EASILY MY HYDRAULIC FEELERS CAN FORM AN UNBREAK-ABLE CAGE AROUND YOU!
HE'S NOT KIDDING! I CAN'T STRETCH 'EM FAR ENOUGH TO GET FREE!
16

IF I DON'T BREAK AWAY SOON, IT'LL BE TOO LATE!
HIS GUN-TOTING STOOGES WILL GET THE NERVE TO TRY AGAIN!!

BUT SOMETIMES HELP CAN COME FROM THE MOST UNEXPECTED SOURCE--
I CAN'T LET HIM GET BEATEN-- WITHOUT EVEN LIFTING A FINGER!!
FOGGY!
HANG ON, DAREDEVIL!! HANG ON!

FOGGY-- WAIT! YOU'LL BE-- KILLED!!
NOT ME! I'M TOO DUMB TO DIE!
ANYWAY, THAT MASKED MANIAC HAS RISKED HIS LIFE PLENTY OF TIMES FOR US!

WHOEVER YOU ARE--STAY BACK! THIS DOESN'T CONCERN YOU!
IT'S FOGGY-- ATTACKING THE BEETLE!
IF HE CAN JUST DIVERT HIS ATTENTION ANOTHER FEW SECONDS--!
I CAN'T HIT THIS FOOL STRANGER!!
I'LL LOSE THE SYMPATHY OF THE AUDIENCE!

BREAK FREE, HORNHEAD!
HE LOOSENED HIS GRIP! NOW'S YOUR CHANCE--NOW!
FTING!
YOU FOOL! YOU DON'T REALIZE WHAT YOU'RE DOING!
I CAN ANNIHILATE YOU IN THE WINK OF AN EYE!

NOT WITH DAREDEVIL FREE, YOU WON'T!
HE DID IT!
GOOD OL' FOGGY ACTUALLY MADE HIM RELEASE HIS GRIP!

BUT I'VE GOT TO STEP IN FAST!
FOGGY WON'T LAST A MINUTE ALONE AGAINST THE BEETLE!
YOU OVERSTUFFED BUMBLER! YOU'VE JUST SIGNED YOUR DEATH WARRANT!

SORRY, WOBBLE-WINGS--YOU CAN'T HOLD HIM TO IT--!
HE HAD HIS FINGERS CROSSED!
I APPRECIATE YOUR HELP, FOGGY--BUT GET OUT--FAST--WHILE YOU CAN!

HOWEVER, BEFORE EITHER MAN CAN MAKE ANOTHER MOVE, EVERYTHING SEEMS TO HAPPEN AT ONCE--!
TOO LATE! THEY'RE ALL ATTACKING EN MASSE!
WHUMP

YOK
BUT THE ADVANTAGE IS STILL MINE!
I'M THE ONLY ONE WHOSE SUPER-SENSES CAN TELL HIM WHICH WAY TO LASH OUT!

ZZOOP!
IT'S THE END OF THE LINE!
LET'S LOOK ALIVE THERE, TROOPS--!

GIVE UP DAREDEVIL--!
--OR I DASH HIM TO THE GROUND!
DON'T WORRY ABOUT ME, MASKED MAN--!
I'M ROUND ENOUGH TO BOUNCE!
ONLY MY BILLY CLUB CAN FIX THINGS NOW!
FTWNNG!

KNOW SOMETHING, MR. NELSON?
IF THIS SORT OF THING KEEPS UP--
YOU'LL JUST HAVE TO JOIN OUR UNION!
YOU--YOU CAUGHT ME!!
SURE I DID, SON!
I COULDN'T LET YOU BUST UP A BRAND NEW FLOOR!

AND NOW-- IT'S TIME TO BRING THE HIGH-FLYING BEETLE BACK DOWN TO EARTH--!

THWAK!
DON'T GO 'WAY, TIGER--
THE PARTY'S JUST BEGINNING!

THIS IS ONE TIME YOU'RE WRONG, DAREDEVIL!
FOR HIM-- THE PARTY'S OVER!
WE LEARNED ABOUT HIS THEFT OF THE REGINA NECKLACE ON THE TRAIN--AND GOT HERE JUST IN TIME!
SO WHAT? YOU'LL FIND NO EVIDENCE!
YOU CAN'T PROVE ANYTHING UNTIL YOU LOCATE THE NECKLACE!

THAT'S EASY, BUG-EYES! IT'S IN A HIDDEN COMPARTMENT OF THE VAN PARKED OUT FRONT!
HOW COULD YOU KNOW?? I HAD YOU BLINDFOLDED WHEN I HID IT!
THAT'S MY LITTLE SECRET!

DID YOU BRING MY SUITCASE FROM THE TRAIN, GIRL?
'NATCH, BOY! WE CHECKED IT IN A LOCKER!

GROOVY, GANG! I'D HAVE FELT TOO CONSPICUOUS MAKIN' THE EXPO SCENE IN MY DAREDEVIL DUDS!
IT'S SO GOOD TO BE TOGETHER AGAIN!
YOU'RE HARDLY A SHRINKING VIOLET IN THAT SPORT JACKET, MURDOCK!
IF FOGGY BROUGHT SOME DOUGH, WE CAN HAVE A BALL!

DON'T YOU EVER CARRY MONEY WITH YOU, MIKE?
HEAVENS NO!! I'M SCARED OF MUGGERS!
IF ONLY MATT WERE HERE WITH US--!
20

WHEN I'M MIKE, SHE MISSES MATT! AND WHEN I'M MATT SHE RAVES ABOUT MIKE!
ONLY A GUY WITH MY SLOPPY LUCK COULD END UP BEING JEALOUS OF HIMSELF!
NEXT
ON THE TRAIL OF-- THE TRAPSTER!

DAREDEVIL SPECIAL
KING-SIZE SPECIAL!
APPROVED BY THE COMICS CODE AUTHORITY
ALL NEW!
HERE COMES...
DAREDEVIL
NOT A SINGLE REPRINT
MARVEL COMICS GROUP
25¢ IND.
1 SEPT
THE MAN WITHOUT FEAR!
ELECTRO AND HIS EMISSARIES OF EVIL!
PLUS!
FEATURES. PIN-UPS! AND A MIXED-UP MEETING WITH STAN and GENE!
FEATURING: A 39-PAGE SLAM-BANG ACTION THRILLER!

DAREDEVIL, THE MAN WITHOUT FEAR!
"ELECTRO,
AND THE EMISSARIES OF EVIL!"
FEATURING: A BRAND-NEW 39-PAGE EPIC OF ACTION
OKAY, YOU GET THE IDEA! OL' FEARLESS IS TAKING A WORK-OUT IN HIS PRIVATE GYM...AND IT'S A GOOD THING HE IS... 'CAUSE HE'S SOON GONNA NEED ALL THE MUSCLE HE'S GOT! JUST WATCH 'N SEE...
DD'S MOST DANGEROUS ADVENTURE... BY: STAN (THE MAN) LEE and GENE (THE DEAN) COLAN
EMBELLISHED BY: JOHN TARTAGIONE LETTERED BY: SAM ROSEN

WELL, I GUESS THAT'S IT FOR NOW!
NO SENSE GETTING OVERTRAINED!
ANYWAY, THINGS HAVE BEEN PRETTY QUIET LATELY!
ALTHOUGH THAT'S USUALLY WHEN I'VE GOTTA BE THE MOST CAREFUL!

A GENT IN MY LINE OF WORK CAN'T TELL WHEN THE NEXT LITTLE CALL TO ACTION IS GONNA POP UP!
AND IT CAN'T BE TOO SOON TO SUIT ME!
DOWN
IT'S FUNNY... I ALWAYS FEEL SORT OF UNHEROIC USING AN ELEVATOR TO REACH MY APARTMENT UPSTAIRS!
BUT, IT CAME WITH THIS BROWNSTONE WHEN I BOUGHT IT...
SO I MIGHT AS WELL GET MY MONEY'S WORTH!

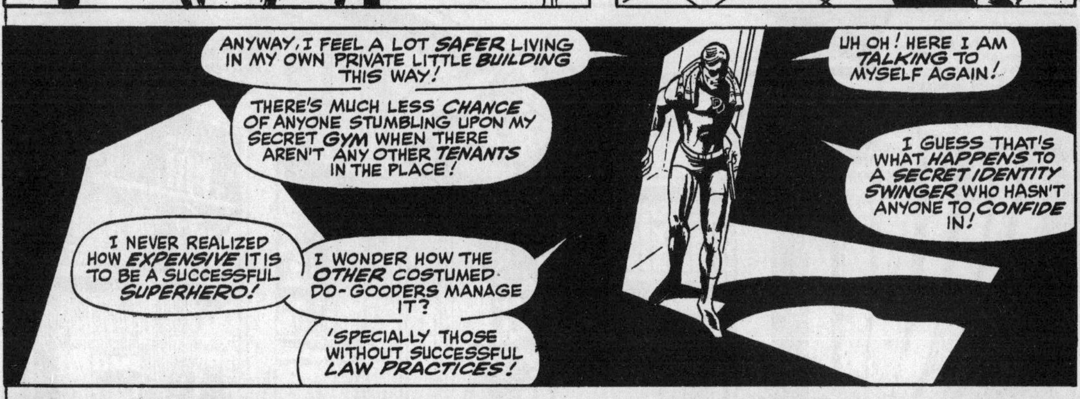
ANYWAY, I FEEL A LOT SAFER LIVING IN MY OWN PRIVATE LITTLE BUILDING THIS WAY!
THERE'S MUCH LESS CHANCE OF ANYONE STUMBLING UPON MY SECRET GYM WHEN THERE AREN'T ANY OTHER TENANTS IN THE PLACE!
I NEVER REALIZED HOW EXPENSIVE IT IS TO BE A SUCCESSFUL SUPERHERO!
I WONDER HOW THE OTHER COSTUMED DO-GOODERS MANAGE IT?
'SPECIALLY THOSE WITHOUT SUCCESSFUL LAW PRACTICES!
UH OH! HERE I AM TALKING TO MYSELF AGAIN!
I GUESS THAT'S WHAT HAPPENS TO A SECRET IDENTITY SWINGER WHO HASN'T ANYONE TO CONFIDE IN!

BUT, I DON'T DARE TAKE FOGGY OR KAREN INTO MY CONFIDENCE!
SHARING MY SECRET COULD BE TOO DEADLY DANGEROUS FOR EITHER OF THEM!
I'M NOT ABOUT TO JEOPARDIZE THE SAFETY OF MY LOYAL LAW PARTNER.. OR OF THE GIRL I LOVE, JUST TO HAVE AN AUDIENCE!
HOW ABOUT THAT! NOTICE THE WAY WE SLIP IN AN ENTIRE SNEAKY SUBLIMINAL SUMMARY OF DD'S LIFE FOR THE BENEFIT OF ANY NEW-COMERS? .. SLY OL' STAN.
I WOULDN'T TRADE THE LIFE I LEAD FOR ANYTHING IN THIS WHOLE NUTTY WORLD...
BUT, IT DOES HAVE ONE PERMANENT DRAWBACK..
IT SURE CAN GET LONELY AT TIMES!
2.

THERE'S A BIG, BLUSTERIN' CITY OUT THERE, WITH EIGHT MILLION PEOPLE RUBBING SHOULDERS NIGHT AND DAY!

AND, AS SOON AS I GET MY LITTLE HORN-HEAD MASK ON, I'M GONNA JOIN THE CROWD...IN MY OWN MERRY WAY!

THERE'S GOTTA BE SOME FASCINATING FEAT OF DERRING-DO I CAN PERFORM, TO KEEP MY HAND IN!

EVEN NABBING A NASTY JAYWALKER WOULD BE BETTER THAN NOTHING!

ANYONE ELSE WOULD USE A BUS, TRAIN, OR TAXI TO GET AROUND TOWN...
CLICK!
BUT I'VE GOT MY IMAGE TO LIVE UP TO!!

SNAP!
AND I CAN'T EVER LET THE PANTIN' PUBLIC DOWN!

THWIPP!
OKAY, LI'L BILLY CLUB...

IT'S TRAVELLIN' TIME AGAIN..!

AND AWAAAAY WE GO!!
OKAY, FRANTIC ONE...HANG LOOSE!! WE'RE LEAVING SMALL TALK BEHIND, AND THERE'S NOTHIN' BUT ACTION AHEAD...!
4.

WE JUST TOSSED THIS IN SO YOU WOULDN'T THINK WE WERE KIDDING..!

SO FAR... NOTHING!
UNLESS MY EVER-LOVIN' RADAR SENSE NEEDS A TUNE-UP, THEY NEED A SUPERHERO DOWN THERE LIKE HERSHEY NEEDS A CHOCOLATE BAR!

A FINE THING! I SPEND MY WHOLE LIFE FIGHTING TROUBLE-MAKERS...
AND THEN, WHEN EVERYTHING'S FINALLY PEACEFUL, I'M JUST PLAIN DISAPPOINTED!
WHOOP!! WAIT A MINUTE!!
I MAY HAVE FOUND SOMETHING!
5.

THOSE TWO HEARTBEATS BELOW.. I COULDN'T MISTAKE THEM ANYWHERE!
AND NOW I HEAR THEIR VOICES!!
THAT CLINCHES IT!
SOMETHING TELLS ME I'VE STUMBLED ONTO LOTS MORE TROUBLE THAN I WOULD HAVE DARED BARGAIN FOR!

IT'S ELECTRO... AND THE MATADOR.. WHISPERING IN THAT ALLEY BELOW...
..AND THEY'RE TALKING ABOUT.. ME!
YOU HAVE MY WORD! I WILL DO MY SHARE TO DESTROY DAREDEVIL!
THE BEAUTY OF MY PLAN IS THE FACT THAT HE SUSPECTS NOTHING!
I SPENT LONG MONTHS, WORKING IN SECRET... CONTACTING THE MOST POWERFUL OF HIS OLD ENEMIES!
AND NOW.. MY EFFORTS ARE ABOUT TO PAY OFF!

WE CANNOT FAIL! EVEN SINGLE-HANDED, WE ARE EACH A MATCH FOR DAREDEVIL!
BUT NOW, THERE WILL BE FIVE OF US... WORKING AS A TEAM...
FIVE OF THE MIGHTIEST EMISSARIES OF EVIL EVER ASSEMBLED!
AND I...THE INVINCIBLE MASTER OF ELECTRICITY, WILL GUIDE US TO VICTORY!

I DON'T CARE WHO DOES THE GUIDING---ALL I WANT IS REVENGE--- REVENGE AGAINST THE ONLY MAN WHO EVER DEFEATED ME!
HOW I WISH HE WERE HERE RIGHT NOW--- TO FEEL THE BITE OF THE MATADOR'S DEADLY BLADE!
YOU MUSTA WISHED ON A STAR, SWEETIE! THIS IS YOUR LUCKY DAY!
WHAT? WHO SAID THAT?!!

JUST THAT LOVEABLE OL' DAREDEVIL... ME!
IT... IT'S HIM!
THIS MEANS WE NEED WAIT NO LONGER!!
6.

HE'S GOT TO BE MINE!! I SAW HIM FIRST!
I SHALL TOY WITH HIM FOR A FEW MOMENTS, AND THEN...OLE!! THE MOMENT OF TRUTH SHALL---UNNHH!!!
HOW MANY TIMES DO I HAVETA TELL YOU, PAL--?
NO MATTER HOW YOU TRY, YOU JUST CAN'T TALK ME TO DEATH!
THAP!
WHY DON'TCHA TAKE A LEAF FROM ELECTRO'S BOOK?
LOOK HOW NICE AND QUIET HE TAKES HIS LUMPS!
LIKE I ALWAYS SAY...NO AMOUNT OF GABBING CAN TAKE THE PLACE OF A SILENT PAINED EXPRESSION!
RIGHT, SPARKY?
THUMP!
BOK!
GLOAT WHILE YOU MAY, DAREDEVIL! NEVER AGAIN SHALL YOU HAVE THE CHANCE!
THWOP!

WITH ALL YOUR SKILL, YOU POSSESS NO DEFENSE AGAINST MY AWESOME ELECTRIC CHARGE!
ZAAT!
ZAT SO?

I'M GLAD YOU TOLD ME!
OTHERWISE, I MIGHT HAVE JUST STOOD THERE...
..INSTEAD OF DUCKING UNDER YOUR BLOTCHY LITTLE BOLT... LIKE THIS!

WOK!
AND, WHILE I'M DOWN HERE...
I MIGHT AS WELL PRACTICE MY CALISTHENICS!
OOPS! SORRY ABOUT THAT!

HAH! YOU FORGOT ABOUT ME, DID YOU?
JUST BETWEEN US, CHUM...
YOU'RE AT THE VERY TOP OF MY LIST OF FORGETTABLE PEOPLE!

KNOW SOMETHING? IF YOU EVER GO BACK TO BULL-FIGHTING...
MY MONEY'S GONNA BE ON THE BULL!
BEHIND ME!! ELECTRO... ABOUT TO STRIKE AGAIN!

TOO LATE TO STOP HIM! ALL I CAN DO IS SPIN AROUND!
I'VE GOTTA SHIFT MY WEIGHT... CATCH IT ON MY SHOULDER... NOW!
ZAAT!
..UHHHH!..

THAT DID IT! QUICKLY, LET US LEAVE, BEFORE THE POLICE ARRIVE!

BUT, WHY NOT FINISH HIM OFF NOW, WHILE YOU HAVE THE CHANCE?

AND CUT SHORT OUR REVENGE?... NO! THAT WOULD BE TOO QUICK... TOO EASY!

WE KNOW HE IS NO MATCH FOR US! WE CAN DISPOSE OF HIM ANY TIME WE PLEASE!

IN THE MEANTIME, LET HIM LIVE... WITH THE KNOWLEDGE THAT HIS DAYS ARE NUMBERED!

WHAT'S WRONG WITH ME?
WHY CAN'T I SHAKE THIS DIZZY FEELING?
GOTTA CLEAR MY HEAD! MAYBE SOME FAST CABLE SWINGING WILL DO THE TRICK!

IT'S NO GOOD! MY TIMING'S OFF!

MY SENSES ARE KEEN AS EVER... I KNOW WHERE I AM... WHAT I SHOULD DO...
BUT... I CAN'T MANAGE TO DO IT!

MISSED MY HAND HOLD... I'M FALLING!!
THERE'S A ROOF... DIRECTLY BELOW ME.. BUT IT'S TOO CLOSE...
NOT ENOUGH TIME FOR ME TO SPIN MY WHOLE BODY AROUND!!
I'M GONNA LAND... HEAD FIRST..!

ONLY ONE CHANCE...
MY HAND!! PUT IT BETWEEN MY FACE...AND THE ROOF...!
IT'LL... CUSHION THE BLOW!!
UNHHH!!
THUD!

THEN, LONG TORTUROUS MOMENTS LATER...
EVERY BONE IN MY BODY... ACHING..!
BUT.. I GUESS I SHOULDN'T COMPLAIN.. I'M LUCKY... TO BE ALIVE!
GOOD THING.. I SPENT ALL THAT TIME... PRACTICING PRATTFALLS... AND TUMBLING!
WELL, THERE'S ONE THING FOR SURE...

TILL FURTHER NOTICE, I'M STAYING AWAY FROM ROOFTOPS..!

IT MAY NOT QUALIFY ME FOR HERO OF THE WEEK, BUT...
TONIGHT, I'M WALKING HOME!

LUCKY IT'S LATE AND THE STREETS ARE DARK...
I WOULDN'T WANT ANYONE TO SEE DAREDEVIL COMING IN THE BACK DOOR OF MATT MURDOCK'S LITTLE HIDEAWAY!

AND NOW, I'VE GOT A LOT OF HEAVY THINKING TO DO..!
CAN'T RELAX FOR A MINUTE TILL I FIGURE OUT WHO THE OTHER EMISSARIES OF EVIL ARE!
11.

PERHAPS DAREDEVIL'S PROBLEM COULD BE SOLVED A BIT SOONER IF HE COULD LOOK INSIDE OF A PRIVATE, CHARTERED JET SPEEDILY WINGING ITS WAY ACROSS THE WIDE ATLANTIC...
I ALWAYS THOUGHT ELECTRO WAS JUST A LEGEND...BUT NOW I KNOW HE REALLY EXISTS!
HE MUST WANT ME PRETTY BAD FOR HIM TO CONTACT THE MAGGIA, ALL THE WAY IN EUROPE, IN ORDER TO GET IN TOUCH WITH ME!
BUT, HIS PROPOSITION INTERESTED ME! I CANNOT RESIST THE OPPORTUNITY TO FACE DAREDEVIL ONCE MORE...AND THIS TIME EMERGE TRIUMPHANT!

EVEN THOUGH HE SPARED MY LIFE LAST TIME WE MET, THE MEMORY OF MY DEFEAT HAS EVER RANKLED ME!*
BUT NEXT TIME THE RESULT IS CERTAIN TO BE DIFFERENT!
*IT WOULD RANKLE US, TOO, IF WE THOUGHT FOR ONE SINGLE MINUTE THAT YOU HAD MISSED THAT YARN IN THE NOW OUT-OF-PRINT DD #23... STRAIGHT-FORWARD STAN.

MINUTES LATER...
MY COSTUME SHOP IS EXACTLY THE WAY I HAD LEFT IT... WITH EVERYTHING STILL INTACT WITHIN THE HIDDEN CHAMBER!

THIS TIME MY COSTUME WILL BE BRAND NEW...
WITH EVERY MIGHTY FACET OF IT MORE DEADLY THAN BEFORE!
CLICK

NOW, DAREDEVIL... YOU MAY LOOK TO YOUR LAURELS..!
ONCE AGAIN YOU'RE ABOUT FACE... THE GLADIATOR!
ELECTRO! THE MATADOR! THE GLADIATOR! BUT, THERE ARE STILL TWO OTHER FOES COMPRISING THE DREADED EMISSARIES OF EVIL! TO SEE ONE OF THEM, LET'S GO BACK A FEW MONTHS, RIGHT AFTER THE END OF DD'S BATTLE WITH...
STILT MAN!! HOW FORTUNATE THAT I WAS NEARBY WHEN HE TOPPLED INTO THE RIVER!
I'LL GET HIM TO SAFETY BEFORE ANYONE CAN FIND US!
HE WILL BE THE FIRST OF THOSE WHO SERVE ME!
AND, A SHORT TIME LATER... IN A STRANGE, LONELY HOUSE ATOP A STRANGE, LONELY HILL... A STRANGE, ARTIFICIAL ELECTRICAL STORM IS CREATED--!
EVERYTHING IS READY!
WITH THE POWER OF ELECTRICITY AT MY COMMAND, I CANNOT FAIL!
REGAIN YOUR POWER, STILT MAN...
YOU WILL NEED EVERY IOTA OF YOUR STRENGTH FOR THE TASK THAT LIES AHEAD--!
FOR THE ULTIMATE DESTRUCTION OF.. DAREDEVIL!
13.

THAT TAKES CARE OF THE INTRODUCTION OF FOUR OF OUR SUPER-MENACES... BUT, BEFORE MEETING THE FIFTH, LET'S VISIT THE NOW-FAMOUS LAW OFFICES OF NELSON AND MURDOCK, WHERE WE FIND...
I HOPE THAT MATT IS ALL RIGHT, FOGGY...
HE'S NEVER BEEN THIS LATE BEFORE!
I'M SURE HE'S OKAY, KAREN!
IF THERE WERE ANYTHING WRONG, YOU KNOW HE'D CALL US!
WHAT A PITY THAT MATT DOESN'T REALIZE HOW LUCKY HE IS!
GIVE ANYTHING IN THE WORLD TO SEE THAT LOOK IN KAREN'S EYES WHEN SHE THINKS OF ME!

PERHAPS I SHOULDN'T WORRY ABOUT MATT SO MUCH, AND YET...
HE SEEMS SO HELPLESS, MAKING HIS WAY THROUGH LIFE WITHOUT THE USE OF HIS EYES!
SO HELPLESS, BUT SOMEHOW... SO WONDERFULLY BRAVE!
NO DOUBT ABOUT IT, HONEY... MATT MURDOCK IS ONE GREAT GUY!

AND I MUST ADMIT, I'M GETTING A LITTLE WORRIED ABOUT HIM MYSELF!
MAYBE WE OUGHT TO JUST GIVE HIM A RING.. AT

BUT, BEFORE THEY CAN REACH FOR THE PHONE...
RR-RING!
MAYBE THAT'S HIM!

THIS IS. SORRY I DIDN'T CALL SOONER, BUT I...EH-- OVERSLEPT!
JUST WANTED YOU TO KNOW I WON'T BE IN TODAY!
HOLD DOWN THE FORT, LADY! I'LL BE IN BRIGHT AND EARLY TOMORROW!
I HOPE!
NO, EVERYTHING'S ALL RIGHT..!
I'VE JUST GOT A FEW PERSONAL MATTERS TO ATTEND TO!

A FEW SECONDS AFTER PUTTING DOWN THE PHONE, THE SIGHTLESS SWASHBUCKLER WASTES NO TIME IN GETTING HIMSELF BACK TO HIS PEAK FIGHTING FORM..!
A GOOD NIGHT'S SLEEP WAS ALL I NEEDED!
I FEEL LIKE I COULD TACKLE A REGIMENT NOW IF I HAD TO!!
AND WITH ELECTRO AND HIS PLAYMATES VOTING ME THEIR TARGET FOR TONIGHT, I JUST MAY HAVE TO!

THUS, FOR THE NEXT FEW HOURS, IN HOMES AND OFFICES THROUGHOUT THE CITY, THIS SOMEWHAT SOUL-STIRRING CRY RINGS OUT...
LOOK! THERE'S DAREDEVIL... SWINGING FROM THE ROOFTOPS ABOVE US!!
WHAT WITH HIM..AND SPIDER-MAN...AND THOR..AND THE HUMAN TORCH ...AND ALL THE OTHER COSTUMED CATS AROUND HERE...
...WE'LL HAVE TO KEEP THE SHADES DOWN TO GET ANY WORK DONE IN THIS TOWN!

BUT, DD HAS FAR WEIGHTIER MATTERS THAN SHADE-PULLING TO WORRY ABOUT..
ALL I CAN DO IS KEEP SHOWING MYSELF--AND WAIT FOR THE FIRST ATTACK!
I'LL START AT THE DOCKS, AND WORK MY WAY ACROSS TOWN!

THEN, A FEW MINUTES LATER...
MY HUNCH WAS RIGHT! HE JUST SWUNG PAST ME!
YOU'LL BE GLAD TO KNOW I'M LEAVING YOU NOW!
THIS IS YOUR PAYMENT FOR ALLOWING ME TO HIDE UPON YOUR BOAT AS I WAITED FOR THIS MOMENT!

DAREDEVIL IS MOVING SLOWLY... AS THOUGH HE WANTS TO BE DISCOVERED!
WELL, THE MATADOR SHALL SEE TO IT THAT HE IS NOT DIS-APPOINTED!

IF ANY OF ELECTRO'S LITTLE FUN BOYS ARE NEARBY, THEY MUST HAVE SEEN ME BY NOW!
I'LL GIVE THEM ANOTHER FEW MINUTES TO SHOW UP BEFORE I TAKE OFF AGAIN!
MAYBE IT'S TOO LIGHT FOR THEM HERE!
I'LL HEAD FOR THE LOWER SECTION OF THE DOCKS... WHERE IT'S MORE SHADOWY!

AHH! THE SETTING IS MADE-TO-ORDER!
WHAT A TOWERING TRIUMPH THIS SHALL BE FOR THE MATADOR!

WELL, LOOKY HERE! SOMEONE TOSSED A CAPE AT LITTLE ME!
HE THINKS I'LL BE HELPLESS... WITH MY EYES COVERED UP!
IF HE ONLY KNEW..!!
THANKS, MATTY! IT WAS GETTING KINDA CHILLY HERE!
SO! YOU KNOW WHO THIS IS, EH?

SURE! WHO ELSE WOULD CARRY AN OVERGROWN HANKY ALL OVER TOWN?
THOK!!
DON'T BOTHER ANSWERING!
..I HATE LONG CONVERSATIONS!
16.

I DO NOT KNOW HOW YOU SAW WHERE TO STRIKE ME...FROM BENEATH THAT CLOTH---
BUT, IT NO LONGER MATTERS!
ALL THAT MATTERS NOW IS---I HAVE FOUND YOU!

I'M ALL SHOOK-UP, BULL-THROWER!
I'LL BET YOU'RE A WHIZ AT PLAYING HIDE-'N-SEEK!
TOO BAD THERE'S JUST ONE LITTLE THING WRONG..!

BOK
YOU DON'T KNOW WHAT TO DO WITH A FELLA AFTER YOU'VE FOUND 'IM!

CARAMBA!! I HAVE DEFEATED THE MOST DEADLY TOROS IN A THOUSAND BULL-FIGHTS!
SAVE YOUR BREATH, BUDDY-- I'M NO BOOKING AGENT!
YOU CAN SHOW ME YOUR SCRAP-BOOK SOME DAY!

STILL YOU MOCK ME!!
STILL YOU DARE TAUNT THE GREATEST MATADOR OF ALL TIME!!
SURE! THINK OF MY REPUTATION..!
THEY WOULDN'T CALL ME DAREDEVIL IF I CHICKENED OUT!

--AND I'M NOT ABOUT TO CHANGE MY NAME NOW--
AFTER ALL THE MONEY I SPENT GETTING MY T-SHIRTS MONOGRAMMED!

WE'RE RIGHT AT THE EDGE OF THE PIER!
IF I CAN JUST GRAB A HANDHOLD... AND THEN SUDDENLY SHIFT MY WEIGHT TO ONE SIDE..!
NOW, DAREDEVIL.. YOU WILL FEEL MY BLADE... FOR THE LAST TIME!

WANNA BET??
SPLUNCH!

NO SENSE GOING IN AFTER HIM! I'LL WAIT TILL HE COMES UP!

WELL, HOW ABOUT THAT? HE'S NOT COMING UP!
I CAN HEAR HIM PADDLING AWAY UNDER THE WATER LIKE A LITTLE POLYWOG!
SO THAT TAKES CARE OF HIM FOR A WHILE!

HEY! DID YOU GET A LOAD OF THAT?
DAREDEVIL POLISHED THAT BOZO OFF WITHOUT EVEN TAKIN' A DEEP BREATH!
MAN! LOOK AT THOSE MUSCLES!! WHAT A DOCK-WALLOPER HE'D MAKE!!

SOUNDS LIKE A CROWD'S BEGINNING TO GATHER --- SO I'D BETTER TAKE OFF!
I'VE A FEELING THAT WHAT HAPPENED JUST NOW IS ONLY THE BEGINNING!
19.

THIS TIME I'LL HEAD FOR THE CENTER OF TOWN AND SEE WHAT TURNS UP!

IN A WAY, I FEEL LIKE ONE OF THE CLAY PIGEONS IN A SHOOTING GALLERY!
BUT THERE'S ONE LITTLE DIFFERENCE...

THIS CLAY PIGEON CAN FIGHT BACK!

AND, SPEAKING OF FIGHTING BACK...
SKRAK

A FELLA CAN'T DO HIS BEST FIGHTING ON AN EMPTY STOMACH!..
AND I HAVEN'T EATEN FOR HOURS!
THAK!
THESE LITTLE NUTRIMENT CAPSULES AREN'T EXACTLY A DINNER AT THE RITZ...

BUT IT'S EASIER THAN TRYING TO ENTER A RESTAURANT UNNOTICED IN THIS GETUP!
AND I DON'T HAVETA WORRY ABOUT WASHING OUT THE GRAVY STAINS!

THEN, AS *EVENING* CLOAKS THE SPRAWLING CITY IN A SHROUD OF SHADOWY SILENCE...

I'D BETTER SKEDADDLE DOWN TO THE *SIDEWALK* NOW!

IF ANYONE'S STILL *LOOKING* FOR ME, THEY'LL NEVER BE ABLE TO SPOT ME UP HERE IN THE *DARK*!

UNLESS THEY *ALSO* HAVE AN ECONOMY-SIZE, GUARANTEED, BUILT-IN *RADAR-SENSE*!

FROM MY VANTAGE POINT UP HERE, IT DIDN'T TAKE ME LONG TO SIGHT YOU...
ESPECIALLY SINCE YOU WERE OBLIGING ENOUGH TO MAKE YOURSELF AS CONSPICUOUS AS POSSIBLE!
AND NOW...IF YOU'LL BE GOOD ENOUGH TO HOLD THAT POSE...
I'LL TRY TO END THIS AS QUICKLY AS POSSIBLE!
IF IT'S ALL THE SAME TO YOU, LONG-LEGS...
I'M NOT IN ANY RUSH!
CAN'T TAKE ANY CHANCES WITH HIM! THAT RAY BLASTER OF HIS MEANS BUSINESS!

ARE YOU BEGGING FOR A ONE-WAY TICKET TO THE HOOSEGOW ON YOUR OWN..?
OR ARE YOU STOOGING FOR ELECTRO... LIKE THE OTHERS?
I'VE TEAMED UP WITH ELECTRO..BUT STILT MAN IS NO-BODY'S STOOGE!
AS YOU WILL SEE.. WHEN I FIRE MY SECOND SHOT!
I'VE GOT NEWS FOR YOU, BIG BOY! YOUR FIRING DAYS ARE OVER!
YOU DIDN'T THINK I TOSSED MY CABLE JUST FOR PITCHING PRACTICE, DID YOU?
IT DOESN'T MATTER WHY YOU DID IT---!
WHIRLING AROUND ME LIKE A GRINNING GORILLA CAN'T DO YOU ANY GOOD!
BITE YOUR TONGUE, TALL MAN!
IF NOTHING ELSE, IT MIGHT HELP ME SHAKE MY HICCUPS!
FOOL! YOU CAN'T GO IN CIRCLES FOREVER!
YOU'VE GOT TO STOP SOME TIME.. AND WHEN YOU DO...
I'LL FINISH YOU..FOREVER!
23.

STILTY, THE TROUBLE WITH YOU IS.. YOU NEVER LEARN!
WE FEARLESS FANATICS ALWAYS HAVE A METHOD TO OUR MADNESS!

YEEOWTCH!!
I SURE OUT-SMARTED MYSELF THAT TIME!!
I FORGOT HOW STRONG HIS ARMOR IS!!
OHHH! MY ACHIN' TOE!!

HAH! PERHAPS NOW YOU REALIZE HOW TOTALLY HELPLESS YOU ARE AGAINST ME!
I CAN WITHSTAND YOUR MOST POTENT ATTACK..AND EFFORTLESSLY SHRUG IT OFF!

IN FACT, SO SURE AM I OF MY POWER...
..THAT I SHALL DESCEND TO YOUR HEIGHT FOR MY FINAL ATTACK!

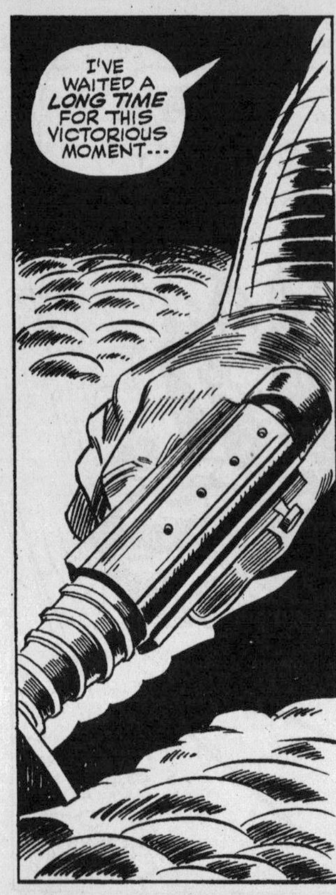
I'VE WAITED A LONG TIME FOR THIS VICTORIOUS MOMENT---

AND, SINCE IT SHALL BE OUR LAST MEETING--- IN THIS LIFE---
I WANT TO SAVOR IT---TO THE FULLEST EXTENT!

MISTER, YOU JUST SAVORED YOURSELF RIGHT BACK INTO THE SOUP!
WHAT DID YOU THINK I'D BE DOING WHILE YOU WERE WAVING THAT POP-GUN AT ME?
YOU ARROGANT FOOL! A MERE OPEN-HANDED TAP CAN'T HURT ME!

GUESS AGAIN, STILTY!
WHAT IF THAT "MERE TAP" HAPPENS TO CLICK YOUR STILT ACTIVATOR BUTTON---SHOOTING YOU FORWARD LIKE A CATAPULT?!!
WELL, I HATE TO BE A PARTY POOP, BUT I THINK I'LL RUN ALONG NOW!

HEY, JOE---DID YOU JUST HEAR SOME-THING LIKE A WALL CAVIN' IN?
YOU KNOW IT, PAL! LET'S GRAB A LOOK-SEE!

SOUNDED LIKE IT CAME FROM THE ALLEY OVER THERE!
GET YOUR GUN! ANYTHING THAT CAN MAKE A RACKET LIKE THE ONE WE HEARD COULD BE MIGHTY DANGEROUS.
POLICE
SAY! WE WERE RIGHT! LOOK AHEAD OF US... THAT RUBBLE OVER THERE..!

IT WASN'T AN EXPLOSION, OR THE WHOLE WALL WOULD'A CAVED IN!
IT LOOKS LIKE A BATTERING RAM JUST PLOWED INTO THE PLACE!
WE MAY NEVER LEARN THE ANSWER! THERE'S NOBODY IN THERE NOW!

BUT, THERE'S ONE MAN WHO KNOWS THE ANSWER... AS HE ARRIVES HOME, NURSING A PAINFUL LEG..!
HOOO BOY! WE COSTUMED CRUSADERS SURE HAVE TO TAKE OUR LUMPS!
...HOPE I CAN LOSE THIS LIMP PRETTY SOON!

SOMETHING ON THE FLOOR... A SMALL BOX!
WHATEVER IT IS, I KNOW I DIDN'T LEAVE IT THERE!
FIN-EST RECORDING TAPE
I'D BETTER GIVE IT THE ONCE-OVER!

FEELS LIKE THE KIND OF BOX THAT RECORDING TAPE IS PACKAGED IN...!
IT COULD BE A MESSAGE FROM FOGGY ..OR KAREN!
FIN-EST RECORD

WELL, I'LL JUST GET OUT OF MY WORKING DUDS FIRST---
AND TAPE UP MY ANKLE BEFORE THE SWELLING GETS TOO PAINFUL!
THEN I'LL GIVE IT A LISTEN!
IF IT'S ANYTHING TO WORRY ABOUT, I'M IN NO HURRY TO HEAR IT, ANYWAY!
I'VE ENOUGH LITTLE PROBLEMS RIGHT NOW TO KEEP ME FROM FEELING NEGLECTED!

OOOOOOOO!!
I'D RATHER FACE A KABOODLE OF CROOKS THAN HAVE TO--OUCH!.. TIGHTEN THIS ANY MORE---
BUT, I'M SUPPOSED TO-- OUCH!--BE FEARLESS-- SO HERE GOES..!

WELL, GLAD THAT'S OVER!
NOW, I MIGHT AS WELL HEAR WHAT'S ON THIS TAPE--!

TRIED TO PHONE YOU, MATT..: BUT YOU WERE OUT!
JUST WANTED TO WARN YOU THAT STILTMAN HAS BEEN SIGHTED IN THE CITY...
SO DON'T COME TO THE OFFICE ALONE---CALL US FIRST!
IT'S FOGGY'S VOICE!
NICE OF HIM TO WORRY ABOUT ME THIS WAY!

BUT, HE CAN REST EASY!
I WON'T VISIT THE OFFICE ALONE..
NOT TILL I'VE PUT THE EMISSARIES OF EVIL ON ICE!
OR VICE VERSA!

THEN, JUST BEFORE TWILIGHT, THE NEXT DAY...
MY SINISTER SPARRING PARTNERS DON'T USUALLY MAKE THE SCENE TILL IT GETS DARK...
SO I MIGHT AS WELL SOAK UP SOME BALMY BREEZES HERE IN THE PARK WHILE I WAIT FOR ROUND TWO TO BEGIN!
27.

MY ANKLE FEELS FINE... MY RADAR SENSE IS WORKING LIKE A CHARM---AND EVEN MY HAIR TONIC ISN'T GREASY!
ALL I NEED IS KAREN PAGE BESIDE ME, AND--- NOPE! I'VE GOT TO GET OFF THAT KICK!
SOME "MAN WITHOUT FEAR" I AM--!
IT SCARES ME TO EVEN THINK OF THE GIRL I LOVE!

WHAT MATT MURDOCK DOES THINK ABOUT FOR THE NEXT FEW MINUTES WILL EVER REMAIN HIS OWN SECRET! AFTER ALL, WE'RE NOT MIND-READERS!
HOWEVER, WITH THE FALL OF DARKNESS, A NEW EVENT OCCURS...TO OCCUPY BOTH MATT AND US..!

REMEMBER US TELLING YOU THERE WERE FIVE EMISSARIES OF EVIL? WELL, WE KIDDED THEE NOT! HERE'S THE MISSING ONE...NONE OTHER THAN THE LOWDOWN, LIGHT-FOOTED LEAP FROG...!

WITH EACH OF US COVERING A DIFFERENT PART OF THE CITY, WE'RE SURE TO SMOKE OUT DAREDEVIL!
AND IT CAN'T BE SOON ENOUGH TO SUIT ME!
I OWE THAT CORNY, CONCEITED CLOWN PLENTY...
AND HE'S GONNA COLLECT IT-- IN SPADES!

THEN, SECONDS LATER...
I CAN'T BE MISTAKEN!!
IT'S THE LEAP FROG!
I'D KNOW HIS FOOTSTEPS ANYWHERE!

HE PASSED RIGHT BY ME... --ALL HE SAW WAS A BLIND MAN ON A PARK BENCH!
WHICH SUITS ME JUST FINE!

HOWEVER, I WOULDN'T WANT THIS EVENING TO BE A TOTAL WASTE FOR HIM..!
SPECIALLY SINCE DAREDEVIL IS PROBABLY THE ONE HE'S SEEKING!
28

HE'S MOVING SLOWLY... HAVING NO REASON TO SUSPECT ANYTHING YET!
BUT AFTER TONIGHT, HE'LL NEVER BE SO CARELESS AGAIN!

HOLD IT, FROGGY!
IT'S NOT POLITE TO COLD-SHOULDER AN OLD FRIEND LIKE ME!
DAREDEVIL!!
GEE, THANKS, PAL! IT'S SO NICE TO BE REMEMBERED!

LOOK OUT!
YOU'RE HEADING STRAIGHT FOR A CLUMP OF POISON IVY!
YOU SURE ARE LUCKY!
I STOPPED YOU JUST IN THE NICK OF TIME!

HEY... WATCH IT!
THAT'S A HECKUVA WAY TO SHOW YOUR GRATITUDE!
YOU LOUSY, LOUD-MOUTHED CREEP!! JUST WAIT...I'LL SHUT YOU UP FOR GOOD!
SPYOKK!
THERE!! WHAT DO YOU SAY TO THAT??
WELL, IF I DIDN'T KNOW BETTER--I'D SAY YOU'RE A VERY UNFRIENDLY PERSON!
OR MAYBE YOU'VE JUST BEEN TRYING TO TELL ME SOMETHING!
I'LL SAY ONE THING FOR YOU..
YOU'VE BEEN A REAL SPORT ABOUT THE WHOLE THING!

HEY... WAIT! I'M OVER HERE!
YOU WANT ME? COME'N GET ME!

HE PROBABLY THINKS I DON'T KNOW HE'S TRYING TO LEAD ME TO THE OTHERS...
WHERE THEY'RE WAITING TO TRAP ME!
BUT, I'VE NOTHING ELSE ON FOR TONIGHT-- AND I HATE BEING BORED!
THANNG!

WELL, WELL-- I SHOULD HAVE SUSPECTED THIS--!
WHAT BETTER PLACE TO SERVE AS A HIDE-OUT FOR ELECTRO--
THAN THE LARGEST ELECTRIC POWER PLANT IN THE WHOLE CITY!

BUT, I DON'T LIKE IT!---I'VE LOST TRACK OF THE LEAP FROG!
ALL THE HIGH VOLTAGE LINES HAVE CONFUSED MY SENSES!! NEED TIME TO--- UNHHH!!
WELCOME, DAREDEVIL!
WE'VE BEEN WAITING FOR YOU!
THE GLADIATOR!!

SORRY WE DIDN'T HAVE TIME TO HIRE A BRASS BAND!
BUT WE'LL TRY TO MAKE YOU FEEL WANTED IN OUR OWN HUMBLE WAY!
TAKE IT EASY, GLADIATOR! WE EACH WANT OUR CRACK AT HIM!
JUST AS I THOUGHT-- THEY'RE ALL HERE!

STAND ASIDE, GENTLEMEN!..
ELECTRO WILL TACKLE HIM NEXT!
MY SENSES ARE BEGINNING TO CLEAR.. TO CUT THROUGH THE THICK BLANKET OF VOLTAGE!
MANAGED TO DODGE HIS ELECTRIC BOLT BY A SPLIT-SECOND!
WAIT! WHAT ARE YOU DOING?
STAY BACK!! ALL OF YOU..!
NOT A CHANCE, MISTER! DAREDEVIL'S TOO SLIPPERY FOR ANY ONE OF US!
WE'RE GONNA TEAR INTO HIM ALL AT ONCE!
THE GLADIATOR'S RIGHT! YOU DON'T TAKE CHANCES WITH ONE SUCH AS HE!
THAT ENOUGH TALK...
LET'S GET 'IM!
NOW I'VE GOT ALL FIVE OF THEM PIN-POINTED!
SO HERE GOES NOTHING!
LOOK OUT! HE'S TENSING.. PREPARING TO DO SOME-THING..!
RELAX! WHAT CAN HE... UNNHHH!
WOULDJA BELIEVE A FAST BACK-FLIP?
32

NOW THAT THE MATADOR SOFTENED YOU UP, BIG MAN...
JUST HOLD THAT POSE..!

I WANNA REMEMBER YOU JUST AS YOU ARE!
THE LEAP FROG... COMING AT ME FROM BEHIND!

NICE TRY, CROAKY..
UH-OH! NOW STILT-MAN IS ATTACKING!
IF I CAN WHIP OUT MY BILLY CLUB IN TIME...!

FOR HEAVEN'S SAKE, STILTY... WAIT YOUR TURN!
FTIK!

AND THAT GOES FOR YOU TOO, YOU HIGH-VOLTAGE HEEL!

GLADIATOR!! HOW MANY TIMES MUST I TELL YOU..?
THAT ARMOR OF YOURS JUST ISN'T BUILT FOR HIGH-SPEED LEAPING!
WHILE MY LITTLE PLAYSUIT IS DIFFERENT!
33.

NO MATTER HOW FAST YOU ARE... NO MATTER HOW AGILE...
NO ONE THAT LIVES CAN LONG RESIST MY SHATTERING ELECTRICAL POWER... NOT EVEN DAREDEVIL!

SIZZZT!
I AGREE WITH YOU, ELECTRO!!
WHICH IS WHY I'D JUST AS SOON DUCK... AND LET ONE OF YOUR OTHER GALLOPIN' GOONS TRY A BLAST... JUST FOR SIZE!

AND, WHILE YOU'RE WAITING TO CHARGE YOURSELF UP AGAIN, I'LL PROVE I DON'T PLAY ANY FAVORITES!
TWO SETS OF FOOTSTEPS.. RUSHING AT ME FROM SEPARATE DIRECTIONS!

SO, I'LL TAKE THE HIGH ROAD... AND LET THEM FIGHT IT OUT!
THOKK!

YOU'RE MAKING FOOLS OF ALL OF THEM, DAREDEVIL!
THAT MAKES YOU A BIGGER FOOL, EH?
BUT, I'M BIGGER.. STRONGER THAN THEY ARE!
STILL YOU MOCK ME, DO YOU?
BUT YOUR JEERS WILL TURN TO PANIC WHEN MY WRIST DISCS START SPINNING!
AND THEY ARE STARTING --NOW!

THANKS FOR THE WARNING, GLADDY!
BAH! YOU CAN'T STAY OUT OF MY REACH FOREVER!

DON'T WORRY ABOUT IT, SON...
I DON'T INTEND TO!

YOU OUT-SMARTED YOURSELF THAT TIME!
NOW THAT YOU'RE ON YOUR FEET AGAIN, YOU CAN NO LONGER DODGE MY DEADLY ATTACK!

IN THAT CASE, I WON'T EVEN TRY!
CAREFUL, CHUM... THESE STEEL BEAMS COST MONEY!
YOU FOOL! THAT USELESS PIECE OF METAL CAN'T HELP YOU!
NOW YOU TELL ME!

HE'S RIGHT!
HIS SPINNING BLADE IS SLICING THROUGH-- LIKE A HOT KNIFE THROUGH BUTTER!
THERE'S NO NEED FOR ME TO RUSH..!
I'LL GIVE YOU TIME.. TO CONTEMPLATE WHAT YOUR FATE WILL BE...IN A FEW MORE SECONDS!

HAH!! YOU MOVED LIKE AN EEL, TRYING TO LOSE YOURSELF AMONG THE OTHERS...
--BUT I WAS TOO CLEVER FOR YOU!
AND NOW...YOU ARE TOTALLY HELPLESS BENEATH MY ALL-CONCEALING CLOAK!!

THUS, IT SHALL BE I... THE MARVELOUS MATADOR.. WHO BRINGS YOU TO BAY!
ALTHOUGH POSSESSED OF LESS SUPER-POWER THAN ANY HERE-- MY SKILL...MY SPEED..HAVE BROUGHT ME THE ULTIMATE VICTORY!

NOW YOU MAY TAKE THE DEFEATED DAREDEV...
THAT'S ONLY YOUR FIRST SURPRISE, BULL-THROWER...
WHA..?!! IT'S.. THE LEAP-FROG!!

THIS IS THE SECOND!!

IT CANNOT BE!
ONE MAN..ALONE AND UNAIDED... CAN'T HOLD US ALL OFF!
NOT EVEN DAREDEVIL!
WE WERE CARELESS.. OVER-CONFIDENT..
BUT NOW IT WILL BE DIFFERENT..!

YOU SAID A MOUTHFUL, ELECTRO!
IT'LL BE DIFFERENT, ALL RIGHT--!!
SINCE I PICKED UP THIS COIL OF WIRE..
IT'S GONNA BE DAREDEVIL WHO DOES THE ATTACKING NOW!

AND THEN, BEFORE THE STARTLED EMISSARIES OF EVIL CAN MAKE ANOTHER MOVE---
HE LASSOED US!
IS HE NAIVE ENOUGH TO THINK WE CANNOT BREAK FREE?
I'LL SPLIT THIS WIRE LIKE A MATCHSTICK!!
SURE, I KNOW HOW EASY IT WOULD BE FOR YOU TO BREAK FREE...
EXCEPT FOR ONE THING--!

I'M ATTACHING THE OTHER END OF THE WIRE TO THE POWER TRANSFORMER...
...IN SUCH A WAY THAT IT REVERSES THE FLOW OF CURRENT!

WHICH MEANS THAT ELECTRO'S OWN POWER WILL ELECTROCUTE HIM---AND ALL OF YOU---IF THE WIRE IS BROKEN!
BUT, DON'T WORRY...THE POLICE WILL SHUT OFF THE CURRENT WHEN THEY ARRIVE---
SO THAT YOU'LL ALL REACH JAIL IN TIP-TOP CONDITION!
THANKS FOR THE WORKOUT, GENTS--IT'S BEEN A BLAST!
38.

AND SO...NOT LONG AFTERWARDS...
I HEARD OVER THE RADIO THAT STILT-MAN HAD BEEN CAPTURED...
MATT! WHERE ON EARTH HAVE YOU BEEN?
WE WERE SO WORRIED ABOUT YOU..
SO I FIGURED IT WAS SAFE ENOUGH TO MEANDER BACK TO WORK TODAY!
FOGGY AND I HAVE BEEN PHONING YOU ALL DAY!

SORRY...I SHOULD HAVE TOLD YOU...
I WAS VISITING BROTHER MIKE...AND I MUST HAVE LOST TRACK OF THE TIME!
KAREN! DID YOU MOVE THE SMALL FILE CABINET AGAIN?
OH NO.. THERE IT IS!

I MUST NEVER FORGET TO ACT LIKE A BLIND MAN...NO MATTER HOW DIFFICULT IT MAY BE!
SAY! YOU STILL HAVEN'T FILED THIS BRIEF!
CAN'T ANY-THING GET DONE AROUND HERE WHILE I'M GONE?

I GIVE UP!
MEN! WHO CAN FIGURE THEM OUT!
WE SPEND THE DAY WORRYING ABOUT HIM---TRYING TO FIND HIM...
AND HE WONDERS WHY WE DIDN'T FINISH OUR WORK!!
I FEEL LIKE A HEEL..BUT AT LEAST THEY SUSPECT NOTHING!

OH, KAREN...KAREN!
IF YOU ONLY KNEW...HOW I LONG TO TAKE YOU IN MY ARMS...TELL YOU WHO I REALLY AM..!
BUT I MUST NOT..I CAN-NOT...I DARE NOT!!
SLAM!
I LOVE YOU TOO MUCH TO ALLOW YOU TO SHARE MY SECRET--AND ITS DANGERS!

NO..MATT MURDOCK HAS ALWAYS BEEN A LONER...AND A LONER HE MUST STAY.. SO LONG AS DAREDEVIL LIVES!!
THE END
...FOR NOW!
39

FABULOUS FAR-OUT FACTS ABOUT THE MAN WITHOUT FEAR!

#1 DD's RIOTOUS RADAR SENSE!

A BUILT-IN "RADAR" ABILITY ALLOWS DAREDEVIL TO "SEE" OBJECTS ALL AROUND HIM BY SCANNING THE AIR WAVES IN HIS IMMEDIATE VICINITY!

#2 DD's TITANIC SENSE OF TOUCH!

SO SENSITIVE ARE DAREDEVIL'S FINGERTIPS, THAT HE CAN "READ" ANY PAGE BY MERELY FEELING THE IMPRESSION WHICH THE INK HAS LEFT UPON THE PAPER!

#3 DD's BUILT-IN LIE DETECTOR!

BEING ABLE TO HEAR A MAN'S HEARTBEAT ENABLES DAREDEVIL TO WHEN A LIE IS BEING TOLD--MERELY BY SENSING THE SUBJECT'S SPEEDED-UP PULSE RATE--LIKE A LIVING LIE DETECTOR!

EVER WONDER HOW A BLIND MAN CAN FIGHT SO EFFECTIVELY?
WELL THEN, WOULDJA BELIEVE--?
MY SUPER-KEEN POWER OF HEARING, COUPLED WITH MY RADAR SENSE, MAKES IT PRACTICALLY IMPOSSIBLE FOR ANY WOULD-BE FOE EVER TO TAKE ME BY SURPRISE!
MY SENSE OF TOUCH IS SO ACUTE THAT I INSTINCTIVELY KNOW JUST WHAT PART OF MY OPPONENT'S BODY TO STRIKE, IN ORDER TO GAIN THE UPPER HAND IN ANY TYPE OF BATTLE!
IN FACT, I OFTEN FEEL SORRY FOR ANY OUT-CLASSED ENEMY WHO HAS ONLY HIS SIGHT TO RELY ON!
MY RAPID-FIRE REFLEXES ALLOW ME TO MOVE FASTER, AND WITH GREATER ACCURACY, THAN ANY NORMAL MAN!
--AND BY THE WAY, ALL THE TIME I SPEND IN MY PRIVATE GYM, WORKING OUT HOUR AFTER, DOESN'T DO ME ANY HARM EITHER WHEN THE CHIPS ARE DOWN!

GATHER 'ROUND, HEROES! THE TIME HAS COME FOR--
AN EXPLANATION!
WE RECEIVE MANY LETTERS FROM NEW READERS ASKING THE SAME BEWILDERED QUESTION-- "WHO IS MIKE MURDOCK?" THOSE OF YOU WHO HAVE JOINED US RECENTLY, SEEM RATHER PUZZLED AS TO WHY MY BROTHER MIKE AND I ARE NEVER SEEN TOGETHER AT ANY TIME!
ALSO, THEY FIGURE OUT HOW A SQUARE LIKE OL' MATTHEW CAN HAVE A SWINGIN' SWEETIE LIKE ME FOR A TWIN BROTHER!
SO, FOR THE BENEFIT OF ALL YOU JOHNNY-COME LATELIES-- AS WELL AS FOR OUR OWN AMUSEMENT, WE'RE GONNA GIVE YOU THE LOW-DOWN-- LIKE RIGHT NOW--!
THUS PROVING THAT, WHILE OTHER MAGS MAY BE BIGGER, PRETTIER, RICHER, OR SMARTER--THE ONE THAT YOU'RE READING NOW IS EASILY THE BIGGEST-HEARTED BOOK OF THEM ALL!
AND NOW, DARING ONE, PREPARE YOURSELF FOR ANOTHER EPIC EXPOSÉ FROM YOUR BATTY BULLPEN--

EVEN OUR NEWEST AND MOST UNINITIATED READER KNOWS BY NOW THAT MATT MURDOCK IS A CAUTIOUS, CALM, CONSERVATIVE COUNSELLOR-AT-LAW!
--WHO ALSO HAPPENS TO BE TOTALLY BLIND!
BUT, BENEATH THIS QUIET EXTERIOR LURKS STILL ANOTHER PERSONALITY...
A PERSONALITY THAT WAS ORIGINALLY CREATED BY YOURS TRULY, IN ISH #25, FOR THE PURPOSE OF CONVINCING FOGGY AND KAREN THAT SOMEONE ELSE IS REALLY DAREDEVIL--!
I DECIDED TO INVENT A TWIN BROTHER FOR MYSELF--ONE WHO WOULD BE A REAL SWINGER!
I FIGURED I COULD PASS HIM OFF TO ANYONE WHO GOT SUSPICIOUS --AS THE REAL DAREDEVIL!
BUT THEN--AS ALL FAITHFUL FEARLESS FANS KNOW FULL WELL--
THE PECULIAR PERSONALITY OF MISCHIEVOUS MIKE REALLY BEGAN TO GRAB ME!
I ENJOYED PLAYING THE ROLL OF MY HIP, HAPPY, HEDONISTIC TWIN!
ESPECIALLY SINCE IT WAS SO EASY FOR ME TO MAKE THE CHANGE FROM MELLOW MATT TO MERRY MIKE!
ALL I NEED DO IS RUFFLE UP MY HAIR--CHANGE TO SOME LOUD, SPORTY THREADS--
AND SWITCH MY FROSTED SPECTACLES FOR A PAIR OF GROOVY SUNGLASSES!
AND PRESTO--I BECOME THE COOLEST CAT IN TOWN--THE ZINGIEST, GLITZIEST LOUDMOUTH YOU KNOW--THE MOST FUN-LOVIN', FRANTIC FRAUD OF 'EM ALL--
THE PEOPLE'S CHOICE--MARVELOUS MIKE MURDOCK, IN PERSON!
BUT, NOW THAT YOU KNOW MY SECRET, TIGER--YOU'VE GOTTA MAKE ME A PROMISE--!
DON'T GO BLABBIN' IT TO STAN OR GENE!
THOSE TWO CORNBALLS WOULD NEVER BELIEVE YOU ANYWAY!
2

A COLORFUL COLLECTION OF DD'S CAST OF CHARACTERS!
ALTHOUGH IT SEEMS SO HOPELESS... A GIRL CAN ALWAYS DREAM!
Yours, till we meet again! Karen Page

A COLORFUL COLLECTION OF DD'S CAST OF CHARACTERS!
AS IF MY PAL MATT WASN'T ENOUGH COMPETITION...
..HIS IDIOT BROTHER MIKE HAD TO CRAWL OUT OF THE WOODWORK!
Oh well, somebody's gotta carry the Spear!
"Foggy" Nelson

A COLORFUL COLLECTION OF DD'S CAST OF CHARACTERS!

A COLORFUL COLLECTION OF DD'S CAST OF CHARACTERS!
HEADS UP, HEROES! HERE'S THE OL' SWASHBUCKLER HIMSELF!
Whatever you do... Wherever you go... always Hang Loose!
—D.D.

A DAZZLING DD MEMORY PAGE!
THE GALVANIZING
GLADIATOR
FIRST APPEARED IN DD #18
THE VERY SIGHT OF THIS BLUDGEONING HUMAN BLOCKBUSTER IS ENOUGH TO MAKE STRONG MEN QUIVER! WITH HIS TWIN WRIST BLADES WHIRLING, THE INCREDIBLY POWERFUL IS CERTAINLY ONE OF THE MOST DANGEROUS FOES DD HAS EVER FOUGHT!

A DAZZLING DD MEMORY PAGE!
THE LARCENOUS
LEAP FROG
FIRST APPEARED IN DD #25
IF A HIGH-JUMPING FROG WERE THE SIZE OF A HUMAN, AND POSSESSED OF A HUMAN BRAIN, HE WOULD BE ALMOST INVINCIBLE!
SO IT WAS WITH THE LEAP FROG --UNTIL HE DARED TANGLE WITH OL' DD!

A DAZZLING DD MEMORY PAGE!
THE OMINOUS OWL
FIRST APPEARED IN DD #3
ORIGINALLY KNOWN AS THE "OVERLORD OF CRIME", THE OMNIVOROUS OWL HAS THE POWER TO ACTUALLY GLIDE THRU THE AIR ON THE SLIGHTEST WIND CURRENTS! BUT, HIS MAIN SOURCES OF MENACE ARE HIS DEMONIAC BRAIN AND HIS MERCILESS HEART!

A DAZZLING DD MEMORY PAGE!
THE MASKED MARAUDER
FIRST APPEARED in DD#16
IN MEMORIAM
OF ALL D.D.'S FOES, THE MASKED MARAUDER CAME CLOSEST TO LEARNING HIS TRUE IDENTITY ...TILL HIS DRAMATIC DEATH ENDED HIS THREAT FOR ALL TIME!

FIRST, YOU'VE GOT TO DIG UP AN INNOCENT-LOOKING *CANE* WHICH COMES IN *TWO SECTIONS*... WHICH CAN BE SNAPPED *TOGETHER* OR WHISKED *APART* IN THE SPACE OF A SINGLE HEARTBEAT!

AT THE STROKE OF MIDNIGHT!

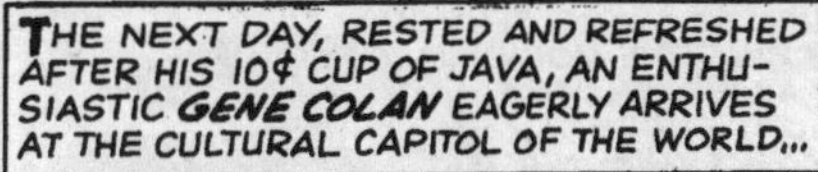

PREEEEESENTING: AN ACTUAL, UNREHEARSED

STORY CONFERENCE WITH STAN AND GENE!

NOW DIG THIS--DD's ON TOP OF THE TALLEST MOUNTAIN IN TIBET!
HOW DID HE GET UP THERE?
YOU CAN FIGURE THAT OUT!
HE'S THERE TO RESCUE POOR, HELPLESS, LOVELY, SCREAMING KAREN WHO'S BEEN CAPTURED BY BARON ZEMO!
BUT, HE'S DEAD! HOW CAN WE BRING HIM BACK TO LIFE?
DON'T WORRY-- YOU'LL THINK OF SOMETHING!

SHEEESH! THIS IS SOME GREAT PLOT YOU'RE GIVING ME!
PLEASE! DON'T EMBARRASS ME WITH YOUR OVERWHELMING GRATITUDE!
I'D DO AS MUCH FOR ANY OF OUR ARTISTS!
NO WONDER THEY'RE ALL NERVOUS WRECKS!

NOW JUST TO MAKE THINGS INTERESTING, THE MOUNTAIN IS REALLY A LIVE VOLCANO-- AND IT SUDDENLY BLOWS UP--IN A GIGANTIC ERUPTION!
YOU MEAN-- WITH DAREDEVIL ON TOP OF IT??
NATCH! CAN'T YOU SEE IT, MAN? IT'LL BE A REAL GAS!

BUT HOW IN THE NAME OF FORBUSH --WILL WE BE ABLE TO SAVE HIM??
SAVE HIM?!!
WHY MUST I ALWAYS BE PLAGUED BY DETAILS??
3

I'M STILL WAITING, LEE!
HMMM--THIS CALLS FOR REAL HIGH-LEVEL THINKING!
MAYBE I'LL ASK MY WIFE--!
WAIT! WAIT! I'M GETTING IT! AHA!! I HAVE IT!
OKAY, CHUM-- WITH DD ON AN ERUPTING VOLCANO-- WHAT DO WE DO NEXT?

IT'LL BE A NEW MILESTONE FOR MARVEL!
WE START A NEW MAG--CALLED: FOGGY, THE MAN FILLED WITH FEAR!
IT'S LIKE LIVING A NIGHTMARE!
THE EVER-LOVIN' BLUE-EYED END!

MARVEL COMICS GROUP

12¢ IND.

35 DEC

APPROVED BY THE COMICS CODE AUTHORITY

HERE COMES...

DAREDEVIL

THE MAN WITHOUT FEAR!

MCG

"DAREDEVIL DIES FIRST!"

DAREDEVIL, THE MAN WITHOUT FEAR!™
"DAREDEVIL DIES FIRST!"
FEATURING-- THE TERRIBLE THREAT OF--
THE TRAPSTER!
--AND GUEST-STARRING--
--JUST TRY TO GUESS!
?
HE CAME HURTLING IN--THRU THE WINDOW!
AH! YOU RECOGNIZE ME! I AM INDEED FLATTERED!
BUT HOW?? WE'RE 15 STORIES HIGH--
--WITH A SHEER CONCRETE WALL ALL THE WAY UP!
HANG IN THERE, ACTION-LOVERS!!
STAN (THE MAN) LEE and GENE (THE DEAN) COLAN
DID THIS ONE JUST FOR YOU!
INKED BY: J. TARTAGLIONE
LETTERED BY: A. SIMEK
AND NOW LET'S MOVE--!!
CRASH
1

QUICK! THE PHONE! WE'VE GOT TO CALL THE POLICE!
I'LL GET IT! I'M CLOSER!
COME NOW! HOW NAIVE CAN YOU BE?
I CAN'T TAKE A HAND WITHOUT GIVING MY SECRET AWAY!
DO YOU THINK I'LL JUST STAND BY QUIETLY AND ALLOW YOU TO SUMMON HELP?? THE TRAPSTER IS ANYTHING BUT A FOOL!
LOOK OUT! HE'S GOT A GUN!
HOW VERY PERCEPTIVE OF YOU, MY FRIEND!

SPLAT
BUT--IT'S FAR MORE THAN A CONVENTIONAL WEAPON--!

IT CAN PUT A VICTIM COMPLETELY OUT OF ACTION--
--WITHOUT CAUSING ANY PERMANENT HARM!
PASTE!! THE GUN SHOOTS PAS--UNHHH!

I DON'T GET IT, TRAPSTER! WHY'D YOU BREAK IN HERE?
WHAT DO YOU WANT WITH US?
INFORMATION, MURDOCK! JUST CALL ME A CLIENT!
BUT WHY US? HOW DO YOU KNOW MY NAME?
EASY--I SIMPLY LOOKED YOU UP!
NOW JUST STAND THERE--AND LISTEN--!

I KNOW YOU'RE BLIND--SO I WON'T BOTHER PASTING YOU DOWN!
I JUST WANT A LEGAL OPINION--AND I BELIEVE IN GETTING THE BEST!
REMIND ME TO TAKE OUR NAME OUT OF THE PHONE BOOK AFTER THIS!
EASY, FOGGY!
OKAY, TRAPSTER! WHAT DO YOU WANT TO KNOW?

IF A MURDER IS COMMITTED--BUT THE BODY'S NEVER FOUND--CAN THE KILLER BE SENTENCED?
YOU MEAN--IF THERE'S NO CORPUS DELECTI--CAN MURDER BE PROVEN?
THAT DEPENDS ON OTHER CIRCUMSTANCES!
DON'T BE TRICKY WITH ME, MURDOCK! I WANT A YES OR NO!
IT'S NOT THAT SIMPLE!
ANYWAY, WHO'S YOUR INTENDED VICTIM?

DAREDEVIL! I'VE FIGURED OUT A WAY TO GET RID OF HIM WITHOUT ANYONE EVER PROVING IT!
I'VE BEEN DEFEATED TOO OFTEN--BY THE FANTASTIC FOUR! I NEED A VICTORY--TO WIN BACK THE RESPECT OF MY OTHER PARTNERS!
SOUNDS TO ME LIKE YOU NEED A GOOD HEAD-SHRINKER!
YOU'LL THINK DIFFERENTLY--AFTER DAREDEVIL IS GONE!
AND NOW I KNOW JUST HOW TO GET RID OF HIM!
HE'S ESCAPING! AND I DARE NOT TRY TO STOP HIM--YET!

I'LL LEAVE NOW--ON MY ANTI-GRAV FLYER!
JUST SEND ME YOUR BILL--WHEN YOU CAN FIND ME!
EVERYONE KNOWS NELSON AND MURDOCK ARE FRIENDLY WITH DAREDEVIL!
THEY'RE SURE TO TELL HIM OF MY THREAT!
THEN HE'LL COME AFTER ME--
SAVING ME THE TROUBLE OF FINDING HIM!

MATT! YOU'VE GOTTA GET THIS PASTE OFF US!
IT MAY TAKE HOURS TO EVAPORATE BY ITSELF!
MATT! REACH BEHIND YOU--ON MY DESK--TRY TO FEEL FOR MY BOTTLE OF NAIL POLISH REMOVER!
THAT MAY LOOSEN IT!

THAT'S IT! KEEP POURING IT RIGHT THERE!
IS IT COMING LOOSE?
YES! LUCKY HE USED A WEAK PASTE MIX-TURE!

YOU'D BETTER CALL YOUR BROTHER MIKE--ON THE DOUBLE--AND WARN HIM, MATT!
OR GIVE ME THE NUMBER --AND I'LL DO IT FOR YOU!
UH OH! THINK FAST, MATTHEW!
SORRY, FOGGY! HIS NUMBER'S UNLISTED! EVEN I DON'T KNOW IT!

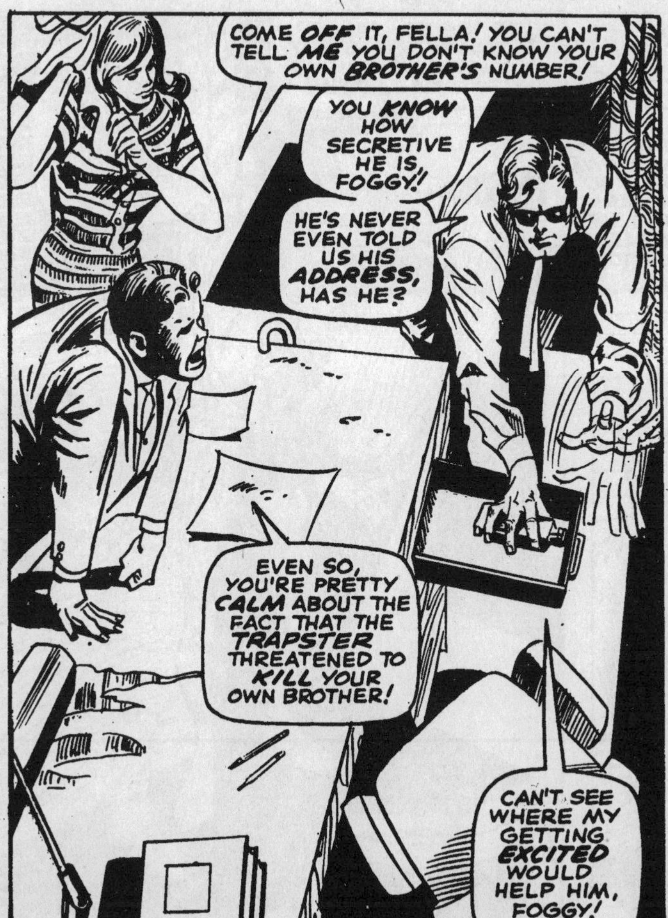
COME OFF IT, FELLA! YOU CAN'T TELL ME YOU DON'T KNOW YOUR OWN BROTHER'S NUMBER!
YOU KNOW HOW SECRETIVE HE IS, FOGGY!
HE'S NEVER EVEN TOLD US HIS ADDRESS, HAS HE?
EVEN SO, YOU'RE PRETTY CALM ABOUT THE FACT THAT THE TRAPSTER THREATENED TO KILL YOUR OWN BROTHER!
CAN'T SEE WHERE MY GETTING EXCITED WOULD HELP HIM, FOGGY!

MATT MURDOCK! WE ALL KNOW THAT YOU'VE VISITED MIKE BEFORE!
YOU MUST KNOW HIS ADDRESS!
HOW CAN YOU BE SO UNCONCERNED ABOUT YOUR OWN BROTHER!
MIKE CAN TAKE CARE OF HIMSELF, KAREN!
YES! NO THANKS TO YOU!

LET'S GO, FOGGY!
AT LEAST WE CAN NOTIFY THE POLICE-- AND THEY'LL KEEP A LOOKOUT FOR THE TRAPSTER!
SURE! AND WE'LL LEAVE MATT HERE! HE CAN ALWAYS "LOOK AFTER HIMSELF!"
HOW CAN I BLAME THEM FOR THE WAY THEY FEEL? I'D FEEL THE SAME WAY!

I'M AFRAID I OUT-SMARTED MYSELF WHEN I TOOK ON A THIRD IDENTITY--THAT OF MY OWN "TWIN BROTHER", MIKE!
I NEVER DREAMED IT WOULD LEAD TO SUCH EMBARRASSING COMPLICATIONS!
NOW, MY PARTNER AND BEST FRIEND THINKS I'M A COWARD--
--AND THE GIRL I LOVE HAS LOST ALL RESPECT FOR ME!
IT'S LUCKY I CAN MAKE IT AS A SUPER-SWINGER--
'CAUSE AS A DIPLOMAT-- I'M ONE BIG WASHOUT!
SLAM!

ANYWAY, WHILE I DON'T DOUBT THAT THE TRAPSTER MEANS TO ATTACK DAREDEVIL--
I CAN'T HELP FEELING THERE'S MORE TO HIS LITTLE PLAN THAN DEFEATING OL' HORNHEAD!
AND THERE'S ONLY ONE WAY TO LEARN WHAT HE'S REALLY UP TO--!

IF THE SO-CALLED TRAPSTER IS OUT THERE SEARCHING FOR DAREDEVIL--
I'M GONNA MAKE SURE THAT THE FEARLESS ONE IS MIGHTY EASY TO FIND!

I'VE GOT TO BE ON MY TOES ALL THE WAY!
I'LL BE FIGHTING A WEAPON THAT CAN PUT ME OUT OF ACTION IF IT HITS ME--
IN THE HANDS OF A KILLER WHO RIDES AN ANTI-GRAV FLYER!
ONE THING'S FOR SURE--A PICNIC THIS WON'T BE!
BUT, ON THE OTHER HAND, I'M NOT EXACTLY A PUSHOVER MYSELF!
IF ONLY I KNEW HOW TO SQUARE MYSELF WITH KAREN AND FOGGY!

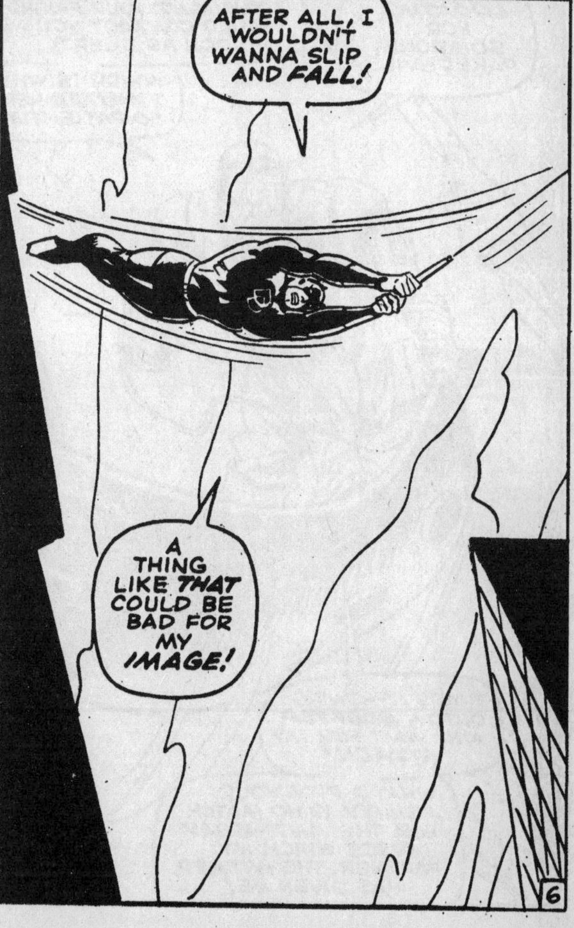

UH OH! THE OL' RADAR SENSE HAS ALREADY LATCHED ONTO SOMETHING--JUST ABOVE ME!
I'LL BET THAT HUMAN GLUE-POT WAS NEARBY ALL THE TIME!
LOOKING FOR SOMEONE, DAREDEVIL??
I THOUGHT YOUR FRIENDS WOULD CONTACT YOU AS SOON AS I LEFT!
WHICH IS WHY I WAITED HERE SO PATIENTLY!
THAT'S IT--SWING ONTO A ROOFTOP AND WAIT FOR MY ATTACK!
WHAT A PITY YOUR AGILITY IS NO MATCH FOR THE ANTI-GRAV DISCS WHICH MY PARTNER, THE WIZARD, HAS GIVEN ME!
THE WINGLESS WIZARD! I'VE HEARD OF HIM!
SO HE PROVIDED THE TRAPSTER'S FLYING DEVICE!
NOW, SINCE I'VE NOTHING AGAINST YOU PERSONALLY, I'LL MAKE THIS AS FAST AS POSSIBLE!

SPAAT!
HOOO BOY! HE'S PLAYIN' FOR KEEPS NOW!
WELL, DD CAN PLAY THAT WAY, TOO!

I MAY BE EARTH-BOUND, FELLA--
FOOL! WHAT GOOD WILL THAT DO YOU?
BUT I DON'T HAVETA STAY THAT WAY!

FOR ONE THING, IT KEEPS ME OUT IN THE FRESH AIR!
AND, FOR ANOTHER--

IT'LL BRING ME CLOSE ENOUGH TO WHUMP THE DAYLIGHTS OUTTA YOU!
LOOK SHARP, LAD--I WOULDN'T WANT YOU TO MISS ANY OF THIS!
SWISH
8

THERE! NOW WASN'T THAT WORTH WAITING FOR, TRAPPY?
S'MATTER, SWEETIE?? CAT GOT YOUR TONGUE?
9

I'VE GOT TO MOVE FAST-- MUSTN'T LOSE THE ADVANTAGE!
IF HE EVER TAGS ME WITH THAT PASTE GUN, I'LL HAVE HAD IT!

ZOK!

UNHH! THAT'S WHAT I GET-- FOR TRYING TOO HARD--!
BUT ONE LUCKY BLOW ISN'T THE FIGHT-- I HOPE!
I'M ASHAMED OF YOU, LAD! AFTER ALL, I'M YOUR GUEST!
SO WHERE'S YOUR HOSTMANSHIP??

NOW, MISTER-- SUPPOSE YOU LAND THIS TUB-- LIKE FAST!
I'LL DO IT! I'LL DO IT! JUST LET GO!

BUT, AS DAREDEVIL RELAXES HIS GRIP, THE WILY TRAPSTER DESPERATELY ROTATES A NEARBY DISC--
CLICK!

WITH THE MAIN ANTI-GRAV DISC THUS DISENGAGED, THE OTHER SUCH DEVICES ALSO BECOME LOOSENED, FALLING OFF, ONE BY ONE--THUS CAUSING THE SMALL FLYER TO SUDDENLY PLUMMET EARTHWARD--

HE MANAGED TO THROW THE SHIP OUT OF CONTROL--

TO FORCE ME TO RELEASE HIM!

HE'S ABLE TO GUIDE IT--TO DIRECT ITS DESCENT--

HE'S HOLDING ON--BUT HE EXPECTS ME TO FALL--!

HE ACHIEVED ONE OBJECTIVE! --I HAVE TO LET HIM GO--

IN ORDER TO BALANCE MYSELF--TO WITHSTAND THE IMPACT!

NOT WHILE I CAN STILL TOSS MY BILLY CLUB, YOU HAVEN'T!

SPAAT!
WHAT?!! YOU DARE MENTION THAT USELESS STICK TO SOMEONE WHO POSSESSES AN UNBEATABLE PASTE GUN!!

SO MUCH FOR YOUR BILLY CLUB!
AND NOW-- I'LL TRAP YOU WHERE YOU STAND!
NOT WHILE I CAN HANDSTAND MYSELF OUT OF THE WAY, YOU WON'T!

NOW--IF I CAN JUST FREE MY CLUB FROM THAT STICKY GOOK BEFORE HE CAN STRIKE AGAIN!!
12

HE'S RIGHT BEHIND ME-- ABOUT TO SHOOT SOME MORE PASTE MY WAY!
NOW-- EVERYTHING DEPENDS ON MY SPEED--!
MY CLUB'S FREE-- SO HERE GOES--!

UNHHH!!
SORRY ABOUT THIS, STICKUMS!

NOT AS SORRY AS YOU SOON WILL BE--!
AN ANTI-GRAV DISC!!
WHAT'S HE UP TO NOW?

HERE, BIG MAN--TRY THIS FOR SIZE!!
THANKS TO MY SPECIAL PASTE FORMULA--
THOSE DISCS WILL STICK TO ANYTHING!!
--ESPECIALLY TO AN OVER-CONFIDENT OAF LIKE YOU!
ZAT
CAN'T-- REMOVE THEM-- FAST ENOUGH!!
THEY'RE BEGINNING TO--LIFT ME-- OFF THE GROUND--!!

AND NOW FAREWELL!!
YOU PUT UP A MOST VALIANT FIGHT-- BUT AT LAST THE TRAPSTER HAS BECOME TOTALLY UNBEATABLE!
THE DISCS ARE ZOOMING ME SKYWARD! I'VE NO WAY TO CONTROL THEM!!
AT THE SPEED I'M GOING UP, I DAREN'T TAKE THEM OFF, EVEN IF I COULD--
--OR I'D FALL TO MY DEATH IN SECONDS!
THIS IS THE PERFECT CRIME I HAD PLANNED FOR YOU!
YOU'LL FLOAT HIGHER-- AND HIGHER--NEVER TO BE SEEN-- OR HEARD FROM-- AGAIN!!
AND NOW, PHASE TWO OF MY PLAN WILL TAKE ME TO-- THE BAXTER BUILDING!!

WITH THOSE TAUNTING WORDS HURLED AFTER THE ASCENDING DAREDEVIL, THE SEEMINGLY TRIUMPHANT TRAPSTER SPEEDILY LEAVES THE ROOFTOP, RACING TO A LONELY HIDEOUT ON THE CITY'S OUTSKIRTS--
EVERYTHING I NEED IS WAITING FOR ME HERE--IN THE WIZARD'S LAB!!
NOW, WITH MY MOST GLORIOUS VICTORY UNDER MY BELT, MY STREAK OF BAD LUCK IS OVER!
THEREFORE, I FINALLY HAVE NEW CONFIDENCE--TO TACKLE THE FANTASTIC FOUR THEMSELVES ONCE AGAIN!

THIS PLASTI-CREAM WHICH THE WIZARD SO KINDLY LEFT FOR ME IS JUST WHAT I NEED!
PLASTI CREAM MAKE-UP PASTE

AFTER ALL, WHY BOTHER TO INVADE THE FF HEADQUARTERS--
--WHEN I CAN JUST AS EASILY BE INVITED TO PARTAKE OF THEIR UNSUSPECTING HOSPITALITY!!
THE PLAN IS PERFECT--UTTERLY FOOL-PROOF!
I'VE LEFT NOTHING TO CHANCE!

THE BAXTER BUILDING--AT LAST!

LET THE FOOLS STARE AT ME! IF THEY THINK I'M DAREDEVIL--THE FF WILL, TOO!
VISI-COMMUNICATOR

DAREDEVIL! WHAT CAN HE WANT WITH US??
BZZZZ
HE SEEMS RELAXED ENOUGH--
IT MUST BE A SOCIAL CALL!

I'LL PRESS THE ELEVATOR-RELEASE BUTTON FOR HIM!
TOO BAD REED, JOHNNY, AND BEN AREN'T HERE--
BUT PERHAPS HE'LL WAIT TILL THEY RETURN!
IT'S BEEN MONTHS SINCE WE'VE SEEN HIM!

I DID IT!!
AND HOW MUCH SIMPLER THIS IS THAN TRYING TO STORM THEIR PENTHOUSE FORTRESS!

THE ELEVATOR STOPPED!
HE'S NOW IN THE OUTER VESTIBULE!
I--WONDER WHY--HE DOESN'T ANSWER?
COME IN, DAREDEVIL! THIS IS AN UNEXPECTED SURPRISE!
CLICK!
16

A SPLIT-SECOND LATER, SUE LEARNS THE ANSWER--
A GUN--POINTING AT ME!! I--I'VE SEEN IT BEFORE--!!
IT'S THE TRAPSTER'S PASTE GUN!!
IT'LL BE FAR MORE OF A SURPRISE THAN YOU IMAGINED, YOU TRUSTING FOOL!!

HOW RIGHT YOU ARE, MY DEAR!
SPAT

THIS TIME I STRUCK BEFORE YOU COULD USE YOUR ACCURSED FORCE FIELD AGAINST ME!
YOUR VOICE!! I SHOULD HAVE GUESSED--!
YOU'RE NOT DAREDEVIL!!
YOU'RE THE TRAPSTER--IN DISGUISE!

HOW CLEVER OF YOU! FOR GUESSING MY SECRET --YOU WIN THIS LITTLE PRIZE!
DON'T BE ALARMED --IT'S MERELY A LETHAL EXPLOSIVE DEVICE!
CLICK!

I'VE JUST TRIGGERED THE SAFETY!
IT WON'T BEGIN OPERATING FOR ANOTHER FIVE MINUTES--
TO GIVE ME TIME TO LEISURELY DEPART!
BUT, AS SOON AS ANY OF YOUR PARTNERS RETURN--
--THEIR OWN BODY HEAT WILL SET IT OFF--WITHIN SECONDS!!
I'LL JUST LEAVE IT IN HERE--SO THE TICKING WON'T DISTURB YOU!

A PITY YOUR DOOMED HUSBAND AND HIS TWO BLUNDERING COMPANIONS WEREN'T IN WHEN I CALLED!
I WAS PREPARED TO DEAL WITH ALL OF YOU AT ONCE!
NOW I MUST FOREGO THE PLEASURE OF WATCHING THE TOTAL DESTRUCTION OF THE FANTASTIC FOUR!
SO FAREWELL, SUE RICHARDS-- FOR THE LAST TIME!
I--I CAN'T FREE MYSELF! HIS PASTE IS SO STRONG, I CAN'T EVEN MOVE!
I CANT--STOP THAT BOMB--FROM DETONATING--AS SOON AS SOMEONE ENTERS--THE ROOM!!

IT'S WORKING!
EVEN THOUGH I'M PLUNGING EARTHWARD-- MY SPEED IS SLOWER THAN IT WOULD BE WITHOUT THE DISC'S EFFECT!
NOW, EVERY-THING DEPENDS UPON MY BILLY-CLUB CABLE!
I'LL ONLY HAVE TIME-- FOR ONE THRUST--!

NOW!

I DID IT!!
I HOOKED IT ONTO A ROOFTOP-- BREAKING MY FALL!!
I DON'T NEED THE DISC ANY LONGER-- I'M SAFE!!

AND THAT'S MORE THAN THE TRAPSTER WILL BE ABLE TO SAY--WHEN I FIND HIM AGAIN!!
WAIT A MINUTE!! HE SAID HE WAS HEADING FOR THE BAXTER BUILDING!!
I'VE GOT TO GET THERE-- AND WARN THE FF!

AND, EVEN AS DAREDEVIL SWINGS EVER CLOSER--
IF ANYONE ENTERS--IT WILL MEAN THE END OF US ALL--BEFORE I CAN WARN THEM!!
TICK
TICK
THE INSTANT THAT ANYONE ELSE'S BODY HEAT IS DETECTED BY THE BOMB--NOTHING ON EARTH WILL BE ABLE TO SAVE US!

THEN, AS MOUNTING PANIC BEGINS TO WELL WITHIN THE HEART OF SUE RICHARDS--
THAT SOUND! A SOFT, MUFFLED THUD ON THE ROOFTOP!!
SOMEONE--IS THERE--!

I SUPPOSE I COULD HAVE TAKEN THE ELEVATOR--
BUT EVERY SECOND MAY COUNT!

EVERYTHING SEEMS QUIET ENOUGH! MAYBE HE HASN'T ARRIVED YET!
YET, WITH SOMEONE LIKE THE TRAPSTER, YOU NEVER KNOW!
I'LL JUST SWING IN THRU THE NEAREST WINDOW--AND MAKE SURE!
AND, AS IF WE HAVE TO TELL YOU...
CONTINUED NEXT ISH!

HERE COMES...

DAREDEVIL

THE MAN WITHOUT FEA

APPROVED BY THE COMICS CODE AUTHORITY

MARVEL COMICS GROUP

12¢ IND.

JAN 36

MCG

THE NAME OF THE GAME IS...

MAYHEM!

DAREDEVIL, THE MAN WITHOUT FEAR!™
"THE NAME OF THE GAME IS MAYHEM!"
MISTER FANTASTIC'S WIFE--GLUED TO THE FLOOR!
THAT MEANS THE TRAPSTER'S BEEN HERE BEFORE ME!
I'VE GOT TO GET INSIDE-- AND HELP HER!
NOW PAY ATTENTION, GANG--'CAUSE THIS IS REALLY COMPLICATED!
LAST ISH, WE SAW THE EVIL TRAPSTER RENDER SUE RICHARDS HELPLESS IN THE HEAD-QUARTERS OF THE FANTASTIC FOUR-- PLANTING A BOMB INSIDE A DRAWER-- WHICH WILL BE DETONATED AS SOON AS ANYONE ENTERS THE ROOM!
AND NOW, HERE COMES AN UNSUSPECTING DAREDEVIL! OKAY? OKAY! THEN LET'S GO--!
TICK TICK
PRODUCED BY: STAN (THE MAN) LEE and GENE (THE DEAN) COLAN
INKED BY: FRANK GIACOIA
LETTERED BY: ARTIE SIMEK
THE REST IS UP TO YOU, TIGER!

SUDDENLY, THE SCARLET-CLAD SWASHBUCKLER STOPS IN HIS TRACKS, AND--
I HEAR THE MUFFLED TICKING OF A CLOCK--AS THOUGH INSIDE A CABINET DRAWER!
TICK! TICK!

BUT WHY WOULD ANYONE KEEP A CLOCK INSIDE A DRAWER--
--WHERE IT CAN'T BE SEEN?
AND THEN AGAIN-- IT JUST MIGHT NOT BE A HARMLESS CLOCK!
TICK!
WHHTTT
WHICH MIGHT EXPLAIN WHY SUE RICHARDS IS HELPLESSLY GLUED TO THE FLOOR!
TICK!

EVEN THOUGH I'M A WALKING BUNDLE OF FEARLESSNESS--
THIS IS ONE TIME OL' DD IS GONNA PLAY IT SAFE!
THERE-- I GOT IT!
TICK!
TICK!

AND NOW, IF IT WAS NOTHING BUT A GIFT-WRAPPED LITTLE TICKOTTY-TOCK--
I'LL BE THE FIRST ONE TO APOLOGIZE!
2

WELL WADDAYA KNOW?
SCRATCH ONE APOLOGY!
MRS. RICHARDS! GLAD TO SEE YOU'VE REGAINED CONSCIOUSNESS!
I'LL HAVE YOU FREE OF THAT GOO AS SOON AS POSSIBLE!
DAREDEVIL!!
BUT--HOW DID YOU GET IN HERE?? WHAT ABOUT --THE BOMB?
I KINDA THOUGHT YOU'D ASK!
THEN, AFTER A BRIEF EXPLANATION--
UNHHH!
HOLD ON-- I THINK WE'RE LOOSENING IT!
THEY JUST DON'T MAKE IT LIKE THEY USED TO!
WHILE, IN THE STREET BELOW--
JOHNNY! THAT BLAST IN THE SKY-- I DON'T LIKE IT!
IT WAS TOO NEAR OUR TOP FLOOR HQ!
AND SUE IS UP THERE-- ALL ALONE!
I READ YOU, LEADER MAN!
LET'S GO!

DON'T FLAME ON YET, JOHNNY-- NOT TILL WE KNOW FOR CERTAIN!
I DON'T WANT TO CHANCE PANICKING THESE CROWDS!
EVERY-THING SEEMS QUIET ENOUGH UP THERE NOW, REED!
WE'LL KNOW FOR SURE IN A MINUTE!

SUE! YOU'RE ALL RIGHT!
AND DARE-DEVIL!
WHAT ARE YOU DOING HERE? WHAT HAPPENED?
WELL, OUR FREE-SWINGING FRIEND SAVED MY LIFE, FOR ONE THING!
WE HAD RATHER A STICKY TIME OF IT, GENTS!
THE TRAPSTER HAD LEFT A BOMB TO GREET YOU WITH!
THEN THAT WAS THE EXPLOSION WE HEARD!

THIS IS THE SECOND TIME YOU'VE HELPED BAIL US OUT, DD!
THAT'S RIGHT! I STILL REMEMBER THE WAY HE FOUGHT SIDE-BY-SIDE WITH US AGAINST DR. DOOM!*
IT'S HOW I GET MY KICKS, GROUP!
--IT KEEPS ME OUT OF THE POOL ROOM!
*WILL YOU EVER FORGET #40 OF THE F.F.? WE DID! --SNIDE STAN.

BUT, HOW DID YOU--?
HOLD IT! I HEAR SOME-THING!

I DON'T HEAR A THING!
EITHER YOU'RE MISTAKEN, OR YOU'VE GOT SHARPER EARS THAN WE DO!
YOU DON'T KNOW THE HALF OF IT, MISTER!
LOOK UP THERE--!

BLAST IT! I THOUGHT I HAD FINISHED OFF THAT SWAGGERING CLOWN!*
BUT IT DOESN'T MATTER!
NOW I HAVE A GOLDEN OPPORTUNITY TO GET THEM ALL AT ONCE!
AND THIS TIME I'M NOT LEAVING TILL I KNOW THE JOB IS DONE!
*ANYONE WOULD HAVE THOUGHT DD WAS KAPUT--WHAT WITH HIM SAILING OFF INTO SPACE WITH THE TRAPSTER'S ANTI-GRAV DISCS! --ANYONE, THAT IS, EXCEPT THE BELIEVERS WHO FOLLOWED HORNHEAD'S ESCAPE LAST ISH!--STEADFAST STAN.

THEY WON'T BE EXPECTING AN ATTACK SO SOON!
I'LL HAVE THEM GLUED TO THE SPOT BEFORE THEY KNOW WHAT HAPPENED!
BUT ONCE AGAIN THE TRAPSTER HAS RECKONED WITHOUT DAREDEVIL'S UNCANNY SENSE OF HEARING--

HE'S SWOOPING DOWN SILENTLY--!
HE HOPES TO TAKE US BY SURPRISE!
BUT HE PROBABLY SEES ME WAITING BY NOW!
HOLD IT, DD! LET US HANDLE THIS!

AT THE RISK OF SOUNDING LIKE A FULL-TIME CORNBALL--
THIS IS A JOB FOR THE HUMAN TORCH!
FLAME ON!

NO-- TORCH!! WAIT!
WAIT, I SAY--!

TOO LATE, DD!! HE DIDN'T HEAR YOU!
BUT WHY THE ALARM?
THE TORCH CAN TAKE HIM!

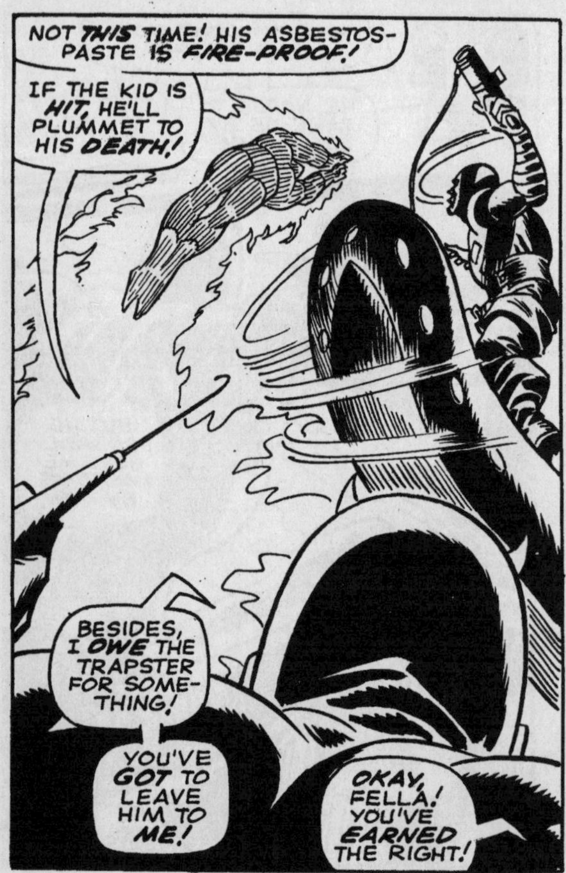
NOT THIS TIME! HIS ASBESTOS-PASTE IS FIRE-PROOF!
IF THE KID IS HIT, HE'LL PLUMMET TO HIS DEATH!
BESIDES, I OWE THE TRAPSTER FOR SOME-THING!
YOU'VE GOT TO LEAVE HIM TO ME!
OKAY, FELLA! YOU'VE EARNED THE RIGHT!

JOHNNY-- COME BACK!
LEAVE HIM TO DARE-DEVIL!
THAT'S AN ORDER, LAD!
NUTS! IT'S GETTING SO THAT YOU HAVETA STAND IN LINE TO FIGHT A BADDIE IN THIS TOWN!

DAREDEVIL, YOU'RE A ***FOOL!***

DON'T YOU REALIZE THAT YOU'RE THE ***WEAKEST,*** THE MOST ***VULNERABLE*** OF THEM ***ALL?!!***

SO FAR AS ***I*** CAN TELL, YOUR ONLY ***SUPER-POWER*** IS A COLOSSAL ***CONCEIT!***

YOU'RE NO SHRINKING VIOLET ***YOURSELF,*** SON!

LOOK OUT!! IF MY ANTI-GRAV ***TILTS--***

--WE'LL BE DASHED TO OUR ***DEATHS!***

Y'KNOW, I NEVER ***SUSPECTED*** THAT YOU HAD SUCH A FLAIR FOR THE ***DRAMATIC!***

YOU WON'T BE SO SMART ONCE I PELT YOU WITH A PASTE BLAST--!
YOU CAN'T KEEP DODGING THESE SHOTS FOREVER!
MAYBE NOT-- BUT I SURE INTEND TO TRY!

SO! YOU'D LIKE TO KICK ME OFF, EH?
THAT'S MIGHTY UNNEIGHBORLY OF YOU, MAN!

ANYWAY, WHEN IT COMES TO FOOT-WORK--
TWO CAN PLAY AT THAT LITTLE GAME!
THUD

NICE TRY, DAREDEVIL--!
BUT YOU CAN'T TALK YOUR WAY INTO A VICTORY THIS TIME!
I'VE GOT TO BRING THE SHIP DOWN, SOMEHOW!
WHILE WE'RE UP HERE, THE ADVANTAGE STILL IS HIS!

--HE'S FAMILIAR WITH THE FLYER--AND THE USE OF HIS ANTI-GRAV DISCS!
HE CAN ESTIMATE EACH SUDDEN MANEUVER FASTER THAN I!
NOW HE'S TRYING TO TILT IT-- TO SHAKE ME OFF--!

SORRY, TRAPPY-- THIS IS ONE RIDE I'M NOT CUTTIN' OUT OF--
--'LESS I TAKE YOU WITH ME!

KNOW SOMETHING, SON? IT'S TOO BAD YOU'RE NOT A BUSINESSMAN!
IF YOU COULD SELL THIS RIDE TO AN AMUSEMENT PARK--
--YOU'D PUT THE ROLLER COASTER OUT OF BUSINESS!

NOW THAT HE'S GOT HIS HANDS FULL--JUST HOLDING ON--
THIS IS MY CHANCE TO KNOCK OFF SOME OF THE ANTI-GRAV DISCS!
IT'S THE ONLY WAY TO BRING THIS BABY DOWN!

THERE! THAT OUGHTTA DO IT!
CAN'T TOSS 'EM ALL OFF, OR WE'LL PLUMMET LIKE A ROCK!

DAREDEVIL!! ARE YOU TRYING TO KILL US??!
WE'RE FALLING TOO FAST!!
WITHOUT THOSE DISCS, WE'LL CRASH! WE WON'T HAVE A CHANCE!!
9

WE DO HAVE A CHANCE, CHARLIE-- BUT ONLY ONE--!
I'VE A BETTER SENSE OF BALANCE THAN YOU --OR THAN ANYONE!
REMAIN PERFECTLY MOTIONLESS AND LET ME GUIDE THIS GADGET DOWN--
I'LL SKIM HER BETWEEN THE BUILDINGS AND BELLY-WHOP HER ON THE SIDEWALK!
ALL YOU HAVE TO DO IS-- FREEZE!
YOU'RE A MADMAN!!
--BUT, I HAVEN'T ANY CHOICE!
HOWEVER, WE DO HAVE A CHOICE-- AS YOU WILL SEE WHEN YOU TENDERLY TURN THE PAGE--

WE'RE FREE TO CHOOSE A SUDDEN CHANGE OF SCENE--AS WE BRIEFLY VISIT THE LAW OFFICE OF NELSON AND MURDOCK, WHERE WE FIND--
I'M EXTREMELY FLATTERED BY YOUR OFFER, GENTLEMEN...
GOOD! GOOD!
THEN WE HOPE YOUR ANSWER WILL BE YES, NELSON!

OUR CITY NEEDS AN HONEST, UPSTANDING DISTRICT ATTORNEY--
AND WE'RE PREPARED TO THROW OUR FULL SUPPORT BEHIND YOUR CANDIDACY--IF YOU'LL AGREE TO RUN!
OF COURSE, YOU'LL DROP THE NICK-NAME FOGGY!
FRANKLIN NELSON--D.A.!!--IT SURE SOUNDS GREAT!

DID YOU HEAR IT, KAREN?
THEY WANT ME FOR D.A.!
I THINK YOU'D BE PERFECT FOR THE JOB, FOGGY!
WILL YOU RUN?

JUST BETWEEN US, GORGEOUS--IT'LL TAKE AN ARMY TO STOP ME!
OF COURSE, I DON'T WANT TO COMMIT MYSELF TILL I'VE SPOKEN TO MATT!
AFTER ALL, HE IS MY PARTNER!
EVEN THOUGH HE HASN'T SHOWN HIS FACE AROUND THIS OFFICE FOR DAYS!
OH, THAT'S RIGHT!
IF YOU GET ELECTED, YOU'LL HAVE TO GIVE UP YOUR PARTNERSHIP!
IT WILL MEAN MATT BEING HERE ON HIS OWN!
BUT HE WON'T MIND!
HE'LL BE AS HAPPY FOR YOU AS I AM!

THERE'S THE PHONE!
MAYBE THAT'S MATT NOW!
I'LL GET IT, KAREN!
RRING

BUT, THE PARTY AT THE OPPOSITE END OF THE LINE TURNS OUT NOT TO BE MATT MURDOCK-- IN FACT, WE CAN SAFELY SAY SHE'S ABOUT THE FURTHEST THING FROM MATT MURDOCK--OR ANY OTHER MALE-TYPE PERSON--!
HEL-LO, FOGGY! CAN YOU TELL WHO THIS IS?
THAT'S RIGHT!
I HOPED YOU'D REMEMBER!

DEBBIE! DEBORAH HARRIS!! I-I THOUGHT YOU WERE STILL IN JAIL!
I'VE JUST BEEN PAROLED, FOGGY!
I WAS WONDER-ING--IF YOU'RE FREE FOR DINNER--
--JUST FOR OLD TIMES' SAKE!
I--EH--AH--THAT IS--I'M NOT SURE!
SUPPOSE YOU CALL ME BACK --DEB--!

YOU ONCE HAD A REAL CRUSH ON HER, FOGGY!
WHAT MADE YOU SHY AWAY NOW?
HOW WOULD IT LOOK, KAREN--TO RUN FOR D.A.-- AND DATE AN EX-CONVICT??

I REMEMBER-- THE TIME I MET HER--AT ABNER JONAS' PARTY--!*
THIS IS AN OLD FRIEND OF YOURS, FOGGY!
I'M DEBORAH HARRIS! WE WERE CLASSMATES AT FILLMORE JR. HIGH!
WOW! WHY DID I EVER LEAVE SCHOOL?!!
*FOR THE SERIOUS ARCHIVIST, WE SUGGEST A CAREFUL RE-READING OF DD #10 & #11! --STATISTICIAN STAN.

"I'LL NEVER FORGET THAT MAD, INCREDIBLE EVENING--IT STARTED WHEN THE LIGHTS WENT OUT AT JONAS' PENTHOUSE PARTY--"
DEBBIE!
DEBBIE!! WHERE ARE YOU--?!!
"BUT, WHEN THINGS RETURNED TO NORMAL, DEBBIE WAS GONE--AND ONLY ONE OF THE ORGANIZER'S MEN WAS THERE IN HER STEAD--!"
IT'S--THE CAT MAN!
HOW DID HE GET HERE?
WHO KNOCKED HIM OUT??
"AND THEN, SECONDS LATER, MY VERY WORST FEARS WERE REALIZED--"
DEBORAH HARRIS IS GONE!
SHE WAS CAPTURED BY ANOTHER OF THE ORGANIZER'S MEN!
THE FLYING BIRD MAN!
"BUT, UNDER CONSTANT GRILLING BY THE POLICE, THE CAPTURED CAT MAN FINALLY BROKE, AND WAS THE FIRST TO TURN AGAINST THE ORGANIZER..."
OKAY--I'LL TALK--I'LL TALK!
THE ORGANIZER AIMS TO GET THE WHOLE CITY UNDER HIS CONTROL--
"THEN, IT WAS JUST A MATTER OF TIME BEFORE DAREDEVIL ROUNDED UP THE REST OF THE GANG--WITH MY HELP--!"
GOOD WORK, FOGGY!
HOLD ONTO HIM--
HE'S THE RINGLEADER!
AND DEBBIE HARRIS WAS IN LEAGUE WITH HIM!
"IT NEARLY BROKE MY HEART TO LEARN THAT DEBBIE HAD BEEN PLAYING ME FOR A FOOL--IN ORDER TO HELP ABNER JONAS--WHO WAS THE UNMASKED ORGANIZER! AND YET--"
WHAT'S THE MATTER WITH ME??
I'D STILL FORGIVE HER--TAKE HER BACK--IF SHE'D HAVE ME!
TAKE 'IM AWAY, FOGGY!
BUT I MUST FORGET HER--I MUST!
13

AND NOW--JUST WHEN I'D ALMOST GOTTEN HER OUT OF MY SYSTEM--SHE'S FREE AGAIN --BACK IN MY LIFE AGAIN--!
DO YOU--PLAN TO SEE HER AGAIN?
I DON'T KNOW! I JUST DON'T KNOW!

HOWEVER, OUR SIGHTLESS SWASHBUCKLER HAS NO SUCH AMBIVALENT FEELINGS AT THE MOMENT! HE KNOWS WHAT HE WANTS TO DO! HIS ONLY PROBLEM IS--HOW TO DO IT--??
I TOLD YOU I'D GUIDE US SAFELY PAST THE BUILDINGS--INTO THE PARK!
AND NOW--WE'RE GONNA HIT!
BRACE YOURSELF, BAD MAN! HERE IT COMES!

SPKOWW!
WE'RE SAFE!

SPEAK FOR YOURSELF, FOOL!
I'M STILL THE ONE WITH THE PASTE GUN!
WELL, GOODY FOR YOU!
YOU'RE ALSO THE ONE WITH THE CRUMMY AIM!
THOP!

I'LL ADMIT I DON'T HAVE ANY GOOEY GUNS--

BUT, FOR WHAT I LACK IN WEAPONS--
I TRY TO MAKE UP IN ENTHUSIASM!

BETTER BE CAREFUL! I DON'T WANNA HAVE TO CARRY HIM TO JAIL!
OOPS! I WAS TOO CAREFUL!
--I MISSED!

ONE CHANCE IS ALL YOU GET WHEN YOU FIGHT THE TRAPSTER--!
AND YOU JUST HAD IT, WISE GUY!

DON'T EXPECT ME TO FIGHT BY THE MARQUIS OF QUEENSBURY RULES, EITHER!
I'M TOO SMART FOR THAT!
OKAY! OKAY! YOU MADE YOUR POINT!

HOWEVER, THERE'S NOT MUCH YOU CAN DO WITH AN EMPTY GUN!
WHA-?--HOW'D YOU KNOW?
I COULD HEAR THE HOLLOW SOUND!
BUT I'M NOT TELLING HIM!
OKAY--MAYBE I CAN'T SHOOT IT!
BUT I CAN STILL USE IT TO STOP YOU COLD!
HE'S SPUN IT AROUND ME-- WITH ITS CONNECTING WIRE!

HAH! BY THE TIME YOU'RE FREE--I'LL BE LONG GONE!
NO ONE WITH MY SUPER SENSE OF TOUCH CAN TAKE LONG TO UNTIE HIMSELF!
DON'T BET ON IT, TRAPPY!
AND AWAAAAAY WE GO--!
I'M SURPRISED THE F.F. HAVEN'T SHOWN UP BY NOW--
ALTHOUGH I'M GLAD THEY DIDN'T!*
HE'S ONE TIGER I WANNA TAME SINGLE-HANDED!
*OF COURSE, IF DD TOOK THE TROUBLE TO STUDY FANTASTIC FOUR #71 HE'D SEE WHY THOSE SWINGIN' STALWARTS AREN'T MAKIN' THE SCENE--BUT ALAS, OUR HERO HAS BEEN NEGLECTING HIS READING OF THE CLASSICS LATELY! --SENTENTIOUS STAN.

HOLD IT, JUNIOR! YOU FORGOT SOMETHING--
NAMELY ME!
SO! YOU FREED YOURSELF, EH?
WELL, IT'LL DO YOU NO GOOD!
I'M STILL FAR TOO CLEVER FOR YOU!
16

MISTER, NOBODY CLEVER HAS TO MAKE HIS LIVING THE HARD WAY--LIKE YOU'RE TRYING TO DO!
DIDJA EVER THINK OF BECOMING A C.P.A.??
EVERYONE LIKES A PROFESSIONAL MAN!
KEEP TALKING, BIG MOUTH!
SEE WHERE IT GETS YOU!

WHAT A BREAK! HE'S OUT IN THE STREET AGAIN!
HE DOESN'T SUSPECT IT'LL BE EASIER FOR ME TO CATCH UP WITH HIM THERE--IN THE OPEN!

HEY, TRAPSTER!!
ONE THING I CAN'T STAND IS A JAY-WALKER!

I HOPE THERE'S A BIG CROWD WATCHING--!
THIS OUGHTTA BE A DOOZY!

GERONIMO!
SYSTEM
AVE. LINE
MANHATTAN
QUEENS
SYSTEM
UP

I'LL SAY ONE THING FOR YOU, TRAPPY--
--YOU SURE MADE ME DO THIS THE HARD WAY!

HEADLONG DOWN THE SUBWAY STEPS TUMBLE THE TWO DESPERATE COMBATANTS-- NEITHER MAN RELINQUISHING HIS GRIP ON THE OTHER-- UNTIL--
HE CAN'T TAKE THIS KIND OF FALL AS WELL AS I--!
I TRIED TO--KEEP HIS HEAD--FROM HITTING THE STAIRS--!
BUT--IN SO DOING --I WRENCHED --MY OWN BACK!
UNHHH!

AND THEN-- AS DRAMATICALLY AS IT HAD BEGUN--THE BATTLE ENDS--!
BTAMM!

LONG MINUTES LATER--
I HEARD POLICE--COMING HERE--PICKING UP TRAPSTER--
BUT--THEY DIDN'T SEE ME!

DIDN'T KNOW--I HAD ROLLED--HERE--UNDER PLATFORM!
COULDN'T CALL OUT TO THEM--TOO WEAK--TOO MUCH--PAIN--!

AT LEAST--I WON! TRAPSTER IS CAPTURED!
BUT--EVERYTHING SPINNING AROUND--HAVE TO HANG ON--!!
AND HANG ON HE DOES--GATHERING UP HIS IRON RESOLVE--HIS DAUNTLESS VITALITY--UNTIL AT LAST--

--OR ELSE--
DOCTOR DOOM!

SURPRISED, TIGER? WE KINDA HOPED YOU WOULD BE!

ANYWAY, IT ALL COMES OUT IN THE WASH
NEXT ISH!!
SO BE HERE--IT'S ONE OF THE GREATEST DD'S YET!!

HERE COMES...

DAREDEVIL™

THE MAN WITHOUT FEAR!

MARVEL
COMICS
GROUP

12¢ IND

37 FEB

APPROVED BY THE COMICS CODE AUTHORITY

MCG

DON'T LOOK NOW, BUT IT'S...

DAREDEVIL, THE MAN WITHOUT FEAR!™
"DON'T LOOK NOW, BUT IT'S.. DR. DOOM!"
LYING WEAK AND WEARY ON THE SUBWAY TRACKS, AFTER HAVING FINALLY DEFEATED THE EVIL TRAPSTER, OUR HERO SUDDENLY FINDS ANOTHER FIGURE APPROACHING FROM OUT OF THE SHADOWS! THE FIGURE OF AN OLD AND AWESOME ARCH-ENEMY--
SILENCE!
YOU WILL NOT SPEAK UNTIL I PERMIT IT!
DOCTOR DOOM!
HOW-- UNHHH!
THE STRONGEST FOE OF ALL-- WHEN I'M AT MY WEAKEST!
WHAT CHANCE DO I HAVE??
LET'S PAUSE JUST LONG ENOUGH TO AWARD A VOTE OF THANKS TO... STAN (THE MAN) LEE & GENE (THE DEAN) COLAN FOR CREATING THIS CONTEMPORARY CLASSIC; AND TO: JOHN TARTAGLIONE, EMBELLISHER AND ARTIE SIMEK, LETTERER!
AND NOW--IT'S ACTION TIME--!
1

LUCKILY, I HEARD OF YOUR BATTLE WITH THE TRAPSTER OVER THE RADIO!
AND IT WAS CHILD'S PLAY FOR ME TO CATCH UP WITH YOU!
SINCE I HAVE RETURNED TO AVENGE MYSELF UPON THE FANTASTIC FOUR-- IT'S ONLY FITTING THAT YOU BE THE CATALYST!
HOW COME I'M USUALLY IN THE MIDDLE WHENEVER ANYONE WANTS TO TACKLE SOME OTHER COSTUMED CUT-UPS?
I WARNED YOU TO REMAIN SILENT IN MY PRESENCE!
LOOK, DOC-- DON'T PUSH YOUR LUCK TOO FAR--!

SURELY YOU DIDN'T THINK YOUR ONE PUNY KICK COULD AFFECT THE ARMOR-CLAD BODY OF DR. DOOM?
TO ME, YOU ARE NO MORE THAN A TRIVIAL, PETTY NUISANCE--
ONE WHICH MUST BE DISPOSED OF--JUST AS I WOULD PERFORCE DISPOSE OF SOME BOTHERSOME FLYING INSECT!
NORMALLY, I DO NOT STRIKE OUT IN THE MANNER OF A PEASANT FIGHTING WITH MY FISTS--
BUT, IT SEEMS POINTLESS TO WASTE ANY OF MY SENSES-STAGGERING WEAPONS ON ONE SO WEAK!
HOWEVER-- BEATEN THOUGH YOU MAY BE--
YOU WILL STILL LIVE LONG ENOUGH-- TO SERVE DR. DOOM!
3

IN A BIG CITY, IT DOESN'T TAKE MUCH TO ATTRACT A CROWD! WITHIN MINUTES, THE PLATFORM ABOVE DR. DOOM AND DAREDEVIL IS FILLED WITH WIDE-EYED, STARTLED ON-LOOKERS--ON THE VERGE OF PANIC--!
HE'S TRYING TO CARRY DAREDEVIL AWAY--INTO THE TUNNEL!
THAT MASK! THAT DREADFUL ARMOR!
HE'S FAR MORE HIDEOUS--MORE REPULSIVE--THAN ONE CAN IMAGINE!
WE'VE GOTTA DO SOME-THING!
WE CAN'T JUST STAND BY AND LET DOOM MAKE OFF WITH DAREDEVIL!
THERE ARE DOZENS OF US HERE! LET'S TACKLE 'IM!
WAIT! WHAT'S HE DOING?
HE WHIPPED OUT SOME SORT OF HAND WEAPON!!
GET BACK!

FOOLS! YOU THINK A MOTLEY CROWD CAN STOP DR. DOOM??
I HAVE POWER ENOUGH--ARMAMENT ENOUGH--TO HOLD OFF AN ARMY--SINGLE-HANDED!
HISS!

WHAT IS IT? WHAT DID HE DO??
HE CREATED SOME SORT OF QUICK-FORMING GLASS WALL--
OUT OF EMPTY AIR!
IT'S MORE THAN GLASS!
FEEL HOW COLD IT IS--HOW IT SEEMS TO VIBRATE TO THE TOUCH!
IT MUST BE A NEW TYPE OF PLASTIC--WHICH HE CREATED AS A BARRIER!
BY THE TIME THE POLICE ARRIVE--HE'LL BE GONE!

AND, EXACTLY AS THE HELPLESS ONLOOKERS HAD PREDICTED--
AH YES--THE SO-CALLED MAN WITHOUT FEAR SHALL AID ME IN ONE OF THE MOST DIABOLICALLY DEADLY PLANS EVER CONCEIVED!
AND, SINCE I AM NOT A COMMON CRIMINAL--
--MY STULTIFYING SCHEME CANNOT FAIL!

ONE THING WE MUST AGREE WITH--WHATEVER ELSE YOU CALL HIM, DR. DOOM MOST CERTAINLY IS NOT A COMMON CRIMINAL--
TAKE ME TO THE EMBASSY--AT ONCE!
YOU NEED NOT CONCERN YOURSELF WITH PETTY TRAFFIC RULES--
SINCE WE POSSESS UNLIMITED DIPLOMATIC IMMUNITY!
YES, EXCELLENCY!

AFTER ALL, HOW MANY COMMON CRIMINALS CAN YOU NAME WHO ARE LEGALLY HEADS OF STATE??
SHALL WE REQUEST AN OFFICIAL MOTORCYCLE ESCORT, EXCELLENCY?
THERE IS NO NEED!
NONE WOULD DARE INTERFERE WITH AN OFFICIAL LIMOUSINE OF THE LATVERIAN GOVERNMENT!

AND, WITHIN THE BULLET-PROOF INTERIOR OF THE GLISTENING BLACK VEHICLE--
SAY! I THOUGHT DOOM HAD BEEN KILLED IN HIS LAST FIGHT WITH THE FF!
WHAT GIVES, ANYWAY?

YOU FELLAS ARE A REGULAR BUNCH OF CHATTERBOXES, HUH?
PULL YOURSELF TOGETHER, DD! YOU'VE GOTTA GET OUT OF HERE BEFORE THEY REACH THEIR EMBASSY!

THE LATVERIAN EMBASSY IS SAID TO BE THE MOST ESCAPE-PROOF BUILDING IN THE STATE!
SO, IF I'M EVER GONNA MAKE A MOVE, IT HAS TO BE NOW!
SO! YOU WONDER THAT I'M STILL ALIVE, DO YOU--?

YEAH!! BUT WE'LL TALK ABOUT IT SOME OTHER TIME!
RIGHT NOW, I'M TOO BUSY KICKING THE FRONT SEAT UP AGAINST THE DASHBOARD!
THONK

I CAN SCARCELY BELIEVE IT!!
ARE YOU WITLESS ENOUGH TO THINK YOU CAN BREAK FREE??
HAVE YOU FORGOTTEN THE PEERLESS POWER OF DR. DOOM--?!!

NOT TO MENTION THE ANGER OF MY TRUSTED AIDES!
WE'LL TEACH HIM TO TRY THAT AGAIN!!

THANKS, FELLAS!
I'M ALWAYS ANXIOUS TO LEARN!
UH OH!! THE DRIVER'S SPINNING AROUND--TOO FAST--!

--CAN'T DODGE HIM IN TI---UNHHH!
SLEEP TIGHT, WISE GUY!

DRIVER! HEY! HE ROLLED WITH THE PUNCH!!
HE GRABBED MY HAND!!
DON'T!! LEGGO!! LOOK OUT-- WE'RE GONNA CRASH!!
SKREEEE

BUT THEN, CALMLY-- UNHURRIEDLY-- DR. DOOM REACHES OUT, AND--
THERE IS NO NEED FOR PANIC!
IT IS SIMPLE ENOUGH FOR ME TO SEIZE THE WHEEL WHILE WE PACIFY OUR GUEST!
YOU-- GRABBED IT-- JUST IN TIME!

AND NOW, GENTLE-MEN--
LET US TAKE NO FURTHER CHANCES WITH OUR COSTUMED CAPTIVE!
WE CAN'T HOLD HIM, EXCELLENCY!
HE'S LIKE-- A TIGER!

HE KEEPS JOSTLING THE DRIVER-- TRYING TO PUT THE VEHICLE OUT OF CONTROL!
I COULD EASILY END HIS FUTILE RESISTANCE--
BUT I HAVE NO WISH TO HARM HIM-- NOT YET!

BUT, THERE ARE MANY WAYS TO SKIN A CAT!
KLIK!

SINCE WE HAVE REACHED OUR DESTINATION, I WILL ACTIVATE THE JET BRAKES!!
SHOOOOSH!

THEIR BLISTERING FORCE IS SURE TO SHATTER THE CONCRETE ROAD--
BUT IT IS SIMPLE ENOUGH TO HAVE A ROAD REBUILT!
SCREEEECH!
SKRAKKK!

ONE MORE MOVE AND I SHOOT!!
NO NEED FOR THAT!
WE HAVE ARRIVED!

FOR THE LUVVA PETE!!
WHAT DO YOU SUPPOSE CAUSED THAT?!!
BEATS ME, CHARLIE!
I COULDA SWORN THIS ROAD WAS OKAY JUST A FEW MINUTES AGO!
QUICKLY--AROUND THE BACK!
WE DO NOT WANT THE AMERICAN POLICE TO SEE OUR UNWILLING PASSENGER!
DO YOU THINK DOOM'S CAR COULD HAVE--?
NAH! IT'S NOT POSSIBLE!
8

SECONDS LATER--
IF I'D KNOWN YOU WERE GONNA GIVE ME A TOUR--
I'D HAVE BROUGHT MY GUIDE-BOOK!
YOUR JUVENILE WITTICISMS LEAVE ME COLD!
YOU WILL WALK STRAIGHT AHEAD-- EXACTLY AS I COMMAND YOU!

YOU MAY TOTALLY ABANDON ANY FOOLISH HOPE OF ESCAPE!
HERE, IN THIS BUILDING, ON THE OUTSKIRTS OF YOUR CITY, I AM TRULY KING--
EXACTLY AS IF I WERE IN MY CASTLE ROYAL IN LATVERIA!
MY EMBASSY BUILDING IS OUT OF BOUNDS TO YOUR OWN POLICE AND MILITARY ESTABLISH-MENTS!
HERE, WITHIN THESE FORTIFIED WALLS--
DR. DOOM IS ROYAL MASTER-- ABSOLUTE!!

WHILE YOU ARE BUT A LOWLY PRISONER!
IN THIS DUNGEON YOU SHALL STAY--TO AWAIT MY PLEASURE!
TALK ABOUT CORNY LINES!
YOU MUST SPEND ALL YOUR SPARE TIME WATCHING OLD BELA LUGOSI MOVIES ON THE LATE SHOW!
--IF ONLY I FELT AS FLIPPANT AS I'M TRYING TO SOUND!
9

WHEN I HAVE COMPLETED ALL PREPARATIONS FOR MY MASTER PLAN--I SHALL COME FOR YOU!
TILL THEN, YOU MAY REFLECT UPON THE UTTER FOLLY OF TRYING TO RESIST THE INDOMITABLE WILL OF DR. DOOM!
SAY! COME TO THINK OF IT--
ARE YOU SURE YOU'RE NOT VINCENT PRICE IN DISGUISE?

NUTS! WHY AM I KNOCKING MYSELF OUT WITH THE BON MOTS!
HE'S GOT AS MUCH SENSAHUMOR AS A HOLLOW HANGNAIL!

THIS IS ONE JAM OL' HORNHEAD ISN'T GONNA BE ABLE TO JOLLY HIS WAY OUT OF!
WHATEVER ELSE HE MAY BE, DOC DOOM ISN'T EXACTLY A PART-TIME PUSH-OVER!

I DON'T KNOW WHAT HE'S GOT COOKED UP FOR ME--OR WHY!
BUT THE ODDS ARE THAT IT'S NOT GONNA INCREASE MY LIFE SPAN BY VERY MUCH!
SO IT'S TIME TO STOP SOLILOQUIZING AND START SEARCHING--!
I DON'T KNOW HOW MUCH TIME I HAVE LEFT--
BUT I DO KNOW I'D BETTER USE IT TO FIND A WAY OUT OF HERE!

IF THERE'S THE SLIGHTEST WEAKNESS ANYWHERE IN THE WALL, MY HYPER-SENSITIVE FINGERS WILL FEEL--WHOOPS!
A TRAPDOOR!
NEVER EXPECTED TO FIND IT SO FAST!
OKAY THEN--NOW THAT I FOUND IT--
I MIGHT AS WELL LEARN WHERE IT GOES--!

THE ONE ADVANTAGE I HAVE OVER DOOM IS THAT HE ISN'T AWARE OF MY HYPERKEEN SENSES!
HE THINKS OF ME AS AN INSIGNIFICENT COSTUMED ACROBAT!
I WONDER WHAT HE'D SAY IF HE LEARNED I'M TOTALLY BLIND?!!
HOW CAN ANY SIGHTED PERSON EVER BELIEVE THAT A MAN IN A WORLD OF DARKNESS CAN BE FAR MORE CAPABLE THAN HE!??

EVEN THOUGH I CAN'T SEE THE SHAFT OF LIGHT AHEAD--
I CAN FEEL ITS WARMTH-- WHILE MY RADAR SENSE PINPOINTS ITS EXACT LOCATION!

I WAS RIGHT! IT'S FROM BEHIND THIS LOOSE STONE--!
BUT, AM I REALLY ESCAPING-- OR--??

AND, FOR THE SINISTER ANSWER TO DD'S UNSPOKEN QUERY, LET'S RETURN TO HIS CHORTLING CAPTOR, IN ANOTHER PART OF THE EMBASSY--
NOW, WHILE I WAIT FOR MY TRANSFORMATRON TO BECOME OPERATIONAL--
--LET THE AMUSEMENT BEGIN!!
11

THEN, AS OUR HAPLESS HERO MAKES HIS WAY INTO THE NEXT CHAMBER, HIS EVERY SENSE REACTS TO THE IMPRESSIONS THEREIN WITH MADDENING BEWILDERMENT--
IT ISN'T POSSIBLE!!
IT'S LIKE SOME GARISH, GROTESQUE NIGHTMARE!!
HE'S MANAGED TO SHRINK ME--TO THE SIZE OF A HELPLESS CHILD!
BUT IF THIS WAS HIS AIM--WHY DID HE DO IT??
WHAT PURPOSE CAN POSSIBLY BE SERVED??
AND YET --THERE'S MORE TO THIS THAN APPEARS ON THE SURFACE!!
EVERY INSTINCT TELLS ME THAT I HAVEN'T CHANGED!
HIS WILL--HIS SELF-CONTROL--ARE INDEED MOST ADMIRABLE!
BUT THE SPECIALLY-PREPARED FESTIVITIES HAVE ONLY BEGUN...
AND NOW FOR OUR NEXT LITTLE TABLEAU--!
SKLAK!
THE ENTIRE ROOM--SPINNING AROUND LIKE A TOP!!
FASTER--AND FASTER--
AS THOUGH IT WILL NEVER END!!
BUT, END IT DOES! AND, WHEN THE WHIRLING STOPS--HURRY! TURN THE PAGE--!
12

ACCORDING TO MY RADAR SENSE--
I-I'M STANDING UPRIGHT--FROM THE CEILING!
EVERY-THING IS UPSIDE-DOWN!
THERE'S ONLY ONE POSSIBLE ANSWER--

IT'S SOME SORT OF WILD SCHEME--CONCOCTED BY DR. DOOM--
IN AN EFFORT TO BREAK MY WILL!
BUT I WON'T LET--WAIT!!
EVERYTHING IS CHANGING!! THE ROOM SEEMS TO BE RIGHTING ITSELF--!
EVEN THOUGH I CAN'T SEE IT--
EVEN THOUGH I KNOW IT'S A TRICK--
MY BRAIN STILL SEEMS ABOUT TO SNAP!

AND, AS THE TORMENTING SECONDS SPEED BY--
I KEEP FALLING BACK--AS THOUGH I'M PLUNGING UP, TO THE CEILING!
I WON'T--LET IT--DRIVE ME MAD--!
HOLD ON, D.D.!--YOU CAN TAKE IT! YOU CAN--!!
I MUST--KEEP REMEMBERING--IT'S JUST AN ILLUSION--!

THEN, SUDDENLY--
EVERY-THING STOPPED!!
THE ROOM IS--BACK TO NORMAL AGAIN!
BUT NOW--I SEEM TO HEAR--
THE SOUND OF MUFFLED LAUGHTER!!

AN ADMIRABLE PERFORMANCE, DAREDEVIL!
A LESSER MAN MIGHT HAVE CRUMBLED BENEATH THE STRAIN!
DOOM! YOU WERE WATCHING IT ALL!
OF COURSE! AND NOW--MORE THAN EVER--
I KNOW I HAVE MADE THE RIGHT CHOICE!
WITH YOUR UNWITTING HELP--
I CANNOT FAIL TO CRUSH THE ACCURSED FANTASTIC FOUR!
THAT'S WHAT THE TRAPSTER SAID--
AND LOOK AT HIM NOW!
YOU FOOL! YOU DARE COMPARE ME WITH SOME ORDINARY COSTUMED CRIMINAL?!!
ME--WHOM THE WORLD-FAMOUS MR. FANTASTIC, WITH ALL HIS SCIENTIFIC PROWESS--COULD NOT DESTROY!
I REMEMBER OUR LAST ENCOUNTER AS IF IT WERE YESTERDAY!
HE USED HIS MOST POTENT FLYING WEAPON AGAINST ME--
MY STRENGTH... BEGINNING TO EBB...!
MY ANTI-COSMIC FLYING WING DIDN'T FAIL US!*
*CONDENSED FROM FANTASTIC FOUR #60--TO PROVE WE HAVEN'T FORGOTTEN! --SQUARE-SHOOTIN' STAN.
IT... STAGGERED ME... BUT IT COULDN'T DOWN ME...!!
MY COSMIC POWER* IS STILL TOO GREAT FOR YOU!
EVEN NOW--MY STRENGTH HAS RETURNED TO ITS MATCHLESS PEAK--!!
*DOC IS REFERRING, OF COURSE, TO THE AWESOME COSMIC POWER HE HAD STOLEN FROM THE SILVER SURFER! AND NOW, YOU'RE AS WELL-INFORMED AS WE--WHICH ISN'T SAYING MUCH! --SMILEY
14

I SHALL PROVE MY UTTER CONTEMPT FOR YOU... AND FOR YOUR INEFFECTUAL SHIP... BY PURSUING IT...
AND THEN, WITH ONE MERE COSMIC BOLT... I'LL REDUCE IT TO TOTAL NOTHINGNESS!
"LEAPING ONTO THE SURFER'S FLYING SURFBOARD, I DIDN'T REALIZE I WAS DOING JUST WHAT RICHARDS WANTED ME TO--"
THE COSMIC WING WAS JUST A DECOY!
THE VITAL PART COMES NOW-- UP THERE!
"NO SOONER HAD I REACHED EARTH'S SUB-STRATOSPHERE, THEN A BLINDING COSMIC EXPLOSION OCCURRED--!"
"AND INSTINCTIVELY I KNEW THAT I HAD STRUCK SOME UNSEEN, IRRESISTIBLE BARRIER--!"
"IN A MATTER OF SECONDS, THE UNCANNY SURFBOARD RETURNED TO MY CASTLE-- EMPTY!!"
"AND THE WORLD BELIBVED THAT DR. DOOM HAD MYSTERIOUSLY PERISHED!"
"KNOWING OF THE DEADLY BARRIER IN SPACE, REED RICHARDS HAD PLANNED IT THAT WAY!"
"BUT, THERE WAS ONE THING HE HAD NOT PLANNED--!"
15.

"THE BARRIER HAD BEEN PLACED IN SPACE BY THE UNEARTHLY POWER OF GALACTUS-- AND WAS THERE FOR ONLY ONE PURPOSE--"
"TO KEEP THE SILVER SURFER IMPRISONED UPON OUR PLANET!"
"THE EXPLOSION SET OFF SOME SORT OF SIGNAL DEVICE WHICH ALERTED GALACTUS, ALTHOUGH HE WAS MANY GALAXIES AWAY--"
"INSTANTANEOUSLY, HIS ASTRAL IMAGE APPEARED--HOLDING ME MOTIONLESS IN SPACE BY A FORCE SO CATACLYSMIC AS TO DEFY ANY MORTAL DESCRIPTION! AND THEN--"
16

"SINCE I WAS NOT THE SILVER SURFER, I REALIZED THAT HE CONSIDERED ME UTTERLY BENEATH HIS NOTICE!"

"SILENTLY, WITH NO SHOW OF EMOTION, HE MADE ONE SINGLE GESTURE--"

"AFTER WHICH --HE VANISHED!"

"AS FOR ME, I FOUND MYSELF ENCLOSED IN A PROTECTIVE MOLECULAR BUBBLE--"

"--WHICH SLOWLY TRANSPORTED ME BACK TO MY KINGDOM OF LATVERIA--!"

IT'S A GREAT YARN, DOOM--

BUT WHEN I NEED A BEDTIME STORY, I'LL ASK FOR ONE!

SAY! HOW--DID I GET IN HERE-- WITH YOU?

ALL IT REQUIRED WAS THE TOUCH OF A LEVER ON MY PART!

BUT, HE DOESN'T SUSPECT THAT I'M BLIND--
SO IT CAN'T AFFECT ME!
I'M BETTING IT'S NOT FOOLPROOF, DOOM!
I'M WILLING TO BET--MY LIFE!

MY DEVICES NEVER FAIL!!
I'LL MERELY INCREASE THE POWER OUTPUT!

YEAH, SONNY--
YOU DO THAT!!

IT'S LIKE HITTING A STEEL TANK!!
HE DOESN'T EVEN SEEM TO FEEL IT!
SPAP!

BACK, YOU BUMBLING BUFFOON!!
MY PATIENCE HAS RUN OUT!

I AM NOT CALLED "*THE MOST* ***DANGEROUS*** *MAN ALIVE*" FOR ***NOTHING!***

YOU MEAN THEY ***PAY*** YOU?

I'M NOT NOT EXACTLY ***MR. PUSH-OVER*** OF '67 MYSELF!

HAD ***ENOUGH??***

--HE ***VANISHED!!***

NO! THERE'S A TRANSLUSCENT CURTAIN OF ***AIR*** BETWEEN US!

DON'T GLOAT ***YET,*** MASKED MAN!

THE VICTORY IS STILL ***MINE!***

OBSERVE!!

I DON'T GET IT!!
HE'S ENCASED HIMSELF IN AN IDENTICAL CYLINDER!!
THANG!

NOW, IT IS TIME FOR YOU TO LEARN WHAT YOUR FATE WILL BE!
FOR THIS IS MY BRILLIANTLY-CONCEIVED MASTER PLAN--!
NONE BUT DR. DOOM HAS EVER SUCCESSFULLY CREATED A WORKABLE BODY-TRANSFERRAL RAY!!

BODY TRANSFERRAL!
HE CAN'T MEAN--SWITCHING BODIES! HOW--??
UNHHH! MY HEAD!! IT--FEELS AS THOUGH--UNHH--!!

I'M--CHANGING!!
I--I CAN FEEL IT--!!

CORRECTION, DAREDEVIL!
YOU'VE ALREADY CHANGED!
MY HANDS--ENCASED IN METAL GLOVES!!
MY HEAD--ENCLOSED IN AN ARMORED MASK!!
NOW YOU KNOW WHY MY PLAN CANNOT FAIL!
BECAUSE, TO ALL INTENTS AND PURPOSES --I AM DARE-DEVIL!!
WHILE YOU--YOU ARE--DR. DOOM!!
NEXT
THE LIVING PRISON!

HERE COMES...

DAREDEVIL

THE MAN WITHOUT FEAR!

MARVEL COMICS GROUP

12¢ IND.

38 MAR

MCG

APPROVED BY THE COMICS CODE AUTHORITY

"THE LIVING PRISON!"

DAREDEVIL, THE MAN WITHOUT FEAR!
"THE LIVING PRISON!"
I CAN SEE AT LAST!
TRAPPED INSIDE OF DOOM'S BODY, HIS EYESIGHT IS MINE!
BUT I'VE GOT TO ESCAPE... BEFORE HE REACHES THE FANTASTIC FOUR!
THAT'S RIGHT, BELIEVER! WITHIN THE IRON-GARBED FORM OF DR. DOOM IS THE DESPERATELY TRAPPED MENTAL ESSENCE OF DAREDEVIL! IT HAPPENED LAST ISH, BUT THERE'S NO TIME FOR REMINISCING NOW!
THE ACTION'S ABOUT TO BEGIN, AND WE DON'T WANT YOU TO MISS A SINGLE ZOK!
REJOICE, O MARVELDOM! STAN (THE MAN) LEE and GENE (THE DEAN) COLAN HAVE DONE IT AGAIN!
STAUNCHLY SUPPORTED BY: FRANK GIACOIA, EMBELLISHER || SAM ROSEN, LETTERER
and
IRVING FORBUSH, APPLE POLISHER
...SO LET'S GET WITH IT..!!

EVEN IF I *DO* BREAK FREE, DOOM'S *EMBASSY GUARDS* ARE ON DUTY UPSTAIRS, AND... *WAIT!!*
HIS *GUARDS!!* THEY'RE MY *ONE CHANCE!*
KNOWING WHAT AN *EGOMANIAC* DOOM IS, HE PROBABLY NEVER BOTHERED TAKING THEM INTO HIS *CONFIDENCE!*
HE TREATS *ALL* HIS UNDERLINGS AS THOUGH THEY'RE *BENEATH CONTEMPT!*
IF THEY'RE *NOT AWARE* OF OUR UNCANNY *BODY TRANSFERRAL...*
THE *SIMPLEST* RUSE OF ALL MAY *WORK!*
I'VE GOT TO *TRY* IT!
GUARDS! GUARDS!!
GET ME OUT OF HERE!! THIS IS DR. DOOM!!

AT THIS MOMENT HE IS ATTEMPTING TO REACH THE FANTASTIC FOUR!
I'VE ALLOWED THE WITLESS FOOL TO THINK HE HAS A CHANCE!
BUT NOW... GO AFTER HIM!
THINK OF HIS FRUSTRATION... WHEN HE IS STOPPED... SO CLOSE TO HIS INTENDED GOAL!

AND, AT THAT VERY MOMENT, WE FIND THE REAL DR. DOOM ARROGANTLY STRIDING THROUGH THE VIRTUALLY DESERTED STREETS...
STRANGE... I SEEM TO SENSE THINGS RATHER THAN SEE THEM!
THE WORLD APPEARS DIFFERENT TO ME THAN BEFORE!
MY VISION IS CLOUDED... YET SHARPENED, AT THE SAME TIME!
PERHAPS IT IS DUE TO THE OPAQUE EYE FILTERS ON THIS COSTUME!

I SUSPECT I HAVE FOUND THE KEY TO DAREDEVIL'S UNIQUE ABILITY!

BY OBSCURING HIS NORMAL VISION, HE HAS FOUND A WAY TO ACTUALLY SHARPEN THE USE OF HIS OWN SENSES!*

*ALTHOUGH HE'S ON THE RIGHT TRACK, EVEN DOC DOOM DOESN'T SUSPECT THE ENTIRE, FANTASTIC TRUTH... NAMELY, THAT DD IS TOTALLY BLIND! -- SECRETIVE STAN.

IT'S MORE THAN I EVER DREAMT OF... MORE THAN I EVER DARED TO HOPE FOR---

I CAN SEE AGAIN!

BUT, NO TIME TO DWELL ON THAT NOW!

I'VE GOT TO MOVE FAST... BEFORE DOOM'S GUARDS REALIZE I'VE TRICKED THEM!

AND NOW, BACK TO THE EMBASSY...

ON THE OTHER SIDE OF TOWN, ATOP THE WORLD-FAMOUS BAXTER-BUILDING, SKILLED HANDS MANIPULATE DELICATE ELECTRONIC CONTROLS, AS WE HEAR---
WATCH IT, LEADER MAN... COULD BE A TRAP!
THAT SURE DOESN'T SOUND LIKE OL' DD!
NOTHING TO FEAR FROM A RADIO MESSAGE, JOHNNY!
LET'S CHECK IT OUT..!
WHY DON'T YOU TWO JOKERS SAY WHATCHER THINKIN'?
WE ALL KNOW THAT WUZ DOC DOOM'S CREEPY VOICE!
MAYBE... WE DON'T EVEN WANT TO ADMIT IT... TO OURSELVES.. BEN!

WE GOT HIM!
ARE YOU MAD?
DO YOU NOT KNOW WHO I AM??

DON'T TRY TO FOOL US, DAREDEVIL!
WE KNOW THAT IT'S REALLY YOU!

IMBECILES!!

CAN DAREDEVIL STRIKE LIKE THIS??!
DOES HE POSSESS THE STRENGTH..??
OR THE NAKED SAVAGERY??

CAN YOU NOT SENSE THAT I AM DR. DOOM?
OF ALL WHO LIVE...
ONLY I AM TRULY... THE MASTER!!

AND, THOUGH OUR BODIES WERE EXCHANGED...
I FIRST REMOVED MY RING IMPERIAL!!
SO, IF ANY ADDITIONAL PROOF BE NEEDED...
THE MIND-BENDING RAYS WHICH ONLY DR. DOOM CAN CONTROL SHALL FURNISH IT WITHOUT HESITATION!
ENOUGH, EXCELLENCY... ENOUGH!!
MERCY, SIRE!! WE INTENDED NO DISLOYALTY!
IT IS NOT YOUR DISLOYALTY I PUNISH...
BUT YOUR IGNORANCE!!
YOU ALLOWED YOURSELVES TO BE DECEIVED BY THE RUSE OF DAREDEVIL!
SUCH UN-MITIGATED INCOMPETENCE CANNOT POSSIBLY BE TOLERATED!
7.

BUT, THERE IS STILL ONE CHANCE FOR YOU TO WIN CLEMENCY!
WE'LL DO ANYTHING, SIRE... ANYTHING!!

THEN RETURN TO THE EMBASSY!!
RECAPTURE DAREDEVIL BEFORE HE MAKES GOOD HIS ESCAPE!
YOU'LL HAVE NO DIFFICULTY FINDING HIM...
SINCE HE IS HOPELESSLY TRAPPED WITHIN MY OWN BODY!
GO!
A SECOND CHANCE!
WE DARE NOT FAIL!

LISTEN!!
METALLIC FOOTSTEPS... FROM AROUND THE CORNER!! IT'S HIM!!
CLANG!
CLANG!

THE FF HAVE BEEN WARNED!
BUT...HOW DO I REGAIN MY OWN BODY AGAIN?
LUCKY IT'S SUCH A LATE HOUR... AND THE STREETS ARE ALL DESERTED!
I COULD HARDLY FIND A SUITABLE HIDING PLACE IN THIS GETUP!
CLANG!
IF ONLY I CAN CATCH UP TO DOOM IN TIME...
ONLY HE HAS THE KEY TO ALL THIS!
8

BUT, NO LONGER POSSESSING THE INFALLIBLE SUPER-SENSES WHICH HIS PURLOINED BODY STILL HOUSES, THE MAN WITHOUT FEAR... WITHIN HIS LIVING, ARMORED PRISON... DOESN'T HEAR THE THREE AGENTS TURNING THE CORNER, UNTIL...
BTANNG!
DOOM'S PLUG-UGLIES, IN PERSON!
THEY MUST HAVE BEEN RETURNING FOR ME!
THAT MEANS HE PUT THEM WISE...
...SO THE PARTY'S OVER!
IT'S HIM... UNHHH!

PERSONAL NOTE: HAVE YOU BEEN ABLE TO FOLLOW THIS TORTUOUSLY TWISTED PLOT THUS FAR WITHOUT LOSING TRACK OF WHO'S WHO? IF SO, CONSIDER YOURSELF HANDSOMELY NO-PRIZED... AND YOU DESERVE IT!
BUT, FOR THE BENEFIT OF THOSE PERPLEXED PILGRIMS (SUCH AS OURSELVES), WHO MAY HAVE TEMPORARILY LOST THEIR WAY...
YONDER IS DAREDEVIL, TRAPPED IN THE BODY OF DOC DOOM...
WHILE THE MASTER OF VILLAINY IS STILL SKIPPING AROUND IN THE GUISE OF OUR FEARLESS FANATIC!
OKAY? THEN BACK TO THE MERRY MAYHEM..!
I'M AT A DIS-ADVANTAGE... CAN'T FIGHT AS WELL IN DOOM'S FORM!
EVEN THE BENEFIT OF HIS ARMORED MIGHT ISN'T ENOUGH FOR ME..!
I'VE DEPENDED TOO LONG UPON MY OWN SUPER REFLEXES... AND MY HYPER-KEEN SENSES!!
ALSO, WHEREAS THE ARMOR SERVED TO PROTECT AND FORTIFY DOOM... ITS CUMBERSOME WEIGHT MERELY SLOWS ME DOW...
UNHHH!!
THE MASTER WILL REWARD US HANDSOMELY FOR THIS!!
LET US BE CONTENT WITH BEING SPARED HIS AWESOME PUNISHMENT!
10

NOW... LET'S FINISH HIM OFF!
I DON'T DARE USE DOOM'S BUILT-IN WEAPONS...
SINCE THEY'RE STRANGE TO ME, THEY MIGHT GET OUT OF CONTROL...

...AND I CAN'T TAKE THE CHANCE OF INNOCENT BYSTANDERS BEING HURT!
SO, THERE'S ONLY ONE THING LEFT TO DO...

BOK!
AND THIS IS IT!

HEAVY THOUGH IT IS, THIS ARMOR DIFINITELY GIVES ME AN EDGE..!

AND, THE MORE I USE IT, THE MORE IT SEEMS TO BECOME A PART OF ME!

IT SURE IS A GREAT FEELING BEING ABLE TO SEE WHERE A ONE-TWO LANDS!
RAP!

HOW ABOUT THAT?!!
A REAL KNOCK-DOWN, DRAG-OUT STREET FIGHT!
IT WON'T LAST LONG---
HERE COME THE POLICE!
LOOK! THE MAN BEING ATTACKED...
I RECOGNIZE HIM!!

IT'S DR. DOOM... THE CHIEF OF STATE OF LATVERIA!!
IF WE DON'T BREAK IT UP, IT COULD CAUSE A WHOLE INTER-NATIONAL INCIDENT!
LOOKS LIKE WE GOT HERE JUST IN TIME!
POLIC

STAND BACK! STAND BACK!
WE'RE IN LUCK! HE DOESN'T SEEM HURT!

OKAY, MISTER... YOU'VE HAD IT!
YOU PICKED YOURSELF THE WRONG SPARRING PARTNER!
UNHAND ME! I AM REPRESENTATIVE OF LATVERIAN EMBASSY!
SURE! SURE! AND I'M MOTHER GOOSE!
YOU CAN TELL IT TO THE JUDGE, MAC!
ARE YOU ALL RIGHT, YOUR EXCELLENCY?
YES! YOU ARRIVED JUST IN TIME!
12

CAN'T TELL THEM I'M NOT DOOM! THEY'D THINK I'M MAD!
WE'LL ESCORT YOU SAFELY TO YOUR EMBASSY, SIR!

NO! THAT'S THE LAST THING I WANT!
I'VE GOT TO FIND THE REAL DR.DOOM... BEFORE HE CAN REACH THE F.F.!

YOUR COMPANY WILL NOT BE NEEDED, OFFICER!
BUT... YOU CAN'T WALK THRU TOWN IN THAT... EH.. THAT GET-UP!
YOUR AUDIENCE IS ENDED!!
STAND ASIDE!

IT'S NOT BAD BEING A HEAD OF STATE!
NO ONE HAS THE RIGHT TO RESTRAIN YOU!
WELL, IT TAKES ALL KINDS!

WHILE, NOT VERY FAR AWAY...
SAME TIME TOMORROW, FOGGY?
WILD HORSES COULDN'T KEEP ME AWAY, DEBBIE!
EVEN THOUGH I KNOW WE SHOULDN'T BE SEEING EACH OTHER!
NELSON AND MURDOCK

I THOUGHT YOU WEREN'T GOING TO SEE DEBORAH HARRIS, FOGGY!
IT WON'T HELP YOU GET THE NOMINATION FOR D.A. IF YOU'RE SEEN DATING AN EX-CONVICT!
BUT NOBODY'S SEEN US SO FAR, KAREN!
AND, I'M NOT FOOLISH ENOUGH TO THINK YOU ASKED ME OUT OF JEALOUSY!

I WISH A CERTAIN SIGHT-LESS PARTNER OF YOURS FELT ABOUT ME THE WAY YOU FEEL ABOUT MISS HARRIS!
POOR MATT! I'M AFRAID HE'S BLIND IN MORE WAYS THAN ONE!
THAT REMINDS ME...
WHERE'S HE BEEN LATELY?
I THOUGHT HE WAS WORKING ON...
FOGGY! LOOK..!!

IT'S HIS BROTHER, MIKE!
RIGHT OUT IN THE STREET... IN FULL COSTUME!
THERE'S DEBBIE! SHE SEES HIM!
SHE'S WALKING OVER TO HIM... TALKING TO HIM!

THEY'VE MET BEFORE... WHEN HE HELPED HER IN THE CASE OF THE ORGANIZER! *
BUT, HE'S RECOILING FROM HER NOW... AS THOUGH SHE'S A STRANGER!
WHY??
IF ONLY I COULD HEAR WHAT THEY'RE SAYING!
*IF YOU DON'T REMEMBER OUR FAMOUS ISHES #'S 10 AND 11, IT'LL SHAKE OUR FAITH IN DARE-DEVILDOM!... SENTIMENTAL STAN.
14.

AND, IF FOGGY COULD HEAR WHAT THEY'RE SAYING...
FOGGY WILL LISTEN TO YOU..!
CAN'T YOU TELL HIM... I'VE REFORMED??
I'D NEVER DO ANYTHING.. TO HURT HIM..!

HE'S THE GENTLEST, MOST WONDERFUL MAN I'VE EVER... OHH!
ENOUGH! YOUR PRATTLE NOW BEGINS TO BORE ME!
I HAVE URGENT MATTERS TO SETTLE!
THE CREEP!! DID YOU SEE HOW HE BRUSHED HER ASIDE??

I WASN'T LOOKING!
ARE YOU SURE YOU DIDN'T JUST IMAGINE IT, FOGGY?
A MAN DOESN'T IMAGINE SOME-THING LIKE THAT!

MEANWHILE, THE REAL DARE-DEVIL (IN THE PERSON OF DOC DOOM, REMEMBER?) FINALLY REACHES HIS GOAL..!
HE'S COMING NOW..!
EVERYTHING DEPENDS UPON THE NEXT FEW MINUTES!

HOLD IT, DOOM! DIDN'T EXPECT ME TO ESCAPE, DID YOU?
NO! I AM CONSTANTLY AMAZED AT YOUR RESOURCE-FULNESS!
BUT, SO LONG AS YOU INHABIT MY FORMER BODY...
YOU CAN NEVER TRULY ESCAPE!

YOU'RE WRONG, DOOM! BUT I CAN'T CONVINCE YOU NOW!
HERE, TAKE THIS TRANSISTOR RADIO!
WHY?
LISTEN TO THE VERY NEXT NEWS BROADCAST!
THEN YOU'LL KNOW HOW I INTEND TO ESCAPE!

YOU'RE MAD, DAREDEVIL!
YOU WON'T THINK SO... LATER!
NO NEED TO PURSUE HIM... OR TO BATTLE HIM!
HE IS TRAPPED IN THAT FORM FOREVER!
HIS PLIGHT IS TOTALLY... ETERNALLY... HOPELESS!

BUT, IS IT?
I'VE GOT TO REACH DOOM'S RADIO ROOM!
HIS MEN WON'T STOP ME!
THEY THINK I'M NOW THE REAL RULER OF LATVERIA!

NOW--- EVERYTHING DEPENDS UPON ME CONTACTING HIS FAR-OFF PRIME-MINISTERS IN TIME!
AND THEN, I HAVE TO HOPE HE'LL TUNE IN TO THE NEWS PROGRAM--- AS I SAID!
BUT, UNLESS I KNOW NOTHING ABOUT HUMAN PSYCHOLOGY--- HE WON'T BE ABLE TO RESIST TUNING IN!
--AND THEN, I'LL HAVE HIM!

HERE'S THE CONTROL BUTTON, I NEED!
LATVERIA
CLICK!
IT STILL FEELS STRANGE TO SEE A DIAL...
INSTEAD OF SENSING IT!
NOW TO SWITCH ON THE TELE-VIEWER..!
NOW ALL I NEED IS A CLOSER FOCUS!
I DID IT! I REACHED HIS CASTLE!
THIS HAS TO WORK!! IT HAS TO!!
16.

I KNEW I'D REACH HIS COUNCIL OF MINISTERS!
A MAN LIKE DOOM WAS CERTAIN TO HAVE MEANS OF INSTANT COMMUNICATION!
AND NOW... THIS IS IT!
THESE ARE MY IMPERIAL ORDERS... TO BE OBEYED IMMEDIATELY--- WITHOUT QUESTION!
YOU WILL DECLARE WAR UPON EVERY NATION THAT BORDERS LATVERIA!
I WANT TOTAL MOBILIZATION!
THAT IS ALL!

AND--- IN A MATTER OF MINUTES...
BULLETIN!! LATVERIA HAS UNILATERALLY DECLARED WAR UPON HER FOUR ADJACENT NEIGHBORS..!
NO! IT IS INSANE!
THEN THIS WAS WHAT DAREDEVIL MEANT!

ONE OF OUR NEIGHBORS IS ALLIED WITH RED CHINA!
WE'LL BE OVER-RUN IN HOURS!!
TAXI

I'VE GOT TO CANCEL THE ORDER---
BUT I CAN'T DO IT IN THE GUISE OF DAREDEVIL!
ONLY AS DR. DOOM WILL MY WORD STILL BE LAW!

COME IN! I'VE BEEN WAITING FOR YOU!
STAND WHERE YOU ARE! DO NOT MOVE!
I WOULDN'T DREAM OF IT! I KNOW WHAT YOU'RE ABOUT TO DO...!
17.

BETTER HURRY, YOUR HIGHNESS!
OR YOU WON'T HAVE A NATION TO RETURN TO!
I NEED NO ADVICE FROM YOU!!

NOW, NOW... TEMPER, TEMPER...
OOOOHH--

I'M BACK IN THE GLASS TRANSFER TUBE AGAIN!
PERHAPS IT IS BETTER THIS WAY!
NONE BUT DR. DOOM IS TRULY FIT TO RULE!

EVERYTHING GROWING HAZY... GETTING HARDER TO SEE...

MY VISION... IT'S GONE!! I--I'M DAREDEVIL AGAIN!!

AND THIS TIME I'LL MAKE SURE I STAY THIS WAY!
KRASH!
18

IT MUST HAVE TAKEN NEARLY A LIFETIME TO BUILD THE TRANSFER MACHINE...
AND, SINCE EVEN DOOM CAN ONLY LIVE ONE SINGLE LIFETIME...
THIS SHOULD INSURE THAT THERE'LL BE NO OTHER VICTIMS... EVER!
SPLASH
BUT, WHAT HAPPENS NOW?
HE'S STILL MANY TIMES MORE POWERFUL THAN I...!
YOU MAY STAND RELAXED, DAREDEVIL!
I HAVE SO RARELY BEEN DEFEATED...
THAT I AM AMUSED BY THE NOVELTY!
YOU MEAN... I'M FREE TO GO?
OF COURSE!
THE KING OF LATVERIA IS NO COMMON MURDERER!
IF I CANNOT MAGNIFICENTLY WIN A VICTORY...
IT AFFORDS ME NO PLEASURE TO MERELY SLAY A FOE!
ONE DAY.. WE SHALL MEET AGAIN!
BUT, MINUTES LATER...
NOW THAT I HAVE CANCELLED MY NATION'S DECLARATION OF WAR...
TRIUMPH SHALL STILL BE MINE!
I SHALL SETTLE MY SCORE WITH BOTH THE FANTASTIC FOUR... AND DAREDEVIL, AS WELL!!

ALL I NEED DO IS EMPLOY MY ELECTRONIC *VOICE MODULATOR!*

AND I WILL *DECEIVE* THE *FF*... JUST AS *DAREDEVIL* DECEIVED MY OWN COUNCIL OF MINISTERS!

IT WILL BE *CHILDS' PLAY* FOR ME TO *DUPLICATE* THE COMMONPLACE VOICE OF THE MASKED CRIME-FIGHTER!

IT IS *CERTAIN* THAT HE WILL NOW HEAD FOR THE *FANTASTIC FOUR!*

BUT *DR. DOOM* SHALL CONTACT THEM *FIRST!*

...WITH THE VOICE OF... *DAREDEVIL!*

AND SO...

IT *SOUNDS* LIKE HIM... BUT I MUST BE *SURE!*

BEN! QUICK... CHECK THIS OUT AGAINST DD'S *VOCA-FILE!*

THE WORLD'S GREATEST COMIC MAGAZINE!
Fantastic Four
APPROVED BY THE COMICS CODE AUTHORITY
MARVEL COMICS GROUP
12¢ IND.
73 APR
MCG
GIANT GUEST STAR BONANZA!

IN WHICH THE FABULOUS F.F. MAKE THEIR DEADLIEST MISTAKE
"THE FLAMES OF BATTLE.."
PAY ATTENTION, PILGRIM--THIS IS IMPORTANT--!
IN DAREDEVIL #38 (NOW ON SALE), WE SAW DD FREE HIMSELF FROM THE PHYSICAL FORM OF DR. DOOM! GOT IT? OKAY!
BUT NOW, THE DEMONIAC DOC HAS TRICKED THE FF INTO BELIEVING THAT DOOM IS ABOUT TO ATTACK THEM--STILL IN THE FORM OF DAREDEVIL!
TAKE YOUR POST, TORCH!
SOUND THE ALARM AS SOON AS YOU SIGHT HIM!
I HOPE I CAN GIT MY PAWS ON 'IM BEFORE YA BELT 'IM WITH THAT SOUPED-UP POP-GUN!
LET MARVELDOM CHEER! LET HUMANITY SHOUT!
STAN (THE MAN) LEE and JACK (KING) KIRBY
HAVE BESTOWED ANOTHER MASTERPIECE UPON MANKIND!
EXOTICALLY EMBELLISHED BY: JOE SINNOTT
LACONICALLY LETTERED BY: ARTIE SIMEK

WITH DOOM ABOUT TO STRIKE, I'M GLAD THERE WAS TIME TO GET SUE SAFELY OUT OF TOWN.!
YOU WON'T HAVETA WORRY ABOUT THAT CREEP--
NOT IF HE GITS WITHIN CLOBBERIN' DISTANCE!

ANYWAY, HOW CAN YA BE SURE THAT OL' HORNHEAD IS REALLY DOOM?
BECAUSE THE REAL DAREDEVIL CALLED TO WARN US!
I SEE HIM--JUST AHEAD!
BUT HOW D'YA KNOW IT WUZ THE REAL DD?
DON'T YOU REMEMBER--?
WE CHECKED HIS VOICE AGAINST THE AUDIO RECORD ON ON OUR VOCA-FILE!

AND, AS WE CONCLUDE OUR SNEAKY, SUBLIMINAL SUMMARY--
IT'S HARD TO BELIEVE THAT DOOM IS REALLY GONE!
BUT, I STILL HAVE TO WARN THE FF--

THERE'S ALWAYS THE CHANCE HE MAY TRY THE SAME TRICK AGAIN--
BUT, ONCE I REVEAL HIS SECRET OF BODY TRANSFERRAL TO RICHARDS, HE'LL-- WAIT!!
IT CAN ONLY MEAN--ONE THING--!
THAT SUDDEN HEAT--ABOVE ME!

ZASK!
THE TORCH! HE'S ATTACKING!
BUT WHY?
WHY USE HIS FLAME AGAINST ME?!!

CAN'T KEEP DODGING HIS STUN BLASTS MUCH LONGER!
MY ONLY CHANCE IS TO TRICK HIM--!

YOU CAN'T ESCAPE ME THAT WAY, DOOM!
SO THAT'S IT!
HE STILL THINKS I'M THE OTHER DD!

IF I HAD THE SENSE OF A GOPHER, I'D TAKE OFF!
I'M NO MATCH FOR THE WORLD'S GREATEST SUPER-TEAM!
BUT, I MUST EXPLAIN--THEY HAVE TO BE WARNED--SOMEHOW!
SOMEONE JUST SWUNG ONTO THE ROOF! IF IT'S--NO!
IT'S SPIDER-MAN!
AM I TOO LATE FOR THE PARTY?
WHAT GIVES, HORN-HEAD?

IT'S NO PARTY, MISTER!
THE FF THINK I'M DR. DOOM--AND THEY'RE AFTER ME--WITH THE GLOVES OFF!
YOU'RE PUTTING ME ON!
THEY THINK YOU'RE DOOM?
IF YOU THINK IT'S A GAG--
THEN CUT OUT! WHO NEEDS YOU?

YOU REALLY MEAN IT, EH? YOU ARE IN A JAM!
OKAY THEN--YOU CAN COUNT ON YOUR FRIENDLY, NEIGHBOR-HOOD SPIDER-MAN!
THWIP!
BUT, IF WE HAVE TO STAND UP TO THE FF--WE'LL NEED HELP!
HOLD IT! I DIDN'T ASK--!
REEE-LAX, SON!

WHILE I WAS CAVORTING AROUND TOWN, I NOTICED JUST THE JOKER WE NEED!
IF HE'S STILL THERE--WE'LL BE IN BUSINESS!

HE'S JUST GETTING UP!
THE BIG FELLA LOOKS LIKE HE'S BEEN THRU A WAR!*
WELL, NOTHING LIKE A GOOD FIGHT TO SHAKE HIM OUT OF IT!
* --HIS BATTLE WITH THE WRECKER, IN THOR #150, TO BE EXACT! --STATISTICAL STAN.

HI, GOLDILOCKS! YOU'RE JUST THE THUNDER GOD I'VE BEEN LOOKING FOR!
SPIDER-MAN! WHAT BRINGS THEE HENCE?
I WAS HOPING YOU'D ASK!

THERE'S TROUBLE BREWING BETWEEN THE FF AND DAREDEVIL, AND--
STILL THY TONGUE! I'LL HEAR NO MORE OF IT!
THE POWER OF THOR IS NEEDED ELSE-WHERE!

WOW!-I NEVER THOUGHT YOU'D TURN CHICKEN!
IF THAT DOTH MEAN WHAT I TAKE IT TO MEAN--
THOU DAREST ACCUSE THE SON OF ODIN-- OF COWARDICE??
YOU FIGURE IT OUT, CURLY!

EVEN AS WE TALK, DAREDEVIL'S LIFE IS IN DANGER--FROM THE FF!
CAN'T WAIT FOR SPIDER-MAN ANY LONGER!
THE BAXTER BUILDING IS JUST AHEAD!

MY RADAR SENSE!! IT JUST REACTED TO SOMETHING! I'D BETTER---UNN!!
TOO LATE! I'VE BEEN SNARED--BY RICHARDS HIMSELF!
HOW DO I CONVINCE THEN I'M THE REAL DAREDEVIL??
IF THEY THINK I'M DR. DOOM --THEY WON'T GIVE ME A CHANCE!
YA GOT 'IM, STRETCH!
BUT, WHAT HAPPENED TO JOHNNY?
THAT'S WHAT WE'LL SOON FIND OUT!
5

LEGGO OF HIM, MISTER!
IT DON'T TAKE BRAINS TO HANDLE A CRUMB THAT!
NO, BEN! WE'VE GOT TO FIND OUT WHAT HE DID TO THE TORCH FIRST!
BEN--STOP!! HOLD IT!
DON'T BE A FOOL, THING!
I'M NOT DR. DOOM!

OH NO?? THEN WHY-- UNNNH!
YER NERVE BLAST RAY!! YA USED IT--AGAINST--ME?!!
I WARNED YOU, BEN!
I HAD A FEELING IT WASN'T MY KICK THAT STOPPED HIM!

LOOK, RICHARDS--USE YOUR HEAD!
IF I WERE DOOM--WOULD I COME HERE?
OF COURSE YOU WOULD--
IF YOU DIDN'T KNOW THE REAL DAREDEVIL HAD ALREADY WARNED US!
BUT--GIVE ME A CHANCE --I'LL PROVE WHO I AM!
HOW?
HE'S RIGHT!! --HOW??
WE BOTH KNOW DOOM HAD A BODY TRANSFERRAL RAY--
SO, HOW DO I PROVE HE HASN'T USED IT ON ME?

LET'S SIT DOWN AND TALK ABOUT IT--LIKE CIVILIZED MEN!
BETWEEN THE TWO OF US WE CAN FIGURE SOMETHING OUT!
FORGET IT, MASKED MAN!
IF YOU ARE DR. DOOM--I WOULDN'T LET MY GUARD DOWN FOR A SECOND!
THEN--WHAT DO YOU PLAN TO DO--
--MURDER ME--JUST ON SUSPICION??
6

THAT DON'T SOUND LIKE A BAD IDEA, FROM WHERE I SIT!
HOLD OFF, BEN! YOUR FULL STRENGTH CAN'T HAVE RETURNED TO YOU SO SOON!
NUTS!! HOW MUCH DO I NEED AGAINST THAT FOULBALL?

I KIND'A HATE TO MESS UP DAREDEVIL'S BODY--SINCE IT DON'T BELONG TO YA--
HAVE TO STRIKE NOW--WHILE HE'S PARTIALLY STUNNED!
--BUT I'LL APOLOGIZE WHEN I SEE 'IM!

UNNHH!!-- EVEN AFTER BEING BELTED WITH RICHARDS' NERVE BLASTER--
HE'S STILL A POWERHOUSE!
THE DEMOLO-GUN--YOU'RE FALLING TOWARDS IT!
RATS!! I TRIPPED OVER STRETCHO'S MILE-LONG LEG!!
LOOK OUT, BEN!
LOOK OUT!

BUT, THE WARNING CRY OF MR. FANTASTIC COMES TOO LATE FOR THE THING TO CHECK HIS FALL, AS--A MICRO-SECOND LATER--
BA-KOW
THE SHOCK MADE HIM RELEASE ME!
THIS IS MY CHANCE TO ESCAPE--
IF I CAN MANAGE TO LIVE LONG ENOUGH!
THE DEMOLO-GUN!!
SMASH IT, BEN--SMASH IT!
7

YOU DID IT!
AND IT WAS JUST IN TIME, OLD FRIEND--
FIRING UNCHECKED, IT MIGHT HAVE DESTROYED THE CITY!
NEVER MIND THE LECTURE!
LET'S GO FIND DOOM!
MEANWHILE--
HEAR THAT BLAST, GOLDEN BOY?
STILL THINK YOU'RE NOT NEEDED AT THE BAXTER BUILDING?
THOUGH OMNIPOTENT ODIN HATH STRIPPED ME OF MY ENCHANTED POWERS--
THOR SHALL BE THINE ALLY!
LET US THEN AWAY!
WELL? WHAT ARE YOU WAITING FOR?
WHERE'S THE OL' PIZZAZZ?
IT CRACKS ME UP TO WATCH YOU FLY, HOLDING ONTO THAT CRAZY HAMMER!
ALAS, I MAY DO SO--NO LONGER!
WITH MY HAMMER'S POWER DENIED ME-- I AM TRULY EARTH-BOUND AS IS ANY MORTAL!
WELL, HANG LOOSE, BIG FELLA--
NO SENSE WASTING OUR MONEY ON CABS!
I DO NOT RELISH THE PROSPECT OF WAGING BATTLE AGAINST THE INDOMITABLE FANTASTIC FOUR!
THEY HAVE EVER ESPOUSED THE CAUSE OF JUSTICE--AND TRUTH!
I DON'T LIKE THE IDEA OF SLUGGING IT OUT WITH THEM EITHER!
BUT MOSTLY BECAUSE THEY'VE GOT A BAD HABIT OF NEVER LOSING!
8

ANY ONE OF THOSE CHARACTERS HAS THE POWER TO HOLD OFF A SMALL ARMY!
EVEN MOISHE DAYAN WOULD THINK TWICE ABOUT TANGLING WITH THEM!
THAT VOICE--SOUNDS LIKE SPIDER-MAN SWINGING OFF TOWARDS OUR HQ!
WHAT'S GOING ON AROUND HERE?
FIRST DOOM ATTACKS US-- IN THE GUISE OF DAREDEVIL--
AND NOW--I SEE THE WALL-CRAWLER, AND-- THAT'S GOTTA BE THOR WITH HIM--!
WHAT IF-- THEY'RE ENEMIES IN DISGUISE, TOO?!!
FLAME ON!
DOOM WAS A MASTER AT CREATING LIFELIKE ROBOTS--!
AND IT'S JUST POSSIBLE THAT THOSE TWO ARE HIS LATEST HANDIWORK!
OKAY, PLAYMATES!! YOU'VE GONE FAR ENOUGH!
GET OFF THAT ROOF BEFORE I BLAST YOU OFF!
THY WORDS WERE TRUE!
THE MADNESS IS SURELY UPON HIM!
IN OTHER WORDS, HE HASN'T CHANGED A BIT!
YOU HANDLE THE THING, CURLY--
A FELLA HIS SIZE IS MORE YOUR SPEED!
I'LL KEEP THE TORCH BUSY!
BUT NOT FOR LONG YOU WON'T!
SO BE IT!
9

STAY THY HANDS!
'TIS THE GOD OF THUNDER WHO DOTH COMMAND THEE!
AT LAST-- SOMEONE BIG ENUFF FER ME TO CLOBBER!
IT COULD BE ANOTHER OF DOOM'S TRAPS, BEN!
HOLD HIM OFF WHILE I SETTLE WITH THE BOGUS DAREDEVIL!
AND YET--WHAT IF HE REALLY IS DAREDEVIL?
HOW CAN I EVER KNOW?
THOR-- SPIDER-MAN-- HERE TO HELP ME!
BUT--AGAINST THE FANTASTIC FOUR-- WILL THE TWO OF THEM BE ENOUGH??

I GOTTA HAND IT TO YER BOSS-- DOC DOOM!
IF I DIDN'T KNOW BETTER, I'D SWEAR YA REALLY ARE OL' GOLDILOCKS!
WHAT?!! THOU DOST TAKE ME FOR A BASE IMPOSTOR?!!
TRULY, THERE BE MADNESS UNBRIDLED AMONGST YE MORTALS!

WATCH YER LANGWICH, CORNBALL!!
THERE MAY BE SOME CHICKS AROUND!
HUH? HOW'DJA DODGE THAT HAY-MAKER?
THINK YOU THE THUNDER GOD BE NOT SWIFT OF EYE AND FLEET OF LIMB?

FOR ASGARD-- AND HONOR IMPERIAL!!
IT'S CLOBBERIN' TIME--RIGHT BACK ATCHA!
11

HAH! I DID IT!! I FLOORED OL' GOLDILOCKS HIMSELF!
BUT, I THOUGHT HIS HAMMER WUZ ENCHANTED!
I JUST REMEMBER --HE SAID HE LOST HIS POWERS!
NUTS! IT'S LIKE HIM BEATIN' PLAIN BEN GRIMM!
HEY! YER STILL AWAKE!
--TRYIN' TO GIT UP!
EVEN WITHOUT YER POWERS-- YOU AINT NO PANTY-WAIST!
EVEN WITHOUT MY POWERS-- STILL AM I THOR--
--SON OF ODIN--WARRIOR OF ASGARD--IMMORTAL BORN!!
OKAY! OKAY! YA WANT I SHOULD COURTSY--OR BOW??
LOOK OUT WITH THAT HAMMER--!
--YER LIABLE TO GIMME A CHARLEY HORSE!
AND, JUST OUTSIDE THE WINDOW--WE FIND--
HOLD IT, WEBHEAD!
YOU'RE NOT GOING ANY-WHERE!
ZIZZZT!
DOESN'T THAT HOTHEAD EVER MISS?
NO MATTER HOW MANY NUTTY WEBS YOU SHOOT--
I'VE FLAME ENOUGH TO SIZZLE ALL OF THEM!
THWIP!
FORGIVE ME FOR NOT APPLAUDING--
BUT I'M KINDA BUSY RIGHT NOW!
12

I FIGURED YOU'D TRY TO LOSE ME AROUND THAT CORNER!
YOU DISAPPOINT ME, WALL-CRAWLER--
DO YOU THINK YOU'RE PLAYING WITH AMATEURS?

ANSWER ME WHEN I TALK TO YOU!!
--OR CAN YOU ONLY TALK WHEN DOOM PULLS THE STRINGS?

HE LANDED ON THE ROOF OF A CHEMICAL PLANT!
GOTTA REACH HIM, BEFORE HE CAN-- UH OH!!
I CAN'T STOP IN TIME--!

THOSE FUMES-- FROM THE CHIMNEY--
WHEN MY FLAME HITS THEM, THEY'LL--
UNNHH!!

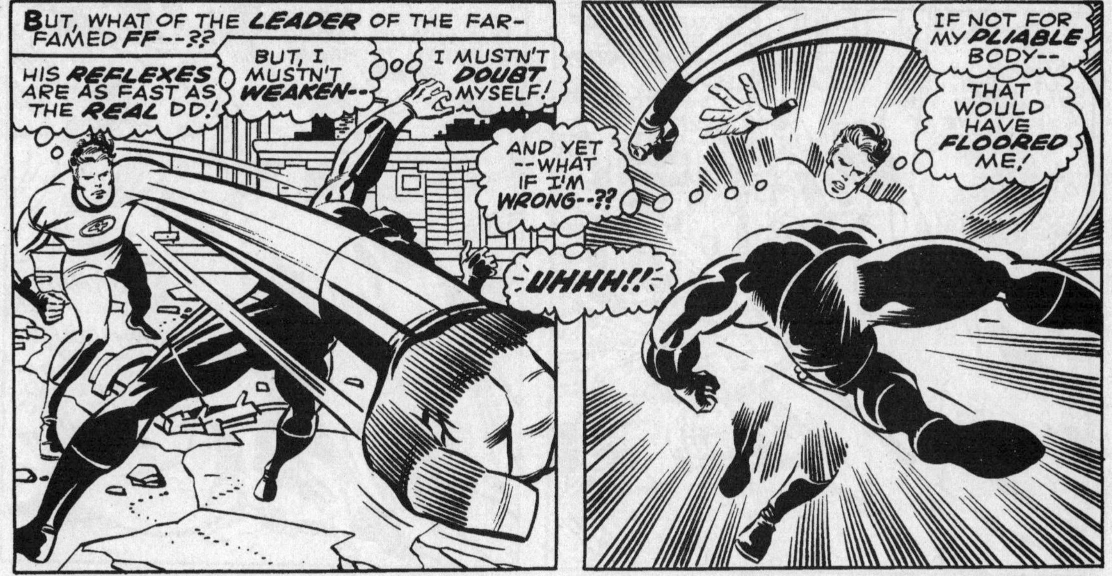
BUT, WHAT OF THE LEADER OF THE FAR-FAMED FF--??
HIS REFLEXES ARE AS FAST AS THE REAL DD!
BUT, I MUSTN'T WEAKEN--
I MUSTN'T DOUBT MYSELF!
AND YET --WHAT IF I'M WRONG--??
UHHH!!
IF NOT FOR MY PLIABLE BODY--
THAT WOULD HAVE FLOORED ME!

THE ROOF--IT'S BEEN WEAKENED BY THE EXPLOSION--
IT'S CAVING IN!
WE'RE FALLING THRU--TO THE LAB BELOW!!

I DON'T WANT TO DO THIS, RICHARDS--BUT--
SAVE YOUR BREATH, MASKED MAN--
YOU WON'T BE DOING IT MUCH LONGER!
I'M THRU HANDLING YOU WITH KID GLOVES--!

PERHAPS I CAN'T MATCH YOUR UNCANNY REFLEXES--OR ACROBATIC SKILL--
BUT, I'VE A FEW LITTLE STUNTS OF MY OWN--SUCH AS THIS--!

BUT, REACHING OUT FROM UNDER THE ENVELOPING BODY OF REED RICHARDS, DAREDEVIL'S UNCANNY SENSES DIRECT HIS HAND TO--
SOME SORT OF ELECTRIC POWER ROD!

I'VE GOT TO SHOCK HIM WITH IT--LONG ENOUGH TO BREAK FREE!
UNHH!
HOW--COULD YOU SPOT THAT ROD--WHEN I HAD YOU--TOTALLY BLIND-FOLDED??

THAT'S MY SECRET!
NOBODY CAN OPERATE SO WELL WITHOUT BEING ABLE TO SEE--
--UNLESS HE HAPPENS TO BE--AN ELECTRONIC ROBOT!
--SUCH AS THE TYPE DR. DOOM EXCELS IN CREATING!

HE DOESN'T REALIZE MY OTHER SENSES MAKE UP FOR MY LIFELONG BLINDNESS!
HE'S MAKING A LASSO--OF HIS ARM!
NOW, DUE TO MY OWN POWER, HE'S SURE TO BELIEVE I'M ONE OF DOOM'S ROBOTS!
ALL RIGHT, MASKED MAN--JUMP!

THANKS! JUST WHAT I WANTED!

AND, AT THAT MOMENT, ANOTHER MEMBER OF THE MULTI-POWERED FF IS ALSO DOING WHAT COMES NATURALLY--
WHAT'S KEEPIN' YA ON YER FEET, CURLEY?
WHEN I BELT A GUY, HE'S SUPPOSED TO STAY BELTED!
YOU TRYIN' TO GIMME A COMPLEX, OR SOMETHIN'?

O, MOST IMPERIAL SIRE--THOUGH THOU HAST MADE ME LESS THAN GODLIKE--
STILL AM I TRULY MORE THAN MORTAL!
THOUGH I HAVE BEEN FORSAKEN BY THEE--
NEITHER MY FAITH--NOR MY TRUST HAVE WAVERED!!

THUS, IN THY NAME--
BECAUSE I BE FLESH OF THY FLESH--BLOOD OF THY BLOOD--
THE VICTORY SHALL YET BE MINE!

SO SPEAKS THOR!!

I DON'T GIT IT!
HOW CAN ANY BLASTED ROBOT MANAGE TO TALK AS CORNY AS THAT--?
YEWWPH!

THIS IS BATTY!!
EVEN THOUGH WE KNOW WE'RE SUPPOSED TA FLATTEN THE WHOLE BUNCH'A YA--
WE KEEP PULLIN' OUR PUNCHES--ON ACCOUNT'A YA LOOK LIKE THE GOOD GUYS!
WITLESS CHURL! DOST THOU TAKE US FOR KNAVES?

THINK YOU WE BE LESS THAN WHAT WE SEEM?
HOW'S A GUY TO KNOW WHAT TO THINK--WITH YOU TALKIN' LIKE A REFUGEE FROM A ROAD-SHOW HAMLET!

I CAN'T MAKE MYSELF TEAR INTA HIM--I JUST CAN'T!
TO THINK THAT THE ONCE-PROUD FANTASTIC FOUR HAVE TURNED TO CRAVEN SAVAGERY!

NOW YA DID IT!
I AINT SURE I KNOW WHAT YA SAID--
--BUT IT SOUNDED TO ME LIKE YER PUTTIN' DOWN THE FF--
AND NOBODY DOES THAT WHILE BASHFUL BENJAMIN'S AROUND!!

MOVING WITH A SPEED BELYING HIS PONDEROUS SIZE, THE NOW-FIGHTING-MAD THING UNLEASHES ONE PULVERIZING BLOW--SHATTERING THE SOLID CEMENT BENEATH HIS FEET--!
FIRST OF ALL--I'LL GITCHA INTO CLOBBERIN' POSITION--!
BTAM!
HAVE A CARE, MORTAL!
THOU ART TOYING WITH POWER FAR BEYOND THY COMPREHENSION!
YEAH--SURE!
I'LL TELL 'IM WHEN HE COMES IN!
AWRIGHT, ROBOT--
HERE'S WHERE I PART YA FROM ALL YER LITTLE COGWHEELS!
SPTANG!
HEY! WHAT GIVES--?
I HIT SOMETHIN'--BUT--IT WUZN'T THOR!
HE'S STILL STANDIN'--LIKE NOTHIN' HAPPENED!
--AND HE LOOKS AS SURPRISED AS I AM!
18

THEN, EVEN AS THE THING STANDS IN MUTE MYSTIFICATION--
I THOUGHT YOU HAD MORE SENSE THAN THE OTHERS, RICHARDS!
I HOPED YOU'D LISTEN TO REASON--!

TRY ME, FELLA!
I'M STILL WAITING FOR SOME PROOF FROM YOU!
BUT, I TOLD YOU--
I DON'T KNOW HOW TO PROVE I'M ME!

SUPPOSE YOU HAD TO PROVE YOU WERE REALLY YOU--
HOW WOULD YOU DO IT?
IT'S A GOOD ARGUMENT, MISTER!
YOU SHOULD HAVE BEEN A LAWYER!

BUT IT SO HAPPENS I KNOW WHO I AM!
YOU'RE THE ONE I'M WORRIED ABOUT!

NOW, TALK!! TELL ME WHERE THE REAL DR. DOOM IS, AND I'LL-- WHA-??!
I DID!
THAT VOICE! IT CAN ONLY BE--!!
WHAT STOPPED MY BLOW FROM LANDING.??

SUE!
BUT--YOU SHOULDN'T BE HERE--!
I HAD TO COME, DARLING--TO SAVE YOU--FROM A TERRIBLE MISTAKE!
HE IS THE REAL DARE-DEVIL!
BUT--HOW CAN YOU KNOW?
19

IT WAS ON THE SIX P.M. TV NEWS! DOOM'S IN LATVERIA--HE WAS ADDRESSING A CONFERENCE OF MINISTERS! THEN, WHEN I LEARNED SPIDER-MAN, THOR, AND DAREDEVIL WERE SEEN AT THE BAXTER BUILDING--AND AN EXPLOSION WAS REPORTED--I COULDN'T STAY AWAY!
I'M SURE GLAD YOU'RE A TV FAN, MRS. RICHARDS!
I GUESS THAT CLEARS THINGS UP, DD!
AND THIS TIME HE MEANS DAREDEVIL--
NOT DOC DOOM!
I FIGGERED IT WUZ YOU GUYS ALLA TIME!
NO BLAMED ROBOTS COULD FIGHT LIKE THAT!

WELL, AS MAYOR LAGUARDIA USED TO SAY--WHEN I MAKE A MISTAKE, IT'S A WHOPPER!
FORGET IT, FRIEND! WHERE ELSE COULD I GET A WORKOUT LIKE THAT!
WORKOUT? WE ALL NEEDED THIS WORKOUT LIKE THOR NEEDS A WIG!
AND, SPEAKING OF THAT ASGARDIAN HIPPIE--
WHERE IS HE?
HE'S HALFWAY ACROSS TOWN BY NOW!
HE SAID SOMETHIN' ABOUT HAVIN' TO FIGHT SOME CREEP CALLED THE WRECKER!*
SHEESH! IT MUST TAKE A LOTTA GUTS TO WALK AROUND TOWN IN A GET-UP LIKE THAT!
*AND FIGHT HIM HE DOES, IN THOR #150!--SNEAK-A-PLUG STAN.

BUT WHAT ABOUT DOOM?
NOW THAT WE KNOW HE'S STILL ALIVE, WHY DON'T WE HIGHTAIL IT AFTER 'IM?
20

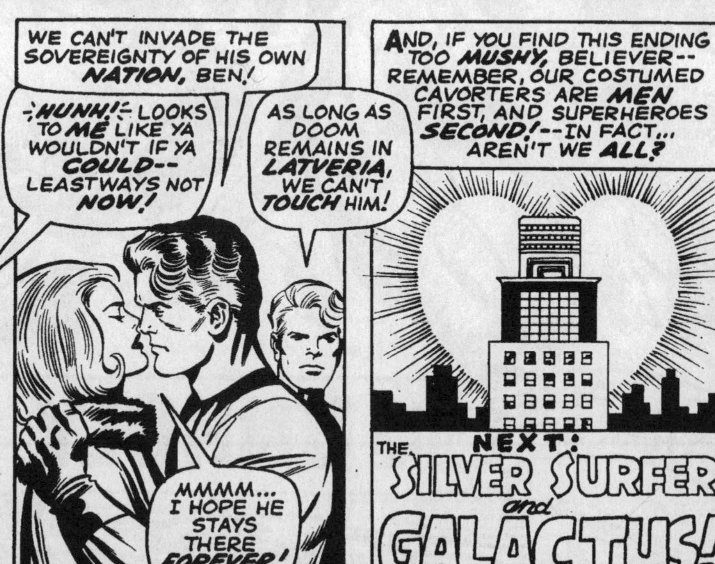
WE CAN'T INVADE THE SOVEREIGNTY OF HIS OWN NATION, BEN!
HUNH! LOOKS TO ME LIKE YA WOULDN'T IF YA COULD--LEASTWAYS NOT NOW!
AS LONG AS DOOM REMAINS IN LATVERIA, WE CAN'T TOUCH HIM!
MMMM... I HOPE HE STAYS THERE FOREVER!
AND, IF YOU FIND THIS ENDING TOO MUSHY, BELIEVER--REMEMBER, OUR COSTUMED CAVORTERS ARE MEN FIRST, AND SUPERHEROES SECOND!--IN FACT... AREN'T WE ALL?
NEXT: THE SILVER SURFER and GALACTUS!

HERE COMES...
DAREDEVIL
THE MAN WITHOUT FEAR!
APPROVED BY THE COMICS CODE AUTHORITY
MCG
MARVEL COMICS GROUP
12¢ IND.
39 APR
DEADLIER THAN EVER...
The UNHOLY THREE!

* THE ORGANIZER--MYSTERIOUS MASTER OF CRIME, WHOSE EVIL CAREER WAS CUT SHORT BY DD IN ISH #11! BUT, THOUGH HE IS STILL IMPRISONED, HIS THREE DEADLIEST HIRELINGS ARE FREE ONCE MORE! --SENSATIONALIST STAN!

I'VE BEEN SWINGING AROUND TOWN FOR HOURS!
I GUESS THIS JUST ISN'T MY --UH OH!
I FOUND WHAT I'M AFTER!

THE OMINOUS THRASHING OF WINGS--
THE HEAVY TREAD OF APE-LIKE FEET--
AND THE MUFFLED FOOTFALLS OF CATS' PAWS!
IT'S THE UNHOLY THREE!

CAT-MAN AND HIS APE-LIKE PARTNER ARE CARRYING SOME SORT OF HEAVY OBJECT--JUDGING BY THEIR PONDEROUS FOOTSTEPS!
I DON'T HAVE TO BE A GENIUS TO KNOW THAT THEY'RE ATTEMPTING TO STEAL A SAFE!
BUT NOT IF OL' DD CAN HELP IT!
HEY, YOU TWO-- LOOK ALIVE!
SOMEONE'S SWOOP-ING DOWN ON US --FROM THE ROOF!
WE SHOULD'A GUESSED--IT'S DAREDEVIL!
2

BUT, SO STARTLINGLY SWIFT IS THE SIGHTLESS SWASHBUCKLER'S ATTACK, THAT HIS THREE FOES ARE SCATTERED LIKE TENPINS BEFORE THEY CAN MAKE ANOTHER MOVE--!
I HATE TO ASK A FOOLISH QUESTION, BUT--
DON'T YOU THREE EVER GIVE UP??
SWISHHH

THEY'RE STILL WEARING THEIR INDIVIDUAL EARPHONE RECEIVERS!
I CAN HEAR THE FREQUENCY IMPULSES CLEAR AS A BELL!
IT MEANS SOMEONE IS RADIOING THEIR INSTRUCTIONS TO THEM!
GO GET 'IM, CAT MAN!

BUT, WHO CAN IT BE? THEIR EX-BOSS, THE ORGANIZER, IS STILL SAFELY IN JAIL!
YOU WON'T ESCAPE US THIS TIME, DAREDEVIL!
BOY, ARE YOU MIXED-UP, TABBY--!

US SWINGIN' SUPERHEROES WOULDN'T BE CAUGHT DEAD TRYING TO ESCAPE--
THINK WHAT IT COULD DO TO A FELLA'S IMAGE!
LOOK OUT!! HE'S SPINNING 'ROUND ON HIS BILLY CLUB!
YOU GET 'IM, APE MAN!
SOUNDS LIKE I'M UP FOR GRABS!
WELL, IT'S BETTER THAN BEING IGNORED!

BUT YOU'LL HAVE TO GRAB FASTER THAN THAT, CURLY!
YOU'RE IN THE BIG LEAGUES NOW!
AND I HAVEN'T EVEN HAD MY INNING YET!
WHERE'D HE GO? WHERE'D HE GO?

I'M RIGHT HERE, CHARLIE--
WE DON'T WANT BIRDMAN TO FEEL LEFT OUT OF THINGS!
NOW'S YOUR CHANCE, APE MAN! I'LL HOLD 'IM!
NO! WAIT!! HE SLIPPED THRU MY FING-- UNNFFF!!
NUTS! HE'S GONE AGAIN!

HEADS UP, DD!
YOU'RE SAILING INTO A PLATE GLASS WINDOW!
HAVE TO THRUST OUT MY ARMS-- TO CUSHION THE IMPACT!
LUCKY THING I SPENT YEARS PRACTICING AND PERFECTING PROTECTIVE FALLS!

A SHORT TIME LATER, AS THE MAN WITHOUT FEAR SILENTLY ENTERS THE PRIVATE TOWN HOUSE OF MATT MURDOCK, ONE NAME KEEPS ECHOING OVER AND OVER AGAIN IN HIS BRAIN--
IT'S THE EXTERMINATOR WHO'S BEHIND THE TRIO'S LATEST CRIME WAVE!
BUT, WHO CAN HE BE?
WITH JONAS STILL IN JAIL, ONLY THE FROG MAN IS LEFT--
BUT HE HASN'T THE BRAINS TO LEAD THESE OTHER THREE!
AND SINCE HE WASN'T WITH THEM--
HE, TOO, MUST STILL BE IN THE POKEY!

WELL, I'D BETTER GET A GOOD NIGHT'S SLEEP!
I'VE GOT TO BE AT THE OFFICE BRIGHT AND EARLY TOMORROW!
THERE'S SOMETHING I HAVE TO TELL MY PUDGY PARTNER!

AS THE EVENING UNFOLDS, DAREDEVIL SURRENDERS HIMSELF TO DREAM-HAUNTED SLUMBER, UNTIL--WITH THE COMING OF DAWN--
THE SUN--SHINING THRU MY WINDOW--WOKE ME UP!
I WONDER IF FOGGY WILL REACH THE OFFICE BEFORE ME?

AND, FOR AN IMMEDIATE ANSWER TO THAT EARTH-SHATTERING QUERY--
SAY WHAT YOU WANT--DAREDEVIL HAD NO RIGHT TO PUSH DEBBIE ASIDE ON THE STREET YESTERDAY!*
NELSON AND MURDOCK ATTORNEYS AT LAW
*IT WAS REALLY DR. DOOM, IN THE GUISE OF OUR HERO, WHOM FOGGY OBSERVED LAST ISH--BUT WE'RE THE ONLY ONES WHO KNOW IT! --SECRETIVE STAN

NOW I REALLY HOPE I'M ELECTED D.A..!
I'LL FIND SOME WAY TO PUT THAT SWELL-HEADED, COSTUMED CLOWN IN HIS PLACE!
7

SECONDS LATER, AS THE FIRM'S BRILLIANT LEGAL TACTICIAN ARRIVES--
COULDN'T HELP OVER-HEARING YOU, FOGGY--
CONSIDERING HOW LOUD YOU SHOUT WHEN YOU LOSE YOUR TEMPER!
AND CONSIDERING THAT I COULD HAVE HEARD HIM IF HE USED THE LOWEST WHISPER!

DAREDEVIL ISN'T YOUR BIG PROBLEM--DEBORAH HARRIS IS!
WHAT DO YOU KNOW ABOUT HER, MATT?
C'MON, FOGGY--DON'T PUT ME ON!

WE BOTH KNOW YOU'VE BEEN DATING HER IN SECRET--
--BECAUSE YOU'RE AFRAID THE PUBLIC WON'T VOTE FOR YOU IF THEY KNOW YOU'RE IN LOVE WITH A FEMALE EX-CONVICT!
BUT YOU UNDER-ESTIMATE THE AVERAGE AMERICAN!
I DO? HOW?
HE'S MUCH MORE UNDER-STANDING THAN YOU SUSPECT!

DATE DEBBIE IN THE OPEN! LET EVERY-ONE SEE THAT YOU'RE WILLING TO FORGET HER PAST--TO GIVE A GIRL A SECOND CHANCE!
THE PUBLIC WILL LOVE YOU FOR IT!
I THINK MATT IS RIGHT!
IT DOES MAKE SENSE TO ME!
AND, NOW THAT THAT'S SETTLED--
HOW ABOUT A DOUBLE DATE TONIGHT?
KAREN AND ME--FOGGY AND DEBORAH!
IT'S TIME WE TOOK AN EVENING OFF FOR FUN!

AND MOSTLY, IT'LL GIVE ME A CHANCE TO BE OUT WITH KAREN AGAIN!
I DON'T DARE EVEN THINK OF HOW MUCH I'VE MISSED HER!--SHE MUST NEVER SUSPECT!
BEST IDEA I'VE HEARD ALL DAY!
HOW ABOUT YOU, FOGGY?
GRRREAT!
I KNEW WE'D MAKE A SWINGER OUT OF MATT--SOONER OR LATER!
8

MEANWHILE, IN A CAREFULLY HIDDEN SANCTUARY, ON THE OUTSKIRTS OF TOWN, WE FIND--
I WAS A FOOL TO ALLOW THE THREE OF YOU TO SERVE ME!
YOU'VE NO CALL TO TALK TO US THAT WAY!
NO WONDER YOUR FORMER EMPLOYER WAS CAUGHT--IF YOU WERE HIS HELPERS!
HAVEN'T I?
ONE SIMPLE SAFE ROBBERY--AND YOU LET DAREDEVIL STOP YOU!
BUT, THAT NO LONGER MATTERS NOW!

BUT, IT AIN'T POSSIBLE! NOBODY CAN REALLY TRAVEL IN TIME!
WHAT DO YOU KNOW ABOUT IT, YOU FUR-BEARING FOOL!
I'M NOT SEEKING TIME TRAVEL--!
MY GOAL IS THE POWER OF--TIME DISPLACEMENT!

IT DON'T MAKE ANY SENSE! WHAT'S TIME DISPLACEMENT MEAN?
YOU WILL HAVE YOUR ANSWER IN SECONDS, APE MAN!
FOR YOU'RE THE ONE WHO'LL BE THE FIRST LIVING BEING TO EXPERIENCE IT!
STAND WHERE YOU ARE! DON'T MOVE!

ALL I NEED DO IS INSERT THIS CYLINDER OF SPECIAL FORMULA T-GAS INTO THE FUELING NOZZLE OF THE DISPLACER RAY!
AND NOW-- ALL OF YOU-- STAND BACK!!

ZZHISST!
HERE IT COMES--!

-HEY!- WHAT GIVES?? WHAT'S GOIN' ON??
THE RAY'S PULVERIZIN' ME--FULL BLAST!!
I DON'T GET IT!! WHAT'S GONNA HAPPEN TO ME??
NOTHING IS HAPPENING TO YOU--!
BUT--THE TIME CONTINUUM IN WHICH YOU--AND YOU ALONE--EXIST--
--HAS SUDDENLY BEEN--DISPLACED!

NEVER MIND THE DOUBLE-TALK LINGO--
HE'S GONE! YOU KILLED HIM!

IF YOU DID THAT TO THE APE MAN--
HOW DO WE KNOW WHICH OF US WILL BE NEXT?
SILENCE, YOU FOOLS!!
HE'S SUFFERED NO HARM!

YOU STILL DO NOT COMPREHEND WHAT YOU HAVE SEEN! CAN'T YOU REALIZE--?
HE NO LONGER EXISTS IN THE SAME TIME AS WE DO!
BUT, WITHIN A HALF-HOUR--HE WILL RETURN!
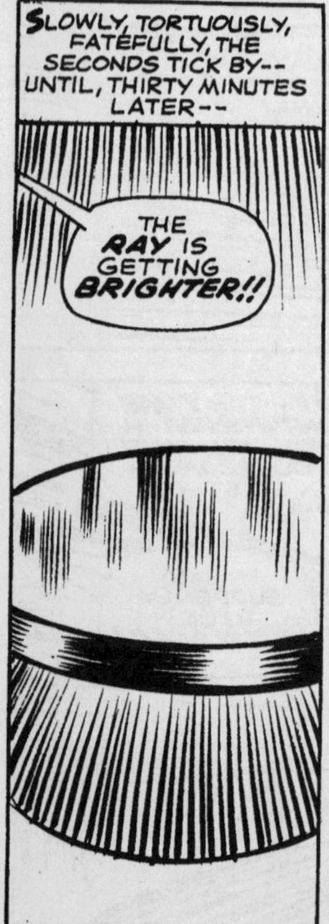
SLOWLY, TORTUOUSLY, FATEFULLY, THE SECONDS TICK BY--UNTIL, THIRTY MINUTES LATER--
THE RAY IS GETTING BRIGHTER!!
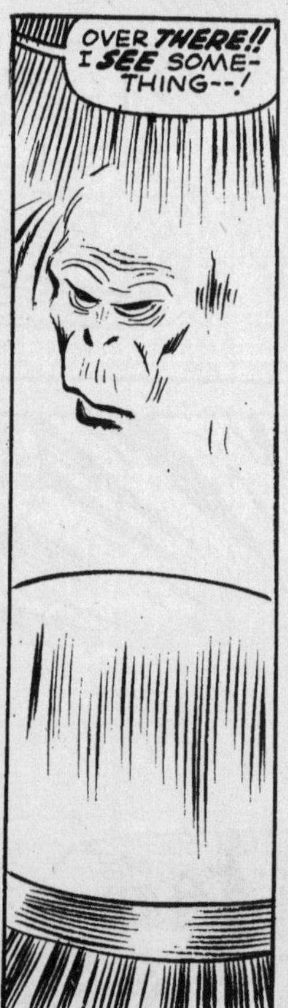
OVER THERE!! I SEE SOMETHING--!

IT'S THE APE MAN!! HE'S ALIVE!
THIS IS--JUST WHAT I DID--
I ALREADY DID ALL THIS--JUST BEFORE!

APE MAN! STAY THERE!
I MAY WANT TO EXAMINE YOU!
THIS WAS ONLY--THE BEGINNING!
12

HEY! NOW I GET IT!
YOU SENT ME-- A HALF-HOUR AHEAD--IN TIME!
NOT EXACTLY! YOU DIDN'T GO ANYWHERE! I MERELY DISPLACED THE TIME DIMENSION FOR YOU!
AND I SET MY DISPLACEMENT DIAL FOR 30 MINUTES--
--WHICH IS HOW LONG IT TOOK TO END THE DISPLACEMENT!
AND, NOW THAT I KNOW MY DISPLACER WORKS--
WE'LL ALL USE THESE PORTABLE, HAND-HELD MODELS!
BUT, AS THE EXTERMINATOR DISCUSSES HIS FUTURE PLANS--IT'S TIME TO TURN OUR ATTENTION TO A SWANK, NOISY NIGHT CLUB, WHERE WE FIND--
THE MUSIC IS SO LOUD, IT'S TORTURING MY HYPER-SENSITIVE EARS--BUT I MUSTN'T LET ON--!
THIS IS A GREAT SPOT FOR PEOPLE WHO DON'T WANT TO TALK TO EACH OTHER, GANG!
RELAX, PARTNER-- LET YOUR HAIR DOWN!
DON'T YOU GET ENOUGH CONVERSATION IN COURT ALL DAY?
I'LL BET MY BROTHER MIKE WOULD DIG THIS SCENE!
DON'T MENTION THAT BUM TO ME!

THAT'S OUR CUE TO DANCE, MATTHEW-- BEFORE FOGGY HAS A TEMPER TANTRUM!
LOVE TO MISS PAGE-- BUT, A FRED ASTAIRE I'M NOT!
WHO'S COMPLAINING? YOU DON'T SEE CYD CHARISSE WORRYING ABOUT LITTLE ME, DO YOU?

DON'T BE CHICKEN, COUNSELOR! DANCE WITH THE LADY!
GIVE US A CHANCE TO TALK ABOUT YOU FOR A WHILE!
WHAT-EVER YOU DON'T KNOW, I'LL TEACH YOU!
BEST OFFER I'VE HAD ALL DAY!

GIVE ME YOUR HAND, MATT--I'LL LEAD YOU TO THE FLOOR!
ISN'T IT GREAT THE WAY FOGGY AND DEBORAH ARE HITTING IT OFF?
FRANKLY, LAWYER MAN, I'D MUCH RATHER TALK ABOUT US!

I'D BETTER PRETEND TO STUMBLE ONCE OR TWICE....!
-OOP!- SORRY, LADY!

EASY, MAN! YOU'RE DOING JUST FINE!
EVERYONE THINKS YOU INVENTED A NEW STEP!
I THINK-- THAT POOR FELLOW IS-- BLIND!
14

OH, MATT--DARLING! IF ONLY SOME MIRACLE COULD RESTORE YOUR SIGHT!

I THINK-- I'M GETTING THE HANG OF IT NOW!
WHEN I'M NEAR HER --LIKE THIS--NOTHING ELSE SEEMS TO MATTER! EVEN BEING DAREDEVIL SEEMS SO--UNIMPORTANT!
WHY, MATT-- WHY CAN'T YOU FEEL ABOUT ME-- AS I FEEL ABOUT YOU??

BUT, AT THAT MOMENT...
THAT'S DEBORAH HARRIS OVER THERE--WITH NELSON, THE GUY WHO'S GONNA RUN FOR D.A.!
I GOTTA HUNCH THE EXTERMINATOR WOULD PAY PLENTY FOR A TIP LIKE THIS!

OF COURSE I'M SURE! THEY'RE HERE WITH NELSON'S BLIND PARTNER, AND HIS SEEIN' EYE SECRETARY!
YOU 'N YOUR BOYS BETTER GIT HERE FAST--AND DON'T FORGET THE DOUGH YA PROMISED ME!
HUH? HOLD IT--I DIDN'T MEAN NO DISRESPECT! HONEST--I WUZ JUST KIDDIN'!
OF COURSE! SURE I TRUST THE WORD OF THE EXTERMINATOR!

STOP WHIMPERING, YOU SPINELESS NON-ENTITY!
WE'LL BE THERE WITHIN THE NEXT TEN MINUTES!
BIRD MAN! ALERT THE OTHERS!

THIS IS A PERFECT OPPORTUNITY TO TEST OUT MY PORTABLE TIME DISPLACER RAYS!
ALSO, WE'LL BE ABLE TO KILL TWO BIRDS WITH ONE STONE!
YOU'LL HAVE A CHANCE FOR REVENGE ON THE GIRL WHO HELPED DAREDEVIL TO SEND YOU TO PRISON!
WHILE I WILL HAVE A HOSTAGE WITH WHICH TO THREATEN NELSON--
--IN CASE HE SHOULD BE ELECTED DISTRICT ATTORNEY!

WHILE, BACK AT THE RANCH--
WHERE ARE FOGGY--AND DEB?
ON THE DANCE FLOOR, MATT!
BUT, HOW DID YOU KNOW THEY WEREN'T HERE?
OH--EH--JUST A WILD GUESS!
CAREFUL, SON! YOU ALMOST GAVE YOURSELF AWAY!

THIS IS THE PLACE!
AND, IN CASE YOU GET ANY WILD IDEAS--
REMEMBER THIS--
THOUGH YOU EACH HOLD A RAY GUN--ONLY I POSSESS THE MASTER CONTROL!
WITHOUT THE EXTERMINATOR, YOUR WEAPONS WOULD BE USELESS!

NOW GO! I'LL GIVE YOU TEN MINUTES TO EXECUTE YOUR ORDERS!
I SHALL REMAIN HERE, IN THE CAR!
WITH THESE T-RAY GUNS, IT OUGHTTA BE A BREEZE!
YOU SAID IT!

C'MON, YOU GUYS--MOVE!
DON'T WORRY ABOUT US, PAL!
WE'RE RIGHT BEHIND YA!

FIRST, I'LL GET THE DOORMAN OUTTA THE WAY--LIKE THE EXTERMINATOR SAID!
I BEEN ITCHIN' TO TRY THIS GIZMO!

HEY, CHARLIE--WATCH THE BIRDIE!
A MAN IN THE AIR--WITH--WITH WINGS!!

YOU SAID THE MAGIC WORD!
SO HERE'S YOUR PRIZE--!

HAH! IT'S WORKIN'! HE'S STARTING TO FADE AWAY!

SLOW DOWN, BIRD MAN! LEAVE SOME OF 'EM FOR US!
DON'T WASTE YOUR BLASTERS ON JUST ANYONE--!
WE GOTTA GET THE GIRL!

DON'T WORRY-- I SEE HER IN THERE NOW!
LET'S GO, APE MAN!
WAIT! YOU TWO COVER ME! I CAN REACH HER FIRST--!

GO ON--YELL, YOU FOOLS!
--FOR ALL THE GOOD IT'LL DO YOU!

LOOK!! IT'S THE BIRD MAN!!
FOGGY! HE--HE'S COMING RIGHT TOWARDS ME!!
18

THEN, BEFORE ANOTHER MOVE CAN BE MADE--
GOT HER!
DEBBIE--!!
I'VE GOT TO CHANGE --TO DARE-- NO!
FOR ONCE-- I'M-- TOO LATE!!

DEB--DEB!! IN THE NAME OF HEAVEN--WHAT'S HAPPENING TO YOU--!??!

SHE'S GONE!!

MATT!! YOUR BROTHER! GET HIM!! DO YOU HEAR ME?? YOU'VE GOT TO GET MIKE!!
HE'S THE ONLY ONE--WHO CAN CATCH--THAT ROTTEN KILLER!!
EASY, FOGGY! GET A HOLD OF YOURSELF!
BUT DEBBIE'S GONE!! HE--HE MURDERED HER!

SHE'S NOT DEAD!
I CAN'T TELL ANYONE--BUT I CAN SENSE HER --ALTHOUGH-- HER IMAGE IS --BLURRED!
ALMOST AS THOUGH-- SHE'S IN--ANOTHER DIMENSION!

I'VE GOT TO GET AWAY--TO THINK!!
I'VE NEVER RUN INTO ANYTHING LIKE THIS BEFORE!
WHAT ARE WE UP AGAINST--??
MAN! I HEARD OF HIGH-FLYIN' CATS--
BUT HE WAS ENDSVILLE!
I MUST FIND THE ANSWER--
HOW CAN DEBBIE HAVE VANISHED--AND YET--I STILL SENSE HER PRESENCE?!!

IT WENT SMOOTH AS SILK, BOSS!
BUT--WHAT DO WE DO NEXT?
NEXT? DAREDEVIL HIMSELF WILL BE ELIMINATED --FOREVER--
--BY THE POWER OF --THE EXTERMINATOR!
20

NEXT ISSUE:
THE FALLEN HERO

HERE COMES...
DAREDEVIL
MARVEL COMICS GROUP
12¢ IND.
40 MAY
MCG
APPROVED BY THE COMICS CODE AUTHORITY
The FALLEN HERO!

DAREDEVIL, THE MAN WITHOUT FEAR!
THE FALLEN HERO!
ACTING UNDER ORDERS OF THE MYSTERIOUS EXTERMINATOR, THE SUPER-POWERED UNHOLY THREE HAVE USED THEIR DREADED T-GUNS TO TRANSPORT DEBORAH HARRIS TO ANOTHER TIME CONTINUUM! AND SO...
...ANYONE WHO UNDERSTANDS THAT MISHMASH CAN NOW GET ON WITH OUR TALE--!
I DON'T KNOW WHAT HAPPENED TO DEBBIE... BUT SHE ISN'T DEAD! I SENSED HER HEARTBEAT EVEN AFTER FOGGY SAID SHE HAD VANISHED!
A MYSTERY WITHIN A PUZZLE, INSIDE OF A RIDDLE! CONFUSED AND COMPOUNDED BY STAN (THE MAN) LEE and GENE (THE DEAN) COLAN
INKED BY: JOHN TARTAGLIONE
LETTERED BY: SAM ROSEN
EXCELSIOR!
AND NOW, LET THE PULSE-POUNDING PANDEMONIUM START TO COMMENCE TO BEGIN...!
WHATEVER THE ANSWER IS, ONE THING'S FOR SURE... DAREDEVIL IS GONNA FIND IT...
...OR KNOW THE REASON WHY!

ONE OF MY FIRST JOBS WILL BE TO LEARN WHO'S THE BRAINS BEHIND THE UNHOLY THREE!
IT'S A LEAD-PIPE CINCH THAT NEITHER THE BIRD-MAN, CAT-MAN, OR APE-MAN HAVE ENOUGH SAVVY TO INVENT A WEAPON LIKE THE ONE THEY USED TONIGHT!
AND THE FACT THAT THEY WERE WEARING EARPHONES OVER THEIR COSTUMES INDICATES THAT THEY'RE IN TOUCH WITH SOMEONE!
SO NOW, I'VE NOTHING LEFT TO DO BUT FIND THEM, DEFEAT THEM, AND LEARN WHO THAT UNKNOWN SOMEONE IS! ...THAT'S ALL!
ANYWAY, IT'S THE LEAST I CAN DO FOR POOR FOGGY!
HE THINKS DEBORAH HAS BEEN DIS-INTEGRATED SOMEHOW... AND IT'S DRIVING HIM MAD!
HE REALLY LOVES THAT GIRL!

IN FACT, HE LOVES HER ENOUGH TO ASK ME TO CONTACT MY BROTHER MIKE... SO THAT DAREDEVIL CAN HUNT THE KILLERS DOWN!

AND, SINCE MIKE AND MATT ARE ONE AND THE SAME...
MY PANICKY PARTNER IS GONNA GET HIS WISH...IN SPADES!!

I'LL KEEP SCOURING THE CITY TILL I FIND THEM!
AND, WHEN I DO...

THOSE THREE COSTUMED CREEPS WILL WISH THEY'D *STAYED* IN JAIL WHERE THEY WERE *SAFE!*
I'M *SURE* I CAN OUT-FIGHT THE WHOLE *PASSEL* OF THEM!
THE ONLY THING I'VE GOT TO BE *CAREFUL* OF IS THAT MYSTERIOUS NEW *WEAPON* OF THEIRS!
...*WHATEVER* IT MAY BE!

LUCKY IT'S SO *LATE!* THE STREETS ARE ALL BUT *DESERTED!*
SO, IT'LL BE A *BREEZE* TO SPOT MY PIGEONS...
IF THEY'RE STILL ON THE PROWL!
I'D BETTER GIVE THE LOCAL *BANKS* THE ONCE-OVER...JUST TO BE *SAFE!*

AND, SPEAKING OF LOCAL BANKS...
WH-WHO...OR WHAT...IN BLAZES ARE YOU??
SHUDDUP... AND GET INSIDE!
BAN

I...I JUST HEARD ABOUT YOU...ON THE RADIO!
YOU'RE THE ONES WHO AIMED THAT RAY GUN AT A GIRL... AND MADE HER VANISH!
I...WON'T GIVE YOU... ANY TROUBLE!
BANK
HAW! YOU BET YOUR LIFE YOU WON'T!

WE WANNA GET TO THE SAFE... AND WE MEAN NOW!
SURE...SURE! IT'S RIGHT IN THERE...THRU THIS IRON GATE...!
HOW FAST CAN YOU GET THE VAULT OPEN?

THE VAULT? I CAN'T OPEN IT! NO ONE CAN!
IT'S A TIME LOCK... AND IT'S SET FOR NINE O'CLOCK...IN THE MORNING!
WAIT! STOP! WHAT...ARE YOU...GONNA DO..??
TAKE A GUESS!

WE'LL SEE YOU *AROUND*, USELESS...

GOOD SHOT! HE'S STARTIN' TO FADE OUT *ALREADY!*

WHEN YOU COME BACK... FROM *NOWHERE!*

NOW, ACCORDING TO WHAT THE *EXTERMINATOR* SAID...

I JUST HAVE TO GIVE THE *ROTATOR* A FULL SPIN, CLOCKWISE...

AND THEN...

CLICK!

THE SAME *FORCE* THAT CAN SHATTER A *TIME BARRIER*...

CAN ALSO SHATTER A *VAULT*... WITH EQUAL EASE!

WE SURE GOTTA *HAND* IT TO THE *EXTERMINATOR!*

YEAH! HE'S A BETTER *LEADER* THAN THE *ORGANIZER* EVER WAS!

WITH *HIM* PLANNING THE CAPERS... AND HIS *T-GUN* TO BACK US UP... WE'RE PRACTICALLY *INVINCIBLE!*

AND OUR *OWN* NATURAL POWER AIN'T EXACTLY *HURTIN'* US, EITHER!

HEY! WHAT'S *THAT..?*

WHAT'S WHAT?
C'MON, SPEAK UP, WILLYA? WE'VE GOTTA GET OUT OF HERE!

LOOKS LIKE... THERE'S GONNA BE... A LITTLE DELAY!
YOU'RE NOT MAKIN' SENSE! WHAT'S BUGGIN' YOU, ANYWAY?
TURN AROUND, AND SEE FOR YOURSELF, BIG MOUTH!
HUH? WHO SAID THAT?!!

YOU!
ATTABOY, BIRDIE...
IF THERE'S ONE THING I LIKE, IT'S A MAN OF FEW WORDS!

HOPE YOU WEREN'T PLANNING TO GO ANYWHERE..!
'CAUSE IT'S KINDA CHILLY OUTSIDE...
AND WE WOULDN'T WANT YOU TO GET A NASTY OL' SNIFFLE NOW, WOULD WE?
CAREFUL WITH THAT CABBAGE, FEATHER-BRAIN...
IF YOU LOSE ANY, I'LL TAKE AWAY YOUR ALFRED E. NEWMAN BUTTON!
I'D BETTER BE CAREFUL!
THE OTHER TWO ARE IN HERE WITH HIM!

GIT OUTTA MY WAY! I'LL BREAK 'IM IN TWO!!
NO NEED FOR PANIC!
MY T-GUN WILL DO THE JOB EASIER... AND IT'LL BE MORE PERMANENT!
THEN HURRY!!
DON'TCHA REMEMBER HOW FAST HE IS?

IT'S OKAY, FUZZY!
I'M ALWAYS GLAD TO REMIND YOU!
CAT-MAN'S ABOUT TO SHOOT... RIGHT BEHIND ME!
HE DOESN'T KNOW I CAN SENSE HIM... WITHOUT LOOKING!

I HOPE THIS WON'T GIVE YOU THE WRONG IMPRESSION OF ME, TABBY!
I'M NOT NORMALLY AGGRESSIVE BY NATURE...!

IN FACT, I'M REALLY A PIPE AND SLIPPERS SORT OF CHAP!
I DON'T EVEN GO TO PEACE RALLIES... 'CAUSE THEY'RE TOO EXCITING!
Y'KNOW, I SOMEHOW SUSPECT THAT I'M NOT GETTING THRU TO YOU!
8

YOU CRUMMY CLOWN... WE LET YA GET AWAY FROM US ONCE...
BUT YOU WON'T BE THAT LUCKY AGAIN!
AH HA! THAT'S WHAT IT IS! WE'RE JUST HAVING A PROBLEM IN COMMUNICATION!
ALL THIS TIME I THOUGHT IT WAS YOU WHO WERE ESCAPING FROM ME!

OOPS! SORRY, TABBY! I DIDN'T MEAN TO MAKE YOU COMMIT A MISDEMEANOR!
YOU CAN GET A SUMMONS FOR LITTERING THE STREETS AROUND HERE!
BAM
GLOAT ALL YOU WANT TO, WISE GUY!
THERE'S STILL NO WAY FOR YOU TO BEAT ALL THREE OF US!
HE'S GOT A POINT THERE, BUT...
SAY! WHAT'S THAT?

MY TRUSTY OL' RADAR SENSE PICKED UP A WEAPON... ON THE FLOOR!
ONE OF THEM MUST HAVE DROPPED IT!

I MIGHT AS WELL BE PHILOSOPHICAL ABOUT ALL THIS!
IF I WAS MEANT TO HAVE A WEAPON, I'D HAVE BEEN BORN WITH A HOLSTER!

HEAR THAT, YOU GUYS?
HE MADE A FUNNY!
GO AHEAD ...YAK IT UP...
IT'LL BE HIS LAST ONE!
THAT SINKS IT! NOW HE'S LATCHED ONTO THE BLASTER!

SO, THIS IS DD'S CUE TO FLIP OUT OF RANGE...
FZZZAT
...BUT FAST!

YER WASTIN' YER TIME, MASKED MAN!
YA CAN'T KEEP DODGIN' MY SHOTS FOREVER!
I DON'T EXPECT TO, JUNIOR...

...I'LL SETTLE FOR THE NEXT HUNDRED YEARS OR SO!
...I HAVE TO GET THAT T-GUN AWAY FROM HIM... SOMEHOW!
I'M A SITTING DUCK UNTIL I DO!

IF NOT FOR THE EDGE MY EXTRA-KEEN SENSES GIVE ME ...
HE'D HAVE PEGGED ME 'WAY BEFORE THIS!
I'M JUST PLAYIN' WITH YA NOW, SMART GUY!
C'MON... C'MON! FINISH 'IM OFF, WILLYA?

IT'S NO USE!
EVEN WITH MY BIG-DEAL REFLEXES...
...I CAN'T GET CLOSE ENOUGH TO HIM!

AND, THOUGH IT MAY NOT BE IN THE BEST TRADITION OF SUPER-HEROING...
...I'M JUST PLAIN BUSHED!

HEADS UP, MATTY BOY! YOU'RE IN FOR IT NOW...!

I GOT 'IM!!
CLASSSK!

I FEEL THE SAME... BUT... MY SENSES ARE CHANGING!
EVERYTHING AROUND ME IS GETTING FAINTER...
AS THOUGH... IT'S ALL FADING AWAY!
BUT, I KNOW NOW... NOTHING ELSE IS FADING AWAY...
I'M THE ONE... WHO'S VANISHING!
AND, JUST TO PROVE HOW RIGHT OUR FEARLESS FRIEND CAN BE... LET'S POST-HASTE PERUSE THE NEXT PULSATING PAGE...
13

IT'S AS THOUGH... TIME ITSELF...IS BEING TWISTED... AND DISTORTED!*
AS IF I'M TRAVELLING FROM NOW... TO THEN...
RATHER THAN FROM HERE...TO THERE!
*SUDDEN THOUGHT! ONE NICE THING ABOUT THESE DRAWINGS IS...NOBODY CAN SAY THEY'RE IN-ACCURATE...UNLESS YOU'VE BEEN THERE YOURSELF! ...SENSES-SHATTERING STAN.

LOOK! ANOTHER HAS COME TO JOIN US!
IT'S...IT'S DAREDEVIL HIMSELF!
THINGS ARE CLEARING NOW!
THAT VOICE... IT'S DEBORAH HARRIS! AND, THERE ARE OTHERS WITH HER!
THEN I WAS RIGHT! YOU AREN'T DEAD! NONE OF YOU ARE!
NO...BUT WE MIGHT AS WELL BE!
WE'RE HOPELESSLY TRAPPED... IN NOWHERE!

BUT, NOT SO THE UNHOLY THREE!
THEY SEEM TO HAVE IT MADE...FOR NOW!
WHAT A DEAL!
WE FINALLY POLISHED OFF DAREDEVIL!
YEAH! AND WE'RE GETTIN' AWAY WITH THE LOOT, BESIDES!

HOWEVER, AT THAT MOMENT...
LOOK! IT'S THE ONES WE'RE AFTER!
EEEE
LET'S TAKE 'EM!
SKREEE

STAY WHERE YOU ARE! WE'VE GOT YOU COVERED!
HOLD IT THERE!
STOP... OR WE'LL SHOOT!
OKAY...WE WARNED YOU...!
POLICE

DON'T WANNA KILL 'EM IF I CAN HELP IT!
I'LL FIRE A BURST OVER THEIR HEADS!
KRAK!

BUT, BEFORE THE CONSCIENTIOUS OFFICER CAN TAKE AIM A SECOND TIME...
OKAY, BLUE-COAT..YOU HAD IT!
ZAT!

CHUCK!! WHA---WHAT'S HAPPENING TO YOU!
UHHHHH..!

CHUCK! HE..HE'S GONE!

LET'S SEE NOW... WE SEEM TO BE RUNNING OUT OF *CHARACTERS!* SO, WHO'S *LEFT?* OH, YES... FRANTIC *FOGGY*...

STILL NO WORD ABOUT *DEBBIE!*

IT'S AS THOUGH THE *EARTH* SWALLOWED HER UP!

SOONER OR LATER *DAREDEVIL* WILL GET ON THEIR TRAIL, FOGGY..!

BUT I CAN'T BE *SURE!*

SO FAR THERE HASN'T BEEN A *SIGN* OF THAT SWAGGERING, MASKED *SHOW-OFF!*

DEBBIE... MY DARLING... I NEVER REALIZED... HOW MUCH YOU *MEANT* TO ME..!

AND THE KILLERS WHO ARE *RESPONSIBLE* ARE STILL AT LARGE!

THEY USED TO WORK FOR ABNER JONAS... BETTER KNOWN AS THE ORGANIZER!
BUT HE'S STILL SAFELY IN THE STATE PEN!
THEY HAVEN'T THE BRAINS TO OPERATE BY THEMSELVES...
SO, PERHAPS I CAN FIND A CLUE TO WHO'S BEHIND THEM.. SOMEHOW!
PROMISE... THAT YOU'LL BE CAREFUL!
CAREFUL? WHAT TROUBLE CAN A SQUARE LIKE ME GET INTO?
--AND DON'T FORGET... YOU HAVE A TV INTERVIEW AT FIVE!

AN INTERVIEW! WHO CARES ABOUT THAT NOW?
THE GIRL I LOVE... MISSING... PERHAPS EVEN... DEAD!
AT A TIME LIKE THIS... HOW I ENVY A MAN WITH THE STRENGTH--AND THE CONFIDENCE OF DAREDEVIL!
BUT EVEN A MAN WHO'S NOT A SUPERHERO... CAN STILL BE USEFUL!
THIS IS WHAT I'M AFTER... OLD CLIPPINGS... WRITE-UPS OF THE CAPTURE OF THE ORGANIZER'S GANG!
NOW, IF ONLY MY HUNCH PAYS OFF...!
NEWSPAPER
WHOEVER IS LEADING THEM NOW...MIGHT HAVE BEEN CONNECTED WITH THEM... IN THE PAST!

THEN, AFTER LONG, DULL, TORTUROUS HOURS OF READING...
I FOUND IT...
HIDDEN AWAY IN THIS FEATURE ARTICLE--
THERE WAS A SCIENTIST WORKING FOR JONAS...
BUT HE LEFT TOWN---JUST BEFORE THE TRIAL!
SINCE HE HAD NOTHING TO DO WITH THE CASE...
NOBODY BOTHERED TO LOOK FOR HIM! HE WAS SOON FORGOTTEN!

WHAT IF THE MISSING SCIENTIST WAS THE REAL BRAINS BEHIND THE ORGANIZER---AND BEHIND THE UNHOLY THREE?
HE MUST HAVE KNOWN THEM WHEN THEY WORKED FOR JONAS!
HE COULD BE THE ONE WHO TEAMED THEM UP AGAIN... AND CREATED THEIR DEADLY WEAPON!
IT ISN'T MUCH... BUT IT MIGHT BE A LEAD! NOW... IF ONLY I KNEW HOW TO FOLLOW IT UP... HOW TO FIND HIM!
MIGHT AS WELL GO TO THE INTERVIEW NOW...
I WOULDN'T BE SO HELPLESS IF I COULD BE ELECTED D.A.!

MEANWHILE, AS FRANKLIN "FOGGY" NELSON TAKES A TAXI TO ONE OF HIS ELECTION CAMPAIGN TV INTERVIEWS, THE POLICE DRAGNET GROWS EVER WIDER---
ATTENTION ALL UNITS! BE ON LOOKOUT FOR THREE MASKED FUGITIVES...
...BEST KNOWN BY THE NAMES OF BIRD-MAN, APE-MAN, AND CAT-MAN...
EEEEEE
...THEY ARE ARMED WITH A NEW, STILL-UNCLASSIFIED LETHAL WEAPON, AND MUST BE CONSIDERED HIGHLY DANGEROUS...
ALL CITIZENS ARE URGED TO STAY OFF THE STREETS UNTIL FURTHER NOTICE...
EVERY AVAILABLE MAN IS ON THE JOB!
BUT, THERE'S NO DEFENSE AGAINST THAT MYSTERIOUS WEAPON OF THEIRS!
AND, WHILE THE CITY TREMBLES, THE ELECTION DAY DRAWS NEARER...

AS YOUR DISTRICT ATTORNEY, I WILL WORK NIGHT AND DAY TO MAKE THE STREETS OF OUR CITY SAFE AGAIN...
AND NOW, THIS IS MY PLATFORM...
TV 4
HBC

BUT, SINCE WE CAN READ ALL ABOUT CANDIDATE NELSON'S PLATFORM IN OUR LOCAL NEWSPAPERS, LET'S TURN ONCE AGAIN TO THE TIME *BEYOND* OUR TIME...

I'VE GOT TO GET *BACK!*

IF I STAY HERE ANY LONGER I'LL GO *MAD!* MAD! ***MAD!***

DEBORAH! WHERE *ARE* WE? WHAT *IS* THIS PLACE? HOW LONG HAVE YOU *BEEN* HERE?

I DON'T KNOW *WHERE* THIS IS!

I DON'T EVEN KNOW *WHEN* IT IS!

ANYWAY, *TIME* HAS NO MEANING HERE!

AT FIRST... I THOUGHT IT WAS A *DREAM*... SOME SORT OF FAR-OUT PSYCHEDELIC *NIGHTMARE!*

IT'S *NO* DREAM! IN SOME FANTASTIC WAY, THAT WEAPON HAS HURLED US INTO ANOTHER *TIME* SPHERE!

BUT, ITS EFFECTS CAN'T LAST *FOREVER*...!

IN FACT, I SEEM TO SENSE A *SHIFTING* IN THE *TIME CONTINUUM* RIGHT NOW!

DAREDEVIL! SOMETHING IS... *HAPPENING*... TO ME... AGAIN!

IT CAN ONLY MEAN...

I WAS *RIGHT!* DEBORAH IS *FADING AWAY* ONCE MORE... RETURNING TO THE *PRESENT!*

DON'T BE AFRAID! YOU'LL BE ALL RIGHT! YOU'RE GOING... *BACK!*

CAN'T SENSE HER ANY MORE! CAN'T *REACH* HER! IT'S *OVER!* SHE'S *RETURNED!*

FOR ONCE, ALL MY POWERS... MY HYPER-KEEN SENSES... CAN DO ME NO GOOD!

TIME ITSELF... WHICH CANNOT BE TOUCHED... CANNOT BE SEEN... IS THE STRONGEST TRAP IN ALL THE WORLD!

I'M CERTAIN THAT I RECEIVED A FAR MORE POTENT BLAST OF THE T-RAY THAN ANY OF THE OTHERS WHO HAVE RETURNED!

THERE CAN BE NO DOUBT ABOUT IT---

THE GREATER THE BLAST... THE LONGER THE VICTIM REMAINS HERE!

WHAT IF THE JOLT I SUFFERED MEANS...

...I MUST STAY HERE... FOREVER?!!

NEXT: THE DEATH OF MIKE MURDOCK!

20

APPROVED BY THE COMICS CODE AUTHORITY
HERE COMES...
DAREDEVIL
THE MAN WITHOUT FEAR!
MARVEL COMICS GROUP
12¢ IND.
41 JUNE
THE DEATH OF MIKE MURDOCK!
RIALTO
NOW PL
"HAM
NO U-TURN

DAREDEVIL, THE MAN WITHOUT FEAR!
The DEATH of MIKE MURDOCK!
OUR SIGHTLESS SWASHBUCKLER HAS BEEN TRAPPED IN AN ENDLESS TIME CONTINUUM BY THE EXTERMINATOR AND HIS THREE BESTIAL HIRELINGS! BUT, THOUGH HIS PLIGHT SEEMS HOPELESS, YOU CAN REST ASSURED HE'LL THINK OF SOMETHING... AFTER ALL, WE'VE STILL GOT TWENTY PULSATING PAGES TO FILL...!!
THE OTHERS FADED BACK TO THE PRESENT WHEN THE T-GUN'S BLAST EFFECT WORE OFF!
BUT I DON'T KNOW HOW POWERFUL A BLAST I RECEIVED... OR HOW LONG IT WILL LAST!
I CAN'T LOSE HOPE... I CAN'T GIVE UP... NOT WHILE THE UNHOLY THREE ARE STILL AT LARGE!
TIME ITSELF.. WHICH CANNOT BE TOUCHED.. CANNOT BE SEEN... IS THE STRONGEST TRAP IN ALL THE WORLD!
...AND I'M CAUGHT IN IT!
BUT THERE MUST BE A WAY OUT... SOMEWHERE... SOMEHOW... THERE MUST BE!
PHANTASMAGORICALLY PRODUCED and PRESENTED By:
STAN (THE MAN) LEE and GENE (THE DEAN) COLAN
EMBELLISHED By: JOHN TARTAGLIONE
LETTERED By: SAM ROSEN
and NOW, LET THE AGONIZIN' ACTION BEGIN...

I'M TRAPPED IN A TIME WARP WHICH IS SOMEHOW OUTSIDE OF NORMAL TIME!

BUT, THERE MUST BE A WAY IN... OR ELSE I COULDN'T BE HERE!

AND, IF THERE'S A WAY IN... THERE ALSO HAS TO BE... A WAY OUT!

I CAN SENSE THE TIME FIBERS CONSTANTLY SHIFTING... CONSTANTLY CHANGING!

AT SOME POINT... IN THEIR NEVER-ENDING MOTION... THERE MUST BE AN OPENING...!

AND, THOUGH IT CAN'T BE SEEN... OR FELT...

A MAN SUCH AS I... WITH HYPER-KEEN FACULTIES...

MAY BE ABLE TO SENSE IT!

EVEN NOW I CAN PERCEIVE A SUBTLE SHIFTING OF THE TEMPORAL RINGS...

THERE'S A SLIGHT LESSENING OF THEIR PRESSURE... AS THOUGH AN OPENING IS BEGINNING TO FORM!

I WAS RIGHT! HERE IT COMES..!

AND HERE I GO..!!

BUT, EVEN AS DD RISKS ALL ON ONE SUDDEN MOVE, DRAMATIC NEW EVENTS ARE TRANSPIRING ELSEWHERE...

BUT, AT LEAST WAIT UNTIL YOU LOCATE MATT!
MURDOCK AND N
WHAT GOOD CAN MY BLIND PARTNER DO ME NOW?
ANYWAY, HE'S JUST LIKE HIS CRUMMY BROTHER, MIKE...
NEITHER OF THEM ARE EVER AROUND WHEN THEY'RE NEEDED!
IF ANYONE CALLS...
I COULDN'T CARE LESS!

POOR FOGGY! I KNOW JUST HOW HE FEELS---HOW WORRIED HE IS ABOUT DEBORAH!
MATT WOULD NEVER HAVE STAYED AWAY THIS LONG---UNLESS HE'S IN SOME SORT OF TROUBLE!
I'VE FELT THAT WAY MYSELF---FOR SO MANY LONG, HEART-BREAKING MONTHS... ABOUT MATT!
SOMEHOW I FEEL THAT HIS DISAPPEARANCE ---AND DAREDEVIL'S--- ARE BOTH TIED UP, IN SOME TERRIBLE WAY... WITH THE ATTACK OF THE UNHOLY THREE!
SLAM
AND, ONE THING I DO KNOW...
I CAN'T STAY HERE ANY LONGER---WAITING--- FEARING---AND DOING NOTHING!
IF MATT NEEDS ME...I'D GIVE MY VERY LIFE... TO HELP HIM!

AND SO, LOVELY KAREN PAGE SPEEDS TOWARDS THE HOME OF MATT MURDOCK, UNAWARE THAT FATE HAS STRANGE NEW PLANS FOR HER, AND FOR THE MAN SHE LOVES---PLANS WHICH WILL GRADUALLY BE REVEALED IN THE WONDERMENT THAT FOLLOWS...

MEANWHILE, A RATHER UNCANNY EVENT IS TAKING PLACE IN ANOTHER NEIGHBORHOOD... UNSEEN BY ANYONE... EXCEPT US...
OKAY! I NOTIFIED THE PAPERS...AND THE RADIO AND TV NEWS PROGRAMS!
THE EXTERMINATOR AND HIS THREE ANIMAL-COSTUMED KILLERS ARE PROBABLY LOOKING FOR ME ALREADY!
FOGGY! FOGGY! IT'S ME..DEBORAH!
WHY DOESN'T HE HEAR ME? WHY DOESN'T HE ANSWER ME?
EVER SINCE I RETURNED...FROM THAT FANTASTIC TIME TRAP...IT'S BEEN THIS WAY!
I'M LIKE... A GHOST! UNSEEN... UNHEARD...UNNOTICED!
HOES

IT CAN ONLY MEAN ...WHATEVER RETURNED ME TO THE PRESENT... SOMEHOW DIDN'T WORK PROPERLY!
INSTEAD OF SENDING ME COMPLETELY BACK TO MY NORMAL TIME...I'M A FEW SECONDS OUT OF PHASE!
BUT, FOR ALL THE GOOD IT DOES ME...
IT MIGHT AS WELL BE A FEW CENTURIES!

MEANWHILE, UNAWARE OF WHAT'S JUST TRANSPIRED...
IF THEY'RE EVER GOING TO SHOW THEMSELVES, THIS IS AS GOOD A PLACE AS ANY!
I'VE GOT A POLICE WHISTLE IN MY POCKET!
THE MINUTE I SEE THEM, I'LL GIVE ONE LOUD BLAST...AND THAT'LL BE THAT!

THERE HE IS...RIPE FOR THE SLAUGHTER!
DID HE THINK WE'D BE AFRAID TO ATTACK HIM?

IF HE DID... HE DESERVES EVERYTHING HE GETS!
UMMF!
IT'S THEM! BUT...HOW DID THEY... ATTACK SO FAST...SO SILENTLY??

OF ALL THE ROTTEN *LUCK!!* MY *WHISTLE*... FELL OUT OF MY POCKET... ROLLING OUT OF *REACH!*

BUT, I'M *STILL* NOT HELPLESS... IF *DAREDEVIL* CAN DO IT...!

WELL, WADDAYA *KNOW!?* THE MOUSE IS *FIGHTING BACK!*

HAH! YOU DIDN'T *EXPECT* THAT, DID YOU?

WHERE'S MY *GIRL?* WHERE'S *DEBORAH HARRIS?* WHAT DID YOU *DO* TO HER?

ANSWER ME, YOU YELLOW-BELLIED *KILLERS*, OR...!

SO! YOU'RE TRYING TO THREATEN *US*, ARE YOU?

UHHH! MY *HAND!* IT..IT'S LIKE HITTING A BRICK *WALL!*

WELL, NOW THAT YOU'VE *HAD* YOUR LITTLE PLAY-TIME..!

...WE'LL SHOW YOU WHAT WE DO TO FLABBY, FAT-FACED WISE-GUYS!
ARE YOU READY, BIRD-MAN?

YEAH! I'M READY!
THEN YOU PUT 'IM TO SLEEP!
IF I HIT 'IM, IT'LL BE OVER TOO SOON!
AND WE WOULDN'T WANT THAT TO HAPPEN!

STOP SQUIRMING, TUBBY!
IT'LL ONLY HURT A MINUTE..!
BRING HIM HERE! LET ME HAVE 'IM..!

MUCH OBLIGED, CAT-MAN!
THINK NOTHING OF IT, FEATHER-HEAD!

BIG DEAL! SO WE MANAGED TO LEAN ON AN OVERWEIGHT MOUTHPIECE!
LET'S GIT 'IM TO THE EXTERMINATOR BEFORE WE HAVETA TACKLE SOME KID ON A TRI-CYCLE!
WHAT'S THE DIFFERENCE WHO WE HAVE TO BATTLE?
SINCE WE POLISHED OFF DAREDEVIL, THERE'S NOBODY WHO CAN STAND UP TO US---
AND EVERYONE KNOWS IT!

HERBERT! DID YOU SEE THAT? THE UNHOLY THREE...CAPTURED A VICTIM --- RIGHT BEFORE OUR EYES!
QUIET, HONEY! NO ONE ELSE SAW IT!
SO LET'S GET OUT OF HERE... BEFORE WE GET INVOLVED!
BUT, IF EVERYONE FELT THE WAY YOU DO...!
THE HECK WITH EVERYONE! I'M JUST LOOKING OUT FOR US!
AND NOW THAT WE'VE SEEN A STIRRING EXAMPLE OF CITIZENSHIP IN ACTION, LET'S RETURN TO DAZZLING DEBORAH HARRIS --- BEFORE WE BECOME NAUSEOUS..!
THEY ABDUCTED FOGGY! AND NO ONE STOPPED THEM --- NO ONE HELPED HIM!
AND, THERE'S NOTHING I CAN DO... NO WAY TO MAKE MYSELF SEEN... OR HEARD!
IT'S LIKE A LIVING NIGHT-MARE! HOW CAN ANYONE FIGHT BACK AGAINST A WEAPON THAT CAN HURL ITS VICTIM INTO ANOTHER TIME??
EVEN DAREDEVIL HAD NO WAY TO DEFEND HIMSELF... AGAINST THAT HORRIBLE T-GUN!
AND, SPEAKING OF THE T-GUN, LET'S SEE WHAT'S GOING ON WITH THE EXTERMINATOR HIMSELF...
SOMETHING IS WRONG WITH MY TIME DISPLACER!
THE PERSONNEL RETURN MECHANISM IS SLIGHTLY OUT OF SYNCHRONIZATION!
THAT'S WHY I HAVEN'T BEEN ABLE TO RETURN MY UNWILLING SUBJECTS TO THE IMMEDIATE PRESENT!
BUT, WHAT DOES IT MATTER?
IT MERELY MEANS I POSSESS A WEAPON EVEN DEADLIER THAN I DREAMED IT WAS!
IT MEANS ANY VICTIM OF THE EXTERMINATOR IS DESTINED TO BE LOST... FOREVER!
8

NO ONE ANSWERED THE BELL!
STRANGE-- THE DOOR IS UNLOCKED!
SINCE I'VE COME THIS FAR... I MIGHT AS WELL...GO IN!

MATT! CAN YOU HEAR ME? IT'S KAREN!
NOT A SOUND! THERE'S NOBODY HERE!
AND YET HE HASN'T BEEN AT WORK...NO-BODY'S SEEN HIM! WHERE CAN HE BE?
HIS BEDROOM DOOR IS AJAR! PERHAPS I'LL FIND SOME CLUE---IN THERE...!

ON THE BED... DARE-DEVIL'S COSTUME!
CAN THAT BE WHY HE'S WANTED NO VISITORS?
BECAUSE HIS BROTHER MIKE HAS BEEN LIVING HERE?
BUT, EVEN SO...WHERE CAN THEY BE NOW?
AND, FOR THE ANSWER TO THAT MOST NATURAL OF QUESTIONS...LET'S GO...!

I DID IT! I MANAGED TO REACH THE PRESENT AGAIN!
BUT... WAIT! I SENSE THINGS DIFFERENTLY... ALL THE IMAGES ARE BLURRED... HAZY... LESS DISTINCT THAN EVER BEFORE!
IT CAN ONLY MEAN ONE THING...
I'M STILL A MERE MICRO-SECOND OUT OF SYNC! I'VE GOT TO CLOSE THE TIME GAP... SOMEHOW!

ANYWAY, BEFORE YOU CAN SAY: FTASSKKK...
I GOT IT!
NOW, IF MY THEORY IS CORRECT..

AND, IF THE CABLE HOLDS..!

AND IF MY UN-SUSPECTING CHAUFFEUR DOESN'T VARY HIS SPEED IN THE NEXT FEW SECONDS..

THERE'S JUST A CHANCE...

---THAT MY FAVORITE HORN-HEADED HERO---
---IS GONNA MAKE IT!!

AND MAKE IT---
PTHOOP!

I DID!!

TSK TSK! CAN'T APPEAR IN PUBLIC WITH A TORN COSTUME!
EERS

IT WOULD BE BAD FOR MY PROFESSIONAL IMAGE!
...AND BESIDES, IT'S DRAFTY!
ANYWAY, IT'S EASIER TO HEAD HOME AND COLLECT MY WITS...
THAN TO TRY EXPLAINING TO TO THAT CROWD EXACTLY WHERE I CAME FROM... OR HOW!

BESIDES, THE EXTERMINATOR AND HIS THREE PLUG-UGLIES HAVE A LOT OF PAYING BACK TO DO...
AND I'M JUST THE JOKER TO MAKE SURE THAT...
UH OH! HOLD IT!

THAT PERFUME! THAT HEARTBEAT! IT'S KAREN! SHE'S UPSTAIRS!
IF..SHE SAW MY SPARE DARE-DEVIL COSTUME..!
SNIF
SNIF
THIS IS IT, MATTY BOY! THINK FAST!
12

I'VE GOT TO BLUFF IT THRU--!
SAY, MATT, DID YOU SEE MY SPARE COSTUME! I CAN'T FIND...
DAREDEVIL! I CAME HERE... LOOKING FOR YOUR BROTHER!
OH! IT'S KAREN!
I GUESS HE MUST HAVE GONE OUT... TO BUY A PIZZA, OR SOMETHING!
THAT LOW HUMMING SENSATION.. FROM THE WINDOW.. I'VE FELT IT BEFORE!
...EACH TIME THE T-GUN WAS USED!

IT'S COMING FROM THE OUTSKIRTS OF TOWN! IT CAN ONLY MEAN ONE THING...!
WHAT'S WRONG, MIKE? WHAT IS IT?

NOTHING, DOLLFACE! I JUST THOUGHT I HEARD SOMEONE!
THE MAIN POWER SUPPLY FOR THE T-RAY ..IS SOMEWHERE NEARBY!
IT'S ABOUT TO BE USED AGAIN... WITH MORE POWER THAN EVER!
AND, IT'S BUILDING UP IN INTENSITY!
I'VE GOT TO TRACE IT... WHILE THERE'S STILL TIME!

MIKE, LISTEN... FOGGY IS TRYING TO FIND THE UNHOLY THREE... ALL BY HIMSELF!
I KNOW HE'S NOT ONE OF YOUR FAVORITE PEOPLE... BUT, IF YOU DON'T HELP HIM..!
RELAX, LADY! I GET THE MESSAGE!

IF THEY FIND HIM FIRST, IT'S BYE-BYE, FOGGY!
YOU MEAN... YOU'LL TRY TO FIND HIM?
YOU BETTER BELIEVE IT! HERE'S YOUR COAT... WHAT'S YOUR HURRY?
I JUST THOUGHT OF SOMETHING! ---THE NUTTIEST IDEA I'VE EVER HAD!
BUT, IF I CAN PULL IT OFF--- IT'LL END MY TRIPLE-IDENTITY BIT...FOREVER!
NEVER THOUGHT I'D TRY TO GET RID OF A CHICK LIKE YOU...
BUT I'VE GOT THINGS TO DO, BABY!
OKAY, PRETTY GIRL---RECESS IS OVER!
13

SECONDS LATER, ATTIRED IN A NEW COSTUME... ARMED WITH NEW RESOLVE ...DD ONCE AGAIN SWINGS TOWARD THE ROOFTOPS...

GOT TO ZERO IN ON THE SOURCE OF THAT HUM...

...BEFORE IT FADES AWAY!

YOU THOUGHT WE'D NEVER GET TO THE ACTION, EH?
I DID IT! I FINALLY GOT THE T-RAY BACK IN SYNCHRONIZATION!
WELL, JUST HANG LOOSE, HERO...!
WHICH MEANS WE ARE NOW READY FOR THE MEDDLESOME MR. NELSON!

HE WILL BE THE FIRST VICTIM TO RECEIVE THE FULL POWER OF A TOTAL RAY BLAST!
QUICKLY... BRING HIM TO ME!

DON'T WASTE YOUR STRENGTH STRUGGLING, FATSO ---
YOU'LL BE NEEDING IT SOON!
I'M SURPRISED AT YOU, NELSON! YOU SHOULD BE PROUD! THINK OF THE CONTRIBUTION YOU'RE MAKING TO SCIENCE!
NO! LET ME GO! LET GO!

AFTER ALL...YOU'RE TO BE THE FIRST MAN EVER SENT BACK INTO TIME---
PAST THE POINT-OF-NO-RETURN!
RELEASE HIM!
THERE'S NO PLACE LEFT FOR HIM TO RUN!
CAN'T MOVE!--I'M STUCK TO THE SPOT!
BESIDES, THE MAGNETIZED METAL DISC BENEATH HIS FEET WILL STOP HIM WHERE HE STANDS!

BUT, BEFORE THE ARMORED MENACE CAN MAKE ANOTHER MOVE, 190 POUNDS OF RED-GARBED, FIGHTING FURY CRASHES INTO THE CHAMBER...
HANG ON, FOGGY! THE INNING'S NOT OVER YET!
VROOM!
DAREDEVIL!!
YOU KNOW IT, MAN!
HE'S MINE! I'LL STOP HIM!
THUMP!
16

MMOPPFFF!
STOP ME??
SURRRRRE YOU WILL!

STILL TOO DUMB TO KNOW WHEN YOU'RE LICKED, EH, HORNHEAD?
WELL, WELL! IF IT ISN'T PUSS 'N BOOTS!
WHICH ONE OF YOUR NINE LIVES IS UP FOR GRABS TODAY?

GO AHEAD, WISE-GUY... KEEP YAKKING!
SEE HOW MUCH GOOD IT DOES YOU!
JUST WHAT I HAD IN MIND, SON!

THEY DON'T CALL ME CAT-MAN FOR NOTHING!
YOU MEAN YOU PAY 'EM?
VER-RY FUNNY! BUT YOU'LL STOP LAUGHING WHEN YOU TRY TO SHAKE ME OFF!
NOW, I'LL JUST APPLY A LITTLE PRESSURE..!
MOVE FAST, DD! HE'S NOT KIDDIN'!

JUST IN CASE NO ONE EVER TOLD YOU...
THERE'S MORE THAN ONE WAY TO SKIN A CAT!
I SUGGEST YOU MAKE NOTES, TABBY! THIS IS GONNA BE AN EDUCATION!
INSTEAD OF PLAYING IT YOUR WAY... AND TRYING TO BREAK YOUR GINCHY LITTLE GRIP...
I'LL JUST HURL MYSELF BACKWARDS ...COMME CA..!

BUT DON'T FRET, PLAYMATE!
...YOUR EXCEDRIN HEADACHE WILL PROBABLY BE GONE BY MORNING!

NOW THE APE-MAN IS COMING TOWARDS ME!
BUT IT'S THE EXTERMINATOR I REALLY WANT!

AND THIS IS ONE WAY TO MAKE SURE I GET TO HIM!
BTOK!

NOW, IF HE'LL JUST *FALL BACK*... EXACTLY AS I *PLANNED*...!

PERFECT!

ONE THING I *LIKE* IS AN OBLIGING ANTHROPOID!

HE PLOWED RIGHT *INTO* THE ELECTRONIC EQUIPMENT!

EVEN *WITHOUT* MY THREE BESTIAL HIRELINGS...

EVEN WITH MY LABORATORY IN *FLAMES*...

MY T-GUN *STILL* MAKES ME THE MASTER OF *DAREDEVIL!*

ONLY IF YOU *NAIL* ME, CHARLIE!

AND *THOSE* DAYS ARE GONE *FOREVER!*

At that very second, a desperate Deborah Harris enters the law office of Nelson and Murdock... unseen by Karen Page...
If anyone can help save Foggy... Daredevil can!
How much longer must I remain a living ghost?
If... it doesn't end... I think... I'll go mad!

But, then...
It's over! I'm myself again!
Deborah!! It's you!
But how? Where did you come from?

And, at the Exterminator's lab...
The T-Ray is destroyed! They're all unconscious... except...
Daredevil!
He's... not here! The explosion... oh, no!
This is all... that's left of him!
Mike Murdock... gave his life... to save mine!

Here comes the police!
Foggy will tell them I died in the blast...
And that gets my "twin brother" out of my hair... forever!
It's easier.. just to be... Matt Murdock!

And so, later that night...
It had to happen... sooner or later!
Mike went out... the way he would have wanted to!
Then this will mean... the end of Daredevil!

Will it? ...I wonder?
Next
The New Daredevil!

APPROVED BY THE COMICS CODE AUTHORITY
HERE COMES...
DAREDEVIL
THE MAN WITHOUT FEAR!
MARVEL COMICS GROUP
12¢ IND.
42 JULY
NOBODY LAUGHS AT...
THE JESTER!

DAREDEVIL, THE MAN WITHOUT FEAR!™
NOBODY LAUGHS at The JESTER!
THE NEWEST, THE MOST CATACLYSMIC CREATION OF SMILIN' STAN LEE and GENIAL GENE COLAN
EMBELLISHED BY: DAN ADKINS
LETTERED BY: SAM ROSEN
NOT MANY MEN CAN LOOT AN UNDERGROUND BANK VAULT, SINGLE-HANDED ...USING ONLY SOME SMALL SLEEP PELLETS AND A HANDFUL OF INNOCENT-LOOKING TOYS!
...BUT THEN, NOT MANY MEN CAN BE... THE JESTER!
AND NOW, LET THE WONDERMENT UNFOLD...!

SINCE MY MISSION IS ACCOMPLISHED, THE TIME HAS COME TO CHANGE THE SCENE!
AND, WHAT BETTER METHOD OF MAKING A SPEEDY EXIT THAN BEHIND THE WHEEL OF A SLEEK SEDAN?
HOWEVER, IT BEHOOVES ME TO WAIT UNTIL THE LIGHT TURNS RED...

FOR, CROSSING AGAINST THE LIGHT IS A MISDEMEANOR...
AND FAR BE IT FROM ME TO SCOFF AT SUCH A LAW!

GOOD EVENING, SIR! CAN I INTEREST YOU IN A YO-YO FOR YOUR CHILDREN?
A STREET HAWKER...IN COSTUME, YET!
NOW I'VE SEEN EVERYTHING!
SORRY, PAL! MY KIDS ARE UP TO THEIR SIDE-BURNS IN YO-YO'S!

BUT, IF YOU WILL PERMIT ME TO DEMONSTRATE...
MINE IS JUST A LITTLE BIT... DIFFERENT!
...OR PERHAPS YOU'VE ALREADY NOTICED!
2.

TSK TSK! IT IS INDEED FORTUNATE THAT I CAME BY WHEN I DID...

FOR, MY SLEEPING FRIEND IS OBVIOUSLY IN NO CONDITION TO DRIVE!

THE PLAY IS ENDED AT LAST... AND IT HAS BEEN A ROUSING SUCCESS!
A PITY THERE ARE NONE TO APPLAUD!

BUT, ALAS... THAT IS ONE OF THE PENALTIES OF A CRIMINAL CAREER...!
I MUST FOREGO THE OVATIONS... AND THE CHEERS!
THE TRIBUTE OF AN AUDIENCE SHALL FOREVER BE DENIED ME!
BUT, EVEN AS THE JOCULAR JESTER REACHES HIS ISOLATED INGLENOOK...'TIS TIME FOR US TO TURN OUR ATTENTION ELSE-WHERE..!
3.

ATTENDEZ! THE LAW OFFICES OF NELSON AND MURDOCK, WHERE WE FIND OUR COLORFUL CREW MOURNING THE "DEATH" OF ONE MIKE MURDOCK...

MATT! HE WAS YOUR OWN BROTHER! HE DIED DEFENDING US!

HAVE YOU NOTHING TO SAY? CAN'T YOU EVEN PUT DOWN THAT BLASTED BRAILLE LAW BOOK FOR A MINUTE?

SORRY, FOGGY! IT'S TOO LATE FOR TEARS... AND WE STILL HAVE WORK TO DO!

MATT, I NEVER THOUGHT YOU COULD BE ---SO COLD-BLOODED!

IF THEY EVER SUSPECTED THAT THEY'RE MOURNING FOR SOMEONE WHO NEVER EVEN EXISTED--!

HIS DEATH... HAPPENED SO QUICKLY..*

IT'S MORE LIKE SOME MAD, IMPROBABLE NIGHTMARE!

DAREDEVIL WAS WINNING! EVERYTHING WAS GREAT!

"AND THEN, MIKE HURLED THE EXTERMINATOR BACK INTO HIS OWN DEADLY RAY MACHINE!"

"I DON'T EVEN WANT TO REMEMBER WHAT HAPPENED NEXT... BUT, I CAN'T HELP MYSELF..!"

*ACTUALLY, IT TOOK A COUPLE OF PAGES LAST ISH, AS WE REMEMBER! --- STICK-TO-THE-FACTS STAN.

Here, among my innocent-looking, specially-modified toys...
I am ready to launch a crime campaign the like of which the world has never known!

THE PUBLIC DESERVES THE FATE IT HAS IN STORE AT THE HANDS OF THE JESTER!
ALL I EVER REALLY WANTED WAS... APPLAUSE... THE APPLAUSE WHICH THEY EVER DENIED ME!

IT'S ALL HERE... IN MY SECRET SCRAP BOOK!
SCRAP BOOK
THE SCRAP BOOKS WHICH NONE BUT I SHALL EVER SEE!
PAGE AFTER PAGE... DEPICTING THE FAILURE OF MY FELLOW MEN TO RECOGNIZE THE GENIUS THAT WAS IN THEIR MIDST!

I HAD STUDIED FOR YEARS... I HAD SLAVED FOR YEARS... UNTIL FINALLY, I WON MY FIRST STARRING ROLE...!
I WAS CYRANO!! I WAS THE GREATEST CYRANO OF ALL TIME!
PLAYBILL
STARRING
JONATHAN POWERS
NANCY FOREMAN

BUT THEY WERE JEALOUS OF ME! THEY WERE ENVIOUS OF ME!
THEY WERE TOO BLIND, TOO STUPID TO GIVE ME THE OVATION I DESERVED!
INSTEAD, THEY BOOED... THEY JEERED...
THEY TURNED MY NIGHT OF TRIUMPH INTO A TIME OF TORMENT!

"I MIGHT HAVE EXPECTED THAT FROM THE STUPID, UNCULTURED PUBLIC... BUT NOT FROM MY OWN FELLOW ARTISTES...!"
THEY ARE FOOLS! BUT, IN TIME, THEY WILL LEARN..!
NOT WITH YOU ON STAGE, THEY WON'T!
YOU'VE HAD IT, POWERS! I MUST HAVE BEEN NUTS TO GIVE YOU THAT ROLE!
TURN IN YOUR FALSE NOSE AND GET LOST!
YOU COULDN'T ACT IF YOUR LIFE DEPENDED ON IT!

"BUT I KNEW HE WAS WRONG! THEY WERE ALL WRONG! I CONTINUED STUDYING... TRAINING... WAITING FOR MY BIG CHANCE!"
THE MORE SWORDS-MANSHIP I KNOW...
THE BETTER CHANCE I'LL HAVE TO STAR IN COSTUME ADVENTURES!
YOU'VE GOT IT ALL WRONG, POWERS!
YOU SHOULD BE STUDYING ACTING! ...THAT'S WHAT YOU NEED!

I'LL LET HIM HAVE IT!
NEXT TIME OPEN YOUR MOUTH, CHARLIE!
GREAT! GREAT! DO IT AGAIN, TUBBY! DO IT AGAIN!

"DAY AFTER DAY IT WENT ON... SHOW AFTER SHOW... WITH THAT UNTUTORED OAF GETTING HIS LAUGHS BY HITTING ME IN THE FACE WITH THOSE COUNTLESS PIES!"
MORE! GIVE 'IM ANOTHER ONE!
DO IT AGAIN, TUBBY! AGAIN!!
I TOLD YOU TO OPEN YOUR MOUTH, CHARLIE!

"UNTIL ONE DAY... I COULD STAND IT NO LONGER..!"
GET YOURSELF ANOTHER STOOGE, YOU CHEAP, LOW-BROW LOUT!

IF LAUGHTER IS WHAT THE PUBLIC WANTS...
LAUGHTER, AT THE EXPENSE OF SOMEONE ELSE...
THEN, I'M GOING TO PROVIDE IT FOR THEM!
...IN A MANNER THAT WILL MAKE ME THE GREATEST STAR OF ALL!
9.

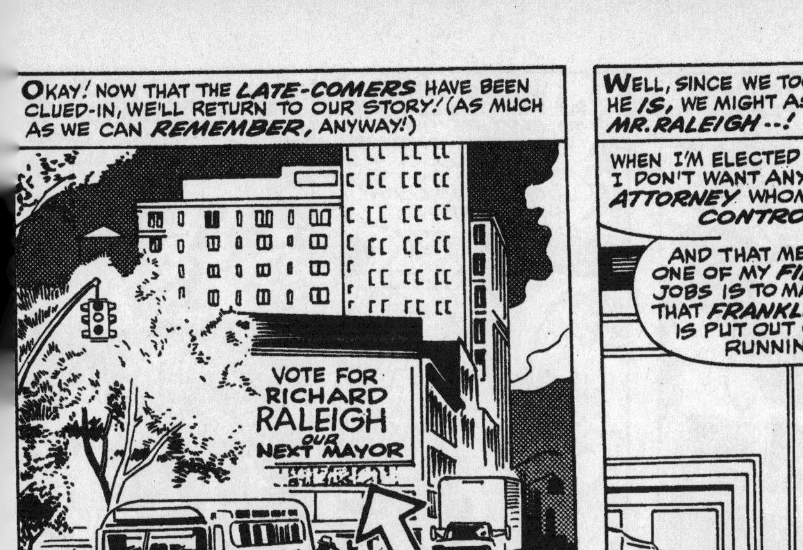
OKAY! NOW THAT THE LATE-COMERS HAVE BEEN CLUED-IN, WE'LL RETURN TO OUR STORY! (AS MUCH AS WE CAN REMEMBER, ANYWAY!)
VOTE FOR RICHARD RALEIGH OUR NEXT MAYOR
IF THE NAME RICHARD RALEIGH LOOKS FAMILIAR TO YOU, HE'S THE CROOKED POLITICAL CANDIDATE YOU READ ABOUT IN THE 35¢ SPIDER-MAN SPECTACULAR (NOW ON SALE)... IT'S EASIER THAN DREAMING UP A BRAND-NEW CHARACTER IN EVERY MAG!

WELL, SINCE WE TOOK THE TIME TO MENTION WHO HE IS, WE MIGHT AS WELL VISIT THE UNSCRUPULOUS MR. RALEIGH--!
WHEN I'M ELECTED MAYOR, I DON'T WANT ANY DISTRICT ATTORNEY WHOM I CAN'T CONTROL!
AND THAT MEANS... ONE OF MY FIRST JOBS IS TO MAKE SURE THAT FRANKLIN NELSON IS PUT OUT OF THE RUNNING!
BUT I'VE GOT TO DO IT CARE-FULLY!
I MUSTN'T TIP MY HAND!

NOBODY MUST SUS-PECT THAT RICHARD RALEIGH ISN'T A PILLAR OF INTEGRITY!
HMMM... THIS LOOKS INTEREST-ING!
Times
CITY PLAGUED BY JESTER'S ONE-MAN CRIME WAVE. POLICE CANCEL ALL LEAVES.
BY STEVEN URBAN

THE JESTER, EH? HE'LL BE JUST THE ONE TO DO MY HANDIWORK FOR ME!
BUT, HOW WILL I BE ABLE TO CONTACT HIM?
BETTER STILL... I'LL LET HIM CONTACT ME!
AND I KNOW JUST THE WAY TO DO IT!

YOU HEARD ME! I WANT TO BUY 15 MINUTES OF TV TIME FOR TONIGHT!
RALEIGH FOR MAYOR
VOTE FOR
I'VE DECIDED TO MAKE A SPEECH!
...ONE WHICH WILL FLUSH OUT THE JESTER!

THUS, LATER THAT NIGHT...
I SHALL NOT REST UNTIL THE JESTER IS SAFELY BEHIND BARS!
THAT IS MY PLEDGE TO THE PEOPLE OF OUR BELOVED CITY!
4

I HAVE DEVISED A PLAN WHICH IS CERTAIN TO CAPTURE THAT COWARDLY, COSTUMED CLOD!
RICHARD RALEIGH SHALL NOT FAIL!
DON'T BET ON THAT, FOOL!

DID HE THINK I'D ALLOW HIM TO THREATEN ME IN PUBLIC THAT WAY?
AFTER ALL, I HAVE MY IMAGE TO THINK OF...

I DON'T KNOW HIS HOME ADDRESS...
BUT I'LL BREAK INTO HIS CAMPAIGN HEADQUARTERS AND WAIT FOR HIM THERE!
THIS IS ONE TIME THAT THE JESTER CAN AFFORD TO BE PATIENT!

NOW, ALL I NEED DO IS...
RALEIGH!
YOU WERE WAITING FOR ME!
BUT SURELY YOU DON'T EXPECT A MERE REVOLVER TO HOLD THE UN-PREDICTABLE JESTER AT BAY?
OF COURSE NOT, MY FRIEND!
I MERELY WANTED TO DELAY YOU LONG ENOUGH TO MAKE YOU AN OFFER..
...WHICH WILL BE OF GREAT INTEREST TO A MAN OF YOUR TALENTS!

I WANT TO HIRE YOU.... NOT CAPTURE YOU!
GET FRANKLIN NELSON OUT OF THE RACE FOR D.A. AND I'LL PAY YOU TEN THOUSAND DOLLARS!
WELL, WHAT DO YOU SAY TO THAT?
SOUNDS LIKE THE EASIEST TEN GRAND THAT'S EVER BEEN OFFERED!
THEN YOU'RE IN?
THE JESTER IS IN!
AND NOW, LET'S SEE IF WE CAN RUSH BACK TO FOGGY BEFORE THE JESTER REACHES HIM...
DEBBIE, WHEN I'M ELECTED D.A., THERE'S A LITTLE QUESTION I'M GONNA POP TO YOU!
YOU WOULDN'T BE PUTTING A LADY ON, WOULD YOU?
OH, MATT...IT'S WONDERFUL TO BE OUT WITH YOU THIS WAY... WITH NO CARES, NO PROBLEMS!
I'M BEGINNING TO THINK I SHOULD HAVE KILLED OFF MY DAREDEVIL IDENTITY LONG AGO!
HOW ABOUT THAT? IT LOOKS AS IF WE JUST MADE IT..!
THERE HE IS NOW!
THIS WILL BE EVEN EASIER THAN I EXPECTED!
THERE'S ONLY NELSON, TWO GIRLS, AND A BLIND MAN TO WORRY ABOUT!
AND, IF YOU'RE BEGINNING TO THINK THAT THIS IS WHERE THINGS START MOVING, GO TO THE HEAD OF THE CLASS, HERO--!
12

AFTER I'VE ACCOMPLISHED THIS LITTLE FEAT---
I'LL HOLD RALEIGH UP FOR TEN TIMES WHAT HE OFFERED ME!
THAT'LL TEACH HIM NOT TO BE SO TRUSTING!

HEADS UP, NELSON! IF YOU'RE OUT FOR A LITTLE EXERCISE, HOW ABOUT LETTING ME FURNISH IT?
THE JESTER!
HE'S ATTACKING FOGGY---IN BROAD DAY-LIGHT!...BUT WHY?
THERE'S STILL TIME FOR ME TO---NO! I DARE NOT GIVE MYSELF AWAY NOW!

ALLOW ME TO DEMONSTRATE THE UTTER FOLLY OF YOUR FUTILE ACT!

ZOK!

BUT, THERE IS NO NEED TO CAUSE YOU FURTHER PHYSICAL INJURY!

I SEE A MUCH SIMPLER MEANS OF ACHIEVING MY OBJECTIVE..!

ALL I NEED DO IS HOLD YOUR SIGHTLESS FRIEND AS A HOSTAGE!

IF YOU EVER WISH TO SEE HIM ALIVE AGAIN...

TAKE YOURSELF OUT OF THE RACE FOR D.A.!

SO THAT'S WHAT'S YOU'RE AFTER!

FOGGY! PROMISE HIM ANYTHING!

DON'T LET MATT BE HARMED!

HE'S GOT MY CANE!

HE MUSTN'T LEARN ITS SECRET..!

I'LL HAVE TO BECOME DAREDEVIL AGAIN--- SOON AS I GET THE CHANCE!

BUT FOGGY AND KAREN THINK MIKE IS DEAD!

BETTER TALK FAST, MATTHEW!

YOU'RE IN FOR A SURPRISE, JESTER..!

DAREDEVIL IS STILL ON THE SCENE! JUST WAIT AND SEE!

IT'S HOPELESS, MURDOCK! WE ALL KNOW THAT HE'S BEEN KILLED!

YES! THE ORIGINAL DAREDEVIL WAS KILLED...BUT HE TRAINED SOME-ONE ELSE---TO TAKE HIS PLACE!

HE NEVER TOLD ANYONE HIS IDENTITY... BUT HE'LL BE SHOWING UP ANY TIME NOW!

THEY DON'T KNOW WHETHER TO BELIEVE ME OR NOT...

BUT AT LEAST I'VE PLANTED THE SEED!

SECONDS LATER...
HE...HE TOOK MATT!
OH, FOGGY... WHAT'LL WE DO?
WAIT! COME BACK!
IT'S NOT MATT HE'S INTERESTED IN!
HE'S JUST USING HIM AS A THREAT... TO STOP YOU FROM RUNNING FOR D.A.!

DON'T WORRY, MURDOCK... NO HARM WILL COME TO YOU!
...SO LONG AS NELSON DOES AS I ORDERED!

BUT, IF HE SHOULD DISOBEY ME...
YOU'LL NEVER LEAVE THIS ROOM ALIVE!
WE'LL SEE ABOUT THAT, BIG MOUTH!

HE'S GONE! LUCKY I CARRIED MY SPARE COSTUME IN MY INNER COAT POCKET!

BUT, SINCE THERE'S NO PLACE TO HIDE MY STREET CLOTHES...
I'LL HAVE TO DESTROY THEM!
AND THIS SMALL VIAL OF VAPOROUS ACID WILL DO THE TRICK!
JUDGING BY THE FOOT-STEPS I HEAR... I'M JUST IN TIME!

EVEN IF YOU ARE BLIND, I'LL PLAY IT SAFE BY TYING YOU UP, AND... UMMPHH!..
YOU'RE TOO LATE, CHUM! I'VE ALREADY GOTTEN MURDOCK SAFELY OUT OF HERE!
BUT YOU CAN TRY TYING ME... JUST FOR KICKS!
DARE-DEVIL! BUT... HOW??
THAT'S MY SECRET, SWEETIE!

OH MAN... IT'S GREAT TO BE BACK IN ACTION AGAIN!
BUT I MUST BE STALE...

HE DUCKED UNDER ME AND SENT ME SPRAWLING INTO A PILE OF TOYS!
TOYS?!!
SO! MURDOCK WAS RIGHT!
THERE IS ANOTHER DAREDEVIL!

BUT YOU ARE FAR CLUMSIER THAN YOUR PREDECESSOR!
AND EVEN HE WOULD HAVE BEEN NO MATCH FOR THE UNBEATABLE JESTER!
THE SOUND OF A NAKED BLADE THRASHING THRU THE AIR!

CAREFUL, SONNY! I DIDN'T BRING ANY BAND-AIDS WITH ME!

YOU ARE MOST ELUSIVE, DAREDEVIL...
BUT YOU CANNOT DODGE MY THRUSTS MUCH LONGER!
I DON'T INTEND TO, CHARLIE!

SERVING AS SOME ODDBALL'S TARGET FOR TONIGHT ISN'T EXACTLY THE WAY I GET MY JOLLIES, PAL!
HE'S A REAL PRO! HE ROLLED WITH MY KICK LIKE A MASTER TUMBLER!
THE ORIGINAL DAREDEVIL MUST HAVE BEEN A GOOD TEACHER!
BUT NOT GOOD ENOUGH!

HE BACK-FLIPPED HIMSELF INTO ANOTHER FIGHTING STANCE WITHOUT A SINGLE WASTED MOTION!
GETTING WORRIED, DAREDEVIL?
JUST BETWEEN US, YOU SHOULD BE!
FACE IT, MATTHEW... YOU'VE GOT A JOB CUT OUT FOR YOU!
IT'S A LUCKY THING HE LEFT ME MY BILLY-CLUB CANE... 'CAUSE I'M GONNA NEED IT!
SURE, TWINKLE-TOES... I'M SHAKING LIKE A LEAF!
BUT I DIDN'T THINK IT SHOWED!
NOW TO SEE HOW HE DOES WITHOUT HIS SWORD!
DON'T PAT YOURSELF ON THE BACK TOO HARD!
THAT SWORD YOU SNARED WAS MERELY A PROP!
I SIMPLY USED IT TO TOY WITH YOU...TO TEST YOUR METTLE!
YOU MAKE IT SOUND LIKE A COLLEGE ENTRANCE EXAM, JESTY!
THWIK!
INDEED? THEN THIS IS ONE EXAM YOU ARE DESTINED TO ABYSMALLY FLUNK!
WHUFFF!
17.

DIDN'T EXPECT ME TO BUTT YOU ACROSS THE ROOM THIS WAY, EH?
I DIDN'T EXPECT YOU TO DO IT ANY WAY!
DID HE HAVE SOME KIND OF LONG-DELAYED CHILDHOOD, OR SOMETHING?
WHAT'S WITH ALL THESE NUTTY TOYS HERE?
AND NOW... I'LL GIVE YOU AN EXAMPLE OF THE JESTER'S UNEXPECTED STRENGTH!
IF IT'S ALL THE SAME TO YOU, I'LL TAKE YOUR WORD FOR IT!
AM I JUST RUSTY, OR IS HE ACTUALLY MORE THAN A MATCH FOR ME?
BECAUSE OF YOUR UNTOWARD INTERFERENCE, I'LL HAVE TO FORMULATE A NEW ATTACK AGAINST FRANKLIN NELSON!
I TRUST I'VE MADE MY POINT, YOU MEDDLING FOOL!
AND THE JESTER DOES NOT APPRECIATE BEING COMPELLED TO CHANGE HIS PLANS!
THOK!

IF... MY OWN SUPER-NORMAL REFLEXES... WEREN'T ABLE TO... MAKE THE BLOW GLANCE OFF ME... I'D BE OUT FOR THE COUNT!
BUT, FOR NOW... I'LL LET HIM THINK I'M UNCONSCIOUS!
THEN, I'LL FOLLOW... AND SEE WHAT HE'S UP TO!

I'VE GOT TO LEARN WHAT HIS PLANS ARE...
AND WHY IT'S SO IMPORTANT TO HIM THAT FOGGY DOESN'T RUN FOR D.A.!

LUCKY HE'S GUNNING HIS ENGINE SO HARD...
HE'S NOT APT TO HEAR ME LAND ON MY CUSHION-SOLED LITTLE BOOTIES!

A SHORT TIME LATER... AT THE PRIVATE, REAR ENTRANCE TO RICHARD RALEIGH'S SANCTUM SANCTORUM ---
THERE'S NOTHING FAMILIAR ABOUT THIS BUILDING! I'VE NEVER BEEN HERE BEFORE!
BUT, JUDGING BY HIS SWIFT AND UN-HESITATING COURSE, THE JESTER KNOWS HIS WAY AROUND!
BUT WHO CAN HE BE LOOKING FOR... AND WHY?

RALEIGH! OPEN UP, BLAST IT! I KNOW YOU'RE IN THERE!
RAP
RAP
THE JESTER ISN'T USED TO COOLING HIS HEELS OUT-SIDE!
RAP
YOU NEVER WARNED ME THAT I'D HAVE TO CONTEND WITH DAREDEVIL ON THIS CAPER!

RALEIGH? HE MUST MEAN THE NEW PARTY'S CANDIDATE FOR MAYOR!
IT BEGINS TO ADD UP! IF RALEIGH'S CROOKED, HE WOULDN'T WANT SOMEONE AS IN-CORRUPTIBLE AS FOGGY TO BE HIS D.A.!
BUT, I HEAR NO SIGNS OF LIFE BEHIND THAT DOOR!
UH OH! THE JESTER'S BREAKING IN..!

HOLD IT, LAUGHING BOY! WE'VE GOT SOME UNFINISHED BUSINESS TO SETTLE!
ON THE FLOOR... A FIGURE LYING... WITH NO HEART-BEAT...NO PULSE!
IT'S RALEIGH ... HE'S DEAD!*
*HOW IT HAPPENED HAS NOTHING TO DO WITH OUR PRESENT YARN, PILGRIM... BUT, IF YOU JUST HAVE TO KNOW, IT'S ALL SPELLED OUT IN THE SPECTACULAR SPIDER-MAN #1, NOW ON SALE! ...SALESMAN STAN.
WAIT, DAREDEVIL! WITH RALEIGH DEAD, WE'VE NOTHING TO FIGHT ABOUT!
HE WAS SUPPOSED TO PAY ME TO TACKLE NELSON... BUT NOW... UNHH!
SO NOW YOU THINK ALL BETS ARE OFF, EH?
WELL, GUESS AGAIN, MISTER!
YOU SHOULD HAVE QUIT WHILE I GAVE YOU THE CHANCE, MASKED MAN!
NOW, IT'S TOO LATE!
K-INK!
MARBLES!
HE FLOORED ME BY DROPPING MARBLES UNDER MY FEET!
THIS ISN'T THE LAST YOU'LL HEAR OF THE JESTER!
NOR IS IT THE LAST YOU'LL HEAR OF ME!
WHEN NEXT WE MEET... YOU WON'T LEAVE THE BATTLE... ALIVE!
CRASH!
HE'S GONE!
BUT, HE SERVED HIS PURPOSE...
HE MADE ME REALIZE... SO LONG AS MATT MURDOCK LIVES... THERE WILL ALWAYS BE... A DAREDEVIL!
NEXT THE CHALLENGE OF... CAPTAIN AMERICA!
20

THE MAN WITHOUT FEAR!
APPROVED BY THE COMICS CODE AUTHORITY
DAREDEVIL
MARVEL COMICS GROUP
12¢ IND.
43 AUG
GUEST- STARRING
YOU-KNOW-WHO
IN THE BATTLE OF THE YEAR!

DAREDEVIL, THE MAN WITHOUT FEAR!™
"IN COMBAT WITH CAPTAIN AMERICA!"
IT'S WRONG-- ALL WRONG!
AND THERE'S NOTHING I CAN DO ABOUT IT!
THWANNG!
SPANNNG!
IN HIS PRIVATE, HIDDEN GYM, A SEETHING, SIGHTLESS SUPER-HERO GIVES VENT TO HIS FEELINGS OF SAVAGE RAGE AND HELPLESS FRUSTRATION--IN THE ONLY WAY HE CAN!
BUT WHY THIS MOOD OF BLEAK DESPAIR? LET'S FIND OUT--
ANOTHER AWESOME EPIC BY:
STAN (THE MAN) LEE
and
GENE (THE DEAN) COLAN
INKING: VINCE COLLETTA
LETTERING: ARTIE SIMEK
FWANG!
1

THE ONLY GIRL I'VE EVER LOVED-- THE ONLY GIRL WHO'S EVER MEANT ANYTHING TO ME--
AND NOW SHE'S GONE!
I'VE LOST HER-- FOREVER!
AND THERE'S NO WAY I CAN GET KAREN BACK!
SHE KNOWS I LOVE HER--SHE MUST KNOW IT!
A GIRL CAN SENSE A FEELING LIKE THAT!
BUT SHE THINKS I WON'T ADMIT IT-- BECAUSE OF MY BLINDNESS!
AND I DARE NOT TELL HER-- THE OTHER REASON--!
SPANG!

HOW CAN I JEOPARDIZE THE LIFE OF THE GIRL I LOVE--
--BY LETTING HER SHARE THE DEADLY SECRET OF DAREDEVIL?

ONLY BY GIVING UP MY CRIME-FIGHTING CAREER --FOREVER--COULD I MARRY KAREN --WITHOUT ENDANGERING HER LIFE!
BUT I CAN'T!! I JUST CAN'T DO IT!
SOMETIMES I THINK I WAS BORN TO BE DAREDEVIL--
AND, MATT MURDOCK IS THE IDENTITY THAT'S NOT FOR REAL!

BUT, WHAT GOOD IS MY MISSION--WHAT GOOD IS ANYTHING--WITHOUT THE GIRL I LOVE?
NO MATTER HOW I KNOCK MYSELF OUT--I'LL NEVER FORGET HER!
--OR THE WAY SHE WEPT--JUST A FEW SHORT HOURS AGO--

I HAVE SOMETHING TO SAY--TO BOTH OF YOU!
I'VE DECIDED TO LEAVE! I CAN'T WORK HERE ANY LONGER!
BUT WHY, KAREN? IF IT'S A MATTER OF MORE MONEY--?
OH NO--NO!
I'D WORK FOR NOTHING--IF ONLY--IF ONLY--!
3

IT'S--BECAUSE OF ME, MY DARLING--ISN'T IT?
I DIDN'T WANT TO TELL YOU! I DIDN'T WANT TO SAY IT!
BUT, HOW CAN I STAY HERE--SO CLOSE TO YOU--AND YET--SO FAR AWAY?
FOGGY AND DEBORAH HAVE EACH OTHER! BUT--EVEN THOUGH YOU CALL ME DARLING--
I CAN'T BEAR--TO KNOW--THAT YOU'LL NEVER BE MINE!
I'VE--NEVER WANTED--TO HURT YOU--!
OH, MATT--MATT--ALL I EVER LONGED FOR WAS TO LOVE YOU--TAKE CARE OF YOU--
BUT YOU LET YOUR BLINDNESS COME BETWEEN US!
AND NOW I KNOW--I'VE GOT TO FORGET YOU!
KAREN! WAIT--!
NO, MATT! I CAN'T WAIT ANY LONGER! THIS IS THE BEST WAY--FOR BOTH OF US!
IF ONLY IT COULD HAVE HAD--A DIFFERENT ENDING!
I'VE GOT TO HELP HER FORGET ME--MAKE IT EASIER FOR HER--
NO MATTER HOW IT HURTS!
WOMEN! YOU'RE ALL ALIKE! YOU TRY TO OWN A MAN!
WELL, NOBODY'S OWNING MATT MURDOCK!
IF YOU'RE GOING--THEN GO!
AND GOOD RIDDANCE!

I'VE DONE IT! I'VE DRIVEN AWAY--THE ONE I LOVE MOST--IN ALL THE WORLD!
SLAM

WHY DID YOU DO IT, MATT? WE BOTH KNOW HOW SHE FELT ABOUT YOU!
DON'T ASK ME, FOGGY! I--DON'T WANT--TO TALK ABOUT IT!

LET'S GO, DEB! THERE ARE TIMES WHEN A FELLA IS BETTER OFF ALONE!
BUT IT'S ALL SUCH A WASTE!
SHE'D HAVE MARRIED HIM--DESPITE HIS BLINDNESS!
THAT'S WHY I HAD TO SEND HER AWAY!
BUT I CAN NEVER EXPLAIN --TO ANYONE!

EACH MINUTE OF MY LIFE--I LIVE WITH DEATH AT MY SHOULDER!
I LOVE HER TOO MUCH TO PUT HER LIFE IN JEOPARDY AS WELL!

NOW IT'S OVER! I'VE MADE MY DECISION! I'VE GOT TO LIVE WITH IT!
BUT WHY CAN'T I FORGET HER?
WHY CAN'T I GET HER OUT OF MY MIND?
5

WHY HAS THE IDENTITY OF DAREDEVIL BECOME THE MOST IMPORTANT THING IN MY LIFE?

NUTS!
WHAT AM I QUESTIONING MYSELF FOR?
WHAT'S DONE IS DONE-- AND THERE'S NO TURNING BACK!
I WAS NEVER MEANT TO BE A BLASTED CASANOVA!
SPTA

I'M A RED-HOT, SWINGIN' SUPERHERO-- AND THAT'S THE WAY I WANT IT!
YEAH--
THAT'S THE WAY--
--I WANT IT....!

MINUTES LATER, EVERY NERVE STRETCHED TAUT, THE AGONIZED ADVENTURER HEADS OUT INTO THE OPEN--
ONLY ONE THING TO DO--I'VE GOTTA KEEP MOVING!
--TILL I FIND A WAY TO OUT-RUN HER MEMORY!

THIS IS WHAT I BARGAINED FOR! THIS IS THE LIFE I CHOSE!
THIS IS WHAT I MUST STAY WITH--FOREVER!
W. 39 ST.
WHAT'S THAT LOUD SPEAKER I HEAR?

--AND, FOR THE BENEFIT OF THE URBAN POVERTY FUND, OUR WORLD-FAMOUS GUEST--CAPTAIN AMERICA--WILL BATTLE ANY VOLUNTEER--IN ANY TYPE OF COMBAT
WELL, WELL --A LITTLE SPORTING EVENT AT THE GARDEN!

IT WOULD BE A BLAST IF I WAS THE ONE TO TANGLE WITH CAP!
BUT I FIGURE I'VE GOT SOME MORE IMPORTANT THINGS TO DO!
AND I JUST REMEMBERED ONE OF THEM--!

THAT COSTUMED CREEP WHO CALLS HIMSELF THE JESTER IS STILL AT LARGE, SOMEWHERE IN THE CITY!*
AND I STILL OWE HIM A LITTLE SOME-THING!

"HE LOOKED LIKE A FULL-TIME, PRACTICING NUT--BUT HE ALMOST DEFEATED ME!"
*AS SEEN AND SAVORED IN OUR SENSATIONAL PRECEDING ISH! --SMOOTH STAN.

"--AND I'M ONE GUY WHO HATES UNFINISHED BUSINESS!"

SO WINGHEAD CAN HAVE HIS FUN AND GAMES--

WHILE I GO LOOKING FOR THAT CORNY, COSTUMED CLOWN!

OH OH! HOLD IT, DD!
THAT SOUNDS LIKE BIGGER TROUBLE!
--STOLEN FROM THE PARKSIDE MEDICAL CENTER--A SMALL, BLACK BAG CONTAINING RADIOACTIVE VIALS--
EXERCISE EXTREME CAUTION! PROLONGED EXPOSURE MAY BE DANGEROUS!

IT HAPPENS ALL THE TIME! SOME BIRD-BRAINED SNEAK THIEF GRABS A DOCTOR'S MEDICAL BAG--
NOT SUSPECTING IT CONTAINS DEADLY RADIOACTIVE MATERIAL!
BUT LUCKILY, IT'S RIGHT UP MY ALLEY--
WITH MY HYPER-KEEN SENSES, I'M LIKE A WALKING GEIGER COUNTER!
IT SHOULDN'T TAKE ME LONG TO SNIFF 'IM OUT!

A FEW MINUTES LATER, JUST AS PREDICTED--
THE SOUND OF RUNNING FEET--FROM THE ALLEY AHEAD--!
AND A STRANGE, BURNING SENSATION--
COMING CLOSER AND CLOSER!
HORNHEAD, YOU FOUND YOUR BOY!

WHEW! WITH THESE ALL-OUT SUPER-SENSES OF MINE--
IT FEELS LIKE I'M STANDING ON TOP OF A CYCLOTRON!

OKAY, TINHORN--THE PARTY'S OVER!
DAREDEVIL!
YOU KNOW IT, SONNY!
9

HEY! YOU'VE GOTTA BE KIDDIN'!
--REACHING FOR A GUN AGAINST ME?!!
ZOCK
HAVE TO GET THIS TO THE MEDICAL CENTER-- FAST!
BUT WHY IS MY HEAD SPINNING--?
WHY IS IT AFFECTING ME SO QUICKLY?
IT REMINDS ME OF-- THAT DAY-- WHEN I WAS JUST-- A KID--

A BLIND MAN-- CROSSING AGAINST THE LIGHT!
WHY DOESN'T SOMEONE STOP HIM?
HEY, MISTER-- LOOK OUT!
THAT TRUCK CAN'T STOP IN TIME! IT'S GONNA HIT HIM!
KKREEEEEEEEE
AJAX MIC LAB
RADIO-ACTIVE MATERIALS
DANGER

I'M THE CLOSEST TO HIM!
IF I CAN'T SAVE HIM-- NO ONE CAN!
"I SAVED THE MAN, ALL RIGHT--BUT THE TRUCK CLIPPED ME--!"

AN OPEN CYLINDER FELL FROM THE TRUCK!
IT HIT THE BOY--NEAR HIS EYES!
HEY, LOOK! IT'S CARRYING RADIOACTIVE MATERIAL!
THAT'S HOW I LOST MY SIGHT--
AND THE ACCIDENT MUST HAVE MADE ME HYPER-SENSITIVE TO RADIATION!
I FEEL STRANGE--DIFFERENT--!
THE PRECEDING WAS BORROWED FROM DD #1--AS IF YOU COULDN'T GUESS! --LOVEABLE LEE.
MINUTES LATER, AFTER RETURNING THE FATEFUL VIAL--
SO! THEY FOUND HIM A FALL GUY, DID THEY?
AND NOW--INNNNNTRODUCING --CAPTAIN AMERRRRICA!
WHAT THAT PHONY NEEDS IS A REAL FIGHT!
AND I'M JUST THE GUY TO GIVE IT TO HIM!
PREEEEEEESENTING--THE WORLD-FAMOUS --STAR-SPANGLED AVENGER!
A MAN WHO HAS BECOME A LIVING LEGEND IN HIS OWN TIME!
IF THIS WASN'T FOR CHARITY, I'D CALL IT OFF!
THAT SCREETCHING SOB-SISTER'S EMBARRASSING ME!
DON'T WORRY, CAP--
HE'LL WEAR 'IMSELF OUT SOONER OR LATER!
11

IF THIS WAS FOR REAL, I WOULDN'T FACE THAT JOE FOR A MILLION BUCKS!

I'VE GOT NEWS FOR YOU, MAN--

IT'S GONNA BE FOR REAL!

HEY! YOU COULD HAVE HURT HIM!

YEAH? WOULDN'T THAT BE A CRYIN' SHAME!

C'MON, GLORY-HOUND! YOU WANTED A FIGHT, DIDN'T YOU?
OR CAN'TCHA TAKE SOME REAL COMPETITION?
WHAT'S GOTTEN INTO YOU? YOU SOUND LIKE--
UNHHH!
HOLD IT! WE'VE GOTTA GET YOU BOTH SOME GLOVES!

JUST LIE THERE, USELESS--IT WON'T BE LONG NOW!
ALL I GOTTA DO IS-- -UNHHH!!-
BTANG!
OKAY, BIG MOUTH-- YOU'VE HAD YOUR FUN--!

MY HAND!!
YOU AND THAT ROTTEN SHIELD OF YOURS!!

I DON'T KNOW WHAT YOUR HANG UP IS, FELLA--
BLANNG!
BUT, IF IT'S A REAL FIGHT YOU'RE AFTER--
YOU'VE COME TO THE RIGHT PLACE!

WELL, WELL-- THE LITTLE TIN SOLDIER IS FIGHTING BACK!
AND THAT'S JUST THE WAY I LIKE IT!

ONLY A MASKED LAMEBRAIN WOULD BOUNCE ME INTO THE ROPES THIS WAY--
THWANNNG
SO I GUESS I OWE YOU A VOTE OF THANKS!

TSK TSK! YOU COULD AT LEAST HAVE SAID "YOU'RE WELCOME"!
ZBOK!
YOU'RE GETTING GROGGY NOW, AREN'T YOU?
WELL, DON'T WORRY, CORNBALL --IT WON'T LAST LONG!
I'LL MAKE SURE OF THAT!
I'VE BEEN TRYING TO HOLD MYSELF BACK... ON THE CHANCE THAT YOU'RE SICK--THAT YOU DON'T KNOW WHAT YOU'RE DOING!
YOU CAN'T BE THE REAL DAREDEVIL! I MUST BE FIGHTING --AN IMPOSTOR!
BUT I'M BEGINNING TO SEE THE LIGHT, MISTER!
AND THAT MEANS--ALL BETS ARE OFF!
15

OH, NO-- YOU DON'T GET AWAY THAT EASY!
CAN'T SOMERSAULT MY WAY OUT OF THIS--
HE'S TOO FAST WITH THAT BLASTED SHIELD!
THE FANS OUT THERE PAID FOR SOME ACTION--
AND NOW THAT YOU'RE HERE--THEY'RE GONNA GET IT--IN SPADES!

I NEVER REALIZED HE WAS SO FAST-- SO STR-- UNHHH!
I DON'T GET IT! YOU CAN'T BE AN IMPOSTOR!
NOBODY ELSE CAN MOVE THAT WAY-- OR ROLL WITH A PUNCH LIKE THAT!

I'LL PRETEND TO BE HELPLESS-- WHILE I STAGGER TOWARDS HIM--
THEN, WHEN HE GETS CLOSE ENOUGH--

WHAT'S WITH YOU, MISTER?
YOU'RE OUT OF THE BUSH LEAGUES NOW!
I'LL STRAIGHTEN UP AND LET HIM--
ARRGHHH!!
16

NOW TALK! HOW COME YOU HAVE ALL OF DAREDEVIL'S POWERS--
BUT YOUR STRATEGY IS LIKE AN AMATEUR'S COMPARED TO HIS!
WHO IN BLAZES ARE YOU, ANYWAY?
I SAID TALK!
GREATEST FIGHT I EVER SAW!
HARD TO BELIEVE IT'S JUST AN ACT!
LOOK! DAREDEVIL'S GETTING UP--
IT STILL ISN'T OVER YET!
WOW! HE'S BUTTING CAP RIGHT OVER THE ROPES--!
YEAH-- BUT CAP DRAGGED 'IM ALONG WITH HIM!
IT'S STILL ANYBODY'S FIGHT!
CAP TOPPLED HIM! HE'S TOSSING HIM OVER--!
THAT STAR-SPANGLED SHIELD-SWINGER KNOWS EVERY TRICK IN THE BOOK!
17

--AND SO DOES DAREDEVIL!
LOOK AT THE WAY HE LANDED--!
I LIKE IT BETTER OUT HERE, WINGHEAD!
I WON'T HAVE THE ROPES TO CRAMP MY STYLE!
SUIT YOURSELF, SON--
I COULDN'T CARE LESS!
AND SO THE BLUDGEONING BATTLE CONTINUES TO RAGE, UNTIL--
UH OH! THEY'RE TOPPLING INTO THE ELEVATOR SHAFT!
GRAB A CABLE, YOU FOOL!
YOU CAN STILL SAVE YOURSELF!
SINCE WHEN DOES DAREDEVIL NEED ADVICE FROM A MASKED HAS-BEEN?
MY HEAD-- STARTING TO ACHE!
FEELS LIKE IT'S ABOUT TO SPLIT OPEN!
WHAT'S HAPPENING TO ME NOW?

MADI
FINALLY, AFTER A SAFE BUT JOLTING DESCENT TO THE BOTTOM OF THE SHAFT--
LOOK--WHY NOT CALL IT A DRAW--BEFORE SOMEONE REALLY GETS HURT!
I DON'T KNOW WHAT YOU'RE TRYING TO PROVE--
BUT I'LL CONCEDE THAT YOU'VE ALREADY PROVED IT!
BESIDES, I SUSPECT YOU NEED MEDICAL HELP MORE THAN A FISTFUL OF KNUCKLES!

HOW ABOUT THAT? JUST SPUN AROUND AND LIT OUT!
NOW HE'S RUNNING OFF!
NOW THAT CAP'S MAD--HE DOESN'T WANT ANY PART OF 'IM!
HOLD IT, MISTER! YOU'VE GOT SOME TALL EXPLAINING TO DO!
I REMEMBER NOW! IT WAS THE RADIUM--IT AFFECTED ME--MADE ME TEMPORARILY GO BERSERK!
BUT, THE EFFECT HAS FINALLY WORN OFF!
MADISON SQUARE GARDEN
CAPTAIN AMERICA
PERFORMS
BOUT FOR CHARITY
PERFORMED AT CAPT. AMERICA'S
AND IT'S EASIER TO CUT OUT THAN TO TRY EXPLAINING A SET-UP LIKE MINE!
I'VE A HUNCH THAT OL' CAP WILL UNDERSTAND!
WALK
NO SENSE GOING AFTER HIM!
IF HE'S WILLING TO CALL IT QUITS--IT'S OKAY WITH ME!
WHATEVER HE DID--I GUESS HE HAD HIS REASONS!
WHAT'S THE LOW-DOWN, CAP? WHY'D DAREDEVIL CHICKEN OUT?
HE DIDN'T! WE ALL WANTED A GOOD SHOW--
AND HE GAVE US ONE!
MEANWHILE, IN ANOTHER PART OF TOWN--
FOR JUST A FEW MOMENTS--IN THE HEAT OF BATTLE--I WAS ABLE TO FORGET--KAREN!
BUT--WHAT HAPPENS NOW--?
CAPTAIN AMER GIVES BENEF AT GARDEN
NEXT DAREDEVIL, WANTED FOR MURDER!

APPROVED BY THE COMICS CODE AUTHORITY
DARE-DEVIL
MARVEL COMICS GROUP
12¢ IND.
44 SEPT
THE MAN WITHOUT FEAR!
I, MURDERER!

DAREDEVIL, THE MAN WITHOUT FEAR!
"I, MURDERER!"
GO, MY LITTLE ROBOT MINIATURE! YOU ARE SMALL ENOUGH TO WALK UNDER THE GUARD BEAM WITHOUT SETTING OFF AN ALARM!
ONLY THE JESTER COULD HAVE CONCEIVED SO BRILLIANT, SO TOTALLY DARING A PLAN!
AHHH, HOW I THRILL TO THE PITTER-PATTER OF YOUR TINY FEET!
STORY: SMILIN' STAN LEE
ILLUSTRATION: GENIAL GENE COLAN
EMBELLISHMENT: VALIANT VINCE COLLETTA
LETTERING: ADORABLE ARTIE SIMEK
APPLAUDING: IRASCIBLE IRVING FORBUSH
TIC
TIC TIC
TIC
1

SLOWLY, SLOWLY, MY ELECTRONIC LITTLE ELF!
WE MUSTN'T JOSTLE YOUR DELICATE TRANSISTORS, MUST WE?
THAT'S IT! CONTINUE TILL THE END OF THE COUNTER --AND THEN--
ACTIVATE YOUR JETS!
TIC
TIC
TIC
PERFECT! NOW APPROACH THE DIAL ON THE SAFE BEFORE YOU--!
YOUR BUILT-IN SONAR SCANNER WILL ENABLE YOU TO DETECT THE FALLING TUMBLERS!
AND YOU MUST BE SILENT ENOUGH TO HEAR MY WHISPERED COMMANDS!
RRRR
CLICK
AND ALL THAT REMAINS, IS SIMPLY ROUTINE!
TIC
TIC
TIC

TO THINK OF THE YEARS I WASTED-- SEEKING FAME AS AN ACTOR!
I--THE GREATEST CRIMINAL GENIUS OF ALL!
WELL DONE, MY UNDER-SIZED LITTLE UNDERSTUDY!
NOW, BACK INTO YOUR RESTING PLACE YOU GO!
JEWEL
HOW CHILDISHLY SIMPLE IT WAS!
EXCEPT FOR MY ONE CARELESS DEFEAT AT THE HANDS OF DAREDEVIL, I'VE BEEN-- WAIT!!
A POLICE SIREN!!
STAY WHERE YOU ARE, MISTER! I'VE GOT YOU DEAD TO RIGHTS!
DO YOU? WE SHALL SEE!!

THEN, AS THE GARISHLY COSTUMED ARCH-FIEND DASHES FROM OUT OF THE SHADOWS--
I MIGHT'A KNOWN-- IT'S THE JESTER!
HOLD IT RIGHT THERE, FUNNY MAN!
JEWELERS
POLICE
NYPD A670Z
DON'T SHOOT! THE SOUND OF GUNFIRE OFFENDS MY EARS!
WHICH IS WHY I PREFER MORE SILENT METHODS--
SUCH AS THIS!
THUD
AND SO THE JESTER TRIUMPHS AGAIN!
HE REALLY IS A FULL-TIME NUT!
HE GOES TO ALL THAT TROUBLE TO GRAB THESE JEWELS-- THEN LEAVES 'EM BEHIND--
AND HE THINKS HE'S WON!

MINUTES LATER--
THE PRIZE ITSELF MEANS ALMOST NOTHING TO ME!
ALL THAT TRULY MATTERS IS THE EXCITEMENT OF THE GAME--THE THRILL OF THE CHASE!
BUT THERE IS ONE THING THAT NOW CONCERNS ME--!
SOONER OR LATER, SOMEONE IS SURE TO LEARN MY TRUE IDENTITY!
AND, WHEN THAT HAPPENS, I'LL BE FAR MORE VULNERABLE THAN I AM NOW!
BUT, IF THE WORLD SHOULD THINK THAT JONATHAN POWERS IS NO LONGER ALIVE--!
AND, EVEN BETTER--
WHAT IF I MAKE IT SEEM AS THOUGH MY OWN WORST ENEMY KILLED ME?
AND, WHILE THE JEERING JESTER CONJURES UP AN IMAGE OF THE MAN WITHOUT FEAR--LET'S VISIT OL' DD IN PERSON--
KAREN MIGHT STILL BE SOME-WHERE IN THE CITY!
AND, IF SHE IS--I'VE GOT TO FIND HER!

I CAN'T BEAR THE THOUGHT THAT I'VE BROKEN HER HEART!
WHEN I ADMITTED WE COULD NEVER MARRY--
I NEVER DREAMED SHE'D TAKE IT SO HARD!
I THOUGHT IT WAS FOR THE BEST-- FOR HER OWN SAKE--
I ONLY DID IT BECAUSE I LOVE HER!
BUT--I REALIZE NOW--EVERYTHING IS MEANINGLESS-- WITHOUT HER!
THE ONLY PROBLEM IS-- HAVE I REALIZED IT--
--TOO LATE?
BUT NOW--SOAP OPERA TIME'S OVER--AS WE VISIT A POLICE STATION THE NEXT DAY--
MY NAME IS JONATHAN POWERS! I HAVE A STATEMENT TO MAKE!
11TH PRECINCT
I JUST THOUGHT THE LAW WOULD LIKE TO KNOW--
I'VE FIGURED OUT THE SECRET IDENTITY OF DAREDEVIL! I KNOW FOR CERTAIN WHO HE IS!
GOWAN INSIDE AND SEE THE SERGEANT!
AND I INTEND TO EXPOSE HIM-- PUBLICLY-- AT THE STROKE OF MIDNIGHT!
YEAH! THAT'S WHAT HE'S THERE FOR!
6

I WILL MAKE AN ANNOUNCE-MENT IN THE CENTER OF THE GEORGE W. SHINGTON BRIDGE--
A LOCATION THAT APPEALS TO MY SENSE OF THE DRAMATIC!
SAY, I HEARD OF JONATHAN POWERS--HE'S AN ACTOR--BEEN IN A DOZEN FLOPEROOS!
THIS MUST BE SOME KINDA PUBLICITY STUNT!
IF YOU KNOW WHO HE IS, MAC, WHY NOT
AH NO! ONLY THE STAR MAY PICK THE RIGHT TIME--THE RIGHT PLACE!
HE SOUNDS LIKE HE MEANS IT, JOE!
IT'S BEEN A SLOW NIGHT SO FAR--WE MIGHT AS WELL CHECK 'IM OUT!
YEAH! WE'VE GOT NOTHIN' TO LOSE--
AND IT COULD BE A PAGE ONE BOMBSHELL!
IT'S PUSHIN' MIDNIGHT NOW-- SO LET'S GO!
WE'LL NEED TIME TO PICK OUR SPOT AND SET UP THE CAMERA!
AND, EVEN AS THE FATEFUL HOUR DRAWS NEAR -
WE INTERRU THIS PROGRA
JONATHAN POWERS, FORMER BROADWAY ACTOR AND COMEDIAN, HAS MADE A STARTLING PUBLIC ANNOUNCE-MENT--
ON THE AIR
HE HAS PROMISED TO REVEAL THE TRUE IDENTITY OF THE COLORFUL, MASKED ADVENTURER WHOM THE WORLD KNOWS ONLY AS--DAREDEVIL!
POWERS HAS CHOSEN AN UNUSUAL SITE FOR THIS DRAMATIC DISCLOSURE--

--HE PROMISES TO DIVULGE HIS INFORMATION ATOP THE GEORGE WASHINGTON BRIDGE AT THE STROKE OF MIDNIGHT!
FM-AM
--OFFICIAL OPINION IS DIVIDED AS TO WHETHER A HOAX IS BEING PERPETRATED, OR--
IT MAY BE A HOAX-- BUT WHAT HAS HE TO GAIN?
All my Love, Karen
AS FAR AS I CAN REMEMBER, I DON'T KNOW ANY JONATHAN POWERS--
SO, WHAT BETTER TIME TO INTRODUCE MYSELF?
IT'LL ACCOMPLISH ONE THING, ANYWAY--
IF NOTHING ELSE, IT MAY TAKE MY MIND OFF KAREN FOR A WHILE!
IT'S ALMOST MIDNIGHT! I'LL BE JUST IN TIME!
BUT-- IN TIME FOR-- WHAT??

FOR THE ANSWER TO OD'S HAUNTING QUERY, LET'S TURN OUR ATTENTION TO A TINY ONE-MAN SUB, SILENTLY APPROACHING THE STATELY BRIDGE--
AS IT DRAWS NEARER, WE NOTICE THAT IT SEEMS TO RESEMBLE A TOY MORE THAN AN ACTUAL, REAL-LIFE UNDERSEA CRAFT--
A RESEMBLANCE WHICH IS FAR MORE INTENTIONAL THAN ACCIDENTAL--
--CONSIDERING WHO THE CREATOR, AND SOLE OCCUPANT IS!
IT'S STRANGE HOW CHEERFUL I SEEM TO FEEL--
--SINCE I PLAN TO BE MOST FOULLY MURDERED DURING THE NEXT FEW MINUTES!
BZZZZ
AND THERE-- DIRECTLY AHEAD-- IS THE PERFECT SETTING FOR SO BRILLIANT A PLOT!
A PLOT IN WHICH DAREDEVIL IS SOON TO BE THE UNWITTING VICTIM!

THEN, AT LAST--
I'M ALMOST THERE!
NOW I'LL LEARN IF POWERS IS A PART-TIME CRANK--
--OR SOMEONE WHO KNOWS MORE THAN IS GOOD FOR HIM!
THERE HE IS-- RIGHT ON CUE!
I KNEW HE WOULDN'T BE ABLE TO RESIST THE BAIT I OFFERED!
AND SO, THE PLAY BEGINS--!
HE SAID HE'D BE AT THE CENTER OF THE BRIDGE!
BUT WHY A PLACE LIKE THIS?
HELP!! HELP!!
HANG LOOSE, DD! YOU'RE ABOUT TO FIND OUT--!
10

SOMEONE'S IN TROUBLE DOWN THERE!
AND THAT MEANS-- I'D BETTER MOVE!
HELP!
11

THERE HE IS, THE STUPID, SWAGGERING, SELF-RIGHTEOUS BUFFOON!
DOWN HERE--QUICK! QUICK! I CAN'T--HOLD ON--ANY LONGER!
LITTLE DOES HE DREAM--THAT THIS IS MY GREATEST--MY MOST MONUMENTAL PERFORMANCE!
WHAT'S THE PITCH, PAL? YOU'RE IN NO DANGER! YOU JUST--HEY!
HOW RIGHT YOU ARE, MASKED MAN!
I'M IN NO DANGER WHAT-SOEVER!
MUST KEEP HIM BUSY--OFF-BALANCE--TILL I'M SURE THERE ARE WITNESSES PRESENT!
A PITY WE CANNOT SAY THE SAME--FOR YOU!
IT'S A TRAP OF SOME SORT! BUT WHO? WHY? WAIT--THAT VOICE!
I'VE HEARD IT BEFORE! IT WAS DIFFERENT--MORE MUFFLED--MORE FRANTIC--BUT IT WAS HIM!
12

STILL, I HEAR SO MANY VOICES-- AND THEY ALL MAKE AN IMPRESSION ON MY HYPER-KEEN SENSES--!
HEY, DD--STOP SPECULATING AND START SLUGGING!
THIS GUY'S GOOD!
I DON'T KNOW WHAT YOU'RE UP TO, CHARLIE--
BUT YOU PICKED YOURSELF THE WRONG PIGEON!
HAVE I? WE'LL SEE ABOUT THAT!
HE COUNTERS MY BLOWS LIKE A PRO--BUT HE'S NOT TRYING TO HIT BACK YET! WHY??
IF SOMEONE DOESN'T GET HERE SOON, I'M IN TROUBLE!
I CAN FIGHT HIM AS THE JESTER--BUT NOW, WITHOUT MY LITTLE PROPS, I--
-UHHH!-
HEY! IT'S A GOOD THING WE SHOWED UP! LOOK!
DAREDEVIL--USING POWERS FOR A PUNCHING BAG!
HE MUST BE TRYING TO SILENCE HIM!
THEY'RE HERE! AND JUST IN TIME!
13

GET THOSE CAMERAS ROLLING!
THIS'LL BE THE SCOOP OF THE CENTURY!
RRRRRRRRRRRRRR
CLICK!
CLICK!
CLICK!
I DON'T GET IT! WHAT'S WITH DAREDEVIL?
LIKE HIM OR NOT, HE'S NEVER ATTACKED AN INNOCENT CIVILIAN BEFORE!
CLICK!
WELL, JUST BETWEEN YOU, ME, AND THESE CAMERAS--HE'S NOT EXACTLY SIGNIN' A PEACE TREATY WITH THAT GUY NOW!
MY TIMING WAS PERFECT!
AND DAREDEVIL IS REACTING JUST AS I KNEW HE WOULD!
WATCH IT, YOU FOOL-- IF I LET GO OF YOU-- YOU'RE A GONER!
GOOD! GOOD! THAT'S JUST WHAT I WANT HIM TO THINK!
AND THE STUPID, MASKED STUMBLEBUM STILL DOESN'T SUSPECT A THING!
HELP! HELP! DAREDEVIL'S TRYING TO KILL ME!

HE'S--
GOING
OVER--!
IT SEEMS
AS THOUGH--
HE WANTS
TO FALL!
HE BROKE
AWAY
FROM ME!
--CAN'T
REACH
HIM!
NOOOOOOOOOOOOOOOO
DAREDEVIL--
NO! NO!
HE'S
GONE!

I'VE GOT TO SWING DOWN-- TRY TO FIND HIM!
KEEP SHOOTING! GET IT ALL ON FILM!
WE'VE ALL BEEN WITNESSES TO A CALLOUS MURDER!
THESE SCENES WILL BE AS FAMOUS AS RUBY'S SHOOTING OF OSWALD!
MY ONLY CHANCE IS TO SWING UP--AND REACH THE SHORE BY RACING ALONG THE UPPER CABLES!
I DON'T DARE DIVE DOWN NOW!
NOT WHILE THEY'RE FIRING AT ME!
HE'S TRYING TO GET AWAY! FIRE! HE MUSTN'T ESCAPE!
CRACK! CRACK!
IF THAT MADMAN IS STILL ALIVE, THE POLICE CAN GET HIM --IN A LAUNCH!
HOLD YOUR FIRE! HE'S OUT OF RANGE!
BUT WE'LL GET HIM --SOONER OR LATER!
EVEN DAREDEVIL CAN'T GET AWAY WITH MURDER!
BY THE TIME THE POLICE LAUNCH REACHES THIS SPOT--I'LL BE GONE!
MEANWHILE, IN A FLEEING, ONE-MAN SUB--
AND, FINDING NO TRACE OF ME--
THEY'LL HAVE TO CONCLUDE THAT DAREDEVIL MURDERED JONATHAN POWERS!

A SHORT TIME LATER, AT THE MIDTOWN OFFICE OF NELSON AND MURDOCK, ATTORNEYS AT LAW, WE FIND A STARTLED FOGGY NELSON CATCHING UP ON THE DAY'S EVENTS--
WHEN MIKE MURDOCK WAS DAREDEVIL, HE'D NEVER HAVE DONE ANYTHING LIKE THAT!
EVEN IF HE WAS AN OBNOXIOUS WISE-GUY, HE WASN'T A KILLER!
WELL, WHO-EVER THIS MASKED MURDERER IS, HE WON'T --WAIT A MINUTE!!
WHAT'S THIS??

A FILMED REPORT OF THE PROTEST DEMONSTRATION THAT WAS HELD ON THE MALL, EARLIER THIS MORNING!
AND, RIGHT OUT IN FRONT-- WITH THE LEADERS OF THE MARCH--IT'S DEBBIE!
ELIMINATE POVERTY AND
OH NO! NOT HER! AND ESPECIALLY --NOT NOW!

MURDOCK AND NELSON
MINUTES LATER--
FOGGY! GUESS WHERE I WAS THIS MORNING!
I DON'T HAVE TO GUESS! I WAS WATCHING TV--I SAW YOU!
ISN'T IT BAD ENOUGH THAT YOU ONCE SERVED A TERM IN PRISON? DO YOU HAVE TO GET INVOLVED IN PUBLIC CONTROVERSY, TOO??
HAVE YOU FORGOTTEN I'M RUNNING FOR D.A. THIS YEAR??
ARE YOU TRYING TO RUIN MY CHANCES?!!

COME OFF IT, LOVE OF MY LIFE!
A PERSON HAS TO STAND FOR SOMETHING THESE DAYS!
IF YOU'D PREFER TO MARRY A VEGETABLE, I'LL STILL LET YOU OFF THE HOOK!
I LOVE YOU, BLAST IT! I WANT TO MARRY YOU! BUT--!!
SORRY, PARTNER! YOU'RE NOT MY TYPE!
MATT!! MAYBE YOU CAN DRUM SOME SENSE INTO HER!
I SURE CAN'T!
HOW CAN YOU EXPECT HER TO BE SENSIBLE? SHE'S A FEMALE!

HE'S ANGRY BECAUSE I WAS PART OF THIS MORNING'S PROTEST MARCH, MATT!
I KNOW HOW CONSERVATIVE YOU ARE, FOGGY--BUT REMEMBER THIS--
IF WASHINGTON WERE ALIVE TODAY, WE'D CALL HIM A PROTESTER!
BUT I'M RUNNING FOR PUBLIC OFFICE--
AND DEBBIE IS MY FIANCEE!
THEN THANK YOUR LUCKY STARS, MISTER!
I WISH--THE GIRL I LOVE--WERE MY FIANCEE!
BUT, SINCE OUR HERO CAN'T HAVE THE ONE HE LOVES, LET'S VISIT A CAT WHO HATES HIM--
KEEP THAT CAMERA GRINDING, IF YOU VALUE YOUR LIFE!
MY LITTLE ROBOTS MAY RESEMBLE TOYS --BUT THEIR WEAPONS ARE AS LETHAL AS THEY LOOK!
YOU CAN'T GET AWAY WITH THIS, JESTER!
SILENCE!
IF ANY SPEECHES ARE CALLED FOR, I WILL MAKE THEM!
NOBODY CAN BREAK INTO A TV STUDIO AND FORCE HIMSELF TO BE VIEWED BY MILLIONS!
YOUR CORNY THREATS CAN'T--UNHHH!
THE JESTER IS FAR MORE QUALIFIED!

NOW HEAR THIS!
I AM ABOUT TO PROVE HOW PUBLIC-SPIRITED THE JESTER IS!
AS A BOON TO THIS FAIR CITY OF OURS, I PROMISE TO CAPTURE THE MERCILESS MURDERER KNOWN AS DAREDEVIL!
2
SOON--VERY SOON--THE WORLD WILL SEE THAT THE JESTER IS TRULY THE "GOOD GUY"!
THE JESTER! I'VE BEEN WONDERING WHEN HE'D SHOW UP AGAIN!
HE'S HEARD WHAT HAPPENED ON THE BRIDGE AND DECIDED TO TAKE ADVANTAGE OF IT!
I NEVER THOUGHT I'D FEEL THIS WAY--
BUT, AFTER WHAT HAPPENED ON THE BRIDGE TODAY, I HOPE THE JESTER WINS!
JUST REMEMBERED --I'M LATE FOR AN APPOINTMENT!
WHOA, PARTNER! WHAT'S THE HURRY?
MAYBE DD CAN REACH THE STUDIO IN TIME!
BUT THEN, MINUTES LATER--
A STRANGE, BEEPING SOUND--IN MY EARS--
NEVER HEARD ANYTHING LIKE IT BEFORE!
BEEP! BEEP!
IT SEEMS TO BE SOME SORT OF SIGNAL--
GUIDING ME TOWARDS CENTRAL PARK!
19

FINALLY, AFTER THE SIGHTLESS SWASH-BUCKLER HAS FOLLOWED THE INSISTENT, HIGH-PITCHED SUMMONS--
AH, I KNEW YOU WOULDN'T DISAPPOINT ME!
BEEP! BEEP! BEEP! BEEP! BEEP!
I DON'T KNOW WHAT YOUR GAME IS, BUT--
THE JESTER!
BEEP!
POP CORN
BEEP!
THEN I'LL BE GLAD TO EXPLAIN!
LAST TIME WE FOUGHT, I PLANTED A TINY RECEIVER ON YOUR COSTUME--
--WHICH I'VE JUST ACTIVATED TO BRING YOU HERE!
BUT, I MUSTN'T FORGET MY MANNERS--!
HERE--HAVE SOME POPCORN!
POP
THE KERNELS ARE--EXPLODING--
THEY'RE--FILLED WITH--GAS!
HOW HIGHLY PERCEPTIVE OF YOU!
A PITY YOU LEARNED--TOO LATE!
YOU MAY ARREST YOUR MURDERER--THE FALLEN DAREDEVIL!
I'VE KEPT MY WORD, GENTLE-MEN!
AND, AS USUAL, THE POLICE ARRIVE--IN THE NICK OF TIME!
NEXT
THE DREGS OF--DEFEAT!

MARVEL
COMICS
GROUP

12¢
IND.

45
OCT

APPROVED
BY THE
COMICS
CODE
AUTHORITY

DAREDEVIL, THE MAN WITHOUT FEAR!
"THE DISMAL DREGS OF DEFEAT!"
DON'T MOVE, DAREDEVIL!
WE'VE GOT YOU COVERED!
HOW ABOUT THAT? THE JESTER TRAPPED 'IM!
TO THINK I CAUGHT THE ELUSIVE DAREDEVIL WITH A FEW CENTS WORTH OF POPCORN!
NO NEED TO MENTION THAT I MIXED MY OWN POWERFUL GAS PELLETS INSIDE THE KERNELS OF CORN!
HERE IS YOUR MURDERER, GENTLEMEN! COMPLIMENTS OF THE JESTER!
I'VE BEEN FRAMED-- FOR MURDER!
BUT, HOW AM I GONNA PROVE IT?
A PANICKY PRODUCTION BY: STAN (THE MAN) LEE and GENE (THE DEAN) COLAN
EMBELLISHED BY: VINNIE COLLETTA
LETTERED BY: ARTIE SIMEK
1

FOR THOSE UNFORTUNATES WHO WEREN'T WITH US LAST ISH (SHAME ON YOU!), THE JESTER, IN HIS CIVILIAN IDENTITY, FOUGHT WITH DD ATOP A BRIDGE, AND THEN FAKED HIS OWN DEATH--IN SUCH A WAY THAT OUR HERO IS ACCUSED OF HIS "MURDER"! AND NOW--
YOU'VE BEEN A BAAAD BOY, DAREDEVIL! WE'RE ALL ASHAMED OF YOU!
OKAY, JESTER-- STAND ASIDE!
WE'RE NOT AIMIN' TO MAKE A FLOOR SHOW OUTTA THIS!
HEY, LOOK! WHAT'S THE BIG SCENE OVER THERE?
DON'TCHA DIG IT? THEY'RE REHEARSIN' FOR HALLOWEEN!
THAT'S NO PUT ON, MAN! IT'S FOR REAL!
IT'S DAREDEVIL! THE FUZZ ARE CLOSIN' IN ON HIM!
AND THERE'S THE JESTER-- TRYIN' TO PUT 'IM DOWN!
REMEMBER THE LAST TIME WE FOUGHT?
I WARNED YOU THAT THE JESTER WOULD HAVE HIS REVENGE!
FORGIVE ME FOR GLOATING, BUT YOU LOOK SO LAUGH-ABLE DOWN THERE!
PERHAPS YOU'D LIKE ANOTHER PIECE OF POPCORN--FOR A PICK-ME-UP?
SO, HE'S STILL GOT SOME MORE OF THOSE GAS CAPSULES, EH?
THAT'S ALL I WANNA KNOW!
SURE, BIG MOUTH-- I'LL TAKE ONE!
THAT'S IT! JUST A LITTLE CLOSER--!
BRACE YOURSELF, DD-- HERE IT COMES--!!

SPAK!
UNHHH!
GOT 'IM!
DIDN'T EVEN GIVE HIM TIME TO HOLD HIS BREATH!
IF I'M LUCKY, THE FUMES WILL MAKE THE BLUECOATS SLUGGISH, TOO!
STOP --OR WE'LL SHOOT!
SEE YA AROUND, GANG!
WHETHER THE GAS FUMES TRULY HAMPER THE LAWMEN'S AIM--OR WHETHER SOME SUBCONSCIOUS INSTINCT PREVENTS THEM FROM HARMING THE MAN THEY HAD ONCE RESPECTED, WE DO NOT KNOW--
BAM BAM
KRAK!
IF I CAN MAKE IT TO THE TREE TOPS, I'LL LOSE MYSELF WITHIN THE FOLIAGE!
--BUT, SUFFICE IT TO SAY, THE VOLLEY OF SHOTS FALL SHORT OF THEIR MARK, AND--

I MADE IT!
YEAH-- MADE IT! --WHAT A LAUGH!
THERE ARE ABOUT 30,000 POLICE IN THIS CITY--AND EVERY ONE OF THEM WILL BE HUNTING ME!
NOT TO MENTION THE JESTER HIMSELF--
--WHO MIGHT JUST BE NARROW-MINDED ENOUGH TO RESENT GETTING KICKED IN THE HEAD!
ALTHOUGH, I MUST ADMIT--
THAT KICK WAS THE BEST PART OF THIS WHOLE SORDID MESS!
BUT NOW, I'VE GOTTA FIND A WAY TO STEER CLEAR OF THE LAW FOR A WHILE--
AS I FIGURE OUT SOME WAY TO PROVE THAT I'M INNOCENT OF MURDERING THAT NUT ON THE BRIDGE!
AND, CONSIDERING I DON'T KNOW WHO THE VICTIM WAS --OR EVEN WHAT THE MOTIVE WAS--
IT LOOKS LIKE I'M GONNA BE A BUSY LITTLE DAREDEVIL!

AND, AT THAT MOMENT--
LET HIM RUN--THE ARROGANT, COSTUMED FOOL!
THERE'LL BE NO PLACE FOR HIM TO TURN-- NO PLACE HE CAN HIDE!
EVEN IF HE ABANDONS HIS DAREDEVIL IDENTITY IN AN EFFORT TO ESCAPE, I'LL STILL HAVE WON!
--FOR I VOWED TO DESTROY DAREDEVIL --AND DESTROY HIM I HAVE!
WHILE MANAGING TO GET IN SOLID WITH THE UNSUSPECTING POLICE AT THE SAME TIME!
IT'S AN ALL-POINTS BULLETIN! THAT FELLA'S FAST!
AND, IN THE HOURS THAT FOLLOW--
IF I COULD BE THE ONE TO CAPTURE HIM AGAIN--
I COULD PROBABLY BE ELECTED MAYOR OF THIS TOWN!
SO--I'LL ABANDON MY OWN CAREER OF CRIME FOR THE NEXT LITTLE WHILE!
AFTER ALL--IT'S FOR A MOST WORTHY CAUSE!

MEANWHILE--*
THIS IS ONE OF THE TIMES WHEN MY SIGHTLESSNESS ISN'T EXACTLY A BLESSING!
I'VE GOT TO HOPE THE ALLEYS I HIDE IN ARE ARE AS DARK AS I THINK THEY ARE!
*WE FEEL A NO-PRIZE IS IN ORDER FOR THE ABOVE CAPTION, SINCE IT IS SO PERFECT A MODEL OF BREVITY, BANALITY, AND TOTAL RESTRAINT! --SAGACIOUS STAN.
AND, AS THE FIRST FAINT FINGERS OF DAWN COME WALKING ACROSS THE CLASSIFIED DIRECTORY OF LIFE--
I CAN'T KEEP SWINGING THRU THE CITY FOREVER!
AND YET, EVERY TIME I TRY TO MAKE IT TO MY HOME--OR EVEN TO THE OFFICE--WHERE I CAN CHANGE TO THE IDENTITY OF MATT MURDOCK--
I HAVE TO TURN BACK--BECAUSE OF THE CORDONS OF POLICE PATROLLING THE NEIGH-BORHOODS!
AND, SPEAKING OF THE OMNIPRESENT MINIONS OF THE LAW--
WHAT HAVE I GOTTEN MYSELF INTO NOW??
THERE HE IS!
HOLD IT, DAREDEVIL! YOU CAN'T GET AWAY!
NOT WHILE THERE'S ANOTHER ALLEY RIGHT BEHIND ME--
I HOPE!
I WAS RIGHT!
BUT, JUDGING BY THE AMOUNT OF RUNNING FEET I HEAR --IT'S NOT ABOUT TO DO ME MUCH GOOD!
6

HE TRAPPED HIMSELF NOW!
THERE'S NO OTHER WAY OUT OF THAT ALLEY!
I HEAR ONE EXCITED SET OF HEARTBEATS ON EACH SIDE OF ME!
AND EVEN A BLIND MAN KNOWS WHAT THAT MEANS!
START THINKING, MURDOCK--LIKE FAST!
I'VE GOT TO STALL--SOMEHOW--TILL I CAN MANEUVER THEM INTO THE RIGHT POSITION!
THEN WHAT ARE WE WAITING FOR?
LET'S TAKE 'IM!
OKAY, MISTER--HOLD IT RIGHT THERE!
SAY! THIS SURE IS AWFULLY FRIENDLY OF YOU!
NOT MANY COPS WOULD TAKE ALL THIS TROUBLE TO MAKE SURE I DON'T GET MYSELF MUGGED IN THIS DANGEROUS NEIGHBORHOOD!
I'VE A GOOD MIND TO RECOMMEND YOU BOTH FOR CITATIONS!
THAT'S MIGHTY NICE OF YOU, PAL! NOW START WALKIN'!
ACTUALLY, GENTS--I'M A LITTLE BIT TIRED!
SO, IF YOU REALLY WANT ME--
7.

I SUGGEST THAT YOU COME 'N GET ME!
THEY'RE BOTH REACHING OUT-- LUNGING TOWARDS ME!
IF I'M EVER TO MAKE MY MOVE-- IT HAS TO BE--
--NOW!
I'M IN THE CLEAR AGAIN!
NOW, I'VE GOT TO FIND A WAY TO MAKE IT HOME --WHERE I CAN CHANGE IDENTITIES!
HOLD IT! COME BACK!
HEY, SAM-- HE'S GETTING AWAY!
A FAT LOTTA GOOD IT'LL DO HIM!
THERE'S NO PLACE LEFT FOR HIM TO RUN!
8

AND, AS TIME RACES BY--
FTWEEEEEEEEEEE
--THE OFFICER'S PREDICTION SEEMS TO BE BORNE OUT--
WHEREVER I GO-- THE SOUND OF THOSE POLICE WHISTLES FOLLOWS ME!
ONLY MY SPEED HAS SAVED ME SO FAR!
FTWEEEEE
BUT I CAN'T KEEP UP THIS PACE MUCH LONGER!
IF I CAN JUST HOLD OUT FOR ANOTHER FEW BLOCKS--
I'LL BE NEARLY HOME WHEN I TURN THE CORNER!
THE ONE THING SAVING ME IS THE FACT THAT THE POLICE-- BLESS THEIR UNDERPAID HEARTS--ARE RELUCTANT TO SHOOT TO KILL!
ONE WAY

BUT, UPON REACHING HIS DESTINATION--
IT'S NO USE! THE WHOLE AREA'S CORDONED OFF!
I SHOULD HAVE ANTICIPATED IT!
EVERYONE KNOWS THAT NELSON AND MURDOCK HAVE BEEN FRIENDLY WITH DAREDEVIL!
SO WHAT'S MORE NATURAL THAN TO PUT A STAKE-OUT AT WHERE WE LIVE--AND WHERE WE WORK!
BAM!
POLIC
THIS MEANS I HAVE TO REMAIN IN MY DAREDEVIL DUDS--
--MAKING ME A COSTUMED TARGET WHEREVER I RUN!
PING!
HOW DID I EVER GET INTO A MESS LIKE THIS?
AND, WHAT'S WORSE--HOW DO I GET OUT OF IT??
WELL, ONE THING'S FOR SURE--
I'VE GOT TO STOP SWINGING--BEFORE MY ARMS PULL A DROP-OUT ACT--
--OUT OF THEIR SOCKETS!

MY BEST BET IS TO LOSE MYSELF SOMEWHERE IN A DIMLY-LIT SUBWAY!
JUST HEARD A TRAIN PULL OUT-- SO THE STATION SHOULDN'T BE TOO CROWDED YET!
SUBWAY
I WAS RIGHT! JUST ONE MAN NEARBY--
AND FROM THE FAINT RUSTLING I HEAR AS HE HOLDS HIS NEWSPAPER--
HE'S WEARING A RAIN-COAT!
DAREDEVIL DASHES FOR FREEDOM!
WANTED FOR MURDER
WITH MY HYPER-KEEN SENSES, I CAN EXERT JUST THE RIGHT PRESSURE--
--TO IMMOBILIZE THIS FELLA-- WITHOUT HURTING HIM!
SECONDS LATER, WITH THE SPEED AND STEALTH OF A STRIKING COBRA--
YOU'LL WAKE UP IN A FEW MINUTES, FRIEND--
AND YOU'LL FIND ENOUGH CASH TO PAY FOR THE COAT IN YOUR PANTS POCKET!
THE PLATFORM'S FILLING UP NOW-- SO I SWUNG IT JUST IN TIME!
I DON'T KNOW WHERE THE NEXT TRAIN'S HEADING FOR-- BUT IT'S NOT LEAVING WITHOUT ME!
I'M NOT SURE IT'S A PERFECT FIT--
BUT THIS IS ONE TIME SARTORIAL MATTHEW WON'T BE TOO PARTICULAR!
11

NOW THAT THE PRESSURE'S OFF FOR A MINUTE--
I CAN REALIZE HOW TIRED I REALLY AM!
I FEEL AS THOUGH I'VE BEEN RUNNING FOR DAYS!
DRAGNET OUT FOR DAREDEVIL
SO FAR THE ELUSIVE DAREDEVIL HAS MANAGED TO ESCAPE THE POLICE
SUDDENLY, SPEEDING AROUND A CURVE, THE TRAIN LURCHES, AND--
WHOOP! --BETTER GRAB THE HANDRAIL--!
IT WOULD BE EMBARRASSING FOR A LAD WITH SUPER-SENSES--
TO FALL FLAT ON HIS FACE IN A CROWDED SUBWAY!
THE MAN IN FRONT OF ME-- WHY IS HE GASPING THAT WAY?
I HEAR HIS PULSE QUICKEN-- HE'S SEEN SOMETHING THAT STARTLED HIM!
OF COURSE!! MY GLOVE!!

I YANKED IT AWAY-- SO QUICKLY--
HE MAY THINK HE IMAGINED IT!
FOR A MINUTE THERE, I THOUGHT--
NAHH! I BETTER FORGET IT!
NO COSTUMED SUPERHERO WOULD BE A STRAPHANGER ON A SUBWAY!
BUT NOW, JUST TO SEE HOW FAR WE CAN STRETCH YOUR CREDULITY --GUESS WHO'S A FELLOW PASSENGER IN THE VERY SAME CAR--?!!
NONE OTHER THAN-- THE JESTER!
--WHICH OUGHT TO WIN US A KING-SIZED NO-PRIZE FOR THE MOST CATACLYSMIC COINCIDENCE IN RECORDED LITERATURE!
IT'S RATHER AMUSING TO TRAVEL WITH THE COMMON FOLK OCCASIONALLY!
BESIDES, WHICH, IT'S FASTER THAN FIGHTING THE TRAFFIC ABOVE!
STRANGE-- I SEEM TO SMELL A FAMILIAR AFTER SHAVE LOTION!
BUT IT'S PROBABLY MEANINGLESS!
THOUSANDS OF MEN USE THE SAME COLOGNES!
I'LL GET OFF AT THE VERY NEXT STATION!
THIS CLOSE PROXIMITY TO SO MANY NOBODYS IS BEGINNING TO DEPRESS ME!
LOOK AT THEM--THE UNTHINKING FOOLS!
NOT ONE OF THEM SUSPECTS THAT I AM REALLY THE FAMOUS JES--WAIT!!
THOSE BOOTS! THEY CAN ONLY BELONG TO ONE MAN--!

DAREDEVIL IS HERE-- RIGHT IN THIS CAR!
GET HIM!!
THAT VOICE! I KNOW IT! IT GOES WITH THE AFTER-SHAVE LOTION!
BUT NO TIME TO THINK ABOUT IT NOW!
MISTER, IN CASE NO ONE'S EVER TOLD YOU BEFORE--
YOU'VE GOT A BIIIIIG MOUTH!
UH OH! SOMEONE MUST HAVE PULLED THE EMERGENCY BRAKE CORD!
BUT, PERHAPS IT'S JUST AS WELL--!
SCRREEEEEEE
THE SUDDEN STOP IS SPILLING EVERYONE TO THE FLOOR--
--EXCEPT DD!
THIS IS WHERE MY SUPER BALANCE SENSE REALLY PAYS OFF!
SKLANKK!

I MUST HAVE BEEN MORE TIRED THAN I THOUGHT!
I SUDDENLY REALIZE WHAT GAVE ME AWAY-- MY BOOTS! I FORGOT THAT THEY'D BE EXPOSED!
EMERG EXIT
BUT ANYWAY, THAT LITTLE REST WAS JUST WHAT I NEEDED!
AND NOW-- I'LL TAKE OFF AGAIN--!
I STILL HAVE TO FIND A WAY TO REACH FOGGY!
AND, SPEAKING OF THAT ESTIMABLE STALWART--
I DON'T GET IT, DEB!
IF YOU KNOW WHERE KAREN IS, WHY WON'T YOU TELL US?
BECAUSE SHE ASKED ME NOT TO, FOGGY!
BUT WHAT ABOUT MATT?
THE POOR GUY'S BEEN WEARING HIS HEART ON HIS SLEEVE SINCE SHE LEFT!
YOU KNOW HOW HE FEELS ABOUT HER!
HE SHOULD HAVE THOUGHT OF THAT --BEFORE HE DROVE HER AWAY!
BUT HE ONLY DID IT BECAUSE HE'S BLIND!
THE BIG LUG THOUGHT HE WASN'T GOOD ENOUGH FOR HER!
AND NOW HE'S GONE-- WITH NO TELLING WHEN HE'LL BE BACK!
AND, I'VE A HUNCH WE'RE GONNA NEED HIM--
--TO DEFEND DAREDEVIL-- IF THE POLICE EVER CATCH HIM!
BUT, IF YOU THINK OUR PLOT'S GETTING COMPLICATED NOW--
JOIN US FOR A LEISURELY FERRY-BOAT RIDE TO BEDLOE'S ISLAND...
...WHERE YOU'LL FIND A COUPLE OF COLORFUL CHARACTERS HIDDEN ON BOARD--!

ONE OF THEM-- THE JEERING, JAUNDICED JESTER--
IF HE THOUGHT ONE PUNCH WOULD STOP ME--
AND THE OTHER--A DESPERATE, THOUGH DETERMINED DAREDEVIL-
IT'S LONELIER OUT HERE THAN IN THE CITY--
AND THE CHANCES ARE IT'S THE LAST PLACE THE POLICE WILL THINK TO LOOK FOR ME!
IN TRUTH, NOBODY DID SEE HIS FACE--BUT THERE'S ONE MAN WHO PLANS TO REMEDY THAT LITTLE OVERSIGHT--
THE STATUE'S DESERTED! IT'LL BE JUST DAREDEVIL-- AND ME!
THAT MAKES IT ALMOST TOO EASY!
IT WAS THE BIGGEST MISCALCULATION OF HIS LIFE!
I'LL STAY JUST LONG ENOUGH TO SWAP A SUIT FOR MY COSTUME!
AND, ALL I CAN DO IS HOPE I MOVED SO FAST THAT NOBODY SAW MY FACE THERE ON THE SUBWAY!
I'LL CLIMB UP TO THE-- SAY! WHAT'S THAT?
A DULL BUZZING BEHIND ME--GETTING LOUDER--!
BUZZ
Z
ZZZ
FLYING DISCS!
THE KIND THE JESTER THROWS!
SQUIRTING SOME SORT OF LIQUID AT ME!
MUSTN'T LET IT TOUCH ME--!
IT'S A POTENT ANAESTHETIC!
HOW RIGHT YOU ARE, DAREDEVIL!

I MIGHT HAVE KNOWN IT WAS THE JESTER!
BUT YOUR KNOCK-OUT FLUID HASN'T TOUCHED ME YET--
AND IT WON'T, SO LONG AS MY SUPER SENSES DON'T FAIL ME!
I THOUGHT YOU'D GET TIRED OF WAITING, LITTLE MAN!
NATURALLY! I WANT THE PLEASURE OF FINISHING YOU OFF MYSELF!
VISITOR ARE NOT PERMITT D ON TORCH
NOW THAT I'M CLOSE TO HIM AGAIN--
HIS HEARTBEAT--HIS VOICE--THE ODOR OF HIS COLOGNE--THEY'RE UNMISTAKABLE!
YOU CAN'T AFFORD TO DAYDREAM WHEN YOU FIGHT THE JESTER!
-UNHHH!-
HE'S RIGHT! I'VE GOT TO CONCENTRATE ON THE JOB AT HAND NOW--!
NAMELY--JUST TRYING TO STAY ALIVE!
AND NOW--OVER YOU GO!!
THAT'S A GOOD IDEA, NEEDLE NOSE--
BUT I'LL DO IT MY WAY--
-YEOOWWP!-

INCIDENTALLY --YOU MAY APPLAUD, IF YOU WISH!
--BUT IT ISN'T OBLIGATORY!
NOW THAT I'VE GOT HIM-- WHAT DO I DO WITH HIM?
18

BUT, BEFORE THAT QUESTION CAN BE ANSWERED--
S-POLICE
CONTACT HQ! WE'VE SPOTTED DAREDEVIL!
AND I COULD'A SWORN THIS JUNKET WAS A WASTE OF TIME!
HOLD HER STEADY WHILE I SECURE THE ROPE!
LOOK! HE'S FIGHTING SOMEONE!
IT'S THE JESTER!
KNOCK IT OFF, YOU MANIAC!
I'M TRYING TO LOWER US TO SAFETY!
THAT'S YOUR PROBLEM, YOU FOOL!
WHY SHOULD I WORRY?
I'M A CHAMPION HIGH-DIVER AND SWIMMER!
BUT, IF I CAN SEND YOU PLUNGING DOWN-- UNCONSCIOUS--!
JOHNSON!! LOOK OUT!!
YOUR ROPE LADDER'S SNAGGING ON THE STATUE'S SPIKES!!
SKRASSK!
HELLP!
SOMEONE'S REALLY IN TROUBLE!
YOU'VE HAD IT, JESTER!
I CAN'T SAVE HIM WHILE YOU'RE HERE!
SO HAPPY LANDINGS!

THE ROPE-- IT SNAPPED!
EASY, FELLA-- I GOT YOU!
YOU-- YOU COULD HAVE GONE SCOT FREE!
YOU DIDN'T HAVE TO-- RISK YOUR LIFE--TO SAVE A STRANGER!
SO, I FEEL LIKE A GRADE-A HEEL FOR THIS--
BUT WE ALL HAVE OUR JOB TO DO!
GOOD WORK, PARTNER! YOU GOT 'IM!
C'MON-- HAUL US UP FAST!
I'M NO DAREDEVIL! CAN'T HOLD ON MUCH LONGER!
A SHORT TIME LATER--IN A PRISON INFIRMARY--
SO THAT'S THE GREAT DAREDEVIL!
HE DON'T LOOK LIKE MUCH NOW!
NOBODY WANTED TO TAKE HIS MASK OFF TILL THEY GOT SOME KINDA WRIT FROM THE JUDGE!
BUT THE JUDGE WON'T BE BACK TILL MORNIN'!
SO IT WON'T DO NO HARM FOR A PLAIN OL' TRUSTEE LIKE ME TO TAKE A PEEK--WHILE HE'S SLEEPIN' IT OFF--!
NEXT
RETRIBUTION!
20

APPROVED BY THE COMICS CODE AUTHORITY

MARVEL™ COMICS GROUP

12¢ IND.

46 NOV

the FINAL JEST!

THE MAN WITHOUT FEAR...
DAREDEVIL
CATACLYSMICALLY CONCOCTED BY:
STAN (THE MAN) LEE and GENE (THE DEAN) COLAN
EMBELLISHMENT: GEORGE KLEIN
LETTERING: ARTIE SIMEK
IN...
N.Y. STATE PRISON
IT'S DAREDEVIL HIMSELF-- BOOKED FOR HOMICIDE!
I'LL NEVER GET ANOTHER CHANCE LIKE THIS--
--TO BE THE FIRST GUY IN THE WORLD... TO LEARN HIS REAL IDENTITY!
AND THERE'S NO ONE AROUND TO STOP ME!
WHAT A REAL SWEET DEAL!
I WAS HOPING--
--HE WOULDN'T TRY THAT!
TRUSTEE

..THE FINAL JEST!
BOK!
NICE TRY, CHARLIE!
BUT THIS IS WHY YOU'LL ALWAYS BE AN ALSO RAN!
ANYWAY, THANKS FOR WAKING ME!
--I FORGOT TO SET THE ALARM!
2

NOW HANG LOOSE AND DON'T MAKE A FUSS--
AND THIS'LL ALL BE OVER BEFORE YOU CAN SAY "I WAS A BAAAAAD BOY!"
DARE DEVIL
BLOOD PRESSURE
TEMPERATURE
PULSE
MON
normal
normal
TUES
normal
WED
THU
FRI
SAT
SUN
LUCKY FOR ME, THAT STRENGTH-DEPLETING GAS OF THE JESTER'S HAS JUST ABOUT ALL WORN OFF BY NOW!
WHICH MEANS MY ONLY PROBLEM IS TO FIND A WAY OUT OF THIS FULL-SECURITY PRISON HOSPITAL-- AND CLEARING MYSELF OF A HOMICIDE CHARGE!
WHAT EVER HAPPENED TO THE GOOD OLD DAYS-- WHEN MY BIGGEST WORRY WAS--WHICH COSTUME TO WEAR?

THAT'S IT FOR NOW, CURLY!
SEE YA AROUND!
THPOOM!
THEN, SECONDS LATER--
HE COULDN'T HAVE GOTTEN AWAY SO SOON!
THERE'S NO TRACE OF HIM IN THE CELL!
AND YET--
GUARD! GUARD! DAREDEVIL'S ESCAPED!
HOW ABOUT THAT OPEN GATE-- AT THE END OF THE HALL?
LET'S GO!
IT WAS A LONG SHOT --BUT IT'S WORKING!
I HAD A HUNCH HE WOULDN'T BEND ALL THE WAY DOWN!
WHAT?!!
HE COULDN'T HAVE!
I'VE BEEN POSTED HERE ALL THE TIME!
THAT'S IT, GROUP!
JUST KEEP GOING THAT AWAY!

NOW, MY NEXT STEP IS TO GET OUT OF HERE--
BEFORE THEY COME CHARGING BACK TO REALLY SEARCH THE CELL!
BUT, HOW FAR CAN I GET IN THESE ZINGY THREADS OF MINE?
THAT ODOR! THE SCENT OF DETERGENT STILL CLINGING TO A FRESHLY-LAUNDERED JACKET!
COULD BE MY TICKET OUT OF HERE!
SOME JOES HAVE TO GO TO MED SCHOOL FOR YEARS TO BECOME A DOCTOR!
BUT I'M TAKING A LITTLE SHORT-CUT--!
I'LL HAVE TO REMOVE MY MASK, AS WELL!
NOT A TRACE OF HIM OUT THERE! I DON'T GET IT!
WHOOPS! I FORGOT THE DOOR WAS STILL OPEN!
LUCKY I'M ON THIS SIDE OF THE ROOM!
THE PHONE! HERE'S WHERE I GO INTO MY ACT!
RRING
SAY, DOC--DID YOU SEE--?
HOLD IT, OFFICER! I'M ON THE PHONE!
WHAT'S THAT? THE MEDICAL SUPPLY ROOM?
I'LL BE RIGHT THERE!

NOW THEN, TALK FAST, PLEASE! I'M WANTED DOWN THE HALL!
WE'RE LOOKING FOR DAREDEVIL, DOC!
SORRY-- I HAVEN'T SEEN HIM!
I THOUGHT HE WAS TRANSFERRED TO THE INTERROGATION WING!
HEY! THAT'S A THOUGHT! LET'S GO!
OKAY, RADAR SENSE--DON'T FAIL ME NOW!
I HAVE TO LOOK LIKE I KNOW WHERE I'M GOING!
TOO MANY GUARDS DOWN THE HALL-- MAY STILL BE WATCHING ME!
I'D BETTER MAKE SURE I FIND THE MED SUPPLY ROOM!
KEEP OUT
BEHIND THIS DOOR--ALL SORTS OF PHARMACEUTICAL ODORS!
I'VE GOT TO CHANCE IT!
IT'S EMPTY-- BUT JUDGING BY THE ECHO OF THE SOUND OF THE DOOR OPENING--
THERE'S ANOTHER ROOM BEHIND IT!
HAVING A BUILT-IN SONAR SENSE CAN BE MIGHTY HANDY AT A TIME LIKE THIS!
COME IN-- COME IN! I THOUGHT YOU'D NEVER GET HERE!
FOR A MINUTE THERE-- SO DID I!
OKAY, DD-- LET'S GO! THIS IS PAY DIRT!

THE NEW SHIPMENT JUST ARRIVED!
IT'S BACK THERE-- READY TO BE CHECKED OUT!
THAT'S IT-- JUST DON'T TURN AROUND!
I'LL GET RIGHT ON IT, DOCTOR!
MEDICIN
ALMOST TOO GOOD TO BE TRUE!
AN EXIT DOOR-- RIGHT BEHIND THE CARTONS!
IT'S JUST AS WELL THAT I DIDN'T CHECK OUT THOSE SUPPLIES!
IMAGINE IF I HAD MISTAKEN NITROGLYCERINE FOR NEO-SYNEPHRINE!
THERE'S WHAT I WANT--
THE SOUND OF A MOTOR RUNNING!
OPEN THE GATE-- FAST! IT'S AN EMERGENCY!
YES SIR, DOC!
--WHEW!-- HE HASN'T BEEN TOLD OF MY ESCAPE YET!
WHAT?--NO SIR! NO SIGN OF DAREDEVIL HERE!
DON'T WORRY! NOW THAT THE DOC JUST LEFT, I'LL KEEP THE GATE SHUT--TILL FURTHER NOTICE!
BZZZ
HUH?
WHICH DOC? SAY--I NEVER THOUGHT TO ASK!
7

SECONDS LATER--
I DON'T DARE REMAIN HERE ANY LONGER!
THE ALARM MUST BE OUT BY NOW!
AL'S TAVERN
AND I WON'T BE SAFE UNTIL I CAN DITCH THESE CLOTHES!
SO START DITCHING, DD!
POLICE
IT MAY NOT BE CHRISTMAS YET--
BUT THERE'S GOOD OL' SANTA UP AHEAD!
SAY, FRIEND-- HOW'D YOU LIKE TO MAKE A FAST TEN BUCKS?
WHAT DO I GOTTA DO?
NO, DON'T TELL ME! DON'T SPOIL IT!
IT'S EASY! JUST SELL ME YOUR CLOTHES!
YOU CALL THESE CLOTHES?
MISTER, YA GOT YERSELF A DEAL!
WE'LL MAKE A QUICK CHANGE IN THAT ALLEY, PAL!
SO LET'S WALK BACK THERE --NICE AND QUIET!
HEY--I'D EVEN WALK OFF A PLANK FOR A TEN SPOT!
LOOK, IF THREADS LIKE THESE ARE YOUR BAG--
I KNOW WHERE YA CAN BUY LOTS MORE-- EVEN CHEAPER!
FORGET IT!
I'M NOT OUT TO CORNER THE MARKET!
THEN, FINALLY--
MATT! WHERE IN BLAZES HAVE YOU BEEN!
THOSE CLOTHES! WHAT'S GOING ON, PARTNER?
SOMETHING --MUST HAVE-- HAPPENED!
OKAY, MATTHEW-- IT'S ACADEMY AWARD TIME AGAIN!
MATT MURDOCK
THEY TOOK EVERY-THING-- EVEN MY SUIT!
I WAS LUCKY TO PICK UP THESE RAGS!
YOU CAN BET SOMETHING HAPPENED!
I WAS MUGGED!
8

MY CANE! WHERE DID I PUT MY CANE?
IN ALL THE EXCITEMENT-- I MUST HAVE DROPPED IT!
THE SOONER I CHANGE THE SUBJECT, THE LESS CHANCE THERE IS OF THEM SUSPECTING MY PHONY STORY!
IT FELL IN THE DOOR-WAY, BEHIND YOU!
I'LL GET IT!
I'VE WARNED YOU NOT TO GO PRANCING AROUND TOWN ALONE THE WAY YOU DO, MATT!
I KNOW HOW YOU LIKE TO BE INDEPENDENT --AND I RESPECT YOU FOR IT--BUT YOU CAN OVERDO THAT LONE WOLF BIT!
I KNOW, PAL! BUT WHAT ABOUT KAREN? HAVE YOU HEARD FROM HER?
I HAVE, MATT!
SHE'S PERFECTLY WELL--BUT SHE STILL DOESN'T WANT YOU TO KNOW WHERE SHE IS!
SO I CAN'T GIVE YOU HER ADDRESS!
I DON'T GET IT, MATT!
YOU TELL THE GAL YOU'VE NO INTENTION OF EVER GETTING SERIOUS WITH HER--
YOU PRACTICALLY DRIVE HER AWAY FROM HERE-- IN TEARS--
BUT, NOW THAT SHE'S GONE--YOU DON'T STOP THINKING OF HER!
YOU'VE NEGLECTED YOUR WORK-- YOU'RE NEVER AROUND WHEN WE NEED YOU--!
OKAY, FOGGY-- OKAY!
DON'T YOU EVER COME UP FOR AIR?
THAT REMINDS ME, FOGGY--
I PROMISED TO ADDRESS A PRAY FOR PEACE FORUM AT THE CIVIC CENTER!
AND I MUSTN'T BE LATE!
WHAT A LIFE! MY GIRL BECOMES A DEMONSTRATOR JUST WHEN I'M RUNNING FOR D.A.--
AND MY PARTNER, AND BEST FRIEND, IS DEFINITELY LOSING HIS MARBLES!
POOR FOGGY! HE DOESN'T KNOW HOW LUCKY HE IS WITH A GAL LIKE THAT!
I PRAY HE NEVER LOSES HER--AS I LOST KAREN!
9

NOW THAT YOU'RE HERE, MATT-- MAYBE WE CAN MAKE A DENT IN SOME OF THE PAPER WORK THAT'S BEEN PILING UP--!
SORRY, PARTNER! I JUST CAME BACK TO CHANGE CLOTHES!
THE DOCTOR SAID I SHOULD GET RIGHT HOME AND TAKE IT EASY--AFTER WHAT HAPPENED!
OH--YEAH, SURE! I, EH, ALMOST FORGOT!
I HATE TO LEAVE HIM IN THE LURCH LIKE THAT--
BUT I CAN'T AFFORD TO WASTE ANOTHER MINUTE!
NOT TILL I FIND A WAY TO CLEAR THE NAME OF DARE-DEVIL!
CAREFUL, NOW! HERE'S THE ADDRESS YOU GAVE ME!
SURE YOU DON'T WANT I SHOULD WALK YOU TO YOUR DOOR?
ON DUTY
TAXI
NO THANKS, DRIVER! IT'S BETTER FOR ME--TO MANAGE ALONE!
BUT, NO SOONER HAS THE SIGHTLESS SWASHBUCKLER REACHED THE SANCTUARY OF HIS OWN PRIVATE GYM, WHEN--
SAFE AT LAST!
I FELT AS THOUGH THE WHOLE WORLD WAS CLOSING IN ON ME!
NOW ONCE MORE I CAN THINK--I CAN MOVE--I CAN BREATHE AGAIN!
THE FIRST THING FOR ME TO DO IS EXONERATE MYSELF!
I'VE GOT TO LEARN WHO TRIED TO FRAME ME FOR MURDER--AND WHY?

WHEN I MOVE LIKE THIS--IT SEEMS TO CLEAR MY HEAD-- SHARPEN MY BRAIN-- WAIT!!
I SUDDENLY REMEMBER-- THAT VOICE I HEARD IN THE SUBWAY BEFORE-- AND THAT FAMILIAR SCENT OF COLOGNE--*
THEY REMINDED ME OF SOMEONE-- BUT I COULDN'T PINPOINT HIS IDENTITY!
AND NOW, AT LAST-- I KNOW!
THEY BELONGED TO THE MAN I'M SUPPOSED TO HAVE MURDERED!!
THAT MEANS HE'S STILL ALIVE!
*IF YOU'VE FORGOTTEN SO SOON, SHAME ON YOU! IT ONLY HAPPENED LAST ISH! --STRAIGHTFORWARD STAN.
WE HAD BEEN BATTLING ON THE BRIDGE--IN FULL VIEW OF WITNESSES--
AND THEN HE FELL--OVER THE RAILING-- BEFORE I COULD STOP HIM!
--ALMOST AS THOUGH HE WANTED TO DIE!
THE POLICE ACCUSED ME OF HIS MURDER! BUT NOW I KNOW--
HE ISN'T REALLY DEAD!
AND, IF MY HUNCH IS RIGHT--
I NOW KNOW HOW TO PROVE IT!
11

AND SO--
THANK YOU-- YOU'RE VERY KIND!
THAT'S THE STORE--IN FRONT OF YOU!
COSTUME
YES, SIR? MAY I HELP YOU?
DO YOU HAVE--A JESTER COSTUME?
IT'S ONE OF OUR HOTTEST SELLING ITEMS!
THEY'VE BEEN IN DEMAND EVER SINCE HE CAPTURED DAREDEVIL!
I'LL JUST SLIP THIS ON OVER MY OWN DD DUDS!
IT'S A BIT LIKE GILDING THE LILY--BUT WHAT THE HEY!
AND NOW--LET'S GET DOWN TO THE NITTY GRITTY, SHALL WE?
IN A HIDDEN HOME --QUIETLY NESTLED ON THE OUTSKIRTS OF TOWN--THE REAL, HONEST-TO-FORBUSH, ONE-AND-ONLY JESTER IS WATCHING TV--
HE FIDDLES FROM CHANNEL TO CHANNEL, UNTIL--
SUDDENLY--SHOCKINGLY--HE SEES--
--AND THAT'S HOW I CAUGHT DAREDEVIL, JOHNNY!
WE'LL BE RIGHT BACK--AFTER THIS MESSAGE--!
SOMEONE'S IMPERSONATING ME!
ME--THE JESTER!
WHEN I GET MY HANDS ON HIM--
I'LL GIVE HIM THE SAME TREATMENT I GAVE DAREDEVIL!!

NO ONE--NO ONE CASHES IN ON THE JESTER'S GLORY!!
ALL THOSE FRUSTRATING YEARS--WHEN I COULDN'T MAKE IT AS AN ACTOR--
WHEN FAME--AND STARDOM--WERE DENIED ME--
I PLANNED--AND WORKED--AND SACRIFICED TO ACHIEVE THIS MOMENT OF TRIUMPH!
AND NO ONE SHALL ROB ME OF IT--NO ONE!
INFORMATIO
WHICH WAY TO THE STUDIO?? QUICK!
BUT--YOU WERE JUST THERE! YOU'RE--ON THE AIR NOW!
OR--I THOUGHT YOU WERE!
IT'S THE THIRD FLOOR--STRAIGHT AHEAD!
GET ME STUDIO THREE! HURRY! IT'S AN EMERGENCY!
CALL THEM--TELL THEM THEY'LL SOON BE DEALING WITH THE GENUINE ARTICLE!
BUT, EVEN BEFORE THE CALL CAN BE COMPLETED--
NO ADMITTANCE
YOU THINK YOU CAN KEEP ME OUT--
WHILE AN IMPOSTOR STEALS MY THUNDER??
HEY--HOLD IT! I--I JUST WORK HERE!
HOW MANY JESTERS ARE THERE, ANYWAY?
ONLY ONE!!
AS THAT SYNTHETIC SCAPEGOAT WILL SOON FIND OUT--TO HIS ETERNAL REGRET!
13

FTAM!!
SO THERE YOU ARE!
NOW WHAT?
IF WE HAVE TO DO THE SCENE OVER AGAIN--!
IT WORKED! HE'S HERE!
HEY! WE'RE FILMING RIGHT NOW!
YOU CAN'T COME IN HERE!
ON THE CONTRARY! IT IS YOU WHO CANNOT LEAVE--TILL I ACQUIESCE!
I THOUGHT YOU'D NEVER ASK!
NOW-- BEFORE I PUNISH MY WITLESS IMPERSONATOR--
LET ME SEE WHO MY VICTIM IS!
YOU!!
YOU SURVIVED OUR LAST ENCOUNTER--
BUT THIS TIME YOU WON'T BE AS FORTUNATE!
YOU'LL HAVE TO DO BETTER THAN THAT, NEEDLE-NOSE--
IF YOU WANNA PLAY IN MY BALL PARK!

NOW--YOU'VE GOT SOME QUESTIONS TO ANSWER!
DON'T HOLD YOUR BREATH WAITING!
PLINK!
HEY! YOU DON'T EXPECT A PING PONG BALL TO STOP ME!
DON'T BET ON IT!
UNNHHH!!
THUMP!
THONK!
IT'S MORE THAN AN ORDINARY BALL!
--BECAUSE IT FOLLOWS ME AS IF IT HAS A MIND OF ITS OWN!
IT KEEPS GROWING WITH EVERY BOUNCE!
AND IT MUST HAVE SOME SORT OF BUILT-IN HOMING DEVICE--!
TAKE COVER, GENTS! THIS IS STRICTLY BETWEEN THE JESTER-- AND ME!
THUMP!
15

MAN! YOU DON'T SEE A SCENE LIKE THIS EVERY DAY OF THE WEEK!
IF I CAN GET IT ON FILM, I'LL BE A CINCH TO GRAB OFF AN EMMY NEXT TIME AROUND!
WHOOSH
FROM THE SOUND OF IT-- IT'S A RUBBERIZED COMPOSITION!
CAN'T KEEP DODGING IT MUCH LONGER!
COME ON, DD--START USING THE OL' NOGGIN!
DESIGNED TO TRAP ITS VICTIM, RATHER THAN HARM HIM!
I HOPE YOU'VE REHEARSED YOUR EXIT SPEECH, DAREDEVIL!
FOR THE FINAL CURTAIN IS NOW ABOUT TO FALL!
HE'S RIGHT! IF IT GETS MUCH BIGGER, I'LL HAVE NO ROOM IN WHICH TO MANEUVER!
WHICH MEANS I'VE GOT TO PULVERIZE IT IN THE NEXT FEW SECONDS-- SOMEHOW!

CLICK
ZZZZIP!
THERE'S ONE SURE WAY TO BUST A BALLOON--
SZPTAK!
AND, SINCE IT'S MORE LIKE AN OVERGROWN BALLOON THAN ANYTHING ELSE--
EVEN AN OVERSIZED, OVERSTUFFED, OVERRATED ONE!
WOW! TALK ABOUT A KICK-BACK--!!
OKAY, JES-- YOU'VE HAD YOUR INNING!
NOW YOU'VE GOT SOME PLAIN TALKING TO DO!
THERE'S NOTHING PLAIN ABOUT THE JESTER--NOT EVEN HIS CONVERSATION!
YOU BRAINLESS, BARNSTORMING, BUMBLING BOOR!
I--FORGOT ABOUT ABOUT--HIS HIDDEN YO-YO!!

TO THINK YOU WOULD DARE PIT YOURSELF AGAINST ME!
GUESS I MUST HAVE LOST MY HEAD!
THERE'LL BE MORE TRUTH TO THAT THAN FICTION--
WHEN I GET THRU WITH YOU!
YOU'RE THRU ALREADY, SON--
BUT YOU DON'T KNOW IT!
I'VE BEATEN YOU BEFORE--
AND I CAN DO IT NOW!
YOU MASKED PHONY--
YOU NEVER BEAT ME!
AND IN CASE YOU WANT SOME PROOF--
YOU CAN TRY THIS FOR SIZE!
18

HIS TIMING'S OFF!
I'M GETTING TO HIM NOW!
GOOD! HE'S STARTING TO TALK!
HE FORGOT THAT THEY'RE FILMING WHATEVER WE SAY AND DO!
AFTER ALL MY PLANNING --ALL MY WORK--
YOU CAN'T SNATCH VICTORY FROM ME NOW!
HE'S DOWN!
AND NOW --WITH THE CAMERAS ON US--
THIS IS MY CHANCE TO CLEAR MYSELF!
THOP
HEY-- LOOK!
THAT'S THE GUY DAREDEVIL'S SUPPOSED TO HAVE KILLED!
I WAS HOPING YOU'D NOTICE!
AND, AT POLICE HEADQUARTERS--
IT WAS A PERFECT FRAMEUP!!
I HAD THE WHOLE COUNTRY CONVINCED YOU HAD MURDERED ME!
HOW DID YOU GET WISE?? HOW?? HOW??
JUST LUCKY, I GUESS!
DAREDEVIL'S INNOCENT!
THE JESTER WAS BEHIND THE WHOLE THING!
WE SHOULD'A KNOWN!
19

GOOD WORK, DD!
NO NEED FOR US TO DETAIN YOU NOW!
SORRY ABOUT THE MIX-UP!
YOU'RE SORRY? LOOK AT THE JESTER!
THERE GOES ONE GREAT GUY!
I'LL BET HE'S HAPPY HE'S BEEN EXONERATED!
YEAH-- HAPPY!
I HAVEN'T BEEN ABLE TO PULL MY WEIGHT BACK AT THE OFFICE FOR WEEKS!
--THEREBY LEAVING MY PUDGY PARTNER IN THE LURCH!
HAVEN'T BEEN ABLE TO HELP HIM--EITHER WITH HIS ELECTION CAMPAIGN--OR HIS LAW PRACTICE --WHEN HE NEEDS IT THE MOST!
AS FOR MYSELF-- THE MOST IMPORTANT THING IN MY LIFE IS-- AND ALWAYS HAS BEEN-- KAREN PAGE!
SO HOW DID I FARE IN THAT DEPARTMENT--?
I'VE MANAGED TO LOSE HER-- FOREVER!
YEAH--IF I WAS ANY HAPPIER-- I COULDN'T BEAR IT--!
NEXT
"STRANGER, TAKE MY HAND--!"

DARE-DEVIL

12¢ IND.

47 DEC

MARVEL COMICS GROUP

APPROVED BY THE COMICS CODE AUTHORITY

BROTHER, TAKE MY HAND!

DAREDEVIL, THE MAN WITHOUT FEAR!
TM
BROTHER, TAKE MY HAND!
HE'LL BE HERE--ANY MINUTE NOW!
WE WANT DAREDEVIL!!
THE SCENE IS VIET NAM-- A FEW SHORT MONTHS AGO! BUT DON'T GET UPTIGHT, PILGRIM--WE'RE NOT TOSSING A WAR STORY AT YOU! STILL, YOU'LL HAVE TO ADMIT-- THIS ONE IS REALLY DIFFERENT--
CONCEIVED, CREATED, AND COMPOSED BY:
STAN (THE MAN) LEE and GENE (THE DEAN) COLAN
EMBELLISHMENT: GEORGE KLEIN
LETTERING: ARTIE SIMEK
1

IS HE *HERE* YET, SAM?
ARE YOU SURE WE'RE NOT TOO *LATE?*
DON'T WORRY, WILLIE! IT'S JUST LIKE I *TOLD* YA--THE SHOW DIDN'T EVEN *START* YET!
I'LL GET US A COUPLE'A THE *BEST SEATS* IN THE HOUSE--
CAUSE WHEN *DD* GOES INTO ACTION, WE WANNA BE UP *CLOSE*, SO WE CAN *SEE* EVERYTHING HE DOES!
WELCOME DAREDEVIL TO

OKAY, GUYS, IF YOU'LL KEEP IT DOWN TO A ROAR, WE'LL GET ON WITH THE SHOW--
YOU GOTTA LOOK AT THE BRIGHT SIDE, SOLDIER!
MAYBE THE DOC WAS WRONG! MAYBE YOUR SIGHT'LL GET BETTER-- INSTEAD OF WORSE!
FORGET IT, SAM!
THEY TOOK TOO MANY TESTS-- CHECKED IT TOO MANY TIMES!
BUT I'M NOT GRIPIN'!
THAT'S LIFE! YOU WIN A FEW--YOU LOSE A FEW!

HEY! CUT THE SPEECHES 'N GET ON WITH THE SHOW!
YEAH! WE CAN HEAR YOU ANY TIME!
WE WANT DAREDEVIL!! WE WANT DAREDEVIL!!
WE WANT DARE-DEVIL! WE WANT DARE-DEVIL!
IF HE DON'T SHOW, WE WANT OUR MONEY BACK!
QUIET, YA DUMMY! WE GOT IN FER FREE!!

I'VE BEEN READY FOR THE LAST HALF HOUR!
WHAT ARE WE WAITING FOR?
THE SPECIAL SERVICES OFFICER WAS WAITING FOR A CERTAIN WOUNDED G.I. TO ARRIVE!

HE'S A REAL FRANTIC FAN OF YOURS--
AND I SEE HE'S JUST BEEN SEATED!
SO, TAKE IT AWAY, DD--
THE STAGE IS ALL YOURS!

HE'S THERE NOW! I CAN HEAR THE CHEERING!
AND I CAN JUST MAKE HIM OUT-- I CAN SEE HIS OUTLINE--IN FRONT OF ME!
HE'S JUST AS BIG, AS POWERFUL-LOOKING, AS I KNEW HE'D BE.
HE'S STANDING THERE--WAVING TO THE CROWD!
NOW HE'S GOIN' INTO ACTION!
MAN! DIDJA SEE THAT SWING?!!
THOSE JOES OUT THERE DESERVE THE BEST--
I'VE GOT TO MAKE THIS GOOD!
IT'S LITTLE ENOUGH TO GIVE--TO GUYS WHO ARE GIVING THEIR LIVES!
I FIGURED IF SINGERS, AND ACTORS CAN ENTERTAIN THE TROOPS--
WHY CAN'T A SLIGHTLY SPRIGHTLY SUPERHERO?
I MISS HER NOW MORE THAN EVER!
ALSO, I KINDA HOPED IT WOULD GET MY MIND OFF KAREN--
BUT IT'S NO GO!
4

WOW! WILLYA LOOK AT THAT!
THE MAN'S TOO MUCH!
IF Y'ASK ME--THE GUY'S JET-PROPELLED!
EVEN WITH THE FASTEST LENS IN THE SECTOR--HE'LL JUST COME OUT A BLUR!
BUT SUDDENLY, OVER THE SOUNDS OF CHEERING, AN ANGUISHED CRY RINGS OUT--
SAM! SAM! EVERY-THING'S FADED!! I CAN'T SEE!
I CAN'T SEE ANY-THING AT ALL!!
AND, EVEN WHILE PERFORMING, THE HYPER-SENSITIVE EARS OF DAREDEVIL HEAR--
WILLIE!
I CAN'T SEE! I CAN'T SEE!!
I'M BLIND--I'M--COMPLETELY BLIND!!
GET 'IM--BEFORE HE FALLS!
BLIND! I'VE GONE BLIND!

LATER, AT THE POST INFIRMARY--
THAT SEDATIVE WILL HELP THINGS NOW!
AND, WHEN IT WEARS OFF, YOU'LL HAVE A VISITOR TO BUOY YOU UP!

THEN, AFTER A BRIEF SLEEP--
KNOCK KNOCK
DOCTOR-- YOU MENTIONED SOMETHING BEFORE-- ABOUT A VISITOR--?
THAT'S RIGHT, SON!
HE'S STANDING AT THE DOOR --RIGHT NOW!

HOW IS HE, DOC?
WHY NOT ASK HIM YOURSELF-- DAREDEVIL?

DAREDEVIL!! DID YOU SAY DAREDEVIL--IS HERE--TO SEE ME?
YOU KNOW IT, SOLDIER!
BRO-THER! WHAT A TIME FOR MY EYES TO CUT OUT ON ME!
YOU'RE NOT MISSING MUCH, WILLIE!
JUST A PAIR OF CRAZY LONG-JOHNS, THAT WOULD LOOK AS GOOD ON YOU AS ME!
ANYWAY, HOW ABOUT US YAKKIN' IT UP FOR A WHILE?

STAY WITH IT, SON! YOU CAN DO HIM A LOT MORE GOOD THAN ANY MEDICINE OF MINE!
DUNNO IF I'M MUCH AT MORALE-BUILDING, DOC--
BUT I'LL SURE DO MY BEST!
THEN, AS THE SLOW, HUMID, VIETNAMESE AFTERNOON DRAGS ON--
AT LEAST YOU DIDN'T LOSE YOUR SIGHT IN VAIN!
YOU MANAGED TO SAVE THE LIVES OF YOUR ENTIRE SQUAD!
NOT MUCH TO TELL, DD! CHARLIE LOBBED A GRENADE SMACK-DAB IN THE CENTER OF MY SQUAD--AND SOMEBODY HAD TO GO FOR IT!
YEAH, I'M SURE TO GET ME A NICE SHINY MEDAL--WHEN THEY SEND ME BACK--TO NOWHERE!
WILLIAM LINCOLN
WHAT DID YOU DO, WILLIE--BACK IN CIVILIAN LIFE?

WAS IT SOMETHING YOU CAN RETURN TO--EVEN NOW?
YOU KIDDING, MAN? HERE'S A LAUGH FOR YOU--I WAS A COP!
OH! I-I DIDN'T KNOW!
WHAT'S THE DIFF? IT DON'T MATTER ANY MORE!
PERHAPS YOU CAN STILL RETURN TO THE FORCE--IN SOME CAPACITY?
NOT A PRAYER, PAL!
EVEN BEFORE THIS HAPPENED--I COULDN'T HAVE GONE BACK!
WHY NOT? WHAT DO YOU MEAN?
SKIP IT, DD! IT AINT A PRETTY YARN ANYHOW!
AND IT'S SOME-THING--I GOTTA 'TEND TO--BY MYSELF!
OKAY, MISTER! I'M NOT ABOUT TO PRY! BUT, LET ME LEAVE YOU WITH THIS THOUGHT--
THERE ARE LOTS OF PEOPLE--WITHOUT SIGHT--WHO LEAD USEFUL, PRODUCTIVE LIVES!
ALL IT TAKES IS GUTS--THE KIND OF GUTS YOU'RE LOADED WITH, WILLIE!

I APPRECIATE WHAT YOU'RE TRYIN' TO DO FOR ME, MAN!
BUT, EVEN THOUGH I FIGURE YOU'RE THE GREATEST GUY GOIN', THIS IS ONE BAG EVEN YOU CAN'T KNOW ANYTHING ABOUT!
IF ONLY--I COULD REALLY TELL HIM!
ANYWAY, WHEN YOU GET BACK TO THE STATES, I'VE A FRIEND YOU OUGHTTA LOOK UP--
HE'S A LAWYER--NAMED MATT MURDOCK!
I THINK YOU TWO WOULD HIT IT OFF PRETTY GOOD!
WAR! THE MOST BRUTAL--MOST IDIOTIC--MOST LOATHSOME MANIFESTATION OF ALL THAT'S WRONG WITH MANKIND!
AND IT'S ALWAYS THE YOUNGEST--THE FINEST--THE BEST OF OUR PEOPLE THAT PAY THE HIGHEST PRICE!
THE WORLD WILL NEVER BE ABLE TO REPAY THE DEBT IT OWES--TO THE COUNTLESS WILLIE LINCOLNS WHO GAVE THEIR LAST FULL MEASURE OF LOYALTY AND DEVOTION!
AND NOW, BACK TO THE PRESENT ONCE AGAIN--
ARE YOU SURE YOU WANNA SEE THE CAPTAIN AGAIN, LINCOLN?
WHY SHOULDN'T I, MAN?
WHAT MORE CAN THEY DO TO ME NOW?
10TH PRECINCT
YOU KNOW HOW I FEEL ABOUT YOU, WILLIE! YOU WERE ALWAYS ONE OF MY BEST MEN!
BUT, THE WAY THINGS ARE NOW--MY HANDS ARE TIED!
BUT HOW? HOW CAN I CLEAR MYSELF--WITHOUT HELP?
THE EVIDENCE AGAINST YOU--WAS MOSTLY CIRCUMSTANTIAL!
THE FIRST THING YOU NEED IS A GOOD LAWYER!
I GUESS YOU'RE RIGHT, CAPTAIN!

THEN, A SHORT TIME LATER, IN ANOTHER PART OF TOWN--
WHERE'S A GUY LIKE *ME* GONNA GET THE BREAD FOR THE KINDA *LAWYER* I NEED?
WELFARE DEPARTMENT
MAYBE SOMEONE IN *HERE* KNOWS WHAT THE *SCORE* IS--!

I DON'T KNOW-- IF I'M IN THE RIGHT *PLACE* OR NOT, MISS PAGE--BUT I SURE COULD USE A LITTLE *ADVICE!*
WHY NOT *TELL* ME ABOUT IT, MR. LINCOLN--AND WE'LL *SEE!*

TO GET RIGHT TO THE NITTY-GRITTY--I WAS *SUSPENDED* FROM THE FORCE FOR TAKING A *BRIBE!*
THE WHOLE THING WAS *RIGGED*--A *FRAME-UP* FROM START TO FINISH--BUT I COULDN'T --AND STILL *CAN'T*-- *PROVE* IT!
I *REMEMBER* THE CASE, MR. LINCOLN! AS A LAWYER'S *SECRETARY*, I FOLLOWED IT WITH GREAT *INTEREST!*

IN FACT, IF *ANYONE* CAN HELP YOU, *MATT MURDOCK* IS THE MAN!

MURDOCK! I'VE *HEARD* THAT NAME--NOT LONG AGO!
BUT *PROMISE*--THAT YOU WON'T TELL HIM THAT IT WAS *I* WHO SENT YOU!
I HAVE--A *PERSONAL* REASON FOR THAT!
WHAT-EVER YOU SAY, MISS PAGE!
9

THEN, A SHORT TIME LATER--
MR. MURDOCK --I'M WILLIE LINCOLN!
TALK ABOUT A SMALL WORLD! BUT, I CAN'T TELL HIM THAT WE'VE ALREADY MET!
A PLEASURE, MR. LINCOLN! LET ME GET YOU A CHAIR, AND YOU CAN TELL ME ALL ABOUT IT!
THERE'S THIS MOB, RUN BY BIGGIE BENSON--THEY TRIED TO GET TO ME--BUT NEVER COULD!
SO THEY DID THE NEXT BEST THING--
THEY GOT ME OUT OF THE WAY--BY FRAMING ME!
SEPT. 5
THEY GOT SOME PATSY TO SWEAR HE SAW ME TAKING A PAYOFF--AND I COULD NEVER BREAK HIS STORY!
AND SO, WILLIE LINCOLN TALKS ON--AND ON--WHILE MATT MURDOCK LISTENS--AND PLANS--UNTIL--
DON'T TELL ME YOU'RE WORRIED ABOUT ONE CRUMMY LITTLE SUMMONS, BIGGIE?
ME WORRY ABOUT A NOBODY LIKE LINCOLN? FORGET IT!
I CAN BEAT THIS THING WITH MY EYES CLOSED!
AND SPEAKIN' OF THAT, I HEAR LINCOLN GOT BLINDED IN THE WAR!
YEAH, BOSS! AINT THAT JUST A REAL, CRYIN' SHAME?!!

I HEAR HE GOT HIMSELF A HOTSHOT MOUTHPIECE!
MEBBE WE OUGHTTA MAKE SURE HE NEVER GETS TO COURT, BIGGIE!
YEAH! WHY DON'TCHA DO THAT LITTLE THING, PAL?

AND SO--MINUTES LATER--
C'MON DOWN, LINCOLN! I KNOW YER THERE!
WE MIGHT AS WELL GET IT OVER WITH FAST!
ONE OF BIGGIE'S HOODS--JUST LIKE I FIGURED!
IT'S LUCKY THESE THICK-DOMED PUNKS ARE SO PREDICTABLE!

SORRY, MAN--WILLIE'S BUSY!
BUT MAYBE I CAN HELP YOU!
ZOK

WHAP!

NOW, CUDDLES, HOW ABOUT DOING ME A LITTLE FAVOR?
--LIKE DELIVER AN EASY MESSAGE--

TELL BIGGIE I'M DISAPPOINTED IN HIM!

I NEVER EXPECTED HIM TO SEND A BOY--TO DO A MAN'S JOB!
YEAH! HE'LL GET A BOOT OUT OF THAT!

THEN, THE VERY NEXT DAY--
BENSON, I PROPOSE TO PROVE THAT WILLIE LINCOLN WAS FRAMED-- AND YOU DID THE FRAMING!
COME OFF IT, COUNSELOR! WE'RE TOO OLD FOR FAIRY TALES!

IT'S NO USE! I CAN FEEL BENSON'S CONFIDENT SMIRK --EVEN FROM HERE!
BUT, IT SEEMS SO HOPE-LESS!
HOW CAN MURDOCK EVER MAKE A CROOK LIKE BENSON CONFESS?
STAY WITH IT, FELLA! YOU'VE GOT THE BEST LAWYER IN THE GAME PLUGGING FOR YOU!
IT'S BEEN ALLEGED THAT WILLIE LINCOLN WAS SEEN ACCEPTING A BRIBE ON THE EVENING OF JULY 6TH OF LAST YEAR!
IS THAT CORRECT, MR. BENSON?
YOU KNOW AS WELL AS I DO, MURDOCK!
IT'S ANCIENT HISTORY BY NOW!
JURY

ISN'T IT TRUE THAT THE WITNESS AGAINST MY CLIENT WAS-- AND STILL IS-- IN YOUR EMPLOY?
SO WHAT? THAT DON'T CHANGE WHAT HE SAW!

OKAY, BIGGIE-- I'M THRU WITH YOU!
CALL WHITEY BARTON TO THE STAND!
WHITEY! HE'S THE WITNESS AGAINST LINCOLN! WHY HIM?
HANG AROUND, MISTER! YOU'LL SOON FIND OUT!

THAT'S VERY INTERESTING--CONSIDERING THE WEATHER REPORT I'VE OBTAINED!
WEATHER REPORT? WADDAYA MEAN? WADDAYA TALKING ABOUT?
EVEN A MAN WITH PERFECT EYE-SIGHT--WHICH YOU DON'T HAVE--COULDN'T HAVE SEEN ANYTHING ON THE FOGGIEST NIGHT OF THE YEAR!
NOW WAIT! YOU AINT HANGIN' A PERJURY WRAP ON ME!

BIGGIE MADE ME SAY IT! HE SAID I'D BE RUBBED OUT IF I DIDN'T! WHAT WAS I TO DO?
YOU FOOL!! HE TRICKED YOU! THERE WASN'T ANY FOG THAT NIGHT! YOU JUST BLEW THE WHOLE THING!
EASY, BOSS! WE'RE IN ENOUGH TROUBLE NOW!

HOURS LATER, THE EARLY EDITIONS HIT THE STREET WITH BANNER HEADLINES--

10¢
DAILY BUGLE
FINAL
New York, N.Y. 10017, Tuesday Sept. 17, 1968 · WEATHER:
Vol. III No. 14
WILLIE LINCOLN CLEARED!
BIGGIE BENTON OUT ON $25,000 BAIL!
MATT MURDOCK, SIGHT-LESS ATTORNEY, PULLS ANOTHER COUP! Story on page 2
COURT STUNNED BY COUNSELOR'S DARING LEGAL TACTIC

BUT, WHAT OF WILLIE LINCOLN? THIS VERY MOMENT, WE FIND HIM IN HIS MODEST APARTMENT, ENTERTAINING A MOST WELCOME VISITOR--
I CAN NEVER REALLY REPAY YOU--FOR WHAT YOU'VE DONE, MR. MURDOCK!
WE'VE KNOWN EACH OTHER FOR A WHILE NOW, WILLIE! SUPPOSE YOU CALL ME MATT!
ANYWAY, NOW THAT YOU'RE CLEARED, YOU'LL BE ON YOUR FEET AGAIN IN NO TIME!
BUT, WITHOUT MY SIGHT--WHERE CAN I GO? WHAT CAN I DO?
IT'S A TOUGH LOAD TO CARRY, WILL--BUT IT CAN BE DONE!
THERE ARE LOTS OF THINGS A BLIND MAN CAN DO!
YOU'VE GOT TO LEARN BRAILLE SO YOU CAN STUDY!
LOOK, MATT, I DON'T WANNA SOUND UNGRATEFUL--
--BUT THAT'S EASY ENOUGH FOR YOU TO SAY!
WILL, THERE'S SOMETHING I NEVER GOT AROUND TO TELLING YOU--
I, MYSELF, AM BLIND!
YOU?!!
BUT--YOU'RE ONE OF THE TOP LAWYERS IN THE COUNTRY!
MAYBE IT'S BECAUSE I HAD TO STUDY--TO WORK--A LITTLE HARDER THAN--
WAIT A MINUTE!!
MUFFLED FOOTSTEPS--COMING UP THE STAIRS!
I'M GETTING BAD VIBRATIONS!
THIS TIME WE GOTTA DO THE JOB RIGHT--FOR BIGGIE!
WILLIE--INTO THE CLOSET--FAST! BENSON'S HOODS ARE ON THE WAY UP!
GRRRR!
14

HE LEFT THE DOOR OPEN!
THIS'LL BE A LEAD-PIPE CINCH!

NO TIME TO CHANGE INTO COSTUME!
LUCKY IT'S PITCH DARK NOW!
WHERE IN BLAZES IS THE LIGHT SWITCH?
I CAN'T SEE A THING!
I'LL HAVE TO FIGHT THEM AS MATT MURDOCK!
IN FACT, THAT GIVES ME AN IDEA!

WHAT DO YOU NEED LIGHT FOR?
I CAN GET ALONG FINE-- WITHOUT IT!
WHA--?!!
ZAK!

COME ON IN! DON'T BE SHY!
THERE'S ROOM FOR YOU, TOO!
IF I CAN STAY IN THE SHADOWS-- KEEP THEM FROM SEEING ME--
MAYBE I CAN CONVINCE THEM I'M REALLY WILLIE LINCOLN!
BOK!

I'VE GOT TO MAKE THEM THINK THAT WILLIE IS MORE THAN A MATCH FOR THEM!
OTHERWISE, HE'LL NEVER BE SAFE FROM THEIR MURDEROUS ATTACKS!
BUT, IF THEY GET A LOOK AT ME, THE JIG'S UP!

SO, I'LL MAKE SURE THE DOOR STAYS SHUT--AND THE LIGHT STAYS OUT!
HERE, IN THE DARKNESS, THE ODDS ARE ALL IN FAVOR OF A BLIND MAN!
SLAM!

MAYBE I CAN'T SEE YOU, LINCOLN--
BUT YOU CAN'T SEE ME, EITHER!
SO THAT MAKES EVERY-THING EVEN!
DON'T COUNT ON IT, SMART GUY!

LIKE THE SAYING GOES--
WE MAY BOTH BE EQUAL--
BUT, I'M A LITTLE EQUAL-ER!

THWUMP!

WELL, WELL! FOUND THE WINDOW, DID YOU?

DON'T YOU KNOW IT'S BAD ETIQUETTE TO HIT AND RUN?!!

IT'S A GOOD THING I WAS PASSING BY--AND HEARD THE RUCKUS!
DAREDEVIL!
THAT'S ALL WE NEED!

IT'S ALMOST UNFAIR OF ME TO PICK ON A COUPLE OF CLOWNS LIKE YOU!
AFTER ALL, IF YOU COULDN'T EVEN HOLD YOUR OWN AGAINST ONE UNARMED, SIGHTLESS VET--
KONK

WHOA, CHARLIE!
DIDN'T THINK I'D FORGET ABOUT YOU?
I'D BETTER WRAP THIS UP NOW!
--AND MAKE SURE THAT WILLIE'S VERSION TIES IN WITH MINE!

HERE--
LET ME
HOLD
YOUR
COAT
FOR
YOU--!
YOU WON'T
BE NEEDING
IT WHERE
YOU'RE
GOING!
PTOK!

YOU CORNY,
COSTUMED
CLOWN!
YOU CAN'T
BEAT ALL
OF US!

H-HOW'D
YOU
DUCK
SO
FAST??
MAYBE
I'LL WRITE
A BOOK!

WATCH
IT,
USELESS!
DO YOU
KNOW
WHAT
THOSE
BLINDS
COST??

OKAY,
MASKED
MAN! THIS
IS THE
WRAP-UP!
IF
THERE'S
ONE
THING
I HATE--
GRRRR!
--IT'S A
CORNY
PUN!
HE COULDN'T
KNOW I HEARD
WILLIE'S DOG--
ABOUT TO LEAP
AT HIM!

LATER--

PRETTY CLEVER OF YOU, HOLDING 'EM OFF THAT WAY IN THE DARK, WILLIE!

YEAH--CLEVER!

WILLIE HATED TO LIE ABOUT HIS PART IN IT, BUT I CONVINCED HIM IT WAS THE ONLY WAY TO INSURE NO FURTHER ATTACKS!

BIGGIE'S HOODS ARE TOO YELLOW TO TACKLE ANY-ONE WHO CAN FIGHT BACK!

BEFORE YOU GO, DAREDEVIL--TELL ME--

WHAT HAPPENED TO MR. MURDOCK?

I GOT HIM SAFELY OUT OF HERE!

HE DIDN'T MIND LEAVING--ONCE HE KNEW THAT YOU WERE OUT OF DANGER!

HE'S ONE RIGHT GUY, THAT FELLA!

FUNNY... HE SAID THE SAME THING ABOUT YOU!

HE SAID HE'S GONNA TALK TO THE COMMISSIONER ABOUT YOU!

THERE ARE LOTS OF JOBS FOR A GOOD COP--

AND YOU WERE ONE OF THE BEST!

Y'KNOW, BOY--JUST A SHORT TIME AGO I THOUGHT I'D REALLY HIT BOTTOM!

BUT THEN I FOUND ME A FRIEND--AND CLEARED MY NAME!

NOW, EVEN WITH-OUT MY EYES--I'M LOOKING FORWARD TO TOMORROW--FOR THE FIRST TIME!

I FEEL LIKE I'M PART OF THE HUMAN RACE AGAIN!

MURDOCK NEVER MADE A BIG DEAL ABOUT IT--

BUT, WHEN YOU GET DOWN TO WHERE IT'S AT--

MAYBE THAT'S WHAT BROTHER-HOOD IS ALL ABOUT!

NEXT FAREWELL TO FOGGY!

DARE-DEVIL

12¢ IND.

48 JAN

HERE COMES...

DAREDEVIL

THE MAN WITHOUT FEAR!

APPROVED BY THE COMICS CODE AUTHORITY

MARVEL COMICS GROUP

HOTEL

DAREDEVIL, THE MAN WITHOUT FEAR!™
"FAREWELL TO FOGGY!"
FOGGY NELSON FOR D.A.
OUR NEXT D.A. FOGGY NELSON
VOTE FOR
A NEW, SPECTACULAR SWINGIN' SAGA BY: SMILIN' STAN LEE and GENIAL GENE COLAN
EMBELLISHED BY: GEORGE KLEIN
LETTERED BY: ARTIE SIMEK
FEATURING: THE SPINE-CHILLING CHALLENGE OF STILT-MAN!

THUMP!
I DON'T MIND A QUIET CITY-- BUT THIS IS RIDICULOUS!
WHAT'S A SWINGIN' SUPER-HERO TO DO ON A NIGHT LIKE THIS?
GUESS I MIGHT AS WELL HEAD HOME NOW--
I KNOW ONE WAY TO KEEP BUSY--
I CAN ALWAYS HELP FOGGY WITH HIS ELECTION CAMPAIGN!
IF HE DOES BECOME D.A., IT'LL MEAN THE END OF OUR PARTNER-SHIP!
HE CAN'T BE A DEFENSE LAWYER AND DISTRICT ATTORNEY AT THE SAME TIME!
AND, ACCORDING TO THE POLLS--FOGGY'S IN THE LEAD RIGHT NOW!
2

UH OH--VOICES! GUTTERAL-- MENACING--WITH AN UNDERWORLD FLAVOR!
AND I DON'T LIKE WHAT THEY'RE SAYING!
THERE'S NOT MUCH TIME LEFT! IF WE'RE GONNA STOP NELSON--
WE GOTTA DO IT NOW!
YEAH! IF HE BECOMES D.A., THINGS'LL GET TOO HOT FOR US!
BUT HOW ARE WE GONNA STOP 'IM?
NOBODY ELSE COULD--AND PLENTY OF 'EM TRIED!
I AWREDDY TOOK CARE OF THAT!
I HIRED THE BEST IN THE BUSINESS--
EVER HEARD OF--STILT-MAN?!!
STILT MAN!! SO HE'S ON THE LOOSE AGAIN!
IF HE GOES AFTER HIM--IT COULD MEAN FOGGY'S LIFE!
I'VE GOT TO LEARN MORE--FOR FOGGY'S SAKE!
AND HERE'S ONE WAY TO DO IT--!

LOOK OUT! IT'S DAREDEVIL!
SO WHERE'S THE BRASS BAND?
HE MUST KNOW SOMETHIN'!
THAT'S THE UNDER-STATEMENT OF THE YEAR!

ONE THING I KNOW IS--
NOBODY'S INTERFERING WITH THE ELECTION FOR D.A.!
AND THAT INCLUDES YOUR BUDDY, STILT-MAN!!
--AS WELL AS THE CREEPS WHO HIRED HIM!

GET IN THE *CAR*, YOU GUYS!
I'LL HOLD 'IM OFF WHILE YA *DO!*
YOU GOT *ROCKS* IN YER HEAD, CHARLIE??
THERE'S ONLY *ONE* WAY TO STOP *HIM*--
CLICK!
MEBBE *SO*, SWEETIE--
BOY! ARE *YOU* AN OPTIMIST!
--BUT *YOU* HAVEN'T FOUND IT YET!
WHIT

NO! WAIT A MINUTE!
I CAN JUST HEAR THEIR VOICES-- OVER THE ENGINE!
TALKING ABOUT STILT-MAN-- AND WHEN HE'LL ATTACK!
GOT TO STAY WITH IT-- AND HEAR THE REST!

GATHERING SPEED! --COMING RIGHT AT ME! CAN'T WAIT--MUCH LONGER--!
TONIGHT!! AT FOGGY'S OFFICE! --THAT'S WHAT I WANTED TO KNOW!
NOW MOVE, DD--!!

AND MOVE--HE DOES!!

THEY'RE NOT SLOWING DOWN!

DON'T WANNA PRESS THEIR LUCK!

BUT NOW I KNOW --WHAT I'VE GOT TO DO!

I HAVE TO MAKE SURE I'M HERE ALONE TONIGHT--

WHEN THE STILT-MAN COMES TO CALL!

THAT FRAGRANCE! THAT SPECIAL PERFUME--!

IT CAN'T BE! AND YET--!

MURDOCK AND NELSON ATTORNEYS

NO! I MUST BE IMAGINING IT!

I'M NOT IMAGINING IT! IT'S NOT ONLY THE PERFUME--
THE HEART-BEAT!! THE MENTAL RADAR IMAGE! IT--IT CAN ONLY BE--
KAREN!! SHE'S RETURNED!

BUT I MUSTN'T LET ON THAT I KNOW! NOT UNTIL-- SHE SPEAKS--!
MATT! I'VE BEEN WAITING FOR YOU--!
WHO--??

HAVE YOU FORGOTTEN ME--SO SOON?
KAREN! IT'S YOU!

YOU--DROPPED YOUR GLASSES --DARLING!
LET ME PUT THEM BACK ON FOR YOU!

YOU'VE COME BACK! THAT MEANS--YOU'VE FORGIVEN ME!
I COULDN'T STAY AWAY FROM YOU-- ANY LONGER!

OKAY, ROMEO! TIME FOR THAT LATER!
RIGHT NOW THERE'S WORK TO BE DONE!
WE'LL HAVE TO STAY TONIGHT AND WORK ON MY CAMPAIGN SPEECHES!
CAN'T! HAVE TO KEEP THEM AWAY FROM HERE TONIGHT-- BECAUSE OF STILT-MAN!
SORRY, FOGGY! I CAN'T HELP!
AND YOU'LL HAVE TO WORK ELSEWHERE! --I PLANNED TO USE THE OFFICE MYSELF TONIGHT--FOR SOME PERSONAL WORK!
MATT! YOU CAN'T MEAN THAT!
IT'S ALMOST ELECTION TIME! THIS IS THE CRUCIAL PERIOD FOR FOGGY!
AND YOU HAVE THE NERVE TO CALL YOURSELF MY FRIEND!
LET HIM HAVE THE OFFICE! WHO NEEDS 'IM?!!
WHAT CAN I DO? WHAT CAN I SAY? FOGGY'S LIFE IS AT STAKE!
MATT! YOU'VE NEVER ACTED THIS WAY BEFORE--!
IT'S MY OFFICE, KAREN! I'VE A RIGHT TO USE IT HOW AND WHEN I WANT TO!
AND I THOUGHT --I'D BEEN WRONG ABOUT YOU!
LATER THAT NIGHT--
IT WAS THE TOUGHEST THING I'VE EVER DONE!
JUST WHEN KAREN HAD RETURNED-- WHEN IT LOOKED LIKE THERE WAS A CHANCE FOR US AGAIN!
I HAD TO BLOW THE WHOLE BIT!
NOW, SHE'S PROBABLY MORE HURT--MORE DISAPPOINTED-- THAN EVER BEFORE!
AND, I CAN'T BLAME FOGGY-- FOR THINKING I'VE TURNED MY BACK ON HIM--WHEN HE NEEDS ME THE MOST!
I CAN JUST IMAGINE WHAT THEY'RE ALL SAYING ABOUT ME NOW!
BUT, I HAD TO DO IT! I HAD TO!
9

DAREDEVIL!
WHAT ARE YOU DOING HERE?
BETTER CHECK ON THE HOODS WHO HIRED YOU, MISTER!
ONE OF 'EM HAS A BIG MOUTH!

SO! YOU WERE TIPPED-OFF THAT I'D BE HERE, EH?
A PITY YOU WEREN'T BRIGHT ENOUGH TO GET OUT OF TOWN!
THIS TIME I WON'T LET YOU ESCAPE UNSCATHED!
NELSON CAN WAIT!
FIRST, WE TWO HAVE A SCORE TO SETTLE--!
AT LEAST I CONVINCED HIM I'M HERE ON A TIP!
DON'T WANT HIM CONNECTING ME WITH MATT MURDOCK!
BUT NOW THAT I GOT INTO THIS--HOW DO I GET OUT AGAIN??
--IN ONE PIECE, THAT IS!

THIS TIME I ATTACK FIRST!
WELL, BULLY FOR YOU!

MEANWHILE, WHAT AM I SUPPOSED TO BE DOING?
OH, YOU WON'T TALK, EH?

I'LL LEAVE THE TALKING --TO YOU!

--WHILE YOU'RE STILL ABLE TO DO IT!
DON'T JUST SIT HERE, DD!! MOVE!

WHA--?? HE SLIPPED AWAY!
--BEFORE I COULD CONNECT!
HEY! OVER HERE, DUMMY!
YOU DIDN'T THINK I'D RUN OFF WITHOUT A FOND FAREWELL?
YOU WOULD HAVE, IF YOU KNEW WHAT'S GOOD FOR YOU!
BUT NOW, IT'S TOO LATE TO SAVE YOURSELF!
SAY! THERE'S AN ORIGINAL PHRASE!
DIDJA THINK IT UP ALL BY YOURSELF, STILTY?

KRAK!
THE FORCE OF HIS KICK--SMASHED RIGHT THRU THE WALL!!
AND, BY GRABBING HIS LEG WHEN I DODGED THE THRUST--
--IT'S TAKING ME RIGHT WITH IT!
SORRY, DAREDEVIL! YOU'RE A BIT TOO HEAVY!
IF HE'S ABOUT TO DO WHAT I THINK--
IT MEANS A 15-STORY DROP!!

I WAS RIGHT!
HE'S PRESSING HIS HYDRAULIC CONTROL STUD--
--RETRACTING HIS MECHANIZED LEG!!
AND I NEVER EVEN LEARNED TO FLY!
WHHH!!
BUT I'M NOT GIVING HIM THE SATISFACTION OF SCOOPING ME UP WITH A BLOTTER!
--NOT IF I CAN WHIP OUT MY BILLY CLUB IN TIME!!
THWITTTT
FASTER, DD-- FASTER!!
GOT IT!
15

PROUD OF YOURSELF, DAREDEVIL?

YOU'VE NO REASON TO BE!

ONCE I SHAKE YOU LOOSE FROM THIS CABLE--

YOU'VE HAD IT!

CAN'T HOLD ON MUCH LONGER!

I'M TOO VULNERABLE HERE!!

HE'S GOT ALL THE ACES!

I'LL DO THE ONE THING HE DOESN'T EXPECT--
A QUICK SNAP WILL CREATE A LARGE LOOP IN MY CABLE--
--WHICH'LL TRAVEL UP TO HIM--WITH INCREASING FORCE--!
UNTIL--

WHA--WHAT'S THIS??
RKO

FTAP!

NOW TO REACH HIM BEFORE HE SNAPS OUT OF IT!

REMEMBER WHEN YOU SAID I HAD IT, STILTY?
WELL, TO SHOW YOU WHAT A SPORT I AM--
I'M GIVING IT RIGHT BACK!
SPOKK!
A
P
I.M
18

WHILE, ON THE STREET BELOW--
QUICK! CORDON OFF THE STREET!
CAREFUL! HE CAN DO ANYTHING WITH THOSE METAL LEGS!
AND, AS IF TO PROVE THE OFFICER'S VERACITY--

I COULD STILL FINISH OFF THAT BUNGLING HORN-HEAD--
BUT LUCK IS WITH HIM AGAIN!
I'M NOT ABOUT TO TANGLE WITH THE POLICE TACTICAL SQUAD, AS WELL!
SO, I'LL JUST RETRACT MY LEGS--
--AND MAKE MY ESCAPE--WITH EASE!
NNNNIIP!

HE WHISKED HIS LEGS UP TO HIM--AND DUCKED INSIDE THE BUILDING!
BUT EVEN WITH HIS HEAD START--
I MIGHT STILL FIND HIM!

OH NO! OF ALL THE SLOPPY LUCK!
THIS IS SOME SORT OF A PERFUME COMPANY SHOWROOM--
AND THE ODORS ARE MUCH TOO STRONG FOR MY SUPER-SENSITIVE NOSTRILS!
THEY'RE CONFUSING ME--OVER-WHELMING ME!
I CAN'T BEGIN TO TRACK HIM DOWN!

CAN'T TELL WHERE HE WENT!
THE PERFUME SCENT IS TOO HEAVY-- MAKING ME ILL! I HAVE TO GET OUT!
BUT, AT LEAST-- FOGGY WILL BE SAFE--TILL AFTER THE ELECTION!
DAREDEVIL WILL MAKE SURE OF THAT!

AND THEN-- AT LAST--
CONGRATULATIONS-- MR. DISTRICT ATTORNEY!
YOU WON IN A LANDSLIDE!
FOGGY NELS
HE HASN'T EVEN SPOKEN TO ME-- FOR DAYS!
AND NOW-- MY JOB REALLY BEGINS!
I'M GOING TO RID THIS TOWN OF CRIME-- JUST AS I PROMISED!

WHAT OF YOUR LAW PRACTICE?
WILL MATT MURDOCK RUN YOUR OFFICE TILL YOU RETURN TO PRIVATE LIFE?
MURDOCK CAN DO WHATEVER HE PLEASES!
NEXT QUESTION!
I NEVER THOUGHT-- IT WOULD END--LIKE THIS!

MR. MURDOCK IS IT TRUE THAT YOU AND THE NEW D.A. ARE PFFFTT!
WAIT! THE PUBLIC DESERVES AN EXPLANATION!
WHAT HAPPENED BETWEEN YOU AND NELSON?
NO COMMENT!

NELSON FOR D.A
NEXT:
D.D. DROPS OUT!

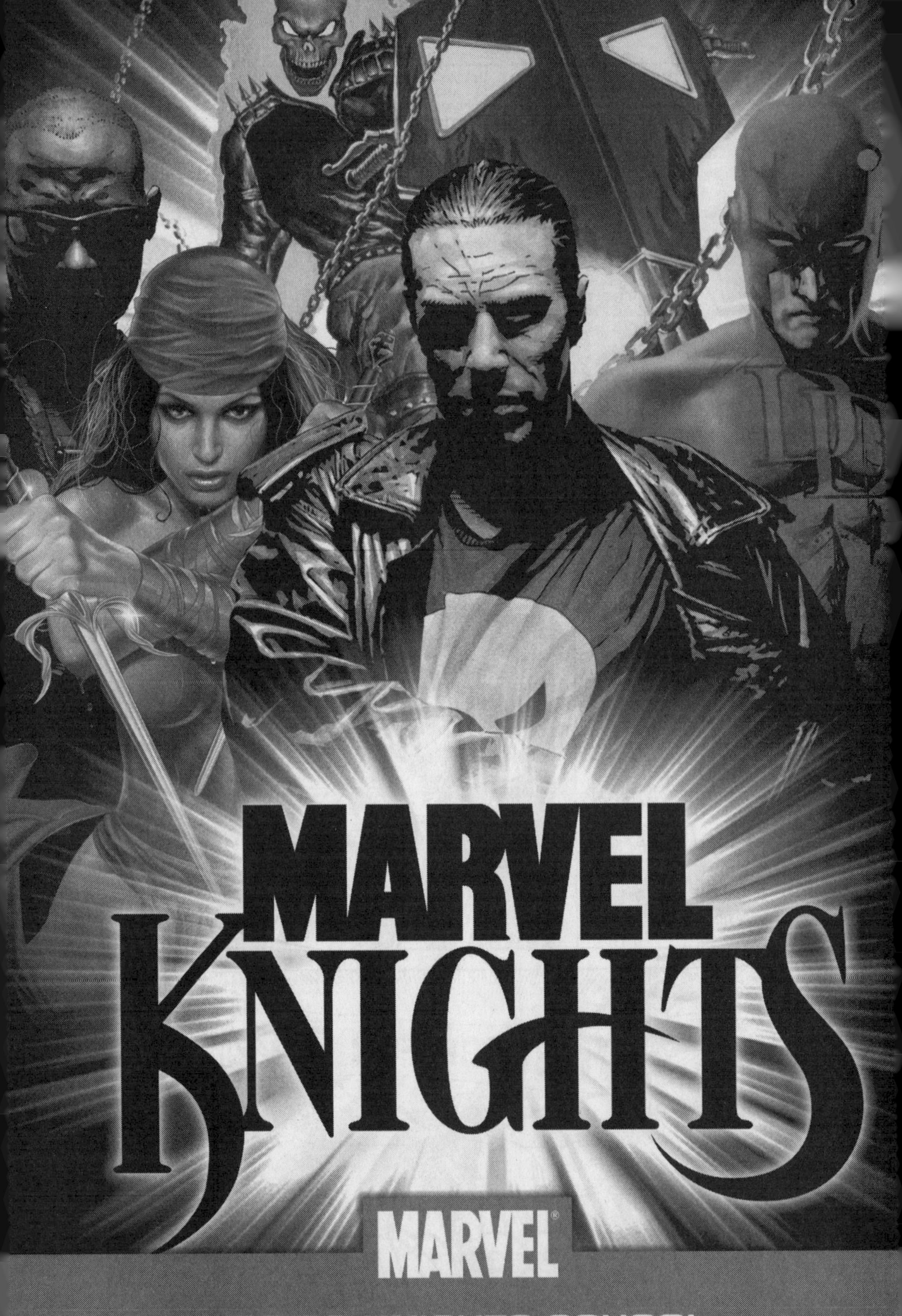
MARVEL
KNIGHTS
MARVEL®

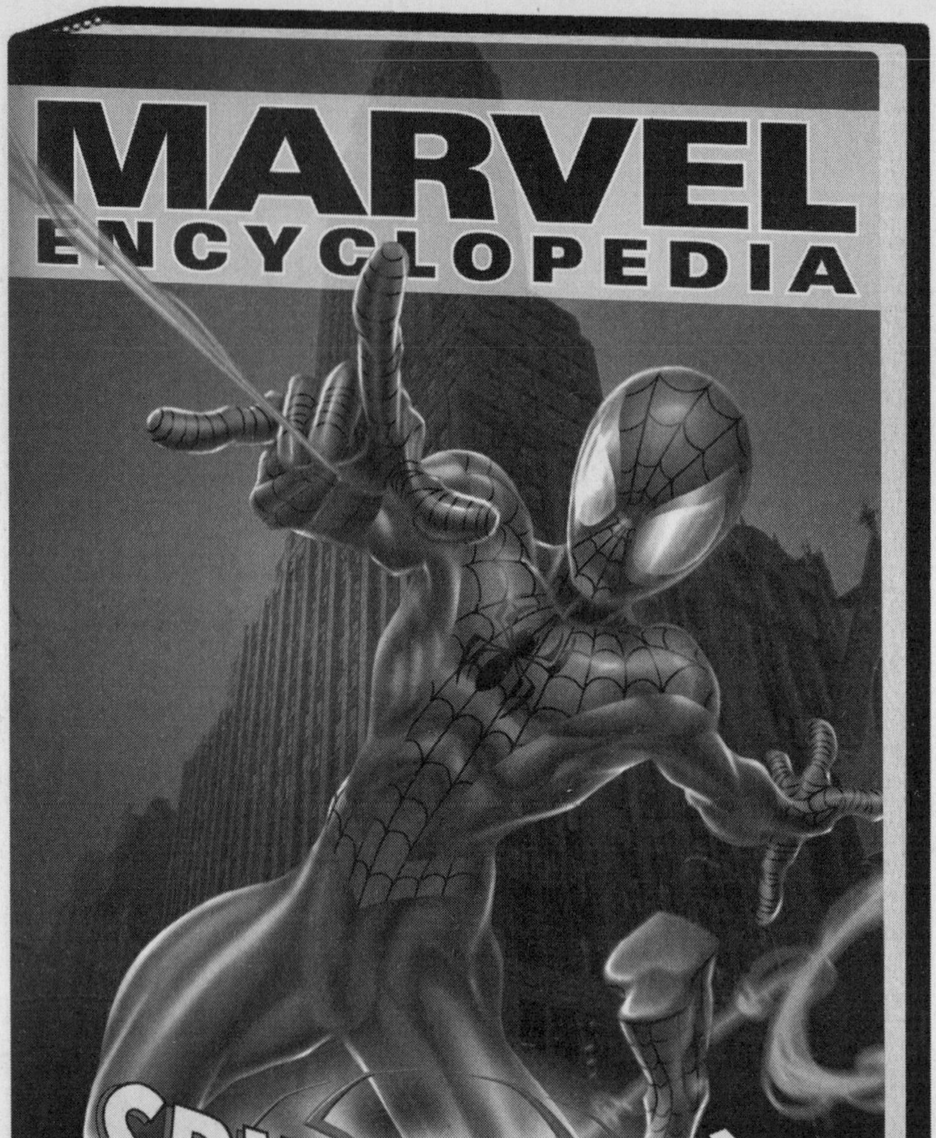

MARVEL
ENCYCLOPEDIA